WHAT EVERY SUPERVISOR SHOULD KNOW

WHAT EVERY SUPERVISOR SHOULD KNOW

LESTER R. BITTEL
Editor-in-Chief, Factory

Cartoons by AL ROSS

McGRAW-HILL BOOK COMPANY, INC.
New York   Toronto   London
1959

WHAT EVERY SUPERVISOR SHOULD KNOW

Library of Congress Catalog Card Number: 58-11161

IV

PREFACE

The truth about supervision. That's what this book might well be called. It's a humble antidote for too much preaching, too little understanding of the problems that challenge first-line supervisors. Ever since I plunged some twenty years ago into my first supervisory job, I've had the urge to put into writing what I believe are the true facts about supervision. To spell out what techniques really work, and which ones are liable to backfire; where a supervisor fits into his organization, and where the doors are closed; how far he can go, and when his freedom is limited. Admittedly, over the years my viewpoint has mellowed. Somewhat sheepishly, I have noted a tendency (slight, I hope) for even this book to idealize the supervisor's role. But in the main, supervisors and training directors alike will find herein a strong cord of reality binding practice to principle.

Problems of supervision constantly change. They demand new techniques and new tools to achieve management goals. The industrial organization in which the foreman works, the management methods and procedures at his disposal, the employees he supervises differ markedly from decade to decade. The welfare of the supervisor's country, be it prosperity, depression, or war (cold or hot), year by year exerts a stronger influence on the supervisor's job. Even more significant is the change in the supervisor himself. No longer does he fit the traditional stereotypes applied to him—"bull of the woods," "messenger boy," or "fall guy." Toward the integration of these changing variables for the supervisor's guidance is this book devoted.

And while the new techniques in supervision are good, they aren't always as good as the old. Consequently what appears in these pages is here for its own sake—not because of its age. Answers to questions, therefore, are in the main based upon my own experience with the success or failure of supervisory principles when judged against the harsh measure of practice.

Then, too, supervision is an imperfect art—but it can also be fun. Few things measure up in pure exhilaration to the joy of a decision well made—or to the satisfaction of rescuing a problem employee, for instance. Leadership in industry combines the tempered pleasure of chess, the quick skill of a second baseman making the pivot in a double play, and the raw courage of a counterpunching boxer in the prize ring. So I have little time for those who view supervision as unadulterated drudgery, or who demand perfection from its practitioners. Worlds don't stop turning or business empires collapse because a foreman backslides occasionally. It will be an objective of this book, therefore, to put the supervisory job into its proper perspective.

Lastly, this book attempts to collect in one place, under a single set of covers, *all* the truly important information a supervisor needs to know about his job of dealing with men, money, machines, material, and himself. This is an ambitious objective—probably too ambitious. It has been impractical to include everything. But it seems safe to say that everything absolutely necessary, and a little bit more, is here.

With these five objectives in mind—realistic helpfulness, integration of change, practicality based upon experience, good-humored perspective, and coverage of the whole job—this book should aid:

Supervisors and foremen as a handy reference manual of methods for handling people, managing their job, and helping themselves to succeed.

Their bosses as an insight into the work problems—human, technical, and personal—as supervisors must see them.

Training directors as a text or guide for supervisory training in employee relationships and in technical job skills as well.

Any student of human affairs in business and industry—as a centralized source of information about the supervisor and his whole job.

A book can never be the work of a single person. A good book about supervision must reflect the work of thousands. It must be the sum of the experiences and observations of hundreds and hundreds of supervisors and managers, training directors and personnel managers, engineers and academicians, psychologists and sociologists, editors and authors. If nothing else, *What Every Supervisor Should Know* meets this criterion of influence. In this book are integrated my personal reactions to the efforts of these thousands of others.

Unfortunately, it would be impossible to single out for recognition every individual who has helped or influenced the author. I'm deeply grateful to all. But it would be a serious omission were I not to mention just a few of whom I can say, "Except for them, this book would not have been written." My salutes to:

Glenn Gardiner, who did so much original thinking about the problems of foremanship and employee training, and whose early writings provided the basis for my awareness of the subject.

David D. Hicks, who, as training director for the Koppers Company, unselfishly taught me everything he knew about industrial training.

Auren Uris, who, through his friendship and encouragement and his remarkable insight into management complexities, bolstered my belief that this book could be written.

Lewis K. Urquhart, who taught me how to write.

Matthew J. Murphy and *Donald H. White,* who, as editor and publisher of *Factory Management and Maintenance,* went far beyond employer-employee responsibilities in encouraging this work. And, through whose efforts, material originally appearing in *Factory* is reproduced here.

Foremen everywhere, the gang who worked with me at the White Tar Company of New Jersey (where I was a foreman myself), the hundreds of foremen and supervisors of the Koppers Company who shared their experiences with me while I was regional training director for that company, and the thousands of other plant operating people I've talked with in my activities as industrial management editor of *Factory.*

It would be an omission, also, to overlook three other very important people, neither foremen, engineers, or authors, without whose influence nothing much would be produced by me:

My father and mother, who helped me find worthwhile things to believe in, and

My wife, who not only did her share of the hard work of manuscript preparation, but who also kept three well-meaning small children from giving me more help than I could stand.

Lester R. Bittel

CONTENTS

PREFACE   v

1 The Supervisor's Job   1

1
ABOUT PEOPLE AT WORK

2 People and Human Relations   13
3 Attitudes and Morale   24
4 Communicating with Employees and Associates   35
5 Public and Community Relations   47

2
SUPERVISING PEOPLE—*The Fundamentals*

6 The Art of Leadership   57
7 Organization and the First-line Supervisor   67
8 Converting Policy into Action   78
9 Manpower Management   86
10 Job Analysis and Evaluation   99
11 Appraising Employee Performance   112
12 Training Employees to Work Well   123
13 The Supervisor's Role in Labor Relations   137
14 Accident Prevention   150

3
SUPERVISING PEOPLE—*Special Techniques*

15 The Knack of Giving Instructions and Orders   167
16 Winning Employee Cooperation   176

17   How and When to Discipline   186
18   Handling Gripes and Avoiding Grievances   197
19   Supervising Women Workers   208
20   Supervising Older Workers   216
21   Supervising Office Employees   225
22   Handling the Problem Employee   233

4

MANAGING YOUR JOB

23   Planning the Work Schedule   249
24   Time-study Fundamentals   259
25   Improving Work Methods   269
26   Figuring and Controlling Costs   284
27   Shop Housekeeping   296
28   Maintaining Machines and Equipment   308
29   Securing Better Quality   315
30   Protecting Your Plant   324

5

HELPING YOURSELF TO SUCCEED

31   Rating Yourself for Self-development   335
32   How to Hold Group Discussions and Lead Conferences   348
33   Writing for Business   360
34   How to Manage Your Time Better   369
35   How to Get Useful Ideas   381
36   Understanding Business Economics   391
37   What a Supervisor's Wife Should Know about His Job
        (for Women Only)   405
38   Getting Along with Your Boss   415

BIBLIOGRAPHY   423

VISUAL AIDS   429

INDEX   439

CORRELATED FILMS FOR GROUP STUDY

The six motion pictures described below have been produced in collaboration with the author of this text. Each film portrays a realistic supervisory situation as it might happen in the shop and is intended for use with supervisory discussion groups. The numbers in parentheses indicate the chapters most closely related to the film problem. The films (together with a *Discussion Leader's Manual*) may be obtained from the Text-Film Department of the McGraw-Hill Book Company, Inc.

Delegating Work (Chapters 7 and 8)

Joe, a shipping room foreman, can't depend upon his employees. In one harrassing day, this causes Joe four unfortunate experiences. The result is that Joe feels overworked and disgusted with his job and himself. *Time: 9 minutes.*

Enforcing Rules and Procedures (Chapters 15, 16, and 17)

Clancy, a maintenance workman, has trouble accepting and following orders from his new boss, Marty. Because of lack of uniformity in rules enforcement, Clancy eventually delays an important shipment. *Time: 9 minutes.*

The Trouble with Women (Chapter 19)

Brad, the supervisor, is fed up with women. The last straw is when the personnel department sends him a bearings inspector who is a girl. Brad recounts his troubles with female employees, wonders what he can do about it. *7 minutes.*

Personality Conflict (Chapters 2 and 3)

Jim, a cocky but competent press operator, and his supervisor, Pete, can't get along. Finally there is a showdown between them. Jim asks for a transfer, but Pete's boss tells Pete he'll have to learn to live with Jim. *Time: 7 minutes.*

The Hidden Grievance (Chapters 13 and 18)

Jake, a machine operator, complains of many ills. It is only toward the end that he voices his real complaint. Larry, his supervisor, tends to minimize it. Jake, dissatisfied, complains to the plant superintendent. *Time: 7 minutes.*

The Personal Problem (Chapters 4 and 22)

The workman in this case is disturbed because of trouble at home. His work suffers as a result. The supervisor tries to get at the root of the trouble, but fails. The employee's work becomes an even greater problem. *Time: 6 minutes.*

WHAT EVERY SUPERVISOR SHOULD KNOW

1 THE SUPERVISOR'S JOB

What is the supervisor's job?

First-line supervisors in industry and commerce represent just about the single most important force in our American economy. Over a million strong, they carry out a management tradition that dates back to the building of the pyramids. And yet time hasn't simplified their work. First the industrial revolution with its division of labor and now mass-production technique with its accelerated mechanization have changed the supervisor's role to one of bewildering and often frustrating complexity.

Today's foreman (supervisor, first-line supervisor, front-line supervisor, section or department manager—call him by any of his names) must be a vigorous leader of men, a shrewd and effective planner of work, a source of technical know-how, and a deft mediator between policy-setting management on the one hand and rank-and-file workers (and their union representatives) on the other. Small wonder that the cry goes up again and again: "We need better supervisors."

Recognition—and acceptance—of the foreman by top management has helped the supervisor to emerge finally as an essential and integrated member of the management group and to assume all the responsibilities of a full-fledged manager. The way hasn't been easy. Too often it has been painfully slow. Even today, there are companies where the supervisor's status is shaky and insecure. But on the whole,

1

no single group of men and women have achieved, and deserved, such stature and attention in so short a time after so long a wait as has the American supervisor.

Where does the term *foreman* come from?

According to Peter Drucker,* the supervisor's job grew out of the lead man who formerly was in charge of a group of tow-rope pullers or ditch diggers. He was literally the "fore man," since he was up forward of the gang. His authority consisted mainly of chanting the "one, two, three, up" which set the pace for the rest of the workers. In Germany, the supervisor is frequently called a *vorabeiter*—fore worker; in England the term *charge hand* is used. Both terms suggest the lead-man origin.

Interestingly enough, the term *supervisor* has its roots in the "master," who was the master craftsman of older days. The master was a real boss with autocratic power in many cases to bid on jobs, hire his own men, work them as he saw fit, and make his own living out of the difference between his bid and the actual costs.

Today's supervisor, observes Drucker, combines some of the qualities of both fore man and master.

How good a manager must a supervisor be?

Just as good a manager as anybody else in the management organization. Make no mistake: The only difference in managerial requirements between the company president and the first-line supervisor is one of degree.

In the intensive Supervisory Development course conducted by the American Management Association, at Saranac Lake, much emphasis is placed upon the concept of the *management cycle*. This cycle is described as a continuous function performed by all managers. It contains three main elements:

Planning. The role of looking ahead and formalizing a course of action both for the immediate problems and for those on the horizon.

Action. The decision-making process, especially the man-to-man contact and direction that gets things done—the products produced, the goods shipped, the letters typed.

Control. The process of observing when things are out of line and taking the necessary action to bring them back under control. Control involves measuring, restraining, or changing.

Now it's a fact that the president's job calls for more planning than the supervisor's does. And in many instances, the president spends

* Peter F. Drucker, *The Practice of Management,* Harper & Brothers, New York, 1954.

more of his effort in controlling. But plan and control the supervisor must, although by all odds his biggest contribution is in the action phase of the management cycle. So see your job as truly a manager's job. And be sure to devote time and thought in appropriate proportion to each of its many demands.

What are the basic objectives of management?

Management serves three important masters:

The *customer* by providing goods and services when they are needed, in the quality required, and at the cost the customer will pay.

The *employees* by meeting the needs of all the people in the company organization by providing equitable wages, good working conditions, and rewarding jobs.

The *community* by providing profit for investors and other risk takers. In turn, profitable enterprise contributes to the needs of the community by providing taxes, jobs, income, and corporate responsibility.

What is scientific management?

Lawrence A. Appley, president of the American Management Association, describes the science of management as "a thoughtful, organized, and human approach to the performance of the management job as contrasted with a hit-or-miss, rule-of-thumb approach."

Scientific management was first described by the great industrial engineer Frederick W. Taylor. He set forth this principle: *Greatest production results when each worker is given a definite task to be performed in a definite time and in a definite manner.* (Note that this idea was considered revolutionary when Taylor conceived of it just after the turn of this century.)

Taylor's concept was soon embellished by such things as job descriptions, instruction cards, stop watches, and time study. Later the idea of financial incentives was added to provide motivation. Others such as Frank and Lillian Gilbreth, who refined time study with micromotion study and Therbligs (symbols for basic human movements), Gantt (whose chart for scheduling is described in Chap. 23), Carl Barth, Halsey, Ramond, to name only a few, also contributed to the development of scientific management.

Nevertheless, by the mid-1930s scientific management—so good in principle—had been far from a success in practice. At about that time, influenced by research into human motivation at the Western Electric Company and elsewhere, leading management thinkers came to realize the missing ingredient in Taylor's concept: *It was consideration for the human element as a human being.* All the systematic approaches in the world won't work, they saw, unless allowances are made for the psychology of human behavior.

As a result, today we think of scientific management as Larry Appley does—as system on the one hand and applied human relations on the other. So in this book, you'll find the elements of scientific management grouped according to applied human relations in Parts 2 and 3 and according to systems and procedures in Part 4.

Where do the supervisor's responsibilities lie?

Few jobs encompass so many responsibilities. It's not difficult to list

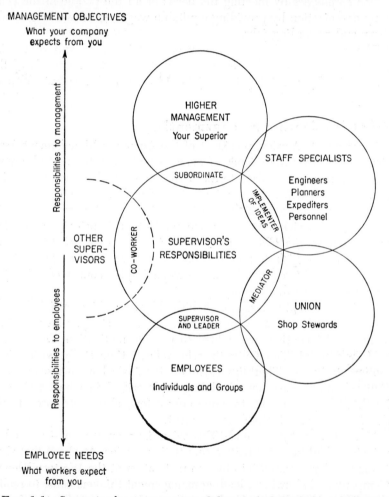

FIG. 1-1 Supervisor's major responsibilities. (Adopted from Robert Saltonstall, *Human Relations in Administration*, McGraw-Hill Book Company, Inc., 1959, with permission from the publisher.)

over a hundred specific duties and responsibilities—as you can see in the answers to the next three questions. But the foreman's main responsibilities lie in five directions (Fig. 1–1) and force him to fill effectively five different roles:

Leader and trainer of his employees.

Implementer of ideas—his own and those originated by staff specialists.

Coworker with other members of the supervisory group.

Subordinate to his own boss and others in middle and top management.

Mediator of employee needs as presented by union stewards.

It takes consummate skill, dedication, and energy for the supervisor to carry out these various roles in dealing with his many separate functions.

On what problems does a supervisor spend his time?

Professor Chester E. Evans of the department of management, Wayne University, Detroit, and consulting psychologist to General Motors for eleven years has given this question (and the next two) considerable first-hand study. He's concluded (as reported in the American Management Association's *Personnel*) that a first-line super-

TABLE 1–1

Activity	Per cent
Production and standards	28
Personnel administration	27
Tools and equipment	18
Quality control	13
Materials	7
Meetings and special activities	2
Miscellaneous	5
	100

visor spends his time as shown in Table 1–1. There's no need to emphasize that the proportions shown will vary from plant to plant, from job to job, and from foreman to foreman. But they should serve you well as a guide for appraising the direction of your own efforts.

With whom does the supervisor spend his time?

Some surprises here, although Professor Evans's conclusions are supported by several other studies—at the Chemical Division of Merck & Co., Inc., Rahway, N.J., for instance, where a survey showed that the average foreman spent only about 25 or 30 per cent of his time in direct supervision. (Corrective measures later raised this figure to approximately 50 per cent.)

Table 1–2 gives Evans's approximate figures for the time spent with various kinds of people by the average foreman. In your role as a

TABLE 1–2

Time spent	Per cent
Alone	33
With own employees	30
With other foremen	8
With superiors	7
With maintenance and service personnel	6
With others	16
	100

supervisor, you should make every effort to arrange your workday and your responsibilities so that you, too, increase the time spent with employees to at least 50 per cent.

On what kind of activities does a supervisor spend his time?

The average foreman spends the bulk of his time talking. No wonder there's so much emphasis placed on improving your communication skills! Table 1–3 shows the approximate time that the foremen surveyed by Professor Evans spent in various physical activities.

TABLE 1–3

Activity	Per cent
Talking	43
Looking	18
Handling, manipulating	12
Writing	7
Walking	6
Showing	3
Listening	2
Reading	2
Sitting	1
Standing	1
Miscellaneous	5
	100

How many employees does a foreman supervise?

This varies widely from company to company according to the company's size and the type of operations performed. In plants employing under 100 employees, the average number of employees supervised by one first-line supervisor is about sixteen. In companies employing from 500 to 1,000 employees, this number is about thirty-eight. In very large companies, the number ranges widely, with many foremen supervising as many as fifty to seventy-five employees.

Generally speaking, a first-line supervisor will direct more employees in a concentrated assembly-type of operation than a supervisor who works in a widely dispersed process-type plant. In other words, foremen tend to supervise more employees in a television plant than in a machine shop. And to supervise more employees in a machine shop than in a bulk chemical plant or oil refinery.

Can foremen join unions?

Technically, yes. And about 1 per cent of all foremen do belong to a foremen's union. But the Taft-Hartley Act reflects management's feeling that foremen are genuinely part of the management group and should not be encouraged to bargain collectively. The Act pointedly excludes supervisory workers from its definition of employees. Consequently, foremen's unions are denied protection by the National Labor Relations Board under the Act. And furthermore, organized foremen must be strictly on their own when dealing with employers; they cannot become members of a union with nonsupervisory employees.

Are there any national foremen's organizations?

The two largest national associations formed primarily for first-line supervisors (although their membership includes a sizable number of middle and top managers) are:

• The National Management Association (formerly the National Association of Foremen), 321 West First Street, Dayton 2, Ohio.

• The National Council of Industrial Management Clubs (affiliated with the Y.M.C.A.), 291 Broadway, New York 7.

Neither of these two organizations acts in any way as a bargaining agent for its members. Their primary purpose is for promoting the status of supervisors generally and in providing educational facilities for members.

In addition, there are hundreds of local foremen's clubs, some independent and many affiliated with either of the above groups.

Can supervisors participate in company suggestions systems?

Here, too, practices vary from company to company. An Employee Relations Bulletin (National Foremen's Institute) survey of 373 companies in 1957 indicates that in companies that have suggestion plans, about half permit their supervisors to participate in some way or other. This participation is usually limited by the kind of award made (usually nonfinancial) and the type of suggestion considered eligible (outside the supervisor's area of responsibility).

Are foremen permitted to do the same work as the people they supervise?

There is no law to stop it. But most companies with unions have a contract clause that prohibits the foreman from performing any work that a union member would ordinarily do (except in clearly defined emergencies).

Here's a point where most managements agree with unions. Few companies *want* you to do the work your employees are hired to do. You are most valuable to your employer when you spend 100 per cent of your time supervising. It makes little sense for a $135-a-week foreman, for instance, to do the work of an $80-a-week laborer.

What happens when a foreman is promoted from the ranks? Can he return to his old job if he doesn't pan out, or if things get slack?

This can become a problem if you work for a company with a union. That's because the company can't act solely on its own accord. It must secure agreement from the union. The Employee Relations Bulletin survey indicates that 55 per cent of all companies now allow foremen to retain their bargaining-unit seniority after being promoted from the ranks. If for some reason the man does not continue as a foreman, he is usually put back on his old job or transferred to a nonsupervisory job outside the bargaining unit. Point here is that most companies today are doing their best to protect the job rights of foremen in order to overcome any hesitancy there may be of union men to accept a change in status.

Can you describe the average foreman?

The Research Institute of America, New York, in 1956 made an attempt to draw a picture of the average foreman in terms of four key qualities. Their survey of 11,598 foremen painted the picture in Table 1–4.

Why do supervisors fail?

When a man (or woman) doesn't pan out as a supervisor, only an examination of the particular situation will pinpoint the real reason. And sometimes the man himself isn't at fault: his boss may never have given him the right kind of training and supervision. But if you'd avoid failure, check yourself against these six supervisory pitfalls, as revealed

TABLE 1–4

Age	Per cent
Under 30 years	7
30 to 39	31
40 to 49	33
50 or over	22
No answer	7
	100

Years with company	
Under 3 years	8
3 to 10 years	28
Over 10 years	57
No answer	7
	100

Education	
Started high school	23
Completed high school	33
Went to college	33
No answer	11
	100

Pay	
Under $4,500	14
$4,501 to $7,500	62
$7,501 to $10,000	12
Over $10,000	4
No answer	8
	100

by the National Management Association after a study of eighty-six companies:

• Poor personal relations with workers or with other management people. This rated highest on the list!

• Individual shortcomings, such as lack of initiative, emotional instability.

• Lack of understanding of the management point of view.

• Unwillingness to spend the necessary time and effort to improve.

• Lack of skill in planning and organizing work.

• Inability to adjust to new and changing conditions.

So if you'd make success your target, look ahead to the pages of this book that follow. And fit the advice to your own job.

ABOUT PEOPLE
AT WORK

2 PEOPLE AND HUMAN RELATIONS

Why isn't good human relations just plain horse sense?

Because this is a dangerous oversimplification. Life and business experiences are full of paradoxes and inconsistencies which show that good intentions and straight-line reasoning are not enough.

Take this example. Joe Smith supervises two men who work side by side on an assembly line in an auto plant. Their job is to attach the garnish (or trim) to the painted body. For some time Ed and Al, the men involved, had been complaining of knicks and cuts received from handling the sharp pieces of metal. Finally, Joe decides the best way to cure the problem is to insist that both men wear gloves on the job. On Monday, he approaches Ed and Al together. "Boys," says Joe, "the safety department has approved the issuance of work gloves for this job. This should prevent the rash of cuts you've been getting. Here's a pair of gloves for each of you. From now on, I'll expect to see you wearing them all the time."

Next day Joe had to ask Ed on three separate occasions to put his gloves on. But Al wore his all the time. At the week's end, Al was sold on the value of the gloves. But Ed just stuck his in his pants pocket. "They slow me down so I can't keep up with the line," he told Joe. But to Ed, he said, "This work-glove idea is just an excuse to justify

13

speeding up the line. If you give in on this issue, they'll put the boots to you on the next."

Why do two men, handled the same way in the same situation, have such differing reactions? After all, weren't Joe's intentions good? Didn't he try to settle Ed's and Al's complaints about the cuts? Wasn't his solution a logical one?

Why *do* people act the way they do?

If you mean, "Why don't employees act the way you wish they would?" the answer will take a long time. But if you are really asking, "Why do people act in such unpredictable ways?" the answer is simple. *People do as they must.* Their actions, which may look irrational to someone who doesn't understand them, are in reality very logical. If you could peer into their backgrounds and into their emotional make-up, you'd be able to predict with startling accuracy how Tom will react to criticism or how Ted will act when told he's changed over to the second shift.

The dog who's been scratched by a cat steers clear of all cats. A workman who's learned from one boss that the only time he's treated like a human is when the work load is going to be increased will go on the defensive when a new boss tries to be friendly. To the new boss, the workman's actions look screwy, against nature. But to the workman it's the only logical thing to do.

So it goes—each person is the product of his parents, his home, his education, his social life, and his work experience. Consequently, by the time a supervisor deals with any workman, he is dealing with a man who has brought all his previous experiences with him to the job.

Then are all people different?

Each person *is* a distinct individual. In detail, his reactions will be different from anyone else's. But to understand human relations, you must know first *why* people do things before you can predict *what* they will do. If you know that Bill dislikes his job because it requires concentration, you can make a good guess that Bill will make it hard for you to change the job by increasing its complexity. If Mary works at your plant because of the conversation she has with her associates, you can predict that Mary will be hard to get along with if she's assigned to a spot on an isolated bench.

The important tool in dealing with people is the recognition that although what they *do* is likely to differ, the underlying reasons for their doing anything are very similar. These reasons, incidentally, are called *motives*, or *needs*.

What is it that employees want from life— and their work?

Employees, like most of us, seek satisfaction from life for what a very famous psychologist, Dr. A. H. Maslow, calls the "five basic needs." * And we seek a good part of these satisfactions at our work. Dr. Maslow outlines the basic needs this way:

We want to be alive and to stay alive. We *need* to breathe, eat, sleep, reproduce, see, hear, and feel. But in America, these needs rarely dominate us. Real hunger, for example, is rare. True, according to Kinsey, most of us men don't get all the sex we need. But all in all, our No. 1 needs are satisfied. Only an occasional experience—a couple of days without sleep, a day on a diet without food, a frantic 30 seconds under water—reminds us that these basic needs are still with us.

We want to feel safe—from accident or pain, from competitors and criminals, from an uncertain future or a changing today. None of us ever feels completely safe. Yet most of us feel reasonably safe. After all, we have laws, police, insurance, social security, union contracts, and the like to protect us.

We want to be social. From the beginning of time, we have lived together in tribes and family groups. Today, these group ties are stronger than ever. We marry, join lodges, and even do our praying in groups. Social need varies widely from person to person—just as other needs do. Few of us want to be hermits. Not too many people are capable of frank and deep relationships—even with their wives or husbands and close friends. But, to a greater or lesser degree, this social need operates in all of us.

We need to feel worthy and respected. When we talk about our self-respect or our dignity, this is the need we are expressing. When a person isn't completely adjusted to life, this need may show itself as undue pride in his achievements, self-importance, boastfulness—a swelled head.

But so many of our other needs are so easily satisfied in America that this need often becomes one of the most demanding. Look what we go through to maintain the need to think well of ourselves—and have others do likewise. When your wife insists you wear a tie to a party, she's expressing this need. When we buy a new car even though the old one is in good shape, we're giving way to our desire to show ourselves off.

* Psychological research is far from completed. Opinions frequently change. But the concept of the five basic needs has stood the test of time very well, although you should be cautioned that few things are more difficult to understand and to apply than human relations.

We even modify our personalities to get the esteem of others. No doubt you've put on your company manners when out visiting. It's natural, we say, to act more refined in public than at home—or to cover up our less acceptable traits.

We need to do the work we like. This is why many people who don't like their jobs turn to hobbies for expression. And why so many other people can get wrapped up in their work. We all know the men who enjoy the hard burden of laboring work—or the machinist who hurries home from work to run his own lathe. This need rarely is the be-all and end-all of our lives. But there are very few of us who aren't influenced by it.

In what way can a man's job satisfy his needs?

It's a fact: Many people are happier at work than at home! Why? Because a satisfying job with a good supervisor goes such a long way toward making life worth living. While all of us may complain about our job (or our boss) from time to time, most of us respond favorably to the stability of the work situation. At home, Jake may have a nagging wife, sick children, and a stack of bills to greet him at the end of the month. At work, Jake can have an appreciative supervisor, a neat job with a quota he can meet each day, and assurance of his pay check (and other benefits) at the week's end. No wonder Jake enjoys himself more at work than at home.

Or look at it this way. A rewarding job with a decent company and a straight-shooting boss easily provides the first two basic needs: (1) a livelihood that keeps the wolf away from the door and (2) a sense of safety from the fears of a layoff, old age, or accidents. Satisfaction from the other three basic needs—to be social, to be respected, and to do the work we like—is often more a function of a workman's supervisor than of the job itself.

A good supervisor can see that a man's job satisfies *the social need* by demonstrating to the rest of the work group the desirability of taking in a new worker. For instance, "Fellows, this is Pete Brown, our new punch press operator. We're glad to have him with the company. And I've told him what a great bunch of guys you all are. How about taking him along to the cafeteria at lunch time and showing him how to get a cup of java?"

To satisfy the *esteem need,* a good supervisor will make sure a workman knows that his work is appreciated. For example, "Pete, here's your locker. I think you'll agree that this is a pretty clean washroom. We feel that if we hire a good man, we've got to give him good conditions to work in so that he can do the best possible work."

To satisfy the *desire to do worthwhile work,* a good supervisor gives a lot of thought toward putting a worker on the job for which he has the most aptitude and training. Like saying, "Since you've worked this type of machine before, Pete, suppose you start on this one. When you've gotten the hang of things around here, we'll see about giving you a chance to learn some of the better-paying jobs."

Is the object of good human relations to have one big happy family?

Have you ever known a family in which there wasn't some discontent? Where one child didn't feel that another one was favored by a parent? Or where there wasn't an occasional spat between husband and wife? Or where there wasn't a disreputable relative hidden somewhere? I can't believe you have. It's the same way in business. As a responsible supervisor, you strive for harmonious relationships with your employees and with the others with whom you associate. But it would be plain foolish to expect that everything is going to be as smooth as cream all the time—or even most of the time. It's only natural for people to have differences of opinions and arguments.

What you should shoot for in your shop is to have the arguments settled in a peaceful and reasonable manner. Keep emotions and epithets out of it. Sure, you can expect occasional name calling—and loud voices and red necks. But the *general* level of human relations in your shop should be friendly. An attitude of, "O.K., Bill, let's pull this issue apart. Call a spade a spade. Tell me exactly what's eating you about this assignment. When I've seen your point, I won't promise I'll agree with you. But I'll be a lot better able to give you a straight answer then." And after your decision, "Don't apologize for making an issue about it, Bill. That's your prerogative. And I'm glad you exercised it to get this matter cleared up. But how about in the future coming to me first before you get so hot and bothered about it."

How far should a supervisor go in calling people by their first names?

Almost as far as he likes and the nature of the situation permits. Some people take to it right away—feel you're stuffy if you don't use their given names. Other people are standoffish about it—feel that first names indicate an intimacy that takes more than an introduction to develop. Important thing is not to make the mistake of assuming that all there is to good human relations is to call a man by his first name and to permit him to do the same to you. First names can grease the ways to easier relationships. But they are only the barest of first steps.

Of course, when talking with your superiors, you should look at the matter in reverse. Follow the custom of your company—whatever it happens to be. But don't be misled into believing that the familiarity of first name usage by your boss means complete acceptance and confidence in you as an individual. You'll have to work to develop these.

Does good human relations really pay off?

Early in your career as a supervisor you'll find this recurrent criticism of the practice of human relations in industry: *It makes good talk, but it doesn't pay the bills. Whenever the squeeze is on to cut costs, all the human relations frills will go out the window.* That's the trouble with human relations. It's been hard for many companies to prove that its practice saves money. And whenever you come across a supervisor who doesn't believe in good human relations (or who mistakes softness for the real thing), he'll be able to quote you lots of examples of the well-meaning supervisor who got trampled on by employees he'd tried to do right by.

On the other hand, the casebooks are full of proof that a supervisor who is intelligent in his dealings with people is able to show more production, lower costs, and greater quality. Good human relations doesn't mean being foolishly soft or weak or negligent of people's intent. But neither does it mean treating people as if they weren't people—which was the mistake of most supervisors for the twenty or thirty years preceding the Great Depression. Good human relations is an art and a science, it's firm yet flexible, and it's the most difficult ambition in the world to achieve. *But be assured that the results are rewarding—in dollars and cents as well as in personnel satisfactions for you and the people you supervise.*

How does a group of employees differ from any single employee in the group?

Take a group of ten employees working in a small can-filling line in a food packing plant. This group is respected and feared by its supervisor as one of the most productive, most likely to strike groups in the plant. Yet in the group are three men who, polled separately, are strong against a walkout. And another three men who, when working with other groups, were low producers. This is typical. Each man in a group may be a fairly strong individualist when working alone. *But when men work in a group, the personality of the group becomes stronger than any single individual in the group.* The group's personality will reflect the outlook and work habits of the various individuals, but it will bring out the best (or worst) in some, will submerge many individual tendencies the group does not approve of.

There is no better example of the power of the group over an individual than the history of the New York Yankees baseball club throughout the 1930s and 1940s. The nonconformists were shipped away from the ball club. Men who joined the club and stayed took on the qualities of the Yankee team. Men who were renegades, trouble-makers, and rule breakers on other clubs somehow walked the straight and narrow in Yankee pinstripes. And improved their batting averages and pitching records at the same time.

Why are some groups influential, others weak?

One union will pull a strike only to see it fizzle out in a week or two. Another union, with a much less clear-cut issue at stake, may go out on strike and stay on strike for months. The first group of strikers was a weak group, the latter a strong one.

Strong groups, contrary to what you might suspect, are ones where there is lots of conflict and frequent arguments. But where arguments are welcomed, agreements are stronger, too. And the pressure to con-form is great.

Weak groups are those groups where the objectives are not very important to most members. Or where a few strong leaders make all the decisions.

In the work groups you supervise, try to find out what the workers want *as a group*. Then help them set these goals themselves. Try to show that your interest is in seeing that group goals are achieved, that *you* aren't the roadblock to job security, better pay, more rewarding work. That way, the work groups you supervise will be strong groups. And properly inspired, their goals will be very similar to yours.

It's when a supervisor sets himself *against* the work group that the group either becomes strongly *against* him and the company or be-comes weak and easily seized by a strong leader who may be against the supervisor or the objectives which best satisfy both company and worker.

How can a supervisor set goals with his work group without sacrificing his authority?

Unless the group of people you supervise believes that what you want them to do is to their advantage as well as yours, you'll have little success as a supervisor. The solution lies in permitting the group to set their goals along with you. And by showing them that these goals are attained through group action—teamwork.

It may be only natural for you to feel that to permit the group to get into the decision-making act will be hazardous to your authority. It needn't be. First of all, make it clear that you'll always retain a veto power over a group decision (but don't exercise it unless absolutely necessary). Secondly, establish ground rules for their participation beforehand—and make these limitations clear. Finally, provide enough information for the group so that they can see situations as you do. It's when people don't have enough of the facts that they rebel against authority.

In dealing with work groups, try to make your role that of a coach. Help employees to see why cost cutting, for instance, is desirable and necessary to ward off layoffs. Encourage *them* to discuss ways of cutting costs. Welcome their suggestions. Try to find ways of putting even relatively insignificant ideas to work. And report the team's achievements frequently. Emphasize that good records are the result of the team's united effort, not your own bright ideas.

(Of course it goes without saying that certain decisions—such as work standards or quality specifications—may be beyond the group's control or even yours. Consequently, you should make it clear at the start what work conditions are off limits so far as group participation is concerned.)

You'll hear a lot about the wonders of participation. And most of what you'll hear is true. In today's employer-employee relations nothing has been so successful in developing harmony and the attainment of common goals as the development of participation by supervision.

Participation is an amazingly simple way to inspire people. And its simplicity lies in the definition of the word: "To share in common with others."

Sharing, then, is the secret. You must share knowledge and information with others in order to gain their cooperation. You must share your own experience so that employees will benefit from it. You must share the decision-making process itself so that employees can do some things the way they'd like to. And you must share credit for achievement.

Once you've learned how to share, participation is self-perpetuating. Supervision becomes easier when employees begin to share responsibility with you. No longer do you alone have to watch for every possibility. An employee will report an overheated motor, raw material with flaws, an impending bottleneck. An employee won't wait for you to tell him what to do in an emergency. You'll find him using his own initiative to keep the lines producing. So sharing pays off as employees share your burdens and their production records with you.

Isn't money the most important thing people get from their work?

People work primarily for money—and what money can buy. Trouble is that today, give or take a few cents, most companies pay the same wages for the same kind of work. To make a job with your company more attractive to an individual than a job with the ABC Company down the road, you've got to look far beyond the paycheck. Remember the famous salesman who sells the sizzle, not the steak? Selling a job to an employee is a lot like that. You must show him how his job brings him prestige among his friends, skill that represents security for him, a feeling of accomplishment.

If you offer Ned Doaks a more difficult job at only a dime more an hour than the easy one he has now, he may turn it down. That is, if you show him only the money. But if you can show him how this job is the stepping stone to an even better job or that it is an important one that even the plant superintendent keeps an eye on, he may take a chance.

All this sound farfetched? According to scientists who have studied why people do things (motivation research), here are a couple of everyday examples that may surprise you. The beauty expert doesn't sell cosmetics—she sells hope. The shoe salesman doesn't sell shoes— he sells pretty feet. A family doesn't buy a food freezer to keep food —it's bought because it symbolizes the bountiful mother we'd all like to have.

Or take everybody's urge to be creative. Millers who sell cake mixes hold out one ingredient (like milk or an egg) which the housewife can add fresh. Thus she feels that when she bakes this cake, she's creative. So don't laugh off the necessity of selling the benefits of the job at your plant rather than the bare bones of the job itself.

What are some of the rewards an employee looks for that aren't in his paycheck (or in his fringe benefits)?

It's an old saw that a man gets two kinds of wages from his job—the pay in his paycheck and the pay that isn't in his paycheck. As discussed earlier, an employee is likely to take the pay he gets in his paycheck for granted. He'll judge the worth of his job by how well his company, and his supervisor in particular, pay him off in other ways. Here are just a few:

Recognition for a job well done. "Ben, that lot of shafts you turned out today was top-notch. I didn't think you could do so well with the sub-par material in that batch."

Fair and impartial treatment. "Last week I let Ted work on that ring job. Ben, your turn comes up next week, and I'll be sure you get the assignment."

Respect for a person's feelings. "Will you come outside and have a smoke with me, Ben? I'd like to talk over that difficulty you had with the No. 6 lathe today. Maybe we can work out a way that will prevent its happening again."

Freedom of speech. "I'm interested in your opinion, Ben. And in your criticisms, too. Be sure to speak up if you feel there's something you don't understand, or if you feel you're not getting a fair shake."

Chance to get ahead. "You won't have to stay on this job forever, Ben. There are better jobs available once you've gained a little seniority and shown you can handle something more difficult. In the meantime, I'll try to help you learn all you can about this one."

To be in the know. "You may see a lot of activity in the shop next week, Ben. Don't get worried about it. It's just an engineering survey to prepare for some new power lines. Should make for a lot fewer interruptions in the future. In the meantime, I'll try to keep you posted."

What happens when a worker doesn't get satisfaction from his job?

His morale will be down, his attitudes not "right." But most important to you, the dissatisfied workman doesn't produce as much or as well as one who finds work rewarding.

Isn't job satisfaction primarily the company's responsibility—not the supervisor's?

The company's stake in good human relationships is just as big as the supervisor's. And when a company helps the supervisor to establish the right climate for good human relations, the supervisor's job with people is much easier. But your relationship with your employees is a very personal one. And no amount of policies and procedures, fancy cafeterias, generous fringe benefits, or sparkling toilets can take the place of a supervisor who is interested in his people and treats them wisely and well. From your point of view, responsibility for employee's job satisfaction is one you share jointly with the company.

The Case of the Three Employees Who Looked Alike. A case study in human relations involving people who appear to be alike, with questions for you to answer.

Lennie, Larry, and Louis began work at the American Specialties plant on the same day. By an odd coincidence, the three men not only were about the same age and came from the same neighborhood, but they also looked somewhat alike. Their coworkers used to say that the only way to tell them apart was to look at their clock numbers. Lennie was 8291, Larry 8292, and Louis 8293.

The first jobs assigned to Lennie, Larry, and Louis were in the labor pool. Under a rather rough-and-ready gang foreman, the three fellows would be sent out on different jobs almost every day. One day they'd be in department A shoveling sand, the next day they'd be in the shipping department loading box cars, and the next day helping the packers on the assembly line to seal up cases. But at the end of each day, the three men would report back to the labor pool to check out with the gang foreman. They liked him and he thought well of them. "These kids are O. K.," he said. "They'll fit in anywhere in the plant."

As the "three musketeers" (that's what they came to be called in the plant) acquired seniority, one by one they were assigned permanent jobs in the plant. Lennie worked as a lift-truck operator in the shipping department, Larry became a pumpman in the processing department, and Louis went into the maintenance shop as a helper.

A year after Lennie, Larry, and Louis had been on their permanent jobs the personnel manager pulled their record cards from his files. What he saw rather surprised him. Lennie, Larry, and Louis had excellent records while they worked in the labor gang. Except for an occasional excused absence, their attendance and deportment had been almost perfect. But today, their records told a different story.

Lennie's personnel record showed that he had been late nine times during the year. He had been absent for one reason or another a total of 27 days. He'd had one lost-time accident and had made over fifteen other visits to the dispensary for various reasons. His boss had issued him two written reprimands for infractions of company rules.

Larry's attendance and safety record was about average for the plant. But while he didn't have a production-type job, his supervisor had reported that Larry was a poor producer. In addition, there was a notation that Larry had come to the personnel office several times during the year to complain about minor troubles in the shop—about a mistake in his pay once, and twice about the kind of work he had been assigned.

Louis' attendance and safety record was also average. But Louis' supervisor had made a special point of noting that Louis was fast and cooperative. In addition, he had recommended Louis for promotion to class B mechanic when the next opening arose.

The personnel manager was frankly puzzled by the difference in the men's records—in view of the fact that they all had shown such promise originally.

1. What sort of experiences at work could have caused Lennie, Larry, and Louis to change?

2. What sort of factors at home or in their lives outside of work could have caused these changes?

3. If you were the personnel manager, what sort of conclusions might you draw about each man's supervisor? Why?

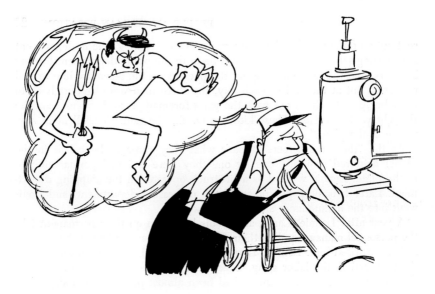

3 ATTITUDES AND MORALE

What is attitude?

An attitude is a person's point of view. It's his way of looking at something. But even more important, an attitude is a person's readiness to react—and to react in a predetermined way.

A baseball batter ready to swing at a pitch, for instance, sets his feet, cocks his bat, keeps his eyes on the pitcher. He's learned from experience that this *attitude* gives him the best chance of getting a hit. In the same way, you—and your employees—learn from your experience to assume a readiness to react when faced with a situation. An employee's attitude toward lateness determines how conscientiously he tries to get to work on time. *Your* attitude toward lateness will determine how much emphasis you place on tardiness as a measure of employee performance.

What causes a bad attitude?

When an employee faces a situation the way you'd like him to—such as accepting your corrections in good grace—you're likely to say of him, "He's got a good attitude." But if the same workman irks you by habitually failing to keep his bench clean, you may find yourself saying, "His attitude is poor." How do you explain this contradiction? How can the same person's attitude be good one time, bad the next?

It could be that the employee's attitudes (from his point of view)

24

are fine. In the first instance, he's learned that you're considerate and helpful when it comes to showing him how to do his job. Your favorable action has developed in him a good attitude toward criticism. In the second instance, this same workman may have learned that you are pretty soft about disciplining him and others for sloppy housekeeping. He's observed, "Joe complains a lot about poor housekeeping, but his bark is worse than his bite." So this workman reacts the way you've taught him to react. His attitude toward housekeeping is the one you've taught him to have—even though it's bad.

Is the foreman always responsible for a worker's attitudes?

No. An employee, just like yourself, has many teachers. His own parents, his boyhood pals, his schoolteachers, the man at the next bench, his union representatives have all been teaching him how to react to things for a long time. These other people may have shown him hundreds of times that he could get away with anything just by giving lip service to what the boss says. So he keeps on doing what he pleases. If that's the case, as it often is, you'll have to try hard to build up new, different experiences with this workman. You'll have to show him that his old attitude won't be a good one in his relationships with you.

You can recognize when others have done a better job of teaching attitudes than you have if you find yourself saying, "I've told him and told him. But he just keeps on doing it the way he wants to." Do you really blame an employee if he continues to find out that he can get away with a bad attitude? For him, the attitude is a good one to assume with you.

Why do people have different attitudes?

For many reasons. First of all, you've seen that each of us has been taught different attitudes by many different people. And each of us goes through widely different experiences as we grow up. This is true even when it doesn't look very different on the surface.

Take Pete and Andy. They grew up on the same street, both went to P.S. 129, both started to work at the same time. Pete and Andy have worked in the same shop now for three years. But Pete's attitude about quality is bad. Andy's is good. Why?

Pete's first job at the plant was as a packer. His foreman put a premium on speed. Just kept after him to get the stuff into boxes. Andy worked on the same line as a material handler feeding the machine operators. His foreman cautioned him from the start that any rough handling would damage the parts being fed to the machines.

And the punch press operators also warned him that damaged parts cut into their earning. As a result, Andy was quality-oriented, while Pete got off on the wrong foot, feeling that speed was the only thing that was important.

Aren't some people more intense in their attitudes than others?

They sure are. Al's attitude toward hunting is one of indifference. He can take it or leave it alone. Harry, on the other hand, is wildly enthusiastic about hunting. He's rabid on the subject. Here's the reason for the difference. The few times Al's gone hunting he's stood around all day without even seeing a target, got his feet wet, and caught a cold. Only thing he likes about it is the day in the open.

Harry's experience has been different. Right from the beginning he had unusual success hunting. He bagged the most ducks, shot the biggest deer, even now always has a great day of it. No wonder that Al's attitude, even though favorable, is mild and that Harry's favorable attitude is rabid!

What has a person's make-up got to do with his attitudes?

If by "make-up" you mean the things about a person that God gave him—and him alone—when he was born, then make-up has a lot to do with attitude. Some people are inherently reserved. Some people are naturally more high-strung than others. A workman with the latter kind of make-up may have his attitudes pretty close to the surface. If you ask him to do a little something out of his line, he's more likely to blow up about the assignment and *show* you what his attitude is. Other employees with similar attitudes, but different natures, may accept such an assignment with apparent good nature, but inwardly fret and fume about it.

Being sensitive to attitudes—even when a workman doesn't wear them on his sleeve—is a big help to a foreman in dealing successfully with workers.

Aren't we all moody sometimes?

Foremen and workers alike all have their good days and bad days. It's natural for each of us to be moody at times. And these moods do affect our emotions and attitudes. For instance, it may be your normal attitude to be calm and collected when dealing with an employee who makes a mistake. But there comes a day—when your emotions aren't up to par—that you blow off steam about something that you normally take in stride.

Primarily, your emotions affect the *intensity* of your attitudes. And likewise, moods have a big effect on the way employees react. It's generally believed that moods are due to the condition of our bodies. When we've had enough rest, are well fed, feel toned up, our attitudes are likely to be more reasonable than when we're out of condition. So watch for mood signs in yourself. And watch for them in your employees. Help them to have more reasonable attitudes by encouraging them to keep in good physical condition.

What can you do to understand more about employee attitudes?

Foremen who are most successful at winning cooperation from their employees are those who have made the most progress in learning why employees feel and act the way they do. But it would be a mistake to think such understanding comes easily. It doesn't. But if you want to hard enough, you can.

To understand a worker's attitude better, you must take an interest in him, not just as a productive cog in the business machine, but as a person who has dreams and ambitions and troubles just as everyone else does. Your interest mustn't be superficial, or he'll recognize it and be harder than ever to get to. In fact you've got to work hard on your own attitudes toward others to get yourself in the mood to want to see each person as a whole.

To begin taking this interest in an employee, first form a habit of inquiring into his nonwork activities. Begin with less personal things like his score in bowling, his do-it-yourself project, or any hobby a man's likely to speak freely about. If you continue to show him you're interested in his pastimes and his success or failure in them, you'll build in him confidence in you. If he has other personal matters he'd like to tell you about—family affairs, financial troubles, etc.—let him bring them up. That way *you* won't be guilty of prying.

Little by little, just listening and showing this sincere interest in an employee will reveal the reasons for his attitude. You needn't attempt to advise him or be overly sympathetic with him in his affairs. It isn't necessary. In fact it can be downright dangerous. For most people, your willing ear is enough.

With most people it's a mistake to use the direct approach—to ask why their attitude is the way it is. More often than not, even they don't know. So it's better to take the roundabout road to discover what an employee's attitudes are underneath—and why he has them.

What can you do to change attitudes?

Quite a lot. Understanding attitudes often points the way to changing them. Employees *learn* the attitudes they have. You can teach them new ones. Don't try this by preaching. Do it by setting favorable examples, by providing employees with favorable experiences.

Suppose Mary is a troublemaker in your department. She complains about her own assignment, continually charges discrimination, stirs up the other girls to make grievances. In your eyes, her actions show her attitude to be bad.

Now you want Mary to change her attitude. But why is Mary a troublemaker? That's hard to say. And it takes experience and understanding to find out. But think for a moment about what Mary's experience shows her about her troublemaking attitude: it provides her with plenty of attention, it makes her a heroine, it wins grudging admiration from her associates.

Now suppose that you could find a way of providing Mary with experiences where her troublemaking didn't get her attention or admiration. And you found other more favorable ways of providing experiences that give her the attention and admiration she desires.

For instance, you might find good reason to compliment Mary openly and frequently about her work. You might ask her opinion about new methods that are under consideration. You might enlist her aid in telling other girls about job changes. All these actions on your part are healthy. And they provide Mary with the type of job satisfaction she looks for. And suppose, for instance, that each time Mary made trouble, you handled her actions discreetly and impersonally. And you avoided any show of emotion or upset. Chances are that the combined effect would be to change her attitudes for the better.

You should be cautioned, of course, that attitudes and behaviors aren't often easy to pin down to actual cause and effect. But if you approach each human relations problem without a preconceived notion, and with real humility and warmth, attitudes can be changed. Point in Mary's case is that you want to help her, not outsmart her.

What can be done to prevent unfavorable attitudes?

Just listening helps to tip you off to unfavorable attitudes before they're really serious—in time for you to do something to correct the situation that causes them. But you can do more. Bad attitudes are often the result of fear—fear of unreal as well as flesh-and-blood things.

Take this example. Workers in Ted's department seemed to be slowing down. The more Ted tried to step up production, the more the gang found reasons to break the rhythm of top-notch performance. Then Ted overheard a conversation in the lunchroom. Jake and Stan were discussing the concrete pads which the maintenance crew in the shop had poured for a huge new piece of equipment. "I heard it's for a super-duper automatic machine that will do the work twenty of us are doing now," said Jake. Ted didn't need to hear any more. The men were worried about the new machine.

Actually Jake and Stan were wrong. The machine was not designed to reduce labor costs. It was being installed to perform a finishing operation that the process hadn't required before. Actually, then, the men didn't know what the machine was for. Left to their own imaginations, they conjured up some pretty terrible consequences. As a result, they adopted a bad attitude, one that put the foreman on the spot.

Ted could have nipped this bad attitude in the bud if he'd been alert to the things that worry workmen. How easy it would have been for Ted to say beforehand to Jake and Stan and others, "You'll see the maintenance crew in here next week pouring concrete. It's for the foundation of a new finishing machine in our shop. This machine will require two new operators. So we'll be posting for two higher-rated jobs soon."

Even suppose the new machine *was* going to displace employees. Just try to keep *that* a secret! Imagine the rumors that would spread! Better for Ted, or you, to lay the facts on the line: "This new machine will cut the shop force—from fifty to thirty-five, not from fifty to fifteen as some people seem to think. Bumping to other jobs will be on the basis of ability and seniority. We're going to make every effort to see that no one gets laid off. But if someone is, I'll be with you to see that you get a fair shake."

Can you always change someone's attitude?

Theoretically the answer is "Yes," but in practice, "No." Some people are just too fixed in their ways to yield very much. Sometimes, you, as a foreman, can do little to change the shop situations that create unfavorable attitudes. And some combinations of circumstances may be too complex to do much about without professional help from the personnel office, or from a psychologist or psychiatrist.

You also should be warned that a fairly large number of workers are emotionally unstable. The cause of their poor attitudes is due to a mental illness that is far beyond the layman's power to improve. And it's very difficult for a layman like yourself to identify. If you suspect such a condition in one of your workmen, don't play parlor psychiatrist with him. Speak to the company nurse or doctor or to the personnel office. And then follow their advice.

What's the foreman's responsibility for the general condition of attitudes in his shop?

A foreman is in the best position logically to control attitudes among rank-and-file employees. Since the foreman's contact is personal and frequent, you can do much toward understanding attitude changes and taking action to improve them or to keep them from getting worse.

It would be misleading, however, not to recognize that middle and top management have a significant effect on attitudes. Foremen are human beings; they're also employees. It's only natural that the foreman should reflect in his attitude the consideration he gets, or does not get, from higher management. And the foreman's attitude—good or bad—is often reflected among first-line employees. But, by and large, the foreman holds the key to employee attitudes in his shop.

What is an attitude survey?

An attitude survey is a systematic way of finding out how employees feel about things—their company, their pay, their supervisors, their working conditions, their jobs, etc.

The most common type of attitude survey is based on a multiple-choice questionnaire. This way a company can take a kind of vote among its employees to find out their attitudes. Questions are phrased something like this:

Check the one answer that most nearly describes how you feel:
There's too much pressure on my job. Do you agree, are you undecided, or do you disagree?

Another typical question:

My boss really tries to get my ideas about things. Do you agree, undecided, disagree?

As many as 100 questions may be asked, with room left for written comments. To make the survey more meaningful, it is kept confidential: no employee signs his name, and the tabulation is done by a university or a consulting firm, so that company officials never see even the handwriting of the employees surveyed.

Questionnaire answers are tabulated and analyzed. Most companies report survey findings either generally or in specific terms to their employees. It's especially important that, once management finds out what employee attitudes are, it take immediate action to improve conditions where these attitudes are unfavorable. For instance, a survey may show that most employees don't feel free to discuss job matters with their supervisors. Most people who have studied the relationship of attitudes to effort feel that such a condition is unhealthy and prevents a foreman from getting the type of cooperation he needs. Consequently the company—and the foreman—should take steps to improve the condition. For you, it may mean changing your own attitude and conduct to show that you will set aside time to listen to employee questions, complaints, or suggestions. And that you will do this listening with interest and welcome the ideas that are presented.

How good is good morale?

You'll never be able to please all your employees all the time. It would be a mistake to try. The foreman's job requires that you enforce rules, mete out discipline, and encourage people to do many things they may not be eager to do. The foreman who strives too hard for popularity may sacrifice some of these important requirements of leadership.

It's fair to ask, though, just how good you can expect morale to get. Studies by the University of Chicago Industrial Research Center of over a half million workers show that two to four out of every ten employees are usually less than satisfied with their lot (Table 3-1).

TABLE 3-1   ATTITUDE YARDSTICK TO MEASURE
MORALE IN YOUR PLANT

Category	Questions asked	Favorable answers, per cent
Job demands	Work pressure, fatigue, boredom, work load, hours of work	72
Working conditions	Annoyances, management's concern for conditions, equipment adequacy, safety measures, effect of these on efficiency	70
Pay	Adequacy, comparison with pay of others in the company and in other local companies, administration of pay system	44
Employee benefits	All benefits, comparison with benefits in other companies, knowledge of program, administration of benefits	74
Friendliness, coopera-tion of employees	Bossiness, friction	77
Supervisory-employee relations	Friendliness, fairness, treatment of suggestions, credit for good work, concern for welfare, follow-through on promises	71
Confidence in man-agement	Belief in management's integrity and its concern for employee welfare, adequacy of personnel policies, friendliness	67

TABLE 3-1   ATTITUDE YARDSTICK TO MEASURE
MORALE IN YOUR PLANT (*continued*)

Category	Questions asked	Favorable answers, per cent
Technical competence of supervision	Administrative skill, knowledge of job, ability to train employees, decision making, work organization	73
Effectiveness of administration	Competence of higher levels of management, efficiency of company operations, cooperation among departments	65
Adequacy of communication	Freedom to express opinion and suggest improvements, complaint handling, information about operations and plans	64
Status and recognition	Standing with the company, fair appraisal of work done, respect for judgment	71
Security of job and work relations	Security from arbitrary discharge and layoff, recognition of length of service, handling of job changes	59
Identification with the company	Pride in the company, interest in its future, sense of belonging and participation with the company	80
Chances for growth and advancement	Opportunities to use one's skills, to grow and develop on the job, to get ahead in the organization	65

And this dissatisfaction will be more so with some things, like pay, than with others, like working conditions. But the University of Chicago study does provide you with a helpful yardstick to measure the attitudes of your workers toward you and your company.

How do employees feel about foremen?

The University of Chicago study shows that workers' attitudes toward foremen are largely favorable. Employees, where supervision warrants it, are quick to acknowledge foremen are good people to work for and know what their job is all about. If your workers don't feel this way, chances are you're below par as a supervisor.

What's more important is to recognize that strong, aggressive supervision doesn't necessarily evoke a poor reaction among employees. If your strength and aggression are turned toward the job—rather than toward the workers themselves—employees find this leadership stimulating and a real force of motivation.

What kind of attitudes do production workers have generally?

Compared with all workers in industry, workers in production jobs have pretty poor morale. They, more than others, seem to find little satisfaction in their work as such. Surprisingly, production workers show better than average reactions to pay and other monetary considerations. But they see themselves as overworked fellows who get little glory from what they do and no real chance to get ahead.

There's no doubt that production workers as a group have a real need for improvement of attitudes. And many of their needs are directly within the foreman's ability to satisfy.

How's your own morale?

Want to measure your own attitudes against those of the average foreman? Then ask yourself these questions: Are you management-oriented? Do you feel rather secure in your work? Do you feel that the company gives you enough recognition and opportunity? To be normal, you should answer "Yes" to all of these.

But do you feel that there's lots more that can be done to improve efficiency? That the company's come a long way but that it has lots more to do before it operates as efficiently as you'd like it to? If you feel this way, chances are you're a pretty good supervisor.

It's normal too for you to be a little sensitive on pay matters—to feel that the men you supervise get almost too much in relation to your own salary. But if you feel that staff departments are out to get you, or that other foremen don't cooperate, you're off the beam. Your attitude is unhealthy and is probably standing in the way of your success.

The Case of the Attitude Survey. A case study in human relations involving employee attitudes, with questions for you to answer.

"Look, Tom," said the personnel manager to the supervisor of the maintenance shop, "see for yourself how our latest survey of employee attitudes shows your department to be at the bottom of the list. Last time we surveyed, you felt certain that the survey was wrong. Or that the results were influenced by a sorehead or two. But now three years have gone by, and you're still low man on the totem pole."

Tom said nothing but looked at the survey report. Sure enough, the facts bore out the personnel manager's words. Employees in his department were far below the plant average in their reaction to job demands, supervisory-employee relationships, adequacy of communications, status, and recognition. On the other hand, their attitude toward their working conditions and pay was as good as the rest of the plant.

"You see, Tom," continued the personnel manager, "Your employees don't complain about their pay or about working conditions. How do you explain that?"

"That's easy," said Tom. "Pay is all these hard-heads are interested in. And why shouldn't they like their working conditions? The company put in new lights and a ventilating fan last year. I'm only surprised they didn't find something else to complain about this year."

Tom went on, "I'll admit that I don't baby the men in my department. But why should I? They're not kids. They're well paid. All I expect from them is a fair day's work. Should I pin medals on a pipe fitter because he happens to make a watertight joint once in a while?

"If I didn't keep after these fellows, you'd find the plant falling apart at the seams. That's how I spend my days: checking, checking, checking! You can't trust a workingman today to do anything right. Especially when the front office treats them with kid gloves. It's no wonder to me that I don't win your popularity contests!"

1. What do you think about Tom's description of the attitude survey as a "popularity contest"? Why do you suppose he feels this way about it?

2. How well do you think the attitude survey reflects Tom's handling of employee relations?

3. If you were the personnel manager, how would you help Tom to improve employee relations in his department?

4 COMMUNICATING WITH EMPLOYEES AND ASSOCIATES

What is the significance of the term *communications* when used in connection with supervision?

The term *communications* is defined as the process in human relations of passing information and understanding from one person to another. As a supervisory responsibility, it is frequently called *employee communications,* although the communicating process is equally important between supervisor and supervisor and between the supervisor and his boss.

How new is employee communications?

As a problem of supervision, employee communications is about as new as the jet plane. It's become a key leadership problem as industrial management has become more and more democratic.

The term *communications* was, of course, originally applied to mechanical means for transmitting and receiving information, such as newspapers, bulletin board announcements, radio, telephone, and television. Employee communications have many of the qualities—and limitations—of mechanical means, but they are infinitely more subtle and complex.

When do human communications get off the beam?

In trying to get our ideas across to others, human communication (like radio or television transmission) systems suffer from poor reception, interference, or being tuned in on the wrong channel. *Poor reception* often occurs when a supervisor gives an order that an employee hasn't been conditioned to expect. *Interference* takes place when a foreman gives conflicting instructions. An employee may be *tuned in on the wrong channel* if a supervisor talks to him about improving the quality of his work when the employee wants to find out whether he can have the day off. Only through skillful communications can these human transmission failures be avoided.

How much must a supervisor know about communications?

A good foreman can't know too much about employee communications. His leadership is affected by what information he can pass on to others through communications. Unless employees know how you feel and what you want, the best management ideas in the world go astray. This is especially true where group effort is essential. *Group* attitudes will depend on how well you can interpret your company's interests and intentions to workers. And you'll need all the communicating skill you can muster to secure the cooperation so necessary from your work team.

Is any one method of communications better than another?

Each situation has its own best method or combination of methods. To show Charlie how much you appreciate his cooperation, all you may need do is give him an occasional pat on the shoulder. But Bill may need frequent vocal assurance. And Tony will believe only that which you put down on paper. So it goes to show that the most successful communication is done by supervisors who know *many ways* of getting their ideas, instructions, and attitudes across.

Should a supervisor use the shop grapevine as a means of communication?

Listen to it. It's one way of getting an inkling of what's going on. But don't depend upon it for receiving accurate information. *And never use it to disseminate information.*

The grapevine gets its most active usage in the *absence* of good communications. If you don't tell employees about changes that will affect them, they'll make their own speculations—via the grapevine. As a result, the grapevine carries rumors and outright lies more often than it does the truth. Surveys show that while an employee may receive a lot of his information from the rumor mill, he'd much rather get it straight from a responsible party—his boss. In fact you build good will by spiking rumors that come to your attention. So show employees you welcome the chance to tell them the truth about plant matters which concern them.

Some authorities, however, believe that if you talk to enough employees and prove yourself to be a reliable source of plant information, the grapevine *will* work for you. This is probably true. But leaking information to the work group deliberately through the grapevine isn't the same thing—and will tend to isolate you from them in the long run.

Some people talk about "three-dimensional" communications. What are they referring to?

Communication should not be a one-way street. For a complex industrial organization to function smoothly, communications must move three ways. Not only must you furnish information downward to employees, but employees must communicate their ideas and feeling upward to you. And since staff and interdepartmental cooperation is so important, there must be horizontal, or sideways, flow of information, too. This *up, down,* and *across* process is called *three-dimensional* communications.

A supervisor can't have the answer to everything that is happening in his company, can he?

No. But it is your responsibility to keep informed on matters of importance. If you don't know what's going on, you can't tell others. This applies to many areas that are of concern to employees—like social security, pension plans, the way an incentive is applied, or a leave of absence policy. When an employee asks you something you don't know about, you'll lose face if every time you have to say that you'll find out from someone else. Soon employees will figure you're not in on the know and will go to someone else—like their shop steward—for information.

When you are caught flat-footed, however, don't bluff. And don't say something like, "How should I know? Nobody tells me anything." Instead, strive to be in a position of confidence with higher management so that you can say, "Ralph, I don't know the answer to that one. But I'll sure as shootin' try to find out and let you know as soon as I can."

Do employees believe what you tell them?

Not all the time, any more than you believe everything *you* hear. But if you shoot as straight as you can in all your conversations with them, they'll look to you as a reliable source of information. Just as important is it that an employee have confidence in the *purpose* of your communications. He should never wonder, "Why did Joe say that?"

If the reason you complimented Al yesterday was so that you could stick him with a tough job today, he'll be suspicious the next time you praise him. If you would build Al's confidence, avoid trickery, and don't blind yourself to the inferences he may draw from what you say. Better to be brutally frank about your purpose: "Al, I'm having this heart-to-heart talk with you now because we're going to crack down on low producers," than to pussyfoot about your intentions: "Al, I want to get your ideas as to what you can do to improve your output."

Is there danger in saying too much to employees?

Yes, although this isn't the most common hazard. Supervisors who run off at the mouth continually, who are indiscreet, or who violate confidences *do* overcommunicate or communicate wrongly. It's much better to speak only about what you are certain of than to get a reputation for being a blabbermouth.

Some supervisors, too, in their eagerness to keep employees fully informed, try too hard. They find themselves spending too much time communicating information that employees don't need or have no interest in.

How can you decide what to talk to employees about?

Talk about those things an employee wants to know—those things that directly affect him or his work. Talk about work methods, shop rules, pay practices, the values in employee benefits, opportunities for advancement, your appraisal of how well the employee is doing his job.

Talk also about shop and company matters that are news—*while they are news.* Your influence as a communicator will be watered down if what a worker hears from you is only a stale confirmation of something he's learned from another workman or from his union representative.

Are there things you shouldn't talk about?

Yes. Politics and religion are dangerous subjects. Steer clear of them—even if an employee brings up the subject.

On the subject of business economics—which should be discussed with employees if they are to get a good perspective of their work environment—be careful to let employees form their own judgments and express their own opinions.

How much communication should you have upward with your boss?

Just as your success as a leader depends upon how freely employees will talk to you and tell you what's bothering them, your superior, too, needs similar information from you. Make a point of keeping your boss informed on:

Matters for which he's held accountable by his superior. This would include performance standards such as deliveries, output, quality, etc. If you see that you're not going to be able to meet a schedule commitment, don't yield to the temptation of trying to conceal it. Instead, build confidence with your boss by saying, "Lou, I want to warn you that Job No. 1257 won't be finished on time. We ran into off-grade material and had to rework some of the units. I *can* guarantee that delivery will be made by next Tuesday, however."

Matters which may cause controversy. If you've had to take action that may be criticized by another department, it helps your boss to know about it so that he can talk intelligently about it if interdepartment disagreements are brought to his attention. Suppose the quality-control section has advised you to shut down a line because production is off-standard, but you've felt that you must keep it running in order to make a delivery date. Better get to your superior fast—with the facts.

Attitudes and morale. Middle and top managers are continually frustrated because of their isolation from the work group. They need your advice and consultation as to how people in the shop feel, generally—or about a specific issue. Make a point of speaking to your boss on this subject regularly. Tell him about good reactions as well as bad. But never, never play the role of a stool pigeon, or go to him with information gained in confidence.

Are talking and writing the only ways to communicate?

They are the ones most frequently used, of course. But regardless of what you say, employees will be most affected by what you communicate to them by *your actions.* What you *do,* how you treat them is the proof of your real intentions. When you go to bat for an employee who is in trouble, that's concrete communication of how well you value his contributions to your production team.

Even on simple matters, such as training an employee to do a new job, the act of showing him how to do it (demonstration) is eloquent even when no words are spoken.

The best kind of communications are generally those that *combine* the spoken or written *words* with *action*. "Show and tell" is a good formula for you to remember.

How can you avoid having an employee take offense over what you say?

Each of us has a great big ego—and some are more sensitive than others. The tone of your voice, your choice of words, your tactlessness may make an employee feel menaced or hurt. Whenever you put something in such a way that he may infer a threat to his pay or status, his personal feelings will get in the way of his thinking.

Take this example: "Well, Smith, you remember I told you they wouldn't approve that transfer you asked for. Well, they won't."

Compare the tone of that statement with this way of saying the same thing: "Pete, I'm sorry but the super won't approve that transfer right now. You recall, we thought it might have to be held up as long as we're short-handed here and they're full in the plating department. But you speak to me about it again in the spring, and we'll try it when we're slack in this department."

Watch out, too, when you start a conversation. Sometimes you can be more aggressive than you intend to be, especially when speaking to a superior. Or when you're afraid you won't get your point across. That's because it sometimes takes courage. You have to push yourself, and some of that push gets into your voice.

Don't start an appeal this way, for example: "Now listen, Mr. Axelson, I know you won't agree with me. But you've *got* to listen." This makes the tone of your message aggressive. It puts *you* on the defensive and may defeat your purpose.

How can you be sure that people understand what you mean?

A very simple device is to ask an employee to repeat back to you what you have told him. If he can't do this, it's the signal for you to tell your story over again.

Another way is to get the employee to ask questions. What he asks will tip you off to areas of weak understanding. And once a conversation is established on a give-and-take basis, communications are always improved.

One reason for poor understanding is that words mean one thing in one relationship, something very different in other situations. Everyone has his own ideas, for instance, of what is meant by "faster," "slower," "harder," "up a little," "bear down." To make the meaning clearer, be more specific. Say, "Go a little slower—down to 2,100 rpm." Or, "George, I want you to bear down a little harder on quality this month. Last month we had complaints about poor finishes on six of the cabinets you turned out. Will you be especially careful about the application of the 00 emery cloth in the future?" Said with this explanation, "bear down" now has explicit meaning.

Should you keep personalities out of the picture?

Don't be impersonal or cold-blooded in your approach to people. In fact, you should tailor your presentation to best fit the person you're talking to. Some employees like rough language. Others feel it is a sign of disrespect. Some employees respond well to an informal request like, "Tommy, when you've got time, will you sweep up the loading dock?" Others want you to be more formal like, "Ted, get a broom and sweep the shipping platform. Start now and be sure it's done by 3 o'clock."

On the other hand, it's a good policy to deemphasize *personalities* in your communications. Think of communications as a process essential to the plant organization. Try to avoid interference from personal factors that don't belong in the picture. Watch your tone so that it is objective and keeps emotional opinions out.

There are helpful ways of rising above personalities. For instance:

"Now let's look at this from the point of view of company policy."

"This isn't between me and you, Bill. This is a question of whether shop discipline will be maintained or not."

"Let's get back to the facts of the case."

"This is really a question of interpretation of the union contract. Let's see what they say in personnel."

What will encourage employees to communicate to you?

Good faith, mutual confidence, welcome for their ideas, a friendly attitude are the foundations on which employees will learn to talk to you. But a more specific way is for you to develop the fine art of listening.

Real communication is two-way. In the long run, people won't listen to you if you won't listen to them. But listening must be more than just a mechanical process. Many employees (in fact, most people) are poor communicators. This means that you have to be an extragood receiver to find out what workers may be trying to say.

Here are a few suggestions that may improve your listening power:

Don't assume anything. Don't anticipate. Don't let an employee think you think you know what he's going to say.

Don't interrupt. Let him have his full say. If you stop him, he may feel that he's never had a real chance to get it off his chest. If you don't have the time to hear him through just then, ask him to stay within a time limit or make an appointment with him (for the same day) when you can get his whole story.

Try to understand his reason. The real need for his talking to you. Often this is quite different from his immediate purpose. For instance, the real reason for his asking for a half-day off may be to test his standing with you against another worker who recently got a half-day off.

Don't react too quickly. We all tend to jump to conclusions. The employee may use a word that makes you see red. Or he may have expressed himself badly. Be patient in trying to be sure you and he are talking about the same thing and that you understand his viewpoint.

Can listening be overdone?

Listening should make up at least a third of your communications. But it shouldn't take the place of definite actions and answers on your part.

When an employee begins to ramble too far afield in his discussions, bring him back to his point with astute questioning.

If an employee is clearly wrong on a point of fact, set him straight— even if it means contradicting him. But watch your tone!

When conferences or group discussions tend to turn into purposeless bull sessions, it's time for you to set talk aside and take action.

Finally, when an employee comes to you with a problem and its solution is clear to you, give him a straightforward reply. It does help him, if you have the time, to permit him to develop his own solution. But when he's come to you by virtue of your knowledge and experience, chances are he wants a direct answer, not a session of hand holding.

What are the pros and cons of the various ways to communicate?

For a supervisor, nothing can beat *face-to-face* communications. This way the common situation is shared with whomever you're talking to. And right at the time, you get a chance to see where your timing, tone, or choice of words has missed fire.

The biggest drawback of face-to-face communication is that it can be awfully time consuming. You may feel at the end of some days that you've done nothing but talk. As a result it can interfere with other work, although actual supervision, for which communication is your biggest tool, should occupy at least three-quarters of your time.

Because person-to-person communication, talking to one person at a time, is so time consuming, you will want to consider some of the many other effective ways for communicating to employees. For this purpose, you'll find this summary check list handy:

THIRTEEN WAYS TO COMMUNICATE *

There are many forms of communication and many more combinations of such forms. Combinations are usually more effective than any one form alone. To help you select the type that best suits your purpose, the general advantages and disadvantages of each of the more popular ways of transmitting plant information are suggested in this summary.

PERSON-TO-PERSON COMMUNICATIONS

The maximum of "custom tailoring" is not only feasible but definitely in order. It becomes increasingly so as the relationship accumulates a common background. That's because an individual who finds himself addressed singly, but as if he were anyone else, is usually resentful in proportion to the degree of previously assumed familiarity.

Spoken. In spoken communication the immediate situation is shared, and the person addressed is aware of the conditions under which the message takes place. Therefore, haste, tone, mood, expression, gestures, facial expression may seriously affect the way he reacts.

1. *Informal talks.* Still the most fundamental form of communication. Suitable for day-to-day liaison, direction, exchange of information, conference, review, discipline, checking up, maintenance of effective personal relations. Even if brief, be sure it provides opportunity for two-way exchange.

Face-to-face communication should always be used (in preference to the telephone) when the subject is of personal importance to either party.

2. *Planned appointments.* Appropriate for regular review or liaison, recurring joint work sessions, etc. The parties should be adequately prepared to make such meetings complete and effective by being up to date, by providing adequate data and information, and by limiting interruptions to the fewest possible.

Many executives have regular planned appointments with each major subordinate—daily (brief), weekly (longer), and monthly (extensive). It's valuable to note the gist of the discussion, for future reference.

3. *Telephone calls.* For quick checkup, or for imparting or receiving information, instruction, data, etc. They play a part in the personal relationship of the individuals concerned which is sometimes overlooked. Your "telephone personality" sometimes contradicts your real self. An occasional personal note can "warm up" the sometimes resented impersonality of routine calls.

* Adapted from William Exton, Jr., "Taking the Double Talk Out of Communications," *Factory Management and Maintenance*, April, 1957, p. 114, McGraw-Hill Publishing Company, Inc., New York, by permission of the publisher.

Written. All messages intended to be formal, official, long-term, or affecting several persons in a related way should be written. Be sure that you use only a written communication to amend any previous written communication.

4. *Interoffice memos.* For recording informal inquiries or replies. Can be of value, too, if several people are to receive a message that is extensive, or when data are numerous or complex. Use of memos should not be overdone.

5. *Letters.* More individualized in effect than a memo and usually more formal. Useful for official notices, formally recorded statements, or lengthy communications, even when addressee is physically available. Often valuable for communicating involved thoughts and ideas for future discussion and development, or as part of continuing consideration of problems.

6. *Reports.* More impersonal than a letter. Usually more formal. Used to convey information assocated with evaluation, analysis, recommendations, etc., to supervisors or colleagues. Most effective when based on conference, visits, inspections, surveys, research, study, etc. Should carefully distinguish objectively determined facts from estimates, guesses, opinions, impressions, and generalizations.

GROUP COMMUNICATIONS

Plant groups that are uniform in status, age, sex, compensation level, occupation, length of service, and other such qualifications provide a valid basis for highly pointed messages. This approach helps avoid the gradually numbing stream of form letters, memos, announcements, etc., that really have meaning for only a few of the recipients. Establishment of such groups on a continuing basis helps to build up a sense of unity and group coherence that fosters favorable group reaction and group response, especially where there is routine personal contact among the members.

Spoken. Effective spoken communication with groups calls for special skills. Those that are effective in a committee of equals may be inadequate in a mass meeting. Ability to conduct a conference of your own staff doesn't mean you will have equal ability to participate effectively as a staff member in a conference called by your superior. Conflicts of interest need more tactful handling than a discussion of factual topics.

7. *Informal staff meeting.* This provides an opportunity for development of strong group cohesiveness and response. Properly supplemented with individual face-to-face contacts, it offers the outstanding means of coordinating activities and building mutual understanding. Hold such brief, informal staff meetings daily (if your schedule permits)—early in the morning, at the end of the day, or at lunch.

8. *Planned conferences.* A relatively formal affair. Commonest error is for the person calling the conference to set up the agenda without previous consultation with those who will attend. It is usually desirable to check with most of the prospective participants in advance; provide time for preparation and the assembling of needed data, information, reports, recommendations, etc.; allow opportunity for suggestions as to agenda and conduct of the meeting.

Properly conducted, a planned conference can be extremely useful. If improperly managed, participation will be limited or misdirected. As a result it can be not only wasteful of time, but even deleterious in effect.

9. *Mass meetings.* Of large numbers of employees or management. Can be a valuable means of celebrating occasions, building morale, changing attitudes, meeting emergencies, introducing new policies or key personnel, making special announcements, etc. Can also be used to clarify confused situations, resolve misunderstandings, or identify dissident elements. But such procedures require of the presiding officer great skill and a forceful personality. And there is always the danger of interference or interruption by individuals, or of adverse demonstrations by groups.

Written. The effect of a single, isolated written communication to a group of employees is generally unpredictable. But a carefully planned program of written communications can develop a desirable cumulative effect.

10. *Bulletin board notices.* For lengthy or formal announcements. Can be used for a series of illustrated messages. Are most effective when readership is constantly attracted by changes and by careful control of content, including prompt removal of out-of-date material. Most bulletin board announcements should be supplemented by other forms.

Some companies believe they have increased readership by placing bulletin boards in washrooms. Many companies feel they build good will by offering a section of each board to employees for announcements of social and recreational events, personals, etc. This points up that much more can be done with boards than is usually attempted.

11. *Posters.* An old standby. Small or large, at suitable locations, used in series, changed frequently, they can do much to supplement your other communication media. Commonest, and most effective subjects: safety, good housekeeping, suggestion system.

12. *Exhibits and displays.* Can serve a useful purpose when appropriate space is available, and when they can be properly prepared. Such preparation is often expensive. Commonest subjects: company products, advertising, promoting quality production, increasing safety, cutting waste and costs, and stimulating suggestions.

13. *Visual aids.* Films, filmstrips, easel presentations, and other special visual materials have great potential value but are only as good as the way they are used. Few are self-administering. A good film will be far more effective, for instance, if presented with a soundly planned introduction and followup. Much material that could be of considerable value will be relatively worthless if not presented appropriately. Careful, competent preparation, planning, and utilization procedures should be applied to the use of all visual materials.

The Case of the Stalwart Foreman. A case study in human relations involving communications, with questions for you to answer.

Sid Banks, assembly-line foreman in an auto accessories plant, is usually well liked by his men. He's a square shooter, goes to bat for them in a pinch, and sees that the work load is fairly distributed. Sid works hard himself and although not a very outgoing person, he's friendly in his own way. These good qualities have stood Sid in good stead with his employees over the years. But in the last few weeks, Sid has noticed a change in the men who work for him.

It began when a team of front-office engineers spent a couple of days observing his department. Three days later there was a notice posted on the departmental bulletin board urging employees to shut off motors and lights during the lunch period. The following week, local newspapers carried a story reporting that a change in automobile models would cancel a major contract held by the company.

During this period, at least three of Sid's men spoke to him in this way, "What's the inside story on the engineering survey? Are they going to change the standards again?" Another workman asked, "Is the heat on to cut costs because of anything new? Is a layoff in the wind? Or is it the same old story?" When the newspaper story about the contract cancellation was published, Sid was asked if he knew whether it was true or not, whether it would affect production schedules at the plant. To all these questions, Sid had little to say. He shrugged his shoulders and said, "I only know what I read in the papers."

Now in actuality the facts were these: The engineering study had been made to draw up plans for installing equipment which would make the plant more flexible. Plans were that in the future the plant could handle a variety of products. The bulletin board notice reflected an increase in power consumption which the plant wanted to get back in line. The newspaper story was true—but it didn't give the whole picture. The company *had* known about the model changeover and had decided to diversify its product line so that it wouldn't have to depend upon only one industry for business. As a result, jobs would become more secure in the plant.

As it happened, Sid knew most of these facts. But he had a natural dislike for gossip. "Let the facts speak for themselves," was his motto.

1. How do you explain the sudden coolness of Sid's employees toward him?

2. What's wrong with Sid's motto?

3. If you were Sid, how much of your knowledge of the situation would you pass along to employees?

5 PUBLIC AND COMMUNITY RELATIONS

Why isn't public relations strictly a front-office responsibility?

Because the public doesn't differentiate between front office and shop management. Nor should you. As a member of management, people outside the plant will regard what you say and what you do to be representative of your company's policy.

Your front office will provide, of course, the *official* spokesman to the public and to the newspaper. In case of strikes, fire, accident, or other emergencies, chances are that people from the community would approach your top management for official information. Civil authorities will also go to the front door when inquiring about air- or stream-pollution problems or other matters which affect the local citizens.

But in the normal course of events, and even in time of emergencies, your community will regard you as an informed person on the subject of what's going on in your plant. Your local grocer may simply ask whether it's true that there's a layoff planned at the plant. A friend may want to know how your company takes care of employees who have been injured on the job. The garage man may ask if your company is a good place for his son to look for a job when he graduates from high school. Or a newspaperman may pry for details as to what lies behind an employee strike. So be prepared to speak intelligently and with discretion.

What should you say to a stranger who asks for details about a strike or other emergency at your plant?

A good rule of thumb: *Give out only that information which you consider to be favorable.* Do not under any circumstances disclose information which is confidential (such as information that you have obtained because of your status as a supervisor). And stick to facts, not opinions. When you say "The starting rate of pay for hourly employees is $1.45 per hour," you are more convincing than when you say, "Our rates of pay are high."

If challenged with a statement like, "We understand that the ABC Company fire was attributed to poor fire prevention," counter with facts: "This is the first fire the company has had in thirty-five years. Twice in the last five years we won an award for our safety record."

When a stranger persists in getting more than the usual amount of information about a crisis, try to find out whether or not he is a newspaper reporter or an investigator from a civil agency. Ask politely for credentials. And if the stranger does prove to have a legitimate right for gaining further information, refer him to your front office. Assure him that he'll get more accurate information if he goes directly to the official source.

Should you withhold information from the press or a newspaper reporter?

Another rule of thumb: either you have the facts or you don't. You do yourself and your company harm if you indulge in idle speculation. So if you don't know, say so.

If you do know the facts of a situation (not rumors or opinions), you may be justified in refusing to talk about them to a reporter. This is a matter of company policy and should be checked with your superior. Certainly you shouldn't tell people about design or process secrets if you know them. Neither should you wash dirty linen about petty squabbles concerning labor relations. Nor should you repeat the unconfirmed opinions of others.

What can be done to help your company avoid bad newspaper or radio publicity?

In the long run, this is a problem your top management will have to handle. However, you can draw some of your own conclusions from what the Du Pont company says about the subject. It says that much unfavorable publicity about industry comes from:

• Insufficient information and misunderstanding rather than from a deliberate attempt by the press to smear the company. When a request for legitimate information is made, management helps its own case by seeing that such information is made available.

• Management's indifference to the press. "Every effort," says Du Pont, "should be made to answer proper inquiries or to get an answer if the information sought is not readily available. The public has a right to certain information, and it is to the company's advantage to supply it."

• Unwise handling of inquiries. "False or misleading information or speculative comment in the papers can be damaging," says Du Pont. "It is far better for a newspaper to get its material direct than through irregular channels. Newspapers much prefer to obtain their information from authoritative sources and will do so unless their questions are avoided or evaded."

Should you tell a reporter something off the record?

No. As a general rule don't tell a reporter anything you don't want printed. Not that reporters can't be trusted, but frequently what you tell a reporter off the record will lead him to another source who may not be discreet. Accordingly, if you tell something to a newspaperman, don't be surprised if you see it in the papers.

What sort of favorable happenings at your plant can make news?

There's good reason for your local news services to look to your company as a source of news items. People in your community know your employees and have an interest in hearing about what happens to them at work, as well as at home. So keep your ears and eyes open for interesting items. Then let your personnel office or public relations office know about them. These people will know how to give the publicity to the papers.

Newspapers will find interest in awards made to employees with long service or exceptional safety records, winners in company campaigns for waste reduction or quality improvement, retirements, promotions, company parties and picnics, and unusual achievements of workers on the job or while taking part in recreational activities.

What can you do in your community that will reflect well on the company?

Just being a quiet, clean-living citizen reflects well on the company, of course. People talk about your good qualities as a homeowner, for instance. They'll say, "Joe Smith is a nice neighbor to have. He never

makes any trouble and he keeps a neat home. Joe is a foreman at the
ABC plant."

Today, however, the trend is for all members of management to
take a more important part in the activities of their community. This
is because their experience as leaders at the plant make them especially well qualified for leadership in social and civic affairs. And this
goes just as much for the front-line foreman as it does for the top brass.
Probably more so, since a supervisor tends to have more off-job free
time.

So look for a chance to do your part in:

Politics. Regardless of political party, government is strengthened
when responsible people from industry play an active part in it. Go to
town meetings. Join the political club of your choice. Run for office:
your party is looking for good men to run at the local level.

Education. Your children will tell you the least you can do is to join
the PTA. But go further than this. Do some committee work. And
express your opinion on educational matters.

Religion. Utilize your leadership in church functions. You set a good
example for young people when you go to church. You become a strong
influence for good when you do more than just attend church or make
monetary contributions.

Recreation. There's a wide-open field of choice for you here. Whether
it's Boy Scouts, the Little League, the American Legion, Elks, or any
other social group, there's a chance to combine fun with leadership
that reflects on your company not only as a good place to work, but
also as a producer of strong leaders and sound citizens.

Beyond providing wages and other incomes, does a company have a worthwhile influence on a town?

Very much so. Carry-over of good habits and favorable attitudes
generated at work are frequently in evidence. Employees who are
alert to quality and allergic to waste in the plant look also for better
performance from their local town officials and have their eyes open
for waste in city government.

Much of the effective education for adults regarding the values of
the capitalistic system, too, has been carried on in American plants.

It's also a matter of record that workers are safer at work, regardless
of how hazardous it may be, than they are in their own homes. In a
notable study made a few years ago, employees of General Electric
Company at Coshocton, Ohio, were found not only to be exceptionally
safe at work but also safer than other townspeople on the highway and
in their homes. GE employees had an accident record while in auto-
mobiles six times as good as the rest of the people in town, sixteen

times as good as the national average. In the home, only 11 per cent of GE people had accidents, compared with 18 per cent of non-GE industrial families and 21 per cent of nonindustrial families. Intensive investigation showed that this safety was a carry-over of what GE employees had learned about safety at work.

Doesn't industry lower property values?

Sometimes. But business is more willing today to cooperate in observing restrictive ordinances. Modern industrial buildings are attractive; their landscaped grounds are often showplaces of a community. Control of air and water pollution has been mastered in most cases. Intelligent zoning can control location of new plants to remote sections of town, may specify the type of power generation, size of equipment to be operated, and the like. The important fact is that today most American business is reasonable, responsible, eager to cooperate in living up to its responsibilities to the community in which it lives.

How can you tell what sort of a business climate your town has?

To hold and attract industry, your community should have a favorable business climate. This shouldn't be interpreted to mean that it should be a company town or that the company should be especially favored by legislation and by prejudicial law enforcement. It does mean that a town should conduct its own business in an efficient and economical way. And that the attitude of civic officials and citizens alike is impartial and unbiased toward business.

You can tell if the climate of your community is favorable by checking to see if new industries are coming to town. This is a good sign. If companies are leaving town, there may be something wrong with the town's attitude toward free enterprise.

Another simple check is to ask yourself whether you are proud of the record of your local government. Has it been honest, efficient, and free from partisan prejudices?

On the more tangible side, a community climate that encourages growth of business is one where there is a good source of labor, where power and transportation are available, where taxes are reasonable, and where there is a good balance of different kinds of industries in town. The latter helps to adjust the ups and down of business fortunes so that all the town's tax-source eggs aren't in one basket.

Many employers look carefully to see what the state of labor-management relations are in a prospective community. A history of strikes and violence will discourage them. Good labor relations experience is far more important in attracting new employers than low wage scales or even the absence of unions. Most companies are resigned to the presence of unions. But they do wish only to deal with unions whose representatives are responsible and progressive.

How will a good business climate benefit you and your family?

When many industries come to your town to stay and prosper, you get a lot personally from their success. You get:

Job security. If your company can grow in your community, it cuts down the chances that economic disaster will force it out of town or out of business—and you out of a job.

Better employees. A good town attracts superior people for business purposes. And if your company has a top-flight reputation in town, your chances of getting the cream of the crop of job applicants is high. Consequently, your task as a supervisor is easier.

Equitable salaries. A good business climate means adequate wages for everyone. It discourages depressed wage scales because there is healthy competition for the labor forces.

Good government. A good business climate encourages economic government. You get more of the kind of services you can use, and these services are more efficiently administered.

Lower taxes. Business pays the lion's share of local taxes in most communities. In towns where industry doesn't exist, the private-property owners have to carry the load.

Greater opportunities. Business growth means more and better jobs. And this increase in opportunities takes place all over town, not only in your own company.

What can a supervisor do to improve the business climate in his community?

You can establish yourself in a position of influence by entering into politics, education, religion, and recreation as outlined above. But you can also do much by speaking up for those qualities that will make your town's business climate attractive.

Unfortunately, business, and big business especially, has acquired a reputation with many people that isn't wholly deserved. Some people are quick to overlook the benefits that industry produces. They assume that when it comes to taxes, there are always "plenty more where that comes from." As a result, many a town has taxed a company right out of town. In addition, for a while it was popular to attribute everything bad to business and to give it little credit for the prosperity it brings. Since World War II, American business has done much to prove its social and community responsibility as well as its economic reliability.

You help your town retain and attract industry when you tell the true story of the effects of business. Stick to facts, not opinions. And don't worry about the global aspects of economics. Talk about what has happened at your own company. Find out (and tell others in town) how much wages have increased in the last fifteen years, how safe the plant is to work in, how much employment has increased while mechanization or automation has been going on. Describe the increase in the number and quality of fringe benefits, the consideration shown employees, the opportunities for advancement. If you can, point out how much your company pays in taxes, not only in town but to state and Federal government. Let people figure out how much their own personal taxes would increase if your company left town.

These down-to-earth facts are your best argument for industry. People are interested in hearing them whether you spread the good news in informal conversation between frames at the bowling alley or present it at a debate on the platform of your civic club.

The Case of the Supervisor at the PTA Meeting. A case study in human relations involving community relations, with questions for you to answer.

Joe Smith, shipping supervisor at the Acme Turnings plant, and his wife Florence attend Parent-Teacher Association meetings in their town regularly. Joe usually sits back and has little to say. But one night last week something came up that made his blood boil.

During the course of the meeting there was a discussion concerning the problem of encouraging high school students to finish their studies. And there was also a lot of talk about the advantages of going on to college for a higher education. All this made sense to Joe, with little to get excited about. That is until a man from the other side of town got up and started talking about how poor the work was that was open to non–college graduates.

"We ought to make it plain to our kids," said the man from across town, "that unless they get a higher education, they'll end up wearing grease-stained overalls and carrying their lunch to work in a box. Then they'll know what it's like to break their hump for a living. And never know from one week to the next whether there's going to be a job and a paycheck waiting for them. Why look at the Acme plant. They laid off seventy-five people last month, and who knows when they'll call them back to work again? Same thing happened last winter. Any kid with ambition won't be satisfied with that kind of a deal."

1. If you were Joe Smith, how would you feel?

2. In what ways do you think Acme's reputation in town can affect the plant?

3. What can Joe Smith do to improve his company's reputation?

4. Should he speak up and defend it at the meeting? If so, what should he say?

2

SUPERVISING PEOPLE

The Fundamentals

6 THE ART OF LEADERSHIP

What is leadership?

Everyone will give you a different answer to this one. My definition is this: *Leadership is the knack of getting other people to follow you and to do willingly the things you want them to do.* Regardless of all the fancy talk you'll hear about leadership, this definition pinpoints the real reason for the high premium on this scarce skill.

Are leaders always popular with the people they supervise?

The best leaders seem to combine the knack of leading and the knack of winning friends. But most leaders must be satisfied with respect and followers. Why? Because many of the decisions you must make as a leader will not always favor everybody. Sometimes they will please nobody. Chances are you won't win any popularity contests among employees.

Why should you want to become a leader?

The job of a leader is an unbelievably tough one. But the rewards are high. You'll find them in increased prestige and status among the people with whom you work, among your friends, and in your community. And to many a leader, the heady exhilaration of making decisions that prove to be correct is reward enough. To others, it's mainly a sense of mission. To still others, it's the satisfaction that power brings. In industry, you can have all these in varying degrees. You may even have more money—since leadership is a quality that business traditionally pays a high price for.

Are good leaders born or made?

Marshall Foch, famous World War I leader, said of leadership, "These are natural gifts in a man of genius, in a born general; in the average man, such advantages may be secured by work and reflection." Foch's statement pretty much reflects the consensus: Some men are born leaders, but *most* leaders are good leaders because they have worked hard and thought hard to become so.

What are the ingredients for good leadership?

In a nutshell, men who prove to be successful leaders are characterized by:

A sense of mission. A belief in your own ability to lead, a love for the work of leadership itself, and a devotion to the people and the organization you serve.

Self-denial. This essential of leadership is often played down. It means a willingness to forego self-indulgences (like blowing your top). And the ability to bear the headaches the job entails.

High character. Few men become successful leaders who aren't honest with themselves and with others, who can't face hard facts and unpleasant situations with courage, who fear criticism or their own mistakes, who are insincere or undependable.

Job competence. There's been too much talk about the insignificance of technical job skill to the foreman. A man who knows the job he supervises has one of the best foundations for building good leadership.

Good judgment. Common sense, the ability to recognize the important from the unimportant, tact, the wisdom to look into the future and plan for it are the added ingredients that make the best leaders.

Energy. Leadership at any level means rising early and working late. It leaves little time for relaxation or escape from problems. Good health, good nerves, boundless energy makes this tough job easier.

Is there only one way to lead people?

Here's where a lot of us have been fooled. Take this situation. Joe Smith supervises three material handlers. Each has become an absentee problem. Listen to how he deals with each person:

To Al: "It's time you get on the ball. I want to see you in here five days a week every week from now on. Otherwise, I'll put you up for discharge."

To Sid: "Your absences are getting to be a headache for me and the rest of us here. You'll have to see that your attendance improves. Let's you and I work out a way to lick this problem."

To Terry: "Take a look at your absence record. Not so hot, is it? I'll leave it up to you to figure out some way to straighten it out."

Which method do you suppose works best? *Answer:* All get good results. Al, Sid, and Terry are no longer attendance problems. The reason? There are three basic kinds of leadership—because there are three basic kinds of people. To be a successful leader, you need to be able to master all three techniques.

What are the three kinds of leadership called?

Autocratic leadership (the type used with Al in the last question). Many people feel this technique is old-fashioned, but it works with many people. The leader makes the decisions, demands obedience from the people he supervises. Trouble is that he better be right.

Democratic leadership (the type used with Sid). Most popular today. The leader discusses and consults. Draws ideas from the people he supervises, lets them help set policy. Makes for participation, strong teamwork.

Free-rein leadership (the type used with Terry). Most difficult to use. Leader acts as an information center and exercises minimum of control. He depends upon employees' sense of responsibility and good judgment to get things done.

Which kind of leadership is best?

Most psychologists and sociologists will tell you that democratic leadership is the best method to use. Fact is that while the democratic way may involve the least risk, you'll hamper your leadership role if you stick only to that one. You *can* play a round of golf with a driver. But you'll get a much better score if you use a niblick in a sand trap and a putter on the greens.

Suppose you have a problem of cutting down on scrap in your department. You may find it better to consult in a group meeting with all your workers to let them decide how they'll approach the problem (democratic leadership); then let the inspector know of what you plan, leaving it up to him to adjust his inspection techniques accord-ingly (free-rein); and merely tell the scrap collector how you want him to sort out the waste (autocratic). You see, you'd be using all three kinds of leadership to deal with the same problem.

Should a leader ever pull his rank?

Authority is *earned,* not inherited as a result of a man's being made a supervisor. In the long run, employees will learn to respect and accept your authority without your having to pull rank on them. To a new supervisor, the wish to pull rank may be a temptation. Resist if you can.

Of course, a particularly sticky situation may arise where an employee refuses to do what you tell him to. In such a case, don't make the mistake of voicing the opinion, "I'm boss around here and what I say goes." Instead, make your demands quietly and firmly. Otherwise, you may make a spectacle of yourself that will take a long time to live down.

How much does personality have to do with leadership?

A good personality helps. Employees react more easily to a supervisor who has a ready smile and who is warm and outgoing. But personality must be more than skin-deep to stand up over the long haul. Much more important is your real desire to understand and sympathize with the people who work for you. Fair play, interest in others, good decisions, and character will help make you a stronger leader than if you rely solely on personality.

Likewise, one kind of leadership may fit your personality better than the other two. And you may rely more upon this kind of leadership than on the others. But work hard to keep from putting all your eggs in the same basket.

What does an employee's personality have to do with the kind of leadership you exercise?

Noted author Auren Uris * advises that you'll find these connections between leadership methods and types of personality:

• The *aggressive, hostile* type of person does better under an *autocratic leader*. His latent hostility must be firmly channeled to confine his work to constructive ends.

• The *aggressive, cooperative* type will work better under *democratic* or *free-rein* leadership. His self-assertiveness takes constructive paths, so that he will head in the right direction when he's on his own.

• The *insecure* type, the man who tends to be dependent on his superior, does better under the firmer hand of the *autocratic* leader.

• The *individualist,* the solo player, is usually most productive under the *free-rein* type of leadership—*if he knows his job.*

What kind of leadership works best in an emergency?

Autocratic leadership is fast. When an emergency arises, say, a live-steam hose breaks loose, is whipping about endangering lives, you wouldn't want to pussyfoot around consulting employees as to what

* Auren Uris, *How to Be a Successful Leader,* McGraw-Hill Book Company, Inc., New York, 1953.

to do. You'd probably shout, "Hey, Smitty, cut the steam valve! Carl, watch the safety!"

Followership? Is that the reverse of leadership?

Not exactly. A good leader must also be a good follower. You may lead your work group, but you follow the leadership of your superior. He, too, may lead seven or eight foremen. But he follows the man who supervises him. And so on. So don't overlook the need to learn how to follow as well as to lead.

Can you tell what kind of a follower you are?

If you can decide what kind of leadership you find most easy to assume, it's a good guess that's the kind of follower you are. In other words, if you exercise authority autocratically, you probably react best to a boss who is decisive. On the other hand, if you tend to give your employees a free rein, you probably put out best for a boss who does likewise.

The root of many of the difficulties between a supervisor who is a successful leader and his boss is that frequently the supervisor expects identical treatment himself. When he doesn't get it, he says, "I can't get along with my boss." What he really means is, "I haven't learned to be as successful a follower as I am a leader."

How many mistakes can you make without being a failure?

The U.S. Weather Bureau, though often derided, is still in business, and it rates itself a success when it's right 85 per cent of the time. If you've got anything on the ball at all, chances are that most of your decisions will be good ones. So don't weaken your leadership by being afraid to commit yourself or by dodging an issue. Learn to reexamine the situation you bungle so that you don't make the same mistake again. Every company needs leaders who have ideas and believe in them, even if some are wrong. It can have little use for men who have no ideas or are too timid to act on them for fear of making mistakes.

Is modesty characteristic of leaders?

General Patton was one of America's most successful and dynamic leaders—and George Patton was not a modest man. Neither was his counterpart in the British Army, Field Marshal Montgomery. Both men were vain to a point. But this vanity was based on ability and confidence. Both used this outward show to inspire their followers. Yes, many leaders are far from modest. But *most* leaders tend to be modest—to be quick to let their associates and employers take credit for what the group has accomplished. Modesty becomes a man. And everyone admires him for it. Just look at the effectiveness and personal popularity of President Eisenhower—a truly humble man. He has received plenty of acclaim without blowing his own horn.

How does a leader win loyalty from his followers?

You win loyalty by being loyal to your employees—by supporting their best interests and defending their actions to others who would discredit them. "We may not have made a good showing this month," a supervisor who is loyal to his group will say, "but no one can say the boys weren't in there trying."

Loyalty is also inspired when you show employees your own loyalty to your superiors. For instance, if you have to pass along an order from your superior, you will breed only contempt among your subordinates if you say, "Here's the new operating instruction from the central office, Tom. I don't think any more of it than you do. But it was sent down from the top, so we'll have to try to make sense out of it, even if they don't know what they're doing."

Is good leadership simply good human relations?

You could say that. Because to be a good leader you must be a student of human nature. Not because you love everybody. Probably you don't. But you must develop shrewd judgment in estimating people's intentions, knowledge, and interests. Even the roughest, toughest industrialists have been keen estimators of human capabilities and have been expert in getting the most from people who work for them.

Employees expect so much from a supervisor. Must he be a superman?

The job of supervising is difficult, but don't expect too much from yourself—all at once, anyway. It's more important to know your own capabilities—and your limitations. Then work hard to round out your own personal inventory of skills. Try to avoid situations which call for skills you lack. But don't damage your leadership by trying to bluff.

You inspire confidence in your integrity when you say candidly, "Frankly, I don't know the answer to this problem. What are your views on it? Perhaps we better get hold of someone who really knows the subject." Of course, if you plead ignorance too often, either you must improve or you must ask for another assignment.

Today it's a sign of strength rather than weakness not to know all the answers. It's smart to solicit guidance from your associates and superiors. Seeking advice from others is good human relations, too. It allows for participation, and it's flattering to those whose opinions are asked.

Is there one single thing that's more important for a leader to do than anything else?

Yes. Lost in the shuffle of platitudes of what a leader should *be* is the reason for leadership in the first place—the need for opinions, decisions, and *action*. Employees won't respond to you as a person unless you can demonstrate to them your courage in stating your views on a problem, your decisiveness in determining what should be done, and finally your ability to get things moving.

Malcolm McNair, a noted authority on the psychology of human beings, puts it this way:

"To *look* is one thing,

To *see* what you look at is another,

To *understand* what you see is a third,

To *learn* from what you understand is still something else,

But to *act* on what you learn is all that really matters!"

How much of a supervisor's job requires leadership?

Today's supervisor is a manager. A manager must first of all be a leader. But he does many other things too. The Methods Engineering Council Division of H. B. Maynard Company, Inc., Pittsburgh, breaks down the manager's job into eleven elements:

• Gather information needed to solve problems.

• Put together the information so that the problem makes sense.

• Plan for the goals to be reached by your group.

• Decide on the course of action to take.

• Organize your work group so that the right person is on the right job.

• Communicate your intentions, issue instructions, keep the group informed.

• Lead and motivate employees to desire to reach the group's goals.

• Direct, guide, and counsel employees through giving suggestions, additional instructions, and information.

• Measure, evaluate, and control by comparing results with what was planned.

• Develop people by proper training and encouragement.

• Look ahead for new areas of improvement, new ways of stimulating your work force.

You can see that some of the eleven elements require more personal leadership than others. That's why many companies provide staff specialists to help a supervisor on the more technical phases of his leadership—like gathering information (record keeping), putting together information (reporting and analyzing data), planning (setting up schedules), and measuring, evaluating, and controlling (auditing performance). But the very best leaders develop their supervisory skills to handle *all* phases of management.

Why is it that some leaders are more poised than others?

Probably because they regard themselves as professional managers and leaders. Even when things seem to be going to hell in a hand-basket, watch how the seasoned leader appears cool and collected. For an immature manager, every day can become a series of crash programs. So begin being a professional by keeping calm at crisis time. Don't waste time blowing your valves. Accept the fact that crises are always bursting in on business. Use your time for study and analysis.

Try to act like the seasoned leader (even if you don't actually feel that way at first). He smiles when things get tough, thinks when problems get mountainous, accepts an occasional defeat as part of the game he's paid for playing. He doesn't get his exercise by jumping at conclusions.

Ask him how he's been able to survive twenty-five years of heavy production schedules, nagging labor problems, and supervision that begets ulcers. He'll answer, "If you can't stand the heat, get out of the kitchen."

Any other tips for leaders?

Advice for leaders is pretty free. There's lots of it lying about. And most of it makes sense for the man who can put it into practice. For instance:

Be predictable. People want to know where they stand with the boss —tomorrow as well as today. You might borrow a page from the books on child psychology. The experts have studied the maladjustments and the frustrations of kids. They suggest one good rule for handling them: *Be consistent.* Praise a child for an act today and bawl him out for the same act tomorrow—bingo, tears. If he tries to help with the dishes, breaks one, and gets a scolding—watch out for tantrums. If you embarrass him in front of others, look out—he may paint the cat green just to make it look ridiculous, too. It's the same thing for adults.

Put yourself in the employee's place. Maybe you recall the last time you were at a ball game. Did you find yourself leaning with every pitch—trying to put body english on foul balls? Do the same thing with people. This mental shift can become a regular and desirable habit. It will help you understand, predict, and direct the responses of people.

Show your enthusiasm. If you sincerely like an idea, the way an employee did a job, your next assignment, show this feeling to others in words and manners. Don't be a cold fish. The personal atmosphere *you* create determines whether people will have the welcome mat out for you or give you the busy signal.

Be interested in employees' welfare. "Men want a foreman, supervisor, or manager whom they can trust in time of need, to whom they can go when they need advice about personal affairs," said Brehon Somervell, late president of the Koppers Company, Inc. "It is a good outfit, indeed when the men say 'My boss told me what to do about it,' or 'You had better ask the boss, he will know.' "

Treat employees equally. Men and women insist on a leader having a sense of fair play. They want to feel they are being given assignments entirely upon their merits and that the boss won't play favorites. Favoritism not only is a sign of weak character, but it can also wreck an organization.

What is there to the group psychology approach to leadership?

As mentioned earlier, there is a large body of authorities on the subject of leadership who feel that success can be attained only through *group-centered* leadership. These authorities base their opinion upon psychological and sociological research studies which seem to show that employees as a whole—and especially taken as a work group—respond most favorably to democratic or free-rein leadership methods. In other words, a group-centered leader never bosses, makes few decisions himself, continually invites the work group to determine what should be done and how it should be done. (This approach is also called "group dynamics.")

Much of this new psychology for leadership makes sense. But it should be approached with caution and used primarily in situations which favor it. It is best used when major changes are planned, when safety campaigns and cost-cutting or scrap-reduction goals are being set. Certainly you should approach this technique gradually until you can note how different employees react to it and adjust your methods accordingly.

The Case of the New Supervisor. A case study in human relations involving leadership, with questions for you to answer.

Adam Force had just been appointed supervisor in a plant manufacturing knitted rayon underwear. Before his elevation to the management ranks, he had been a loom fixer for five years. His work on that job had consistently been of superior caliber.

Except for a little good natured kidding, Adam's coworkers had wished him well on his new job. And for the first week or two most of them had been cooperative—even helpful—while Adam was adjusting to his supervisory role.

Late Friday afternoon of Adam's second week as a supervisor, a disturbing incident took place. Having just made the rounds of his department, Adam stopped in the men's washroom. There he saw two of his old buddies—Mick and Bob—washing up.

"Say fellows. You shouldn't be cleaning up this soon. It's at least another 15 minutes until quitting time," said Adam. "Get back on the floor and I'll forget I saw you in here."

"Come off it, Adam," said Mick. "You used to slip up here early yourself on Fridays. Just because you've got a little rank now, don't think you can get tough with us." To this Adam replied, "Things are different now. Both of you get back on the job or I'll make trouble." Mick and Bob said nothing more, and they both returned to the shop.

From that time on Adam began to have trouble as a supervisor. Mick and Bob gave him the silent treatment. The loom operators seemed to forget how to do the simplest things. Every few minutes there was a machine shutdown. By the end of the month, Adam's department was showing the poorest record for production.

1. How do you think Adam should have handled the washroom incident? Why?

2. What do you suggest Adam could do about the silent treatment he got from Mick and Bob?

3. If you were Adam, what would you do to get your department's production up?

7 ORGANIZATION AND
THE FIRST–LINE SUPERVISOR

Is the foreman the middleman
in the management organization?

Too often, the foreman (and occasionally his superiors) sees himself only as a middleman put in an awkward position to serve as a buffer between the company and the workers. The upper group wants him to put the pressure on; the lower group wants him to be a good Joe.

A good foreman in a good organization is much more than just a middleman. He's really the key man. Situated where he is, the first-line supervisor can clear the way for intelligent top-management actions directed toward the rank and file and also serve as the key man in letting top management know how workers feel. Acting as a key man, he knits the whole organization of management and workers together.

A particularly bad situation is one where the foreman has no real status, where he's a figurehead who is bypassed by both managers and workers. This can be sheer torture.

Not being just a middleman or a figurehead depends upon two things—your company's attitude toward foremen and your own attitude toward yourself. Most companies truly want supervisors to be full-time managers who think and feel and act at the department or section level the way other executives do at middle- and top-management levels.

67

Surprisingly, more supervisors than companies have shirked this responsibility. These are the supervisors who continually complain of being sold down the river or of being whipping boys. The record will show that most foremen determine for themselves whether they will be key men or merely men in the middle.

What is organization?

An organization is a grouping of people together so that they can work effectively toward a goal which members of the group want to achieve.

The goal of a business organization is primarily profits for stockholders and wages and salaries for managers, supervisors, and employees. There are other important goals, too, like supplying goods to the general population or producing military materials for our defense in time of war. And members of the organization all aim for less material satisfactions, too, such as the sense of fellowship, accomplishment, and prestige.

Why organize?

We'd have nothing but havoc without it. We take organization for granted because we have lived so long with it at home, in church, and at school. Little we do together would be effective if we didn't agree among ourselves as to *who* should do *what*. And since business organizations are under tremendous pressures to be effective, their organization tends to be more formal and rigid.

Are all organizations formal?

No. In a good many of our activities, even in manufacturing plants, some people just naturally take over responsibilities and exercise authority without anyone ever spelling it out. Chances are that in a group of fifteen employees who you might imagine are all at the same level, you'll discover some sort of informal organization. It may be that Bob, who sweeps the floors, actually swings weight in that group. His staff assistant may be Ted, the lift-truck driver, who acts as his informant. The rest of the group may either work hard or stage a slowdown at a nod from Bob. No one gave Bob his authority, but he has it as surely as if the company president had published a special order giving him a title.

So beware of informal organization—among the employees you supervise, in the supervisory group itself, and in the entire management structure. Don't go off half-cocked until you know the ropes in your own situation.

Which comes first, the organization or the job?

If there were no job to do, there would be no reason for having an organization. So don't make the mistake of being organization-happy and trying to set up an elaborate organization just for the sake of having one. The best organization is a simple one that puts people together so that the job at hand gets done better, more quickly, more cheaply than any other way.

In business, the job at hand for a manufacturing plant is a very big and complex one. The number of people involved is large, and their different skills are many. Some authorities say that the business organization must manage four big M-jobs:

Men. The people who manage others, as well as those who do the work.

Machines. The machinery, buildings, and equipment that enable the men to produce the goods and services.

Material. The raw materials and other goods that go into the product or are used to refine it.

Money. The dollars and cents that provide the machines and materials for men to manage and work with.

Your job, too, is one that involves management of the four Ms. Your place in the company's organization should be designed to help you do that management job better. But recognize that the big organization can't be tailormade to the last inch to suit all of your preferences. Within the framework of your own department, however, it's up to you to see that your organization is tailormade to the job as well as it possibly can.

What's the difference between line and staff?

An organization works best when it gets many related jobs done effectively with the minimum of friction. This requires coordination and determination of *what* to do and *how* to do it. Those managers and supervisors whose main job it is *to see that things get done* are usually members of the *line* organization. Other management people who *help them to decide* what to do and how to do it, and assist in coordinating the efforts of all, are usually called *staff* people.

Production departments, sales departments, and occasionally purchasing departments are the most common line activities. The production foreman or first-line supervisor is likely to be a member of the line organization.

Departments which help the line departments control quality and maintain adequate records are typically staff activities. Industrial engineering, maintenance, research, accounting, industrial and personnel relations are some examples of typical staff activities.

It may help you to think of line people as the doers, staff people as the advisors. Each function is important in its own way, even though there has often been rivalry between line and staff for credit and recognition.

On an organization diagram, line functions are usually connected by vertical lines, staff functions by horizontal lines (Fig. 7-1).

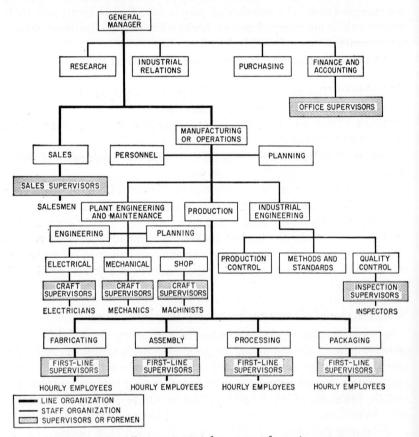

Fig. 7-1   Line and staff organization for a manufacturing company.

Are authority and responsibility the same thing?

No. Authority should go hand in hand with responsibility, but the two are no more alike than the two sides of a coin.

Your *responsibilities* are those things you are held accountable for—

like costs, on-time deliveries, and good housekeeping. Responsibilities are also spoken of as your duties—like checking time cards, investigating accidents, scheduling employees, or keeping production records.

Authority is the power you need to carry out your responsibilities. A supervisor's authority includes the right to make decisions, to take action to control costs and quality, and to exercise necessary discipline over the employees assigned to him to help carry out these responsibilities.

It's an axiom that you shouldn't be given a responsibility without enough authority to carry it out. If foreman Brown is given responsibility for seeing that quality is up to specifications, he must also be given authority to stop the production line when the quality falls off or to take any steps he feels necessary to correct it.

Where does authority come from?

Authority, like responsibility, is usually handed down to a supervisor from his immediate boss. The boss, in turn, has received his authority and responsibilities from his immediate superior. And so it goes, on up to the company president who has received his dual assignments from the board of directors.

The biggest chunk of authority and responsibility rests with the company president. He may split this chunk in as few as three pieces (to the vice presidents of production, sales, and financing) or as many as twenty (to vice presidents in charge of twenty different products). As the responsibilities and authorities come down the line to you, the chunks get smaller and smaller. But they also get much more specific.

Your plant superintendent may have the responsibility "for producing goods in sufficient quantities to meet sales requirements," while your responsibility may be "to see that ten milling machines are operated at optimum capacity so that 200,000 product units are produced each month." Similarly, the plant superintendent's authority may permit him to "exercise broad disciplinary measures," while yours may be limited to "recommending disciplinary action for employees who break rules or whose output is not up to production and quality standards."

Most companies try to make the responsibilities and authorities at each level of management fairly consistent. For instance, a foreman in department A should have the same general responsibilities as a foreman in department Z. And their authorities would be generally the same even though the specific duties of each might differ widely.

Figure 7–2 is a check list which might help you and your boss to decide duties, policies, and actions for which *you* are held responsible.

SUPERVISORY RESPONSIBILITY SURVEY

Do you feel it is your responsibility to . . .		YES	NO	DON'T KNOW
. . . select and train your employees?	1. Request that additional employees be hired as neded?			
	2. Approve new employees assigned to you?			
	3. Explain benefit plans such as group insurance and hospitalization to new employes?			
	4. Tell employees about upgrading and pay ranges?			
	5. Make sure employees know rules of conduct and safety regulations?			
	6. Train an understudy?			
	7. Hold regular safety meetings?			
. . . make work assignments and maintain discipline?	8. Prepare employee work schedules?			
	9. Assign specific duties to workers?			
	10. Assign responsibilities to assistants or group leaders?			
	11. Delegate authority?			
	12. Discipline employees?			
	13. Discharge employees?			
	14. Specify the kind and number of employees to do a job?			
	15. Determine amount of work to be done by each employee in your group?			
	16. Authorize overtime?			
	17. Enforce safety rules?			
	18. Transfer employees within your department?			
. . . handle employee problems with the union?	19. Interpret the union contract?			
	20. Process grievances with shop stewards?			
	21. Prepare vacation schedules?			
	22. Recommend changes in the contract?			
	23. Lay off employees for lack of work?			
	24. Grant leaves of absence?			
. . . know how pay and incentive systems work?	25. Explain to employees how their pay is calculated?			
	26. Determine allowances for faulty material or interruptions to be paid pieceworkers?			
	27. Approve piece rates or standards before they become effective?			
	28. Answer employee's questions regarding time studies or allowances?			
. . . make these production decisions?	29. Start jobs in process?			
	30. Stop jobs in process?			
	31. Authorize set-up changes?			
	32. Approve material substitutions?			
	33. Requisition supplies to keep your department running?			
	34. Determine whether material should be scrapped or reworked?			
	35. Replan work due to breakdowns?			
	36. Take unsafe tools out of service?			
	37. Correct unsafe working conditions?			
. . . tie in with other departments?	38. Know how an order flows through the plant from start to finish?			
	39. Understand what the staff departments do? Your relationship to them?			
	40. Authorize maintenance and repair jobs?			
	41. Requisition tools?			
	42. Investigate accidents?			
. . . be concerned with the way the job gets done?	43. Make suggestions for improvements in manufacturing procedures in your department?			
	44. Recommend changes in layout?			
	45. Suggest materials handling methods to be used in your department?			
	46. Discuss with staff the manufacturing problems caused by proposed design changes?			
. . . think about how much things cost?	47. Cut down on waste of materials and supplies?			
	48. Keep adequate production records for checking output per machine and per manhour?			
	49. Participate in setting up your department budget?			
	50. Investigate charges against your budget?			

FIG. 7-2 Supervisory responsibility survey. (Hector E. Macdonald, "Do Your Supervisors Really Know What's Expected of Them?" *Factory Management and Maintenance*, McGraw-Hill Publishing Company, Inc., New York, October, 1954.)

Who can delegate authority and responsibility?

Any member of management, including the foreman, can usually delegate some of his responsibility—*and his authority*. Remember, the two must go together.

A foreman, for instance, who has responsibility for seeing that proper records are kept in his department may delegate that responsibility to a records clerk. But the clerk must also be given the authority to collect time sheets from the operators and to interview them if the data seems inaccurate. The foreman wouldn't, however, delegate to the records clerk the authority to discipline an employee. Likewise, a foreman can't delegate *all* the responsibility for seeing that accurate records are kept.

What's the chain of command?

The term *chain of command* is a military term used to imply that orders and information in an organization should originate at the top, then proceed toward the bottom from one higher management level to the next lower without skipping any levels or crossing over to another chain of command. The same procedure would be followed by information and requests going up the line.

Is it a bad practice to go out of channels?

It's best to conform to the practice in your company. "Channels" is just a word to indicate the normal paths that information, orders, and requests should travel when following the chain of command. The channel for customer orders to travel from the sales manager to the production foreman might be from the sales manager to the production manager, from the production manager to the department superintendent, and from the department superintendent to the foreman. It would be going out of channels if the sales manager gave the order directly to the foreman.

Going up the line, the channel for a supervisor to ask for a raise might be from him to his department head, from the department head to the production manager, and from the production manager to the manufacturing vice president. The foreman would be going out of channels if he asked the vice president for a raise without having seen each one of the other managers in progression.

Since authority and responsibility are delegated through the channels of a chain of command, for the most part it's better to handle your affairs (especially decisions) through them, too. It avoids having you make changes without letting your boss know what's going on. And prevents others from feeling another manager is going over his head.

On the other hand, there are occasions when chain-of-command channels should be circumvented. In emergencies, or when time is essential, it makes sense to get a decision or advice from a higher authority other than your boss if your boss is not readily available.

For purposes of keeping people informed and for exchanging information, channels sometimes get in the way. There's really nothing wrong with your discussing matters with people in other departments or on other levels of the company—so long as you don't betray confidences. If you do cross channels, it's a good practice to tell your boss you are doing so, and why. That way, he won't think you are doing something behind his back.

Why do staff people have so much influence?

Staff departments exert influence, rather than real authority, because their responsibility is to advise and guide, not to take action themselves.

Before the days of staff departments (and when manufacturing plants were smaller) the plant manager or shop superintendent tried to be informed on all kinds of subjects related to manufacturing. These subjects included personnel management, industrial engineering, cost control, quality control, etc. As plants grew larger, and the manufacturing processes became more complex, many managers found it was wiser to employ assistants who could devote their full time and attention to becoming authorities in each of these phases of manufacturing. These assistants have become known as "staff assistants" and the departments they manage, "staff departments."

It's a mistake to assume (in most cases) that a staff department tells you how to do something. More often than not the staff department suggests that you do something differently, or advises that your department is off the beam (on quality for instance), or provides information for your guidance. This isn't weasel-wording. It's an honest recognition that the line people must retain the authority to run the shop, but that to stand up to today's competition, you need the counsel of a specialist in these side areas.

If a supervisor is smart, he'll make every use he can of the staff department's knowledge. If you were building a house yourself for the first time and someone offered to furnish you free the advice of a first-rate carpenter, a top-notch mason, a heating specialist, and a journeyman painter, you'd jump at the chance. The same holds true in accepting the advice and guidance available from the staff departments and other specialists in your plant when tackling a management problem.

How can you do a better job of delegation?

Start by seeing yourself as a manager, not a hired hand. Recognize that no matter how good a man you might be, you'll always have more responsibilities than you can carry out yourself.

The trick of delegation is to concentrate on the most important matters yourself. Keep a close eye, for instance, on the trend of production costs: that's a big item. But let someone else check the temperature of the quenching oil in the heat-treat. That's less important.

Trouble begins when you can't distinguish between the big and the little matters. You may feel you can put off checking the production record: it can wait until the day of reckoning at the end of the month. You may feel that unless the quenching oil temperature is just right, the heat treater will spoil a $500 die today. But in the long run you'll lose your sanity if you don't see that the small jobs must get done by someone else.

When should you delegate?

Delegate when you find you can't personally keep up with everything you feel you should do. Just giving minor time-consuming tasks to others will save your time for bigger things. Let Joe double-check his production report, for example, or send Al down the line to see who wants to work overtime.

Be sure to have certain jobs taken over when you're absent from your department in an emergency or during vacation. Keep it to routine matters, if you will, and to those requiring a minimum of authority. But do try to get rid of the task of filling out routine requisitions and reports, making calculations and entries, checking supplies, and running errands.

Should you delegate everything?

Don't go too far. Some things are yours only. When a duty involves technical knowledge that only you possess, it would be wrong to let someone less able take over. And it's wrong to trust confidential information to others.

What should you tell an employee about a job delegated to him?

Give him a clear statement of what he's to do, how far he can go, and how much checking up you intend to do. Let the employee know the relative importance of the job so that he can judge how much attention it should receive. There's no point in letting him think that making a tally will lead him to a promotion if you consider it just a routine task.

Tell a man why you delegated the job to him. If it shows you have confidence in him, he'll try that much harder. But if he thinks you're pushing off all the dirty jobs on him, he may deliberately make a botch of it.

Don't mislead an employee about his authority. You don't want him trying to crack your whip. But do define the scope of the task and see that others in your department know that this new task isn't something that he's assumed on his own. Let them know that you handed him the assignment and that you'll expect that they'll give him cooperation in carrying it out.

Why should an employee accept a delegated job?

An employee who accepts a delegated job outside of his own job responsibilities is really taking the job on speculation. He has a right to know what's in it for him:

• An employee who takes on an extra duty gets a chance to learn. If he's never seen how the individual records in the shop are tabulated, here's a chance for him to get a better perception of what's going on.

• A delegated job provides more job satisfaction. Employees thrive on varied assignments. This is a chance to build interest by letting an employee do something out of the normal as far as he's concerned.

• Delegation is sometimes a reward for other work well done. If you can truthfully say that you wouldn't trust anyone else with a certain delegated task, this will help build an employee's pride and feeling of status.

The Case of Andy Jacobs. A case study in human relations involving organization, with questions for you to answer.

In an electronics plant in the Southwest, changes in manufacturing techniques have been the order of the day. Hardly a month goes by that there aren't changes in the circuitry design, revisions of specifications, or substitution of new components for old ones that were new only a short while before. When Andy Jacobs, subassembly foreman, walks into the shop with a revised set of operating instructions, his gang frequently greets him with, "Here we go again!"

Employees in Andy's shop (all men) are a pretty flexible group. They have come from all over the country attracted by the climate and the opportunities in a growing industry. Taken as a lot, they're above average in intelligence and education. Only a very few are not high school graduates.

Andy is considerably older than the men he supervises, even though he's only fifty-one. He got into electronics work with one of its pioneers in

Chicago and grew up with the industry. Andy got most of his technical learning on the job and from correspondence schools. He manages to keep pretty well up on things, but he's not brilliant.

Last year the plant got its first ultrasonic manufacturing equipment—a soldering pot that fuses aluminum-foil capacitors to wire leads by agitating the oxide off the aluminum so that the two metals make a clean contact. When the pot was installed in Andy's department, Andy was too busy to pay much attention to the engineers who were checking it out. Accordingly, they spent most of their time demonstrating its operation to the plant's methods engineer, Bob Smith. Bob is a college-trained electronics engineer being groomed for a higher management position.

The new soldering pot worked fine for several months. Then one day the inspection department started rejecting subassemblies from Andy's department because of improper joining of the capacitors. Bob wasn't around at the time, so Andy and two of the men on the soldering operation played around with the sonic pot for a couple of hours without finding out what the trouble was.

By that time, a dozen or so operators were watching Andy experiment. He was getting lots of advice and red in the face, too. Just then Bob returned to the department. With him was Andy's boss. "What's the delay here, Andy?" asked his boss. While Andy was explaining the difficulty, Bob tinkered with the soldering pot. Suddenly Bob asked, "How long has it been since this pot's been cleaned?" One of the operators volunteered that it hadn't been cleaned for several weeks because of the heavy demand on it for production. "Well, that's the trouble," said Bob. "All it needs is a cleaning."

With that, Andy's boss turned to Andy, "You better keep an eye on this so it doesn't happen again. It costs us plenty to have a crew like this stand around doing nothing just because there's a slip-up in supervision." Then he clapped Bob on the shoulder, "It's good to have you around, Bob. We need young fellows like you to keep us oldtimers on the ball."

When Andy's boss had left, Andy called Bob into his office. "Why didn't you speak up and tell the boss you were handling the sonic pot?" asked Andy. "You put me in a devil of a spot. You do that once more and I'll have your hide!"

1. Who do you think was at fault, Andy, Bob, or the boss? Why?

2. If you were Bob, what would you say to Andy?

3. If you had been Andy, how would you have settled the situation?

4. What do you think of the boss's attitude?

5. Why, after so many months, do you suppose Andy hadn't learned the operation of the sonic pot?

6. What do you think Andy's age had to do with the situation? His education?

8 CONVERTING POLICY INTO ACTION

What is meant by company policy?

Company policies are broad rules or guides for action. At their best, these rules are a statement of the company's objectives and its basic principles for doing business. They are intended as a guide for supervisors and managers in getting their jobs done. Many policies give the supervisor the opportunity to use his own best judgment in carrying them out. Others are established by firm rules, which the supervisor must observe if he is to run his department in harmony with the rest of the organization.

Is policy only high-level stuff?

Policy is generally set by managers high up in the company organization. But policy can be no more than a collection of high-sounding words unless the foreman translates them into action on the firing line.

Take an example of a disciplinary policy. Here's how it might sound as it works its way down from the front office to first-line action by the foreman:

Company president: "Our policy is to exercise controls to regulate the conduct of our employees."

Manufacturing vice president: "The policy on attendance in this plant is that habitual absenteeism will be penalized."

Plant superintendent: "Here are the rules governing absences. It's up to you foremen to keep an eye on absences and to discharge any employee absent or late more than three times in three months."

Foreman: "Sorry, Joe. I'm going to have to lay you off for three days. You know the rules. You put me in a bad spot when you take time off on your own without warning or getting approval."

Note that no real action takes place until the foreman puts the words of the policy into effect.

What sort of matters does policy cover?

A company may have a policy to cover almost every important phase of its business—from regulating its method of purchasing materials to stipulating how employees may submit suggestions. As a foreman, you will probably be most concerned with policies that affect (1) employees and (2) the job practices of your department.

Employee policies most commonly formalized are those affecting wages and salaries, holidays and vacations, leaves of absence, termination of employment, safety, medical and health insurance and hospitalization, service awards, and retirement and pensions.

Shop practices most often reduced to policy are requisitioning of supplies, preparation of records, timekeeping, safeguarding classified materials, cost-control measures, quality standards, maintenance and repair, and acquisition of new machinery and equipment.

These listings are not all inclusive. Some companies have more, others less.

Is policy always in writing?

Far from it. Many a rigid policy has never been put down in black and white. And many firm policies have never been heard to be repeated from an executive's lips. But employees and foremen alike recognize that matters affected by such a policy must be handled in a certain manner and usually do so.

The existence of so much unwritten policy has led many authorities to the conclusion that all policy is better put into writing so that it may be explained, discussed, and understood. Nevertheless, there are many companies that don't subscribe to this way of thinking, and their policies remain implied rather than spelled out.

Does policy apply only to rules and regulations?

No. One of the great misunderstandings about policy is the belief that it's always something negative like "Don't do that" or "Do it this way or you'll get in trouble."

Policy is also something positive, encouraging, and uplifting. Just examine the written policy of the Esso Standard Oil Co. as expressed in a booklet published by its board of directors:

Importance of the individual. We believe the actions of business should recognize human feelings and the importance of the individual and should insure each person's treatment as an individual.

Common interest. We believe that employees, their unions, and management are bound together by a common interest—the ability of their unit to operate successfully—and that opportunity and security for the individual depends upon this success.

Open communications. We believe that the sharing of ideas, information, and feeling is essential as a means of expression and as the route to better understanding and sounder decisions.

Local decisions. We believe that people closest to the problems affecting themselves develop the most satisfactory solutions when given the authority to solve such matters at the point where they arise.

High moral standards. We believe that the soundest basis for judging the "rightness" of an action involving people is the test of its morality and its effect on basic human rights.

Words? Yes. Policy? Definitely! And as an official guide to action committed in print by the top officers of the organization, an excellent example of the positive side of policy.

Should a foreman change policy?

No. That's a very dangerous thing for him to do. Policies are set to guide his action. It's his responsibility to act within policy limits.

A foreman can *influence* a policy change, however, by making his thoughts and observations known to his boss, the personnel department, and top management. After all, the foreman is in the best position to feel employees' reactions to policy—favorable or otherwise. You do your boss and your company a service when you accurately report employees' reactions. And that's the time to offer your suggestions for improving or modifying the policy.

Does a foreman ever set policy?

In a way, the foreman *always* sets the policy at the shop level. His application of policy is his interpretation of how the broader company policy should be carried out when he deals with his employees. It's important for you to recognize that company policy usually allows you discretion at your level—even though this discretion may be limited.

Suppose your company has a policy that forbids bookmaking in the shop. Anyone caught will be fired. You can carry out that policy many ways at the shop level. You can bait a trap, hide behind a post, and fire the first fellow you catch. Or you can quietly size up the most likely violator, and warn him that if you catch him there won't be a second chance. You can put a notice on the bulletin board calling employees' attention, generally, to it. Or you can hold a group meeting and announce how you will deal with bookmakers. You can choose to regard only taking of horse-racing bets as bookmaking, or include professionally run baseball, basketball, and football pools. Or you can rule out any kind of gambling. Whatever you decide, so long as you carry out the intentions (and the letter where it's spelled out) of the company policy, you are setting your own policy.

Are some policies more important than others?

A better way to look at this problem is to say that some policies are set more specifically at the top of the organization than others and are carried down the line in the same language. An example of this is the safety regulations at the Armco Steel Company. The company has only four general safety regulations. These apply anywhere in the company and in every part of the plant. No "discretion" is permitted at any level. But the company does have another fifty or sixty safety regulations that apply to specific situations and are initiated at various levels of the organization. Some will originate with the plant superintendent and cover his whole operation. Others originate with the foreman and apply only to his department. But it would be a distortion of fact to say that one safety policy was more *important* than another simply because one had broader application than the other.

How responsible will employees hold you for company policy?

If you have done a good job of convincing employees that you fully represent the management of their company, your actions and company policy will be one and the same thing in their eyes. Naturally, you will sometimes have to carry out policy that you don't fully agree with—policy that may be unpopular with you or with your employees. Resist the temptation to apologize for your actions or to criticize the policy to employees. When you do, you weaken your position.

If you have to reprimand George, don't say, "I'd like to give you a break, George, but that's company policy." Or when sparking a cleanup campaign, don't say, "Mr. Jones wants you to get your workbench in order." Handle such matters positively. Give the policy your own personal touch, but don't sell the company down the river or you're likely to be caught in the current yourself.

How can you prevent your policy interpretations from backfiring?

Try protecting your actions in policy matters by asking yourself questions before making decisions:
- Is policy involved here? What is the policy?
- Am I sure of the facts? Do I know all the circumstances?
- How did I handle a similar matter in the past?
- Who can give me advice on this problem? Should I ask for it?
- Would my boss want to talk this over with me first?
- Does this problem involve the union? If so, should I see the union steward or should I check with the labor relations people first?

Many foremen complain that policy puts them in a strait jacket, makes their life miserable. Is this true?

Most of the time, no. Policy is another of those famous two-way streets. The formulation of policy and the conduct of the top-level people in a company do much to determine how this policy will affect the foreman's authority. But the foreman is just as often to blame for policy that tangles his authority as others higher up in the organization.

The good thing about policy is that once it has been established, and a decision made through its interpretation, you don't have to go through the agony of making that decision over and over again. If the company policy is to discipline workers for producing off-quality goods and you set the practice in your shop of giving two warnings, then a layoff, then that's it. Each time a malpractice comes up, you handle it the same way. You don't have to debate with yourself whether this time you'll fire or this time you'll overlook it.

Foremen who gripe loudest about policy taking the power out of their hands are those who make the least effort to understand the *intent* of the policy. If you find out the reason behind the policy, it will work for you. If you don't make a point of understanding it, you'll be in trouble. You'll either be practicing it with tongue in cheek or simply going through the motions. In either case employees soon lose respect for you, and respect is the strongest force in your authority.

If you buck the policy and try to do things your way only and contrary to what is consistent with what other foremen are doing, of course you'll pull the management rug out from under your own feet.

How much leeway does a foreman have in making decisions?

You can't draw a hard-and-fast rule to follow. Generally speaking, a company may establish three rough classifications of authority for a supervisor, within which he can make his decisions:

Class 1. Complete authority. A foreman can take action without consulting his superior.

Class 2. Limited authority. A foreman can take action he deems fit so long as he tells his superior about it *afterwards.*

Class 3. No authority. A foreman can take no action until he's first checked with his superior.

If many decisions fall into class 3, the foreman will become little more than a messenger boy. To improve this situation, first learn more about your company's policy and then spend time finding out how your boss would act. If you can convince him that you would handle matters as he might himself, he's more likely to transfer class 3 decisions into class 2, and as you prove yourself, from class 2 to class 1.

Note that the existing company policy would still prevail. The big change would be in permitting the foreman's discretion. And this would be because he has demonstrated that he is qualified to translate front-office policy into front-line action.

For suggested ways to pin down your responsibilities for carrying out employee relations policies, see chart on p. 190.

Must you consider more than one policy at the same time?

Yes. Frequently you'll be called upon to handle a shop situation that involves several policy matters simultaneously. For instance, suppose you were informed that the company was dropping a product from its line. It will mean reducing labor costs in your department 25 per cent, since the work volume will fall off the same amount. When one of your employees hears of the cutback, he asks whether instead of laying off people, the work can be shared—that you retain all the employees but have them all work fewer hours per week. You check with your boss. He says, "Joe, the company's policy (and it's written into our agreement with the union) is that we will not 'share work.' The employees we retain must work a full forty-hour week. But anything else you can do to reassign work is all right with me—as long as it's in line with company policy."

What can Joe do? Company policy knocks out a work-sharing plan. How about keeping the most skilled workers and laying off the less skilled? No. Can't do that. Company policy is that in "permanent" layoffs, men with least seniority will go first. How about reducing the number of material handlers? That's okay. Nothing to prevent Joe from doing that. How about having the setup man double as an inspector? Oops, policy says, "Quality will be considered before every other operating policy except safety."

"Well," says Joe to himself, "what I propose to do needn't sacrifice quality, so I'll make the double-up move.

"Now what can I do with my direct labor? I can drop ten from the gang if I can work four men to an assembly instead of our usual six. Let's see, the union contract specifies that the number of men needed to staff an assembly job operation cannot be changed except when changes in work load warrant a reduction. That seems like pretty clear policy to me. But I better check with the shop steward to see if there's some angle I've overlooked."

Before Joe has made his final plans, he's had to check them—and adjust them—against five company policies. Yet Joe makes his own decisions. And runs the shop as he sees fit—except that he is guided by the rules set down for integrating his action with that of all the other departments of the company.

What is a foreman's policy manual?

Many companies have actually taken their general company policies and written down interpretations as a specific guide to foreman action. Those written guides for foremen are usually placed in a loose-leaf folder and called a "Supervisor's Manual" or a "Foreman's Manual." Supervisors use these manuals as references whenever a policy question comes up that they aren't certain about handling. If your company has such a manual, and it's up to date, it's an invaluable aid in handling your job.

What do employees want to know about policy?

Employees are rarely concerned with nice phrases. General statements of policy will mean little to them. But they do have a keen—and critical—interest in the specific and concrete aspects of policy whenever it hits home.

If your company's policy is to "treat employees equitably in disciplinary affairs," this will be about as clear as mud to them. You can help a lot if you rephrase the broad statements of policy (which may necessarily be generalized) into language that every workman understands. In this case, "We intend to give everyone a fair and square deal if he breaks a rule."

But even such a clear summary of a regulation still doesn't answer for an employee, "What does this mean to me?" You'll have to be still more specific: "Paul, if more than three out of every hundred pieces you turn out don't measure up to standards, I'll give you a warning the first time. The second time, you'll be given time off without pay. If it continues, you may be discharged." You wouldn't get far with policy, for instance, if you say, "Paul, if the quality of your production is substandard, we may have to take disciplinary action." Paul may very well ask himself, "What's quality? What's my production? What's substandard? What's disciplinary action?"

The Case of the Excused Absence. A case study in human relations involving company policy, with questions for you to answer.

"The company's policy regarding time off from work is a reasonable one, Dick," said the plant superintendent to Dick Deeds, the new supervisor in the stamping room. "If an employee has a personal emergency to take care of during working hours, we're only too glad to let him punch out and take care of it. However, we frown on the practice of granting time off to fish or hunt or to take care of any other personal matters which can be done after working time."

Three weeks later, Tad Wade, a machine operator, asked Dick if he could report in late the next morning. He needed to do so, he said, because he had just bought a new car and wanted to register it at the motor vehicle agency. There was always a long line of applicants at the lunch hour or in the afternoon. "Sure you can," said Dick. "But come to work as soon as you have tended to your business."

The following morning while Dick was lining up the day's schedule, Ray Featherstone, supervisor of the mixing department, stopped by Dick's desk. "You certainly put me in a tough spot with a couple of my people today. The boys got wind of the fact that you let Tad off today to register his new car. I've never accepted an excuse like that. I tell my people that so long as it's urgent, I'll let them go. But nix on rearranging work schedules just to suit one man's convenience."

1. Do you think Dick was right in letting Tad have the time off? Why?

2. What do you think of Ray's interpretation of company policy? Of Dick's?

3. Would it be better if Dick's boss had been more explicit in explaining the policy to Dick? Why?

4. What can Dick do to avoid having this situation arise again?

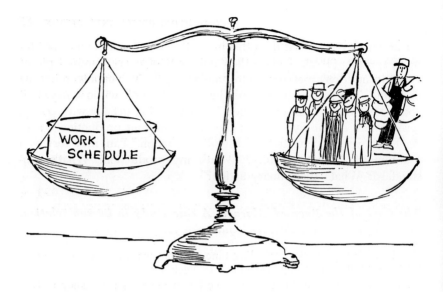

9 MANPOWER MANAGEMENT

What are the symptoms of poor manpower management?

Costs so high that they don't allow your department to operate at a profit are the most obvious symptom. And your first corrective step should be to see that you have only the right *number* of employees on the job.

Signs of inefficient manpower management also include a high turnover rate, excessive absences and lateness, lots of grievances, poor quality of work, and lowered output. Each one tells you that there's a big chance you don't have the right person working for you, or if you do, he isn't working on the right job at the right time.

How much does it cost to keep an employee on the payroll for a year?

A conservative estimate of the cost of keeping a semiskilled factory worker on the plant payroll in 1956 was $4,840 per year, according to Industrial Psychology, Inc., Phoenix, Ariz. Figure it this way. A man's salary runs about $3,000 a year. It costs an average of $500 to train him and bring him up to normal production. Another $150 to offset the cost of the one out of three employees who don't pan out. Add $740 in fringe benefits that don't show up in his salary. And cap this with another $450—cost of the depreciation on the capital investment that makes his job possible.

Consequently, each employee who works for you must return about $5,000 in productive efforts before the company can break even. If you supervise ten employees, you can figure you're managing a payroll of at least $50,000 per year. That's why manpower management is so important.

What does it cost to hire a new employee?

One aircraft manufacturing company on the West Coast found that it cost over $1,000 for one net addition to its labor force at the assembly worker level. This is not unusual when you consider costs of running want ads, operating an employment office, handling paper work, and breaking the new man in.

What phases of manpower management concern the foreman most?

The foreman's chief responsibilities for a plant's manpower management could be summed up by saying he should have the right worker on the right job at the right time. How can he do this? By making accurate forecasts of the number of workers he'll need to staff his department, by taking an active interest in the kind of employees the company hires, and by maintaining working conditions that attract and hold the best employees.

How do you forecast manpower requirements?

It's really a matter of looking ahead—and applying simple arithmetic. Time studies, labor standards, and the like all make a forecast more accurate, but you can do very well without them.

Step 1. Find out what your department is scheduled to produce for the next week, month, quarter, or as far ahead as you can determine. If you don't know that, chances are slight that you'll make efficient use of the people who work for you.

Step 2. Calculate how much the work schedule means in terms of total man-hours. You can do this by getting an estimate from the time-study, industrial engineering, or planning and scheduling department—if one exists at your plant. Their schedules are certainly based upon machine time and manpower estimates.

If man-hour requirements aren't available elsewhere, you'll have to make your own estimate. Do this either by checking times for previous or similar jobs or by making careful estimates of the time required for *each* job. Keep your figures in terms of man-hours, man–half days, or man-days. But be specific and allow time for setups and teardowns. Try to recall delays associated with each job and allow time for these.

Where jobs are machine-controlled (that is, the job can't be done any faster than the speed at which the machine runs), make your estimates based upon (1) how long the machine will take to do each job—allowing for breakdowns, idle time, etc., and (2) how many operator-hours are needed to run the machine.

Step 3. Convert your totals to man-hours and divide by 8 to see how many man-days it will take you to complete your schedule for the period you've selected.

Step 4. Divide the total man-days by the number of working days during the period to find the number of operators you'll need. But don't stop here.

Step 5. Check how many indirect people—sweepers, material handlers, setup men, etc.—you'll need to service the required number of operators during this period (unless you included these in step 2).

Step 6. Add the number of operators (direct labor) to the number of indirect people to get the total needed.

Step 7. Make allowances for absences. How many days absent per month do employees in your department average? How many man-days a month do all your employees combined lose? Suppose, for example, it's 5 man-days a month. That's just the same as saying that you can expect to be short-handed 5 days a month, which may interfere with meeting your schedule. If you add an extra employee, you can expect to be overstaffed 15 days a month—which is costly.

EXAMPLE OF FORECASTING MANPOWER REQUIREMENTS

1. Suppose your schedule shows that during July your department must produce 1,000 widgets, 250 gadgets, and 60 umphlets.
2. Widgets and gadgets are hand assembly jobs. Umphlets are produced on a machine. Previous production records, or time studies, or standards show the following:

   Widgets: Average 50 per day with 10 employees

   $$\frac{1,000}{50} = 20 \text{ days} \times 10 \text{ employees} \times 8 \text{ hours} = 1,600 \text{ man-hours}$$

   Gadgets: Average 10 per day with 2 employees

   $$\frac{250}{10} = 25 \text{ days} \times 2 \text{ employees} \times 8 \text{ hours} = 400 \text{ man-hours}$$

   Umphlets: Average 3 per day, allowing for down time, require 1 operator

   $$\frac{60}{3} = 20 \text{ days} \times 1 \text{ operator} \times 8 \text{ hours} = 160 \text{ man-hours}$$

   Total: 2,160 man-hours

3. Convert to man-days:

   $$\frac{2,160 \text{ man-hours}}{8 \text{ hours per day}} = 270 \text{ man-days per month}$$

4. Average number of employees needed for month:

$$\frac{270 \text{ man-days}}{20 \text{ days/month}} = 13\tfrac{1}{2} \text{ employees for the month}$$

5. Add number of indirect employees. Three material handlers take care of the gadget and umphlet operation. A combination setup man and packer handles the widget line. That's 4 employees each day all month.
6. Average number of employees needed in July:

$$
\begin{array}{rl}
13\tfrac{1}{2} & \text{direct} \\
4 & \text{indirect} \\
\hline
17\tfrac{1}{2} & \text{employees}
\end{array}
$$

7. Allowance for absences. Record for department shows your employees lose on the average of a half-day per month:

$17\tfrac{1}{2}$ employees $\times$ 4 hours per month absent = 72 hours absent per month
72 hours is about one-half of one employee for a month. So

$$
\begin{array}{rl}
17\tfrac{1}{2} & \text{employees needed} \\
\tfrac{1}{2} & \text{employee for absences} \\
\hline
18 & \text{employees needed for the month of July}
\end{array}
$$

Should you overstaff or understaff?

That depends. If you plan for too many employees, department costs will go up unless your schedule and machine availability will permit you to assign them to productive jobs. It's bad, too, to have idle people in the shop or to use them on make-work jobs. Overstaffing, however, does allow you to step up production in emergencies and assures your meeting delivery dates.

Understaffing can be just as bad. It can get you behind in schedule and in trouble on deliveries. It can also give employees the feeling of being overworked. And it doesn't give you much flexibility.

Your company can minimize either overstaffing or understaffing by pooling the manpower estimates of each foreman and maintaining an optimum-size labor pool as a cushion against unpredictables—such as unusual absences or a sharp upward adjustment in schedules.

How far ahead should you plan?

As far as you can—even a year ahead if possible. Demands by labor unions for a guaranteed annual wage have mainly been for a guarantee of a more stable job.

Job stability is just as desirable to management as it is to labor. Layoffs and rehiring are costly. One very good way to minimize both is to make your forecast of manpower requirements accurate and to make them as far ahead as possible. That way you can iron out the hills and valleys of your labor requirements. There's little point in laying off five workers this week if you're going to need ten more workers a week from now. It's much better if you can level out the scheduling in your department so that you keep, say, seven or eight of these employees working continuously all the time.

It's recognized that such optimum forecasting cannot always be done—that interruptions in supply, restrictions to storage capacity, and unpredictable demands by customers interfere with the best plans.

How do you measure turnover?

"Turnover" is the name given to the measure of how many people come to work for you and don't stay for one reason or another. Turnover includes employees who are hired or rehired and employees who are laid off, who quit, or who are discharged. It also includes those who retire or die.

You can compute turnover in your department by adding (1) all the employees who were hired during the month or came back to work to (2) all the employees who were separated from the payroll for any reason during the month.

The *rate of turnover* is calculated as follows:

$$\frac{\text{Turnover} \times 100}{\text{Average size of work force}} = \text{Turnover per cent}$$

For instance, if you had an average of 50 employees during the month, but you hired 2 and laid off 3, the turnover would be 5. Your turnover rate would be $\frac{5 \times 100}{50} = 10$ per cent per month.

If that rate persisted, your turnover rate for the year would be 120 per cent.

Turnover rates vary from department to department, from company to company, and from industry to industry. The national average for all business in the United States in 1956 was 6.9 per cent per month, or 81 per cent per year!

What causes turnover?

Turnover is generally considered to be the single best measure of morale. Poor morale can result from many things. Two of the most important of these are poor supervision and having the wrong person on the wrong job. The wrong person on the wrong job can mean poor hiring procedures—or poor placement procedures after a good person is put on the payroll. This chapter will discuss the latter cause. For discussions of how to improve turnover through better morale, see Chaps. 3 and 16.

What's so bad about absenteeism?

Absences (like turnover) are costly—to the company as well as to the employee himself. If it costs about $5,000 per year to keep a man on the payroll, then each day he's absent could cost your department something like $20. Even the direct cost doesn't tell the whole story. Absences frequently cause overtime, delays in getting an operation started or a machine running. And every foreman can testify to the aggravation absence and lateness cause. It's the biggest obstacle you have in your manpower planning—from day to day or from month to month.

Absence and lateness, like turnover, can be controlled by good supervision. But it's better to avoid this demand upon your supervisory time and skill if you can. And you can, by screening out applicants who have displayed these undesirable characteristics in the past or are likely to develop them on the job in your plant—simply because they are unsuited for the work they were hired to do.

How can better hiring reduce turnover and absences?

Selecting the proper person to fit first the company and then the available job opening hits at the turnover and absenteeism problem at its source. There are hundreds of thousands of people looking for work who would be misfits almost anywhere. But there are millions who would be out of place in your plant. Joe doesn't like close work. Pete can't stand heavy work. Tony wants a job with lots of room for initiative. Alma wants a job where she doesn't have to think. And so on. Turnover and absences show that Joe, Pete, Tony, and Alma didn't find work to suit them in your plant.

To complicate the matter further, Tony may want a job that allows for initiative, but maybe he doesn't have the native ability to produce without close supervision. Alma wants a job where she doesn't have to think, but maybe all those jobs call for someone who can work rapidly and Alma is slow as can be.

A third complication, and perhaps the most serious, is that the ability to handle the human side of the job varies widely with different people. And of course the human relations requirements of jobs vary, too. If you put a man who likes to be one of the gang back in the corner of the shop where he spends most of his time alone baling scrap, he won't be happy no matter how well he likes that kind of work or how skillfully he can perform. Similarly, a person who has never been able to get along well with his superiors won't be much of a help on a job where he has to take a lot of close supervision.

In what ways can hiring be improved?

Just formalizing the employment procedure and making it system-atic helps rule out the big boo-boos that often occur during haphaz-ard hiring. For instance, every applicant should fill out some sort of form before he's given consideration. On such a form the applicant should furnish critical information about his age,* physical character-istics, work experience, education. A glance at the form will rule out people who are too old or too young or don't meet educational or job-experience requirements.

The application form can tell you something more. A work record will show up the job hopper who has held a dozen jobs in three or four years. He's always a big employment risk. Periods of prolonged employment are good indicators of stability, even if the indicator doesn't always prove reliable.

Chances are that in your company, your responsibility will be lim-ited to cooperating with the employment or personnel department. If you understand what they are trying to do for you, they'll be able to do a better job for you.

Will tests help select better employees?

Yes. Properly selected, administered, and evaluated, tests are a big help in picking better workers. Tests may be simple and direct, such as tests that show whether an applicant can read and write or perform the simple arithmetic that record keeping on the job may demand. Tests may also enable an applicant to show that he can actually per-form the skills your job requires. Anyone can *tell* you he can operate a multiple-spindle automatic. A 10-minute tryout will *prove* whether he's exaggerating or not.

Job tests need not necessarily be accomplished on actual equipment. Some testing can be done through asking questions—either directly or in writing.

For many semiskilled and skilled jobs, aptitude tests will help pre-dict whether an applicant will *be able* to perform well on the job—even if he has never done the work before. Such tests, based upon psychological research, are not 100 per cent accurate. But they can improve your chances of getting the right worker from say one in three (that's average) to two or three out of five. Some tests score even better than this.

* No longer permitted in some states unless the employer can demonstrate a direct and justifiable relationship between age and the work to be performed.

How good are physical examinations?

As a supervisor, you'll want to know whether a man assigned to your department has any limitations on what he can do physically. There's no way of actually finding out about poor eyesight, a hernia, or a heart condition, for instance, without a complete physical examination. A physical defect doesn't necessarily rule out an applicant, but it does assure his being put on a job where he can do the best work and is least likely to aggravate his condition.

People talk of the normal person. What does that mean?

A concept of the "normal" or "average" person, or of "normal" or "average" personal characteristics is a good one to have. It helps you understand psychological testing and your chances of getting good employees.

Take any personal characteristic—a person's height, weight, length of his arms, size of his foot. If you measured any one of these characteristics you'd find that the bulk of the people have about the same size. But a few people have a very small size and an equal number have a very large size. In shoe sizes, for instance, three-quarters of the American men may wear a shoe size from 8 to 11½. Only one-eighth of the American male population would wear a shoe size smaller than 8; only one-eighth wear a size larger than 11½. Shoe manufacturers know this. That's why it's so easy to get fitted if you're in the middle group.

This distribution of sizes is called a *normal distribution*. Plotted on a distribution chart that shows how many people there are in each size group, it takes a bell-shaped appearance. (For an interesting example of this bell shape, see Fig. 9–1.) And this normal, or bell-shaped, distribution (most people in the middle and relatively few at either extreme) is typical of most personal characteristics—including a job applicant's ability to become a skillful workman.

Consequently, your chances of getting the best workmen will depend upon how well you can predict in advance whether an applicant will be above normal, average, or below normal in any desired quality. Psychological tests work toward making reliable predictions possible.

Who gives the tests?

Most companies employ either a psychologist or someone professionally trained to administer tests to job applicants. But it's important that the supervisor know what the tests are trying to prove and about how reliable they are at selecting employees who will be successful on the job.

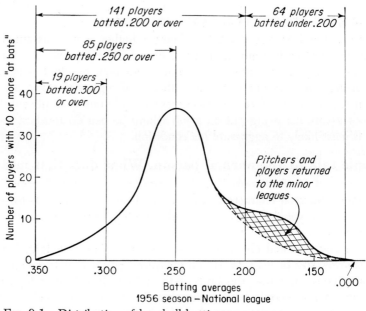

FIG. 9-1   Distribution of baseball batting averages.

What can the foreman do to improve the selection process?

Whenever the foreman is given a chance to interview a prospective job candidate, that's a golden opportunity for the foreman to help make sure he gets a first-rate employee.

Interviewing points that apply most directly to selecting employees are reviewed here:

Know what kind of man you want. Don't describe him vaguely as "a good worker who will stick on the job." That doesn't tell you a thing about the qualities you are looking for to suit the job that is open. Try making a check list of necessary or desirable qualifications like:

• Experience—he ought to have worked a couple of years on multiple-spindle drill presses even though they weren't exactly like ours.

• Blueprint reading—he'll have to be able to work directly from prints.

• Speed—this job doesn't require a fast man so much as it requires a steady, consistent worker.

• Initiative—can his previous experience show that he's worked on his own without close supervision?

• Attendance—how's his health, has he a good record of attendance, because this job needs someone who's going to be here every day?

See enough candidates. Your personnel department will probably screen out the obvious misfits before an applicant is sent to you for approval. But if you do the hiring directly, make a point of interviewing at least three candidates before making up your mind. That way you get a chance to make comparisons and to get the feel of the prevailing labor market. For some hard-to-fill jobs, you may have to see as many as twenty to thirty people.

What should you talk about to job candidates?

Preview the job for the applicant. It's a great time saver to tell the applicant what the fixed requirements of the job are. Mention such things as job title and relationships to other jobs, and the main activities involved in the job like walking, standing, sitting, heavy work. Tell him what kind of materials and machines he'll work with, and describe the working conditions.

It's especially wise to forewarn an applicant about any undesirable conditions like fumes, dampness, night work, etc. Don't scare him, but be sure he knows the facts ahead of time. Better that he turn down the job than walk off it after three days.

You *can* describe the good parts about the job, what kind of advancement there is, the company's benefit programs, etc. This is the place to do some sound, factual selling.

What sort of questions should you ask the applicant?

Don't turn the interview into a third degree by asking too many point-blank questions—especially those that can be answered by a simple "Yes" or "No." The job seeker is likely to be on his guard during the interview anyway. He will ordinarily answer "Yes" to a question like, "Did you get along well with your boss in the last place you worked?"

Ask questions that begin with what, where, why, when, who. This gives the applicant a chance to talk, and while he's talking, he's more likely to show you the kind of person he really is. If he does most of the talking and you do most of the listening, you'll have lots of time to size him up.

Ask questions like these:

"What about your education? How do you feel that it would help you do the kind of work we do here?"

"Where did you get your most valuable experience? Suppose you tell me about your working experience, starting with your first job."

"Whom did you report to in your last job? What sort of a supervisor was he?"

"When did you first decide you liked to do this sort of work? What have you found most difficult about it? Most pleasant?"

"How would you describe your health? What kind of an attendance record have you maintained during the last year?"

"Why did you leave the job at the XYZ Company?"

In addition, ask questions about the applicant's trade. If he says he's a toolmaker, you can find out pretty quickly whether he's exaggerating or not. And if you discover that some of the applicant's facts don't jibe, ask to have him clarify the discrepancy. Say something like:

"Let me see now, who was it you said you worked for in 1953?"

"What did you do just before you took that job at GM?"

What do you look for while interviewing an applicant?

Besides the factual things you obviously need to know about an applicant's skills and know-how, you'll want to be alert to what the interview tells you about his:

Background. Do his education and experience, and even the place he lives in, the kind of people he associates with off the job indicate that he will be happy working with the people in your plant? If education isn't Joe's strong point and his main hobbies are bowling and baseball, he won't find many friends among employees who take their education seriously and spend their spare time discussing opera and stamp collecting.

Characteristics. What are his achievements? Has he done anything outstanding? Can he say that he worked five years at the XYZ Company without missing a day?

How about his *interests?* If Joe tells you the jobs he's liked best in the past have been outdoor ones, like truck driving, why is he looking now for a confining job on an assembly line?

Try to spot his *attitude.* Does he act mature, or does he sound as if he's given to childish boasting? Does he listen to what you say? An example of an attitude you'll want to steer clear of is one where the man goes out of his way to criticize the last company he worked for, the people he worked with, or the quality of the product. You'll probably be making no mistake to conclude he's the kind of person who'd find everything wrong at your plant, too.

You can tell a lot about a man's *physical condition,* too, from the interview. If he sounds as if he's got all he can do just to go back and forth from work, or if he appears slow-moving and lethargic, he may have no oomph on his job either. Remember, most people looking for work are trying to put their best foot forward. If a man can't show you a very good side during the interview, there's a chance that he won't show you any better on the job.

Whom should you hire?

Deciding which applicant to hire isn't easy. But you can make a better decision if you separate *facts* from *hunches*—not that you should ignore your hunches or inferences. It's a good idea to take 5 minutes after you've interviewed an applicant to jot down what you feel are the significant facts about him, and list your hunches too.

Facts may show that he has had ten years' experience on a milling machine, that his health is good, that he can read blueprints. But your conversation may have brought out the feeling that he's stubborn and boastful and that he'd be a hard man to supervise. Only *you* can tell which items you'll give most weight to. Some supervisors don't mind having a prima donna on their staff so long as he can produce. Others fear that a prima donna is likely to upset teamwork. And of course your hunches can be wrong.

You can be sure, however, that your choice will be better than flipping a coin if you've gone about your interview in a systematic way. And you've kept personal prejudices as to race, religion, or nationality out of your figuring.

Should you check employee references?

Absolutely yes! It's foolhardy to hire anyone without checking with his last employer to find out about the actual job the applicant held, his attendance, and his honesty. Most employers cooperate if the information is kept confidential. (It's a good practice to tell the applicant that you are going to verify his references.) Checking can be done either by telephone or by letter.

Personal references are usually not of much value. No one is going to supply the name of a person who will say something bad about him. And school references are of value primarily to verify whether the employee actually has the education he claims.

The Case of Too Much Overtime. A case study in human relations involving manpower management, with questions for you to answer.

"This overtime has got to stop," stormed the plant superintendent to Jake Barnes, supervisor of the finishing department in a toy factory. "You've had to schedule overtime three times already, and the month has only just begun. What's the trouble out there?"

"Well, boss, it's this way," said Jake. "When the pressure was on to pare costs to the bone, I let three of our finishers go. According to the schedule we got from sales, we would have been able to produce all they required without putting on any overtime. But the sales manager has been out here every day moving up orders. And increasing some, too. We'll still be in good shape by the end of the month. But right now I don't have as much help as I need to get the stuff out as fast as sales is calling for it."

"Jake, I've told you time and again not to accept delivery changes from sales without first making sure you can handle them. It's easy for sales to make promises. But the way you're running up overtime, we're the ones who will have to pay for those promises."

"To tell the truth," said Jake, "I thought we'd be able to move up those orders—and we would have, except that we had four girls out this week. Seems as if the flu is knocking out more people every day. I can't predict things like this. You tell me to keep my labor force down to the minimum. I don't want to recall anyone for just a few days. I think that if the company wants delivery, we'll have to schedule the overtime."

"Jake, I still don't think you've handled this problem well at all. There's going to be the devil to pay if you don't bring your labor costs into line."

Two days later, the finishing department was still in trouble. At 3 P.M. the phone rang. It was the sales manager. "Jake, the shipping department tells me you're holding up the McWorth order. It's got to go out tomorrow for sure. Can I call McWorth and promise the order will be shipped?"

1. What do you think of the instructions Jake got from his boss?

2. What do you think of the sales manager's request?

3. What do you think Jake should have said to his boss when the overtime problem arose?

4. If you were Jake now, how would you handle this situation?

5. What would you do to avoid the problem in the future?

10 JOB ANALYSIS AND EVALUATION

What's the purpose of job evaluation?

The purpose of job analysis and job evaluation is to determine systematically the relative worth of jobs and positions within a plant.

Have you ever wondered how the job of a washroom sweeper can be compared in terms of wages with that of a machine operator? Do the unpleasant duties of the sweeper's job make it worth as much as that of the machinist who has better working conditions but needs more skill? Or how would you compare the dollar value of a foreman who supervises seventy-five people with that of a quality-control engineer who supervises only two people but who needs much more technical education than the foreman? Would you pay a steeple jack more than a toolmaker in order to reward the steeple jack for the risks he takes?

Job evaluation is designed to form a systematic basis for answering such questions.

Is job evaluation foolproof?

No. Job evaluation is a systematic art, but it is not a science yet. In job evaluation, you still have to exercise judgment to appraise the worth of jobs. But job evaluation is the most reliable and fair way we know of to compare the value of one job with that of another. Its checks and balances help rule out personal prejudices and see that each job is measured by the same set of yardsticks.

What good comes from job evaluation?

When jobs are rated fairly, and employees paid accordingly, there are usually fewer grievances about pay rates. It's said that employees are not so much interested in "how much I get" as in "how much the fellow next to me gets." Job evaluation assures that people doing the same work under the same conditions get the same pay.

In addition, job evaluation provides a structure so that an employee may progress within defined lines to a higher wage grade. The same structure can be used to rate a new job quickly when it is added. And it can be used to compare the pay for jobs within the company with those in nearby or similar plants.

What is the relationship between how much a person gets for his job and how it is rated under a job-evaluation plan?

Under a job-evaluation plan, the job's rating should be the major factor in determining its pay, but there are other influences. The total wage can be affected by the prosperity of the company, the industry involved, or its geographic location. For instance, in 1958 a machinist in an auto plant in Detroit might receive anywhere from 20 to 50 cents more per hour than a machinist with the same classification in a textile plant in Columbia, S.C.

Another factor that influences wages is the power of the individual or of the group to bargain for higher wages. And where wage incentive plans exist, two workers with identically rated jobs may draw the same base rate but have different earnings because of differences in their effort and output.

Which is rated, the man or the job?

First big principle of job evaluation is that only the job is rated—not the individual who performs it. Here's why: Suppose Lou and Tom have identical jobs and turn out about the same quality and quantity of work. But Lou has a better education than Tom. So far as the jobs are concerned, both should still be rated the same. In job evaluation, what is important is *only what the job demands*, not what extra personal qualities the man may or may not bring to it. After all, if Lou's job requires only a grammar school education or its equivalent, what purpose would be served in paying him extra for his college education when he can't apply this extra education to that job?

How do you find out what the job entails?

The basic tool of job evaluation is a job analysis. It is a method for finding out in an orderly way the duties, requirements, and skills of a job.

Job titles, in and of themselves, mean very little. In one plant a machinist is a lathe operator, in another a grinding machine operator. Even in the same plant, a grinding machine operator in Dept. B will work to 0.002 inch on routine work. In Dept. C, he'll work to 0.001 inch on custom jobs. In Dept. G, he may operate a horizontal grinder, in Dept. H, a centerless grinder.

Only real way to find out what a job involves is to study it in detail.

How is a job analysis made?

Information is gathered for a job analysis by any of three methods:

• Sending a questionnaire to supervisors and employees who fill the survey form out in detail. Accuracy and comprehensiveness of this method depend almost entirely on the foreman and the employee.

• Interviewing supervisors and employees and recording significant facts on a survey form. This method is more accurate than the first one, but it depends upon good cooperation from the people interviewed.

• Actually observing the job as it is performed. This is the most dependable way, although there can be a loophole if the operator performs a variety of jobs and the observer doesn't see a representative sample of all of them.

Who can make a job analysis?

Anyone, properly instructed, can make a job analysis. But most companies either employ a professional specialist to do this job or train someone to do it on a full-time basis.

What's included in a job description?

The job description or job analysis is *not* a step-by-step account of the way a job is done. It summarizes in more general terms what the job entails.

A typical job description for a light assembly job might read something like this:

Work performed. Assembles small electronic components like capacitors, resistances, tubes, rheostats, shunts, etc., to radio chassis. Works with hand tools like socket wrenches, screw drivers, and pliers and with overhead power-driven wrench. Refers to instruction sheets and diagrams. Keeps tally sheet of units worked on. Keeps work place clean and performs miscellaneous related duties. Is under close supervision of foreman.

How clearly are job requirements spelled out in a job description?

Through interviews with the employee and his supervisor and through comparisons with other jobs, the analyst determines specifically what the performance requirements are. For instance, in the light assembly job described in the last question, the analyst might enter on the job description:

Responsibilities. Is responsible for assembling parts according to specifications. Is responsible for care of tools and housekeeping.

Job knowledge. Must know how to read from job instructions and diagrams, must know how custom changes are handled.

Mental application. Requires moderate concentration. Must recognize poor fit or parts that are faulty mechanically.

Dexterity and accuracy. Requires high degree of dexterity.

Machines or tools used. Hand tools and power-driven screw driver.

The analysts will also specify other requirements such as:

Experience required. None.

Training data. One week vestibule training.

Education requirement. Equivalent of two years of high school.

Relation to other jobs. Transfer from other assembly work. Transfer to other assembly work like soldering and wiring. Promotion to lead assembler.

Supervision. Under supervision of department foreman.

Finally, the analyst will run through a checklist of over 100 items which describe *physical activities* (like walking, stooping, carrying, hearing, color vision, etc.), *working conditions* (like hot, cold, dusty, noisy, or toxic conditions, electrical hazards), and *occupational characteristics* (like strength of hands, ability to work rapidly for short periods, memory for written instructions, arithmetic computation, tact in dealing with people).

How does a job analysis become a job evaluation?

Data collected during the analysis becomes the raw material for job evaluation. But without the analysis, job evaluation on a large scale is practically impossible. The more accurate the data, the better the evaluation.

Four principal methods are used to convert the job analysis data into a job-evaluation system. The first three are described only briefly here because only about one-fifth of all companies having job-evaluation plans use any of them.

Ranking is the simplest and earliest form of job evaluation. Simple title and descriptions of each job are written on separate cards. Then a committee sorts the cards, ranking them from highest to lowest worth. Trouble here is that it's nearly impossible for everyone on the committee to know each job or to agree on the importance of the various factors like working conditions, supervision required, etc.

Classification is a refinement of the ranking methods. The committee begins by classifying all possible work at the location into grades of work: like A—messenger-boy work, B—simple clerical work requiring no training, C—requires recognized clerical ability or considerable experience on certain machines, etc. Next the committee slots the existing jobs into the various grades. Here again, the committee must guard against thinking of *man* rather than job. Nevertheless, this system is simple and is used effectively in most government jobs.

Factor comparison is a reliable, but complicated, method of evaluating very different types of jobs—like comparing manual jobs with jobs requiring creative thinking. Essentially, the method consists of ranking about twenty key jobs according to several different factors common to all jobs. A proportionate amount of the present wage for a key job will represent each of the factors. The sum of the amounts paid for each of the factors is the money rate for the job. This is the only job-evaluation method that brings money into the calculations before the job classifications are determined.

What is the most popular method for evaluating jobs?

The point method. Point plans have been installed in several thousand plants—small and large.

Under the point method, jobs are defined in terms of factors which are common to all—like responsibility, skill, education, effort required, and so on. The amount of each factor will vary according to the job. So the first step is to take the job analysis or job description and transfer the data to a point-system job-rating sheet (see Fig. 10–1.)

For each of the factors (eleven are in the illustration), there is a range of points (see Table 10–1). According to the demands of the particular job upon each of the factors, the job will get a certain amount of points. To determine just how many points, it is common to rate each factor for each job according to the degree of demand for that factor (see Table 10–2).

For example, in the case of the engine lathe operator's job, look at the description of Responsibility for Material or Product. The basis for rating (obtained from the original job analysis) says that the probable losses are seldom over $250. On Table 10–2 this is considered a third-

---

Job Name __LATHE OPERATOR – ENGINE (Up to 30")__ __Class__ __A__

FACTORS	DEG.	BASIS OF RATING
EDUCATION	3 (42)	Use shop mathematics, charts, tables, hand book formulas. Work from complicated drawings. Use micrometers, depth gauges, indicator gauges, protractors. Knowledge of machining methods, tools, cutting qualities of different kinds of metals. Equivalent to 2 years high school plus 2 to 3 years trades training.
EXPERIENCE	4 (88)	3 to 5 years on wide variety of engine lathe work, including diversified set-ups.
INITIATIVE AND INGENUITY	4 (56)	Wide variety of castings and forgings of complicated form. Close tolerances. Difficult set-ups of irregular shaped parts. Considerable judgment and ingenuity to plan and layout unusual lathe operations, select proper feeds and speeds, devise tooling, for varying materials and conditions.
PHYSICAL DEMAND	2 (20)	Light physical effort. Set-ups may require handling of heavy material mounting on face-plate. Machine time greatest part of cycle. Most of time spent watching work, checking, making adjustments.
MENTAL OR VISUAL DEMAND	4 (20)	Must concentrate mental and visual attention closely, planning and laying out work, checking, making adjustments. Close tolerances may require unusual attention.
RESPONSIBILITY FOR EQUIPMENT OR PROCESS	3 (15)	Careless set-up or operation, jamming of tools, dropping work on ways, jamming carriage, may cause damage seldom over $250.
RESPONSIBILITY FOR MATERIAL OR PRODUCT	3 (15)	Careless set-up or operation may result in spoilage and possible scrapping of expensive castings, forgings, shafts, etc., e.g., machining below size, inaccurate boring of diameter and depth. Probable losses seldom over $250.
RESPONSIBILITY FOR SAFETY OF OTHERS	3 (15)	Flying chips may cause burns, cuts or eye injuries. Improperly fastened work may fly from face plate or chuck. May injure another employe when setting work in machine.
RESPONSIBILITY FOR WORK OF OTHERS	1 (5)	None.
WORKING CONDITIONS	2 (20)	Good working conditions. May be slightly dirty, especially in set-ups. Some dust from castings. Usual machine shop noise.
UNAVOIDABLE HAZARDS	3 (15)	May crush fingers or toes handling material or from dropped tools or clamps. Possible burns, cuts or eye injury from flying chips and particles. Finger or hand injury from rotating work.
Remarks	311-4	

Fig. 10-1 Example of job rating sheet. (A. L. Kress, "How to Rate Jobs and Men," *Factory Management and Maintenance,* McGraw-Hill Publishing Company, Inc., New York, October, 1939.)

JOB RATING SUMMARY BY LABOR GRADES

PRODUCTIVE JOBS – MACHINE SHOP

OCCUPATION	LABOR GRADE NO.	TOTAL POINTS	EDUCATION DEG/PTS	EXPERIENCE DEG/PTS	INITIATIVE AND INGENUITY DEG/PTS	PHYSICAL DEMAND DEG/PTS	MENTAL/VISUAL DEG/PTS	EQUIP. OR PROCESS DEG/PTS	MATERIAL OR PRODUCT DEG/PTS	SAFETY OF OTHERS DEG/PTS	WORK OF OTHERS DEG/PTS	WORKING CONDITIONS DEG/PTS	HAZARDS DEG/PTS
						Labor Grade 2							
Lay-Out Man	2	347	4 56	5 110	4 56	2 20	4 20	2 10	4 20	3 15	1 5	2 20	3 15
Boring Bar-Horizontal		343	3 42	5 110	4 56	3 30	4 20	3 15	3 15	3 15	1 5	2 20	3 15
Assembler-Group Leader		341	3 42	4 88	4 56	3 30	4 20	2 10	2 10	3 15	5 25	3 30	3 15
							Labor Grade 3						
Inspector-Mechanical	3	335	4 56	4 88	4 56	2 20	4 20	3 15	3 15	3 15	3 15	2 20	3 15
Set-Up Man-Welding		331	3 42	4 88	4 56	3 30	4 20	2 10	2 10	3 15	3 15	3 30	3 15
Sheet Metal Worker		331	3 42	4 88	4 56	3 30	3 15	3 15	3 15	3 15	1 5	4 40	3 15
Lay-Out Man		327	4 56	5 110	4 56	2 20	4 20	2 10	2 10	2 10	1 5	2 20	2 10
Grinder-External		326	3 42	4 88	4 56	3 30	4 20	3 15	3 15	3 15	1 5	3 30	3 15
Grinder-Internal		326	3 42	4 88	4 56	3 30	4 20	3 15	2 10	3 15	1 5	3 30	3 15
Lathe Operator-Turret		326	3 42	4 88	4 56	3 30	4 20	4 20	2 10	3 15	1 5	3 30	3 15
Planer Operator		326	3 42	4 88	4 56	3 30	4 20	4 20	2 10	3 15	1 5	2 20	3 15
Boring Mill Operator		321	3 42	4 88	4 56	3 30	4 20	3 15	3 15	3 15	1 5	2 20	3 15
Lathe Operator-Engine		321	3 42	4 88	4 56	3 30	4 20	3 15	3 15	3 15	1 5	2 20	3 15
Lathe Operator-Engine		316	3 42	4 88	4 56	3 30	4 20	3 15	3 15	3 15	1 5	2 20	3 15
Lathe Operator-Turret		316	3 42	4 88	4 56	3 30	4 20	3 15	2 10	3 15	1 5	2 20	3 15
Milling Machine Operator		316	3 42	4 88	4 56	3 30	4 20	3 15	2 10	3 15	1 5	2 20	3 15
Milling Machine Operator		316	3 42	4 88	4 56	3 30	3 20	3 15	2 10	3 15	1 5	2 20	3 15
								Labor Grade 4					
Welder-Arc	4	314	3 42	3 66	4 56	3 30	3 15	2 10	4 20	3 15	1 5	4 40	3 15
Boring Bar-Horizontal		307	3 42	4 88	3 42	3 30	4 20	2 10	3 15	3 15	1 5	2 20	3 15
Lay-Out Man		306	4 56	4 88	3 42	2 20	4 20	2 10	3 15	3 15	1 5	2 20	3 15
Heat Treater		305	3 42	3 66	3 42	3 30	3 15	4 20	3 15	3 15	1 5	4 40	3 15
Drill Press Operator-Radial		302	3 42	4 88	3 42	3 30	4 20	3 15	2 10	3 15	1 5	2 20	3 15
Miller – Worm Thread		300	3 42	3 66	4 42	4 40	4 20	3 15	3 15	3 15	1 5	3 30	3 15
Milling Machine Operator		299	3 42	3 66	4 56	3 30	4 20	3 15	3 15	3 15	1 5	2 20	3 15
Punch Press-Set-Up Man		296	2 28	3 66	3 42	3 30	3 15	2 10	2 10	3 20	3 15	4 40	3 15
Sheet Metal Worker		295	3 42	3 66	3 42	3 30	3 15	3 15	2 10	3 15	1 5	4 40	3 15
Inspector-Mechanical		294	4 56	3 66	3 42	2 20	3 15	3 15	2 15	3 15	3 15	2 20	3 15

FIG. 10-2 Example of a master job rating summary sheet. (A. L. Kress, "How to Rate Jobs and Men," *Factory Management and Maintenance*, McGraw-Hill Publishing Company, Inc., New York, October, 1939.)

degree demand for that factor. Table 10–1 allocates 15 points for third-degree demand for this factor.

Points on the job-rating sheet are totaled, and the total for the job plus each of the point scores for each factor is posted to a master summary sheet (Fig. 10–2). The analyst, together with the foreman, can then compare the factor rating of each job with others that are similar and next, the total points for each job with total points for other jobs.

Final step in classifying the job under the point system is to convert the points into a labor grade. Minimum and maximum point ranges are established for each labor grade. The point total for a particular job, like the engine lathe operator job, is slotted into the appropriate labor grade.

In this case, note that two extremely different types of jobs might have similar point totals and appear in the same grade—jobs such as a setup man in welding and the engine lathe operator's job.

Where does the foreman fit into this picture?

A foreman or any other supervisor can be of great help to the job-evaluation specialist. First, he can aid the job analyst in getting the true picture of the job. After all, the foreman probably knows better than anyone else how a job might vary from time to time. And since

TABLE 10–1 POINTS ASSIGNED TO FACTORS

	First degree	Second degree	Third degree	Fourth degree	Fifth degree
Skill					
1. Education	14	28	42	56	70
2. Experience	22	44	66	88	110
3. Initiative and ingenuity	14	28	42	56	70
Effort					
4. Physical demand	10	20	30	40	50
5. Mental or visual demand	5	10	15	20	25
Responsibility					
6. Equipment or process	5	10	15	20	25
7. Material or product	5	10	15	20	25
8. Safety of others	5	10	15	20	25
9. Work of others	5	..	15	..	25
Job conditions					
10. Working conditions	10	20	30	40	50
11. Unavoidable hazards	5	10	15	20	25

SOURCE: A. L. Kress, "How to Rate Jobs and Men," *Factory Management and Maintenance,* McGraw-Hill Publishing Company, Inc., New York, October, 1939.

he looks at *many* jobs, his opinion as to the degree of the various demands is likely to be more objective than the employee's.

The foreman is especially helpful in determining the degree to be assigned the various factors for each job. And when the summary sheets are analyzed to compare job points, he can spot when a job is

TABLE 10–2 RESPONSIBILITY FOR FACTOR NO. 7
(MATERIAL OR PRODUCT)

Degree	Requirements
First	Value of material which may be wasted, damaged, or lost is small (maximum $10), or possibility of loss or damage is slight
Second	Probable loss due to damage or waste of materials or product is low (maximum $100)
Third	Probable loss due to damage or waste of material or product is limited (maximum $250), or if amount of possible loss is high, probability of occurrence is exceedingly low
Fourth	Probable loss due to waste or damage of material or product is high (maximum $500)
Fifth	Value of material which may be wasted, damaged, or lost by the employee is very high, up to several thousand dollars

SOURCE: A. L. Kress, "How to Rate Jobs and Men," *Factory Management and Maintenance*, McGraw-Hill Publishing Company, Inc., New York, October, 1939.

out of line. For instance, he may have felt originally that the experience factor for a heat treater was fourth degree. But when comparing this factor on the summary sheet with other jobs, he sees that a layout man's job is rated fourth degree also. He might now say, "No, the heat treater's experience isn't quite as necessary as that of the layout man, so let's drop the heat treater's rating back to third degree."

Are all point systems the same?

No. Even if your company uses a "standard" plan like the National Metal Trades Association (NMTA) plan, there's a good chance that the plan has been adjusted slightly to fit better the jobs peculiar to your plant.

Are job-evaluation plans different for white-collar jobs?

Most of the time a different scale of points is used for white-collar jobs than is used for factory workers. Some white-collar or "salaried" job-evaluation plans also include supervisor positions. Additional factors like "number of people supervised" and "type of supervision" are added. However, not many plans (other than factor comparison and ranking) extend very high up into the management organization.

When are the money values assigned to the various job classifications?

Only after the labor grades have been assigned. That way, the ratings are liable to be fairer because the raters up until now have been talking only in terms of the job itself—not the man currently performing it or the wages he should receive.

How are actual wages determined?

Job evaluation ratings are usually converted to wages rates in three steps:

• Plot a chart of money paid employees *now* against the evaluation job grade. This shows up the current inequities in payment. It's not uncommon to find two men working in the same job classification— one getting $2 per hour, another $1.50. This is the type of situation that job evaluation corrects.

• Make a "wage survey" of wages paid by comparable companies in the plant's community. In making this survey, the job-evaluation specialist is careful to compare job descriptions—not just job titles, since titles are misleading.

• Combine the study of actual wages paid with wages other companies in the area pay to develop a pattern for paying wages in the particular plant.

What are rate ranges?

Rate range is the term typically applied to the minimum and maximum wage rate for each job grade. Many companies, however, pay only a single rate to wage-roll employees in each grade and have rate ranges for salaried, white-collar, and supervisory jobs only.

What's a red-circle rate?

When the wage-rate pattern is determined, the wages paid certain individuals working on certain jobs will stick out from the new pattern. For example, if the rate for a grade 3 job falls in line at $2.35 an hour and engine lathe operators are in grade 3, then all engine lathe operators must be paid $2.35 an hour. If the job-evaluation specialist discovers that an engine lathe operator is being paid *more* than what the rate calls for, say $2.50 an hour, he circles that rate in red.

A red-circle rate then means that the individual on that job is being paid more than the new wage pattern calls for. Usually, the company will pay him (the incumbent) that rate, but not a new employee who comes onto the job. The red-circle rate employee is being paid more than the job is worth, and it is good management to try to find another job for him to do in a higher rate (if he is qualified), so that his rate will match the job.

Does the wage pattern always remain the same?

Under job evaluation, the difference in pay rate between a higher grade job and a lower one provides an incentive for employees to take jobs which demand more from them. So the steps between rates are very important. This becomes a problem, and a management decision to be made when general increases or across-the-board increases are negotiated with the union or otherwise put into effect. If the company decides to pay everyone 10 cents an hour more than he now receives, this has the effect of lowering the *percentage* difference between steps.

Take an example. In a foundry in 1945 the lowest paying job was at $1.00 per hour, the top job at $1.75. The difference between the two was 75 per cent. During the ensuing years, all the raises had been across the board and had accumulated to a total of 50 cents. Now the percentage difference between the bottom rate $1.50 and the top rate $2.25 has been reduced to 50 per cent. And the percentage difference between each job grade has been narrowed accordingly.

To avoid the narrowing of pay differentials, many companies try to apply general wage increases as a percentage of the current rate. Instead of giving 20 cents an hour across the board, the raise might be 10 per cent of each grade's wage rate. So 10 per cent would mean a raise of 15 cents for the lowest job and 22½ cents for the highest. This would maintain an incentive for employees to move up in grades.

Has a cost-of-living raise anything to do with job evaluation?

Not directly, although cost-of-living raises can affect differentials between grades as shown in the last question. Cost-of-living, or escalator, raises usually are introduced to gear wages to rises and falls in the Consumer Price Index of the U.S. Bureau of Labor Statistics, commonly referred to as the "cost-of-living" index. In some companies, if the Index rises one full point, all wages go up 1 cent—or some agreed-upon fraction of a per cent.

How much should employees know about job evaluation?

Job evaluation takes the mystery out of why some jobs pay more than others. Nothing can destroy morale more than the thought that someone else is getting more for doing the same job that you are doing. So, within the limits of your company's policy, job-evaluation methods should be an open book to employees. And each foreman ought to make it his business to know more about how his company's plan works than any of his employees. That way the foreman remains the employees' main source of information. And the foreman can do much to explain what may appear to be discrepancies and thus keep grievances from growing.

In discussing job evaluation with employees, emphasize these points:

• Job evaluation rates the job, not the man.

• Many factors are compared and evaluated—not just the one that seems most important to the particular individual.

• The same set of yardsticks is used to measure every job.

• Job evaluation is based upon the gathering of factual evidence, not just a casual description of the job.

• Job titles are misleading and can mean different things in different parts of the company. Descriptions are what count.

• While judgment still plays a role in determining a job's worth, it has been held to a minimum because the method is systematic and involves enough people so that discrimination or favoritism is practically ruled out.

Can a job be changed from one grade to another?

Yes. Whenever there is a significant change in the content of a job, it's the supervisor's responsibility to report this to his boss or the personnel department. It will take a job-evaluation specialist to determine (with your help) whether the change has altered any of the factors in a degree—either up or down. But you should caution an employee that even though a factor may be changed, that the grade of the job is not necessarily changed unless the total points added (or subtracted) move it from the point range of his present job to another.

What happens to an employee's pay when he moves from one job to another job in the same grade?

A transfer from one job to another in the same job grade is not considered a promotion, even though an employee may feel it is and consider one job more preferable. He'll continue to get the same rate he had on his old job. Only way for him to get more money (if there are no rate ranges) is to be promoted to a higher job grade.

The Case of the Lift-truck Operator. A case study in human relations involving job evaluation, with questions for you to answer.

"Say, Smitty," said Bill Todd to his foreman one day, "I thought we had a job-evaluation system here that guaranteed that everybody with the same job got the same pay. How come I don't get the same money as Abe Tower over in Department 303? He and I got talking at the bowling matches the other night, and I find out that he and I do the same work. Except he gets 12 cents an hour more than I do. Don't I know the right people?

"First I thought Abe was off the beam—or giving me the needle. But we're both lift-truck operators. We both work for the same company. And he showed me his pay envelope. He gets $77.50 base pay for 40 hours while I get only $72.70.

"Furthermore, Abe's got it lots easier than I. His boss leaves him pretty much on his own. And he can go in and out of the warehouse without getting an O.K. But you know how I have to work—I've got every operator in the department on my back all day.

"What I want to know is, who do I have to see to get a square deal around here?"

1. Do you think Bill is right in his request for more money? Why?
2. What kind of information will Smitty need to know in order to judge this request?
3. What sort of answer do you think Smitty should give Bill?
4. Could this situation have been avoided? How?

11 APPRAISING EMPLOYEE PERFORMANCE

What's the difference between job evaluation and merit rating?

In job evaluation, only the *job* is considered. In merit rating, you are measuring how well an *employee* does on that job.

Should you let other employees help you make a merit rating or employee performance appraisal?

Evaluation of an individual's performance and ability is a definite management responsibility. You cannot properly share it or delegate it to someone else outside the managerial ranks. It's perfectly all right, however, and often helpful, to discuss your opinions with your boss or occasionally with your associates (like an assistant foreman). But management alone can determine the relative value of individual employees and their place in the organization.

What factors do you consider when rating an employee's performance?

The specific characteristics to be rated will vary from company to company. But they follow much the same pattern. The National Metal

Trades Association says a supervisor should answer these three questions about an employee's performance:
  • What has he done?
  • What can he do?
  • Can you rely on him?

A typical employee performance rating form is shown in Fig. 11–1.

EMPLOYEE'S NAME_____CLOCK NO._____DEPT. NO._____

CLASSIFICATION_____PRESENT RATE_____HIRE DATE_____

SATISFACTORY: The employee's performance with respect to a factor meets the full job requirements as the job is defined at the time of rating. A satisfactory rating means good performance.

THIS IS THE BASIC STANDARD FOR RATING ANY FACTOR BELOW

FAIR: The employee's performance with respect to a factor is below the requirements for the job and must improve to be satisfactory.

VERY GOOD: The emloyee's performance with respect to a factor is beyond the requirements for satisfactory performance for the job.

UNSATISFACTORY: The employee's performance with respect to a factor is deficient enough to justify release from present job unless improvement is made.

EXCEPTIONAL: The employee's performance with respect to a factor is extraordinary approaching the best possible for the job.

RATE FACTORS BELOW	UNSATISFACTORY	FAIR	SATISFACTORY	VERY GOOD	EXCEPTIONAL
QUALITY: The volume of passable work regularly produced.	Quality too poor to retain on job without improvement. ☐	Work in some respects below job requirements. ☐	Work fully satisfies job requirements. ☐	Quality High, work very well done. ☐	Extraordinary accuracy & thoroness. ☐
QUANTITY: The extent to which work produced meets established standards of quality expected on this job.	Output totally inadequate to retain in job without improvement. ☐	Output in some respects below job requirements. ☐	Output fully satisfies job requirements. ☐	Output more than satisfies job requirements. ☐	Extraordinary speed and volume of output. ☐
DEPENDABILITY: Extent to which you can count on him to report on time, stay on job, care for company property and carry our instructions.	Too unreliable to retain in job without improvement. ☐	Dependability not fully satisfactory. ☐	Fully satisfies dependability demands. ☐	Superior to normal job demands. ☐	Extraordinary dependability in all respects. ☐
JOB ATTITUDE: Amount of interest and enthusiasm shown. Cooperation given those he must work with.	Attitude too poor to retain in job without improvement. ☐	Attitude needs improvement to be satisfactory. ☐	Favorable attitude. ☐	High degree of enthusiasm and interest. ☐	Extraordinary degree of enthusiasm and interest. ☐
JOB KNOWLEDGE: Possession of information and understanding of all types of work which he must perform.	Knowledge inadequate to retain in job without improvement. ☐	Lacks some required knowledge. ☐	Knowledge fully satisfies job requirements. ☐	Very well informed on all phases of work. ☐	Extraordinary beyond that which present job can utilize. ☐
JUDGMENT: Ability to decide correct course of action when some choice can be made.	Judgment too poor to retain in job without improvement. ☐	Decisions not entirely adequate to meet job demands. ☐	Makes good decisions in various situations arising in job. ☐	Superior in determining correct decisions and actions. ☐	Extraordinary beyond that which present job can utilize. ☐

FIG. 11-1   Typical employee performance rating sheet to be completed by the supervisor.

How often should you rate an employee?

Twice a year is a happy medium. If you rate too often, you're likely to be too much impressed by day-to-day occurrences. If you wait too long—you're likely to forget many of the incidents that ought to influence your appraisal. Even if your company has a plan that calls for rating only once a year, it's good practice on your part to make an informal appraisal more often.

Where employees are rated for quality of work, won't an employee on a high-skill job always get a higher rating than one on a job requiring less ability?

Watch out for making this mistake. Measure the employee's skill against the job he's on, *only*. Quality standards will obviously differ from job to job. Ask yourself only to what degree the employee measures up to standards of the job he's on *now*.

For example, external grinding may require very close tolerances up to 0.0005 inch and a fine finish. Both conditions are mostly within the control of the operator himself. Compare this with a punch press, where the work may be set up by a setup man, the quality standards less rigid and mainly controlled by the machine itself. Regardless of the differences in skill required, it would be entirely possible to give the same quality performance rating to operators of each machine. It's the same as saying "Tom is a top-quality performer on the external grinder job. Pete is also a top-quality performer on the punch press job." This *does not* mean that Pete would also be a top-quality performer on the grinding job.

Doesn't an employee's rating represent only his supervisor's opinion?

A good performance rating includes more than just a supervisor's opinion. It should be based on facts, too. In the consideration of quality, what is the employee's scrap record? As to quantity, what do the production records show? Dependability, what's his absence and lateness record? Can you cite actual incidents where you may have had to discipline him or speak to him about the quality or quantity of his output? Answering these questions makes your rating less opinionated, consequently more valid and worth while.

How can you make sure your ratings are consistent from employee to employee?

One good way to make sure you rate each employee fairly is to make out a check list with the name of each of your employees down one side of a sheet of paper and the factor to be rated across the top. Look at only one factor at a time. Take quality, for instance. If you have previously rated Tom only "fair" and Pete and Ted "good," decide whether Pete and Ted should still be rated "good" when compared with Tom's rating. Perhaps you'll want to drop Pete's rating to "fair" because Pete and Tom produce about the same quality of work, while Ted's quality is consistently better than either of the other two.

Another way to check your ratings for consistency is to see whether there is a variation of appraisals, or whether you have rated all your employees the same. In any group, there should be a variety of performances. Roughly speaking, three-quarters of your employees should be in the middle ratings—say "fair" to "good." About one-eighth will stand out at the top with "very good" to "exceptional." And another eighth will be at the bottom rated from "fair" to "unsatisfactory" (see the normal distribution curve in Fig. 9–2).

How do you convert employee performance ratings to money?

This is strictly a matter of your company's policy. About the only generality that can be drawn is that employees whose ratings are less than satisfactory should not be recommended for increases. Where a company has a rate range (maximum and minimum wage rates) for each job, many people believe that only workers who are rated "very good" or "exceptional" should advance to the maximum rate for the job.

If you can't give an employee a raise, why rate him at all?

Merit rating is so often associated with money that supervisors and employees alike lose sight of the other important benefits. Periodic performance reviews help a supervisor to:

• Point out strengths and weaknesses to an employee so that he can cultivate the former and correct the latter.

• Provide a fair and unbiased method for determining qualifications for promotions, transfers, and rate increases.

• Recognize those employees who have exceptional ability and deserve training for higher positions and responsibilities.

• Weed out those who aren't qualified for the work they are doing and help assign them to more suitable work. Or, if they are wholly unqualified, to separate them from the company's payroll.

Why should you bother to tell an employee where he stands?

People like to know how they shape up, as long as your evaluation is fair and constructive. The actual rating is like a doctor's diagnosis.

It doesn't do the patient any good until the therapy is prescribed. In the case of merit rating, this cure takes place when the supervisor sits down with the employee to show him where he stands and what he can do to improve.

Informal discussions of ratings with an employee will:

• Give him a clear understanding of how well his boss thinks he is doing his job.

• Provide him with a chance to ask questions about your opinion and give his views on his own efforts.

• Clear up any misunderstandings about what you expect from him on the job.

• Set a course for an employee to improve his attitudes and his job skills.

• Build a strong relationship based on mutual confidence between supervisor and employee.

Don't employees resent being told?

Biggest fear in most supervisor's minds is that an employee will dislike being criticized. Surprisingly, this fear is unfounded—if the appraisal is based on facts rather than opinion only and you display a willingness to change ratings if an employee can show you you're wrong. People want to know where they stand—even if it isn't good. But don't interpret this to mean that appraisal interviews are easy, or that an employee will make it easy for you. Chances are he won't.

How do you handle charges of discrimination or favoritism?

Unfavorable criticism stings an occasional employee so hard that it's not unusual for him to react by charging you with favoritism. Don't try to argue him out of it. He probably won't accept your direct denial anyway. Instead, try acknowledging that possibly you have erred in making your rating of him.

For instance, say, "Tony, why do you think I might be favoring Sam? If I've given you that impression, perhaps you can help me see where I've been wrong." So Tony says, "Well, you give Sam all the easy jobs, and I get all the junk that no one else wants."

Your reply ought to be along these lines: "I don't agree that I give Sam the easy jobs, but I do find that I ask him to do lots of jobs that need first-rate attention. He seems easier to get along with when I need something done in a hurry. On the other hand, I've been hesitating to ask you to do anything out of the ordinary. That's because you act as if I'm taking unfair advantage of you. Don't you agree that it's just human nature on my part to lean on people who show they want to cooperate? Maybe it's been my fault that you feel I've favored Sam. I'll watch that in the future. But how about your pitching in and taking your share of the load? Will you try it that way with me, Tony?"

How can you tell a man his work is way below par?

Don't be too tough on a poor performer. Be especially sure that your treatment of him has encouraged the best kind of performance. Otherwise he may feel that his poor showing is more your fault than his.

Your guides should be these: *Be firm. Nothing is to be gained by being soft. If his work has been bad, tell him so.*

Be specific, such as, "Harry, we've been over this before. During the last six months I've made a point of showing you exactly where you have fallen down on the job. Remember the rejects we had on the X-56 job? And the complaints on the motor shafts? Only last week you put the whole shop in a bad light by the way you mishandled the shaft job again. It looks to me as if you just aren't cut out for machine shop work. So I'm recommending that you be transferred out of this department. If there's no other suitable work available, I guess you'll have to look for work elsewhere."

Don't rub it in, though. Leave him his self-respect. End the discussion by summarizing what you have found satisfactory about him as well as the things that are unsatisfactory.

Isn't it true that no matter how well some employees do their job, there's little chance of their getting a better job?

Yes. It's especially tough on a good workman who is bucking a seniority sequence and who knows that until the man ahead of him gets promoted or drops dead, he's not going to move up. Suppose a No. 2 operator on an oil still said to you, "Each time I get reviewed, you tell me I'm doing a good job. But this hasn't done me any good. I'm getting top dollar for the job I'm on, and until the No. 1 operator changes jobs, I'm stuck. All the merit review does to me is to rub salt in the wound!"

A good way for you to handle this gripe is to admit the situation exists, but don't oversympathize. Try saying something like this: "Sure, I agree that it's hard waiting for your chance. But some workers make the mistake of depending entirely upon seniority for their advancement. I don't want you to fall into that trap. When the next better job opens, I hope both of us can say that you're fully qualified. That's one of the good things about performance ratings. You can find out where your weak spots may be and correct them. For a fellow who has your ability and does as well on the job as you do, there's no reason why you have to limit your ambitions to the No. 1 operator's job either. Maybe you'll be able to do what Pete did. He jumped from a No. 2 job to a foreman's spot."

Should you discuss one employee's rating with another employee?

Not if you can possibly help it. Avoid comparisons when you can. And be sure that each employee knows that you treat his rating as confidential. Try to establish the entire procedure on the basis that it is a confidential matter.

Where should you carry on merit rating or appraisal interviews?

Do it privately, in your own office or in a private room. You'll want to be able to give the interview your undivided attention. And you won't want to be in earshot of other employees either. Allow yourself enough time—at least a half hour. Otherwise the whole procedure will be too abrupt.

Can you tell ahead of time how an employee will react?

You should be the best judge of how one of your employees will take what you have to say to him. Try to estimate his reactions ahead of time so that you're not taken by surprise. The interview gets out of control mainly when the supervisor is shocked by an employee's unexpected antagonistic or hostile attitude. If you expect it, you can plan ahead of time what to say—or at least be prepared to hear out his objections.

What's the "sandwich" technique for telling an employee about unfavorable aspects of his work?

The sandwich technique means simply to sandwich unfavorable comments between favorable comments: "Alice, I've been pleased with the way you've stepped up your output. You've made real improvement there. I am a little disappointed, however, by the quality of what you produce. The records show that you're always near the bottom of the group on errors. So I hope you'll work as well to improve quality as you did quantity. I feel sure you will, since your attitude toward your work has been just fine."

The same technique is a helpful guide to the entire merit review discussion. Use it by starting the talk off with a compliment. Then discuss the work which must be improved. Finish by finding something else good to say about the employee's work.

Should you leave room for an employee to save face?

Call it what you want, but give an employee every chance to tell you what obstacles stand in the way of his making good. Don't interrupt or say, "That's just an excuse, John." Instead, take your time. Let him talk. Often the first reason he gives isn't the real one. Only if you listen carefully will you discover underlying causes for poor attitude or effort.

Confidence in you as a supervisor and in the merit rating system is important. So don't be too anxious to prove that he's wrong. Above all, don't show anger, regardless of what kind of remark the employee makes. That advice goes even if he blows his stack.

Isn't it dangerous to tell an employee you've given him a high rating? Won't he get a swelled head as a result, or expect to get an immediate raise or promotion out of it?

Knowledge of where he stands with the boss is just as important to a top-notch performer as it is to a mediocre employee—maybe even more so. If you fail to show your recognition of a good job, a workman is likely to feel, "What's the use of doing a good job? No one appreciates it."

Good workers are hard to come by. They should know how you feel, even when you can't show them an immediate reward. Remember, people work for lots more than what they get in the pay envelope.

What's the halo effect? How can you avoid it?

Nearly everybody has a tendency to let one favorable or unfavorable trait influence their judgment of an individual as a whole. This is called the *halo effect*. A supervisor may feel that Carl is a hard person to socialize with, that his attitude is wrong. This becomes a halo effect if the supervisor lets this one trait color his whole judgment of Carl so that he forgets that Carl's workmanship is outstanding or his attendance is good. In the other direction, a supervisor may be so impressed with a workman's loyalty that he may tend to overlook his other shortcomings. Either kind of halo effect is bad.

To avoid the halo effect, it's helpful to rate all employees on one of the rating factors before going on to the next factor.

What are some common errors a supervisor may make when appraising employee performance?

Plain old bias or prejudice is something that will ruin an otherwise good appraisal unless you make a definite effort to keep it out. Ask yourself, am I measuring this man's performance only against his job? Or am I dragging in the way he dresses, his accent, his color or nationality, the twist of his nose, the shape of his chin, or the "cut of his jib"?

Overemphasizing a single incident will also distort your rating. Guard yourself against saying, "Merlin is one of the best men we have. I remember three years ago when he saved our skin by turning out the Thompson job in six hours." Or, "Mack will never be any good. He proved that to me last year when he botched the Smith job."

Can you be too lenient?

Few employees are good in everything—or poor in everything. Most of us rate high in some qualities, not so good in others. If you overrate your employees, you're not being fair to the men who are really top-notch. And this lack of judgment on your part will show up when someone up the line, like the plant manager, reviews ratings for consistency. It will be hard for him to believe that everyone in your department is outstanding.

Can you be too tough?

Yes. It's foolish to expect the impossible from people. And it's unwise to be so strict in your standards that no one can please you. It's no pleasure to work for a supervisor who takes good performance for granted. So try to make your ratings fair. Not so tight that employees will say, "Regardless of how good a job you do, Joe can always find some fault with it."

What sort of follow-up should a supervisor make after the performance rating interview?

Merit rating isn't something that's done today and finished. To be of lasting value to you and your employees, you should follow up the appraisal interview this way:

Stick to your side of the bargain. If you have promised to examine an employee's work more carefully to see if you've given him a fair rating, do so. Check his past record and show him any of the data he's questioned. If you must change your rating, do it promptly and let him know that his point of view has been supported.

Provide ways for his development. An employee will need your help to improve—especially his skills. Give him the kind of instruction your review indicated will help him. If he needs more versatility, broaden his assignments by giving him different and challenging jobs to do. If his workmanship is inferior, study what he's doing wrong and show him how to do it right.

Continue to show interest in his work. Drop by the employee's work place occasionally with a view toward letting him know he's improved —or gone downhill—since the interview. If he's making progress, give him credit. If he's slipping, point out where you're dissatisfied.

What's a good guide to follow when discussing an employee's performance rating with him?

Before talking to an employee about his rating, try this check list:
• What sort of a reaction do you think he'll have? Have you thought of how you'll handle it?
• Will you be able to support your rating with facts? Can you cite a number of instances that back up your opinion?
• What are the good points you'll want to compliment him about?
• Which of his important weaknesses are you prepared to discuss?
• What sort of corrective action do you want the employee to take?
• Have you developed a training plan for his skills improvement?
• Which of his personal traits do you want to encourage him to develop? How will you help him do this?
• In what way will this rating affect his chances for a raise or for a promotion?

The Case of the Overheard Conversation. A case study in human relations involving employee performance, with questions for you to answer.

Red Bonnard, supervisor of M shop, ducked into a doorway to light a cigarette as he left the plant office. As he did, two of his employees walked past. Neither noticed Red. Red started to wave hello when he realized they were talking about him. "What a line of malarkey Red gives you," said the first employee. "He got me in the corner this afternoon and told me he couldn't run the shop without me. That I was his number-one boy."

"He told *you* that, too?" responded his companion. "Maybe in your case he means it. But I don't pay any attention to his compliments any more. I found out he gives everyone the same pep talk. Even when I blow a job and expect to catch the devil for it, he's just as sweet as sugar."

"To tell you the truth," said the first employee, "I wish he would let me know for real how I stand. It may be fine to have a boss who talks nice to you. But I'm always afraid he tells me one thing and then runs me down to someone else in the shop. You know how lousy a job Pete does on ring polishing? Well, Red picked up Pete's tote box the other day and even he was shocked. There were at least three burned rings in the lot. Pete looked up and said, 'Anything wrong, Red?' You know what Red said? 'Nope. Glad you got this job out on time.' But here's the clincher! Red came over to my machine to chew the rag and in less than five minutes he's telling me how he can't trust Pete with the ring jobs. He'll have to give them to me in the future. Why doesn't he straighten Pete out, anyway?"

"That's the trouble with Red, all right. He's so eager to make people feel happy that he never levels with you."

"I'm not worried about Pete," said his companion. "What I worry about is what Red tells others about me that he can't tell me to my face."

As the two men walked away Red tossed his unsmoked cigarette into the gutter. He turned back into the building and went back to his office. He sat down at his desk without lighting the light. Then he began to think.

1. What do you suppose Red was thinking about?

2. What was wrong with Red's approach to dealing with his employees? Was he all wrong?

3. If you could advise Red, how would you tell him to improve his status among his employees.

12 TRAINING EMPLOYEES TO WORK WELL

Will employees learn without being trained?

Yes. That's the danger. Regardless of whether you train an employee or not, he learns anyway. Even if you do it and don't do it the right way, someone else is likely to do it the wrong way for you. It's a sad story that employees who learn by trial and error or from fellow workers and shop stewards are rarely trained to do the job efficiently.

Why should a supervisor have to do the training? Isn't this job better done by a training specialist?

Make up your mind that training is your baby and one of the most important ones. It needs to be done day in and day out. For training is the only sure-fire way to build a work force that returns full value for every dollar invested in labor cost. As a supervisor, you no longer work with your hands. You are judged by your ability to get the people who work for you to produce accurately and well and to turn out more goods at lower costs. Employee training is your biggest tool.

When can you tell training is needed?

Training needs give themselves away easily if you look for them. Even if the relationship between the symptoms and the cause isn't always obvious. Here are some of the more common conditions that point up the need for employee training:

High scrap record	Unusual tardinesses
Excessive absences	High accident rate
Too many quits and fires	Too much overtime
Low production	Poor employee morale
Abnormal amount of complaints	Lack of cooperation

Whenever you spot one of these conditions, check your training efforts before you crack down on your employees' performance. By and large, a workman who is well trained doesn't create these problems.

Are there any special rewards for a supervisor who does a good job of training his workers?

In addition to making a better showing for your department in terms of better quality and quantity of output, training puts you in a favorable light in other ways. Smart employee instruction:
• Helps you handle transfers better.
• Actually gives you more time for planning and scheduling your work.
• Provides a reserve of trained manpower in your department for emergencies.
• Automatically helps you win the cooperation of your workers.
• And, perhaps most important of all for a supervisor who wants to get ahead, training makes you "available" for advancement.

When does good training begin?

When a new employee is hired. Getting a new worker off on the right foot is like a baseball team that gets off to a ten-run lead in the first inning. There's a darn good chance of eventual success.

Training recently hired workers, called *induction training,* or sometimes *orientation training,* is a little like introducing a friend at a lodge meeting where he is a stranger. You'd want to introduce him around and try to make him feel at home. You'd show him where to hang his hat and coat, where the rest rooms are. If you wanted to have him think well of your lodge, you might tell him something about its history and the good fellows who belong to it. If you had to leave him for a time to attend to some duty or other, you would come back occasionally to see how he was getting along. It's the same way with a new employee who reports to you. Treat him as someone you'd like to think well of you and feel at home in your department.

What should you tell a brand-new employee about his job?

An induction talk should cover the following subjects, where they apply:

> Pay rates, pay periods, how employees are paid—by cash or by check, day first pay is received, and pay deductions
>
> Hours of work, reporting and quitting time, lunch periods, washup time
>
> Overtime and overtime pay
>
> Shift premium pay
>
> Time cards, where they are located, how to punch in and out
>
> How to report out sick
>
> What to do when late
>
> Location of lockers and washrooms
>
> Location of first-aid facilities and how to report accidents
>
> Basic safety rules
>
> Tour of department or plant
>
> Introduction to fellow workers
>
> Assignment to work station

Just this basic information is a lot for a new employee to swallow at once. So don't be afraid to repeat what you tell him several times. Better still, give him some of the more detailed information in small doses. Some today, a little more tomorrow, and as much as he can take a week from now.

Note that in many companies, a new employee receives an induction talk from a central service, like the personnel or training department. As valuable as this talk may be, it won't help the new man half as much as an informal, straight-from-the-shoulder chat with you.

How do you get down to the real business of training an employee to do a job the way you want him to?

Training can be either the simplest—or the most difficult—job in the world. If you can grasp just four fundamentals, you can be a superior trainer. If you don't buy this approach, you'll spend the rest of your life complaining that employees are stupid, willful, or not like workmen used to be in the good old days.

The foundation of job training has four cornerstones:

Step 1. Get the worker ready to learn. People who want to learn are the easiest to teach. So let a man know why his job is important, why it must be done right. Find out something about the employee as an individual. Not only does this make him have more confidence in you, but it reveals to you how much he knows already about the job, the amount and quality of his experience, and what his attitude toward learning is. This familiarization period helps the trainee to get the feel, or "heft," of the job you want him to do.

Step 2. Demonstrate how the job should be done. Don't just tell him how to go about it or say, "Watch how I do it." Do both—tell *and* show him the correct procedure. Do this a little at a time, step by step. There's no point in going on to something new until the trainee has grasped the preceding step.

Step 3. Try him out by letting him do the job. Let the employee try his hand at the job—under your guidance. Stay with him now to encourage him when he's doing right and to correct him when he's wrong. The mistakes he makes while you're watching him are invaluable, since they show you where he hasn't learned.

Step 4. Put him on his own—gradually. A man doing a new job has to fly alone sooner or later. So after he's shown you that he can do the work reasonably well while you're standing by, turn him loose for a while. Don't abandon him completely, though. Make a point of checking on his progress and workmanship regularly. Perhaps three or four times the first day he's on his own, than once or twice a day for a week or two. But never feel he's completely trained. There's always something he can learn to do, or learn to do better.

How much should you teach at a time?

This depends upon (1) the speed with which a trainee can learn and (2) how difficult the job is. Each learner is different. Some catch on fast. Others are slow. It's better, therefore, to gauge your speed to the slow person. Try to find out why he has trouble learning. With a new employee, it may simply be that he's nervous and trying so hard that he doesn't concentrate. So be patient with him. Give him a chance to relax. And when he completes even a small part of the task successfully, be sure to praise him.

Going ahead slowly is especially important at the start, since learning is like getting a three-speed car into motion. You first warm up the engine, then start slowly in low gear. You shift into second only as the car picks up speed, and finally into high when it's rolling along under its own momentum.

What can you do to make the job easier to learn— and to teach?

Jobs that seem simple to you because you're familiar with them may appear very hard to a workman who has never performed them before. Experience has shown that the trick to making jobs easier to learn is to break them down into simple steps. That way, an employee needs to learn only one step at a time rather than try to grasp the whole job in a single piece.

Breaking a job down for training purposes involves two elements:

First you must observe the job as it is done and break it into its logical steps. For instance, if the job were to in-feed grind on a centerless grinder, the first step would be to place the piece on the plate against the regulating wheel. The second step is to lower the lever-feed and grind. Third step is to raise the lever-release. And so on until the job is finished.

Second, for each step in a job breakdown, you must now consider the second element—called the *key point.* A key point is anything at a particular step that might make or break a job or injure the worker.

JOB BREAK-DOWN SHEET FOR TRAINING MAN ON NEW JOB	
Part ____Shaft_____ Operation	In-feed grind on centerless grinder
IMPORTANT STEPS IN THE OPERATION Step: A logical segment of the operation when something happens to ADVANCE the work	**KEY POINTS** Key point: Anything in a step that might Make or break the job Injure the worker Make the work easier to do, i.e., "knack," "trick," special timing, bit of special information
1. Place piece on plate against regulating wheel	"Knack" - don't catch on wheel
2. Lower lever-feed	Hold at end of stroke (count 1-2-3-4) Slow feed - where might taper Watch - no oval grinding
3. Raise lever-release	
4. Guage pieces periodically	More often as approach tolerance
5. Readjust regulating wheel as required	Watch - no back lash
6. Repeat above until finished	
7. Check	

FIG. 12-1   Sample job instruction breakdown. (The Training Within Industry Report, War Manpower Commission, Bureau of Training, Training Within Industry Service, Washington, D.C., 1945.)

Essentially, it's the knack or know-how that an experienced workman has that makes the job go easier for him. The key point for the first step in the centerless grinding job in the previous paragraph would be to know the knack of not catching the work piece on the wheel. For the second step it would be the knowledge of how to avoid tapering or oval surfaces.

Figure 12–1 shows how this centerless grinder job might be broken down into seven steps for training purposes.

How soon should you expect an employee to acquire job skill?

This, too, depends upon the employee and upon the job being learned. But, regardless, it's smart to set a timetable for learning. This

	Drill	Bore	Ream	Face	Taper Turn	Burr and Burnish	Etc	Etc	Etc
White	√	√	√	√	√	√			
Nolan	√	√	√	11-10	–	=			
Smith	11-1	11-20	–	√	√	12-1			
Jones	–	–	√	11-15	12-1	12-8			
Etc.									

√ means the worker can already do the job.

– means he doesn't need to know the job.

11-1, 11-15, etc., indicate the dates the supervisor has set for himself when he plans to have his men TRAINED to do the jobs required.

FIG. 12-2   Sample job instruction timetable. (The Training Within Industry Report, War Manpower Commission, Bureau of Training, Training Within Industry Service, Washington, D.C., 1945.)

can be a very simple one like Fig. 12–2, or it can be as detailed as you like. The important thing is to use it to:
- Record how much the worker knows already.
- Indicate what he doesn't need to know.
- Plan ahead for what he has to learn.
- Set definite dates for completing his training in each phase of the job.

In what sequence must a job be taught?

Best way to teach a job is to start with the easiest part and proceed to the most difficult. This isn't always possible, of course. But if you can arrange your employee training in this sequence, learning will go more smoothly and teaching will be easier.

A sample training sequence for making eye-glass lenses appears in Fig. 12–3.

These separate jobs are arranged in the order best suited for training a man by successive assignments, on each of which he will develop more skill and knowledge on one or more of the progress factors as shown.

Operations are to be assigned in numerical order from # 1. Fully trained man	0001'' and fractions of minutes on angles	Color Test Perfect	Highest	$15 per piece and up	Complex
15. Polish. 14. Fine grind. 13. Cement crown and flint elements together. 12. Center and edge to diameter (finished)	↑	↑	↑	↑	↑
4th Level					
11. Grind 1st radius. Grind 2nd radius. 10. Grind to rough diameter. 9. Grind to thickness. 8. Cut on saw if necessary.	Accuracy in Working to Dimensions	Quality of Surface Produced	Care Required in Handling Finished Surfaces	Increased Value Due to Previous Processing	Set-up – Adjusting Equipment
3rd Level					
7. Block lens on blocking tool. 6. Inspect. 5. Inspect before polishing. 4. Remove and clean.					
2nd Level					
3. Place sealing wax buttons on polished side. 2. Grind bevel. 1. Grind one side flat.					
1st Level					
Green Man	.050''	Rough	Ordinary	Low	Simple

FIG. 12-3   Sample training sequence of jobs for making optical glass eye lens. (The Training Within Industry Report, War Manpower Commission, Bureau of Training, Training Within Industry Service, Washington, D.C., 1945.)

Does the supervisor have to do all the training himself?

No. Actual instruction is a job he can delegate to another employee—*if the employee is a qualified trainer.* Just as you must know the ins and outs of teaching a job, any employee you appoint to instruct another must also know how to train others. This means that he should have completed a course in Job Instruction Training (JIT) or have been thoroughly indoctrinated by you or by the company's training director in how to train. Nothing is worse than bringing a new employee over to the bench of an older employee and just turning him loose. If the older worker doesn't know how to train, chances are 1,000 to 1 that the new employee will never learn the job correctly. And the training process itself will be slow and costly. So never depend upon old Jake to "show young Bob the ropes."

Caution: Even if you have a qualified job instructor in your department, you can never completely delegate your training responsibility to him. It's up to you to show a personal interest in the trainee's progress and to supervise his training just as you supervise any other of your responsibilities.

Can you depend upon an employee to learn a job by reading an equipment manufacturer's instruction manual?

Absolutely not. It's a very exceptional person who can apply himself to an instruction manual and learn how to operate equipment solely on that basis. Instruction manuals are valuable training aids, however. And they will help you draw up job-breakdown sheets. But they are no substitute for personal instruction.

How much training can be done through outside reading and by correspondence instruction?

If an employee is ambitious to learn and improve himself—and if he's the rare person who can absorb knowledge and skills through reading and self help—he can learn much through reading or through correspondence courses. But make no mistake about it, this is the hard way! Few employees are up to it. And despite the claims of many of its advocates, the percentage of industrial workers who have learned their jobs this way is very small.

This is not to say, however, that outside reading *combined* with personalized instruction by the supervisor is not effective. It is, but the two must go hand in hand.

How good is group training?

Personalized training seems to be best for job skills, but it is expensive and time-consuming. Training employees in groups is obviously less expensive. And for many purposes, it is just as effective as individualized training. For some purposes—like explaining the theory behind an operation—it's even better.

There are many training methods. Each has its good and bad points. And the more training ideas you have in your bag of tools, the better trainer you'll be. So give some thought to using any or all of the eight methods shown in Table 12–1.

TABLE 12–1   EIGHT TRAINING METHODS *

Method	Use	Example
Individual instruction	Teach important or complicated skill	Running machine; assembly work
	Change method of work or bad habit	Correcting experienced operator
Group instruction	Give basic facts that can be told off job	Telling importance of operation or reasons for new method
Lecture	Give basic or supplementary information on specific subject	Usually technical information: mathematics, job evaluation, electronics
Demonstration	Clarify grasp of manual skills, high-light key problem or principle	Show right way to hold tools. Solution to plant layout problem
Conference	Solve problems, direct or change attitudes	How to control absenteeism; how to prevent waste
Meeting	Exchange information, get ideas of group, solve immediate problem	Supervisory production meeting; department safety meeting
Written instruction	Give important information in permanent form for immediate or later use	Procedure for punching time clocks; policy on night shift bonus
Oral directions	Give information needed at once—in short form	What job to work on next; where to send special order

* M. J. Murphy, "How to Start a Training Program from Scratch," *Factory Management and Maintenance*, June, 1951, p. 128, McGraw-Hill Publishing Company, Inc., New York, by permission of the publisher.

How quickly do people forget what they have learned?

According to the Research Institute of America the startling figures in Table 12–2 indicate how fast our learning disappears unless we keep at it.

TABLE 12–2

Time interval since learning	Per cent forgotten	Per cent retained
⅓ hour	42	58
1 hour	56	44
8¾ hours	64	36
1 day	66	34
2 days	72	28
6 days	75	25

So for an employee to become expert at the job you're teaching him, he must practice constantly. And you must keep repeating the important things that these figures show he's likely to forget.

Why all the fuss about following up your training effort?

If what is taught isn't used, all the time and effort you've devoted to training will be wasted. It's up to you to follow up to see that training is used. Try a simple tickler system, like jotting down the trainee's name on your calendar at a date 30 or 60 days from when he finished training. Then make a point of observing his performance when that date comes up. Discuss his job with him. Find out where he feels he could use further instruction.

What's the purpose of visual aids?

The corny old Chinese proverb still tells the story best: "One picture is worth 1,000 words." Any device that helps a trainee visualize what you're telling him speeds up the learning process. After all, most of us use our eyes to pick up 80 per cent of what we know. So it's only natural for training that utilizes the visual senses to be more effective.

Visual aids may include a variety of devices such as transparencies, slides and filmstrips, motion pictures, and opaque projectors; charts and chart boards, posters, flannel and magnetic board presentations; simulated equipment and mockups, cutaway models of machines, and actual displays of products, materials, etc.

Visual aids may also be simple and obvious, such as writing on a blackboard or demonstrating a point on a shop machine. Practically nothing beats making the demonstration right on the equipment a worker will use.

How good is apprentice training?

Traditionally, the top-notch, all-round skilled craftsmen have been schooled through apprenticeship. This is a long, thorough, and costly practice. It may take anywhere from 12 months to four years. A man who has learned his trade through an approved apprenticeship program will be able to handle with skill almost any kind of job that occurs within his skill class. But as jobs in industry have tended to become more and more standardized, much of what the journeyman (a tradesman who has completed his apprenticeship) knows never gets used. For this reason, the percentage of employees trained through apprentice programs gets less and less. Most employees today are trained for only one specific job at a time. As a result, the training is more to the point, is done faster, and costs less. But if you were to examine apprentice training, you'd find that over the long haul, it incorporates the four points of job training outlined previously. The main difference lies in the length of the training period and the variety of skills learned.

What's vestibule training?

When an employee is trained by the company on the kind of work he's hired to perform before he begins to work on in-production materials, the training is called "vestibule" training. It gets its name from the fact that such training is often done outside the shop or plant—as if it were performed in the vestibule of the company before actual entry into the working part of the shop.

Can you teach old dogs new tricks?

Yes. Older workers can and do learn new methods and new jobs. And while they may learn at a slower rate than younger workers, this is mainly because older workers frequently have to "unlearn" what was taught them in the past. Older workers often don't have the same incentive to learn that younger ones do. They tend to feel more secure in their jobs and have less interest in advancement. For these reasons, *Step 1—Getting the worker ready to learn*—is of prime importance when teaching older workers.

How do you get employees to want to learn?

An employee must see how training will pay off for him before he pitches into training with a will. So show the younger employee how training helped others to get ahead, how it built job security for them and increased their incomes. For older workers, stress the prestige that skill gives them with other workers. Show them how learning new jobs or better methods makes the work more interesting.

Telling workers *why* a job is done a certain way is often the key to securing their interest. To see the necessity for training, a workman needs to know not only *what* to do and *how* to do it, but *why* it needs to be done. This process may be compared with a technical problem in transmitting color television. As you may know, the picture is broken down into three separate channels, one of which carries the red, another the green, and the third the blue part of the picture. Unless all three are transmitted in harmony, the picture is blurred and distorted. So, too, unless all three requisites of training are transmitted to the employee, it makes little sense to him.

Do labor unions object to training programs?

Few unions are opposed to the principle of training. How you set up your training activities and how you carry them out is where suspicion might arise. It's a good idea for you to lay your training cards on the table so that the shop steward knows exactly what you propose to do. Aim for his cooperation, since mutual confidence and trust between you and the union representative help make your training efforts successful. Explain to them how training will benefit employees in security, pay, pride, etc.

How smoothly should the training process proceed?

The learning process doesn't go smoothly for most people. We all have our ups and downs. Expect a trainee to learn quickly for a while, then taper off on a plateau temporarily. He may even backslide a little. That's the time to reassure him that his halt in progress is normal. Don't let him become discouraged. If necessary, go through demonstration again so that he can get a fresh start. And pile on the encouragement.

For smoothing out the learning process for difficult jobs, see Fig. 12-4.

If the supervisor is responsible for training, what's the purpose of the company's training department?

The function of a plant training department will vary from company to company. But almost all training directors are agreed that unless the supervisor is sold on training as his responsibility, the efforts of the training department won't be very effective.

Generally, the training department people are *experts in teaching methods:* they won't lay claim to technical skill about the job (except in cases where technical specialists are employed for certain types of instruction, such as blueprint reading and the like). The training department serves best as an aid and a guide to the supervisor in improving the skills of his workers.

For example, the training director can be of real help in determining the training needs. He can help you recognize and interpret the training symptoms mentioned previously. You'll want his help, too, in learning how to be a good instructor and in training some of your key employees to be trainers. And the training department is invaluable in getting you started in making job breakdowns and training-time tables.

Certain employee training is best done by a central training group. Such general subjects as company history and products, economics, and human relations are naturals for them. Other classroom-type instruction (like arithmetic, work simplification, etc.) lends itself to centralized training, too. But when the training department does these jobs for you, you must still assume the responsibility for requesting this training for your employees and for making sure they apply what they learn to their work.

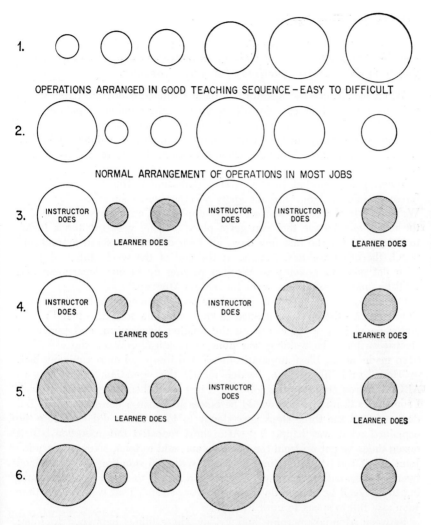

1.

OPERATIONS ARRANGED IN GOOD TEACHING SEQUENCE – EASY TO DIFFICULT

2.

NORMAL ARRANGEMENT OF OPERATIONS IN MOST JOBS

3. INSTRUCTOR DOES   LEARNER DOES   INSTRUCTOR DOES   INSTRUCTOR DOES   LEARNER DOES

4. INSTRUCTOR DOES   LEARNER DOES   INSTRUCTOR DOES   LEARNER DOES

5.   LEARNER DOES   INSTRUCTOR DOES   LEARNER DOES

6.

FIG. 12-4   How to teach the difficult operation. If a job can be taught by proceeding from the easy steps to the difficult, teaching becomes easier. Few jobs, however, have their working sequence arranged in an order of increasing difficulty as shown at the top of the chart. Instead, the difficult parts of the job are usually mixed in with the easy ones, like the second line on the chart. These steps have to be done on the job in the correct order, and therefore they should be learned in that order. What can the supervisor-instructor do? He can keep the job in proper sequence and still teach the easier parts first by setting up his teaching plan as shown by the dark spots in each row of the chart. The instructor does the difficult, or white, spots while the worker does the easy, or black, spots, thus maintaining a learning sequence even in a difficult or long operation. (*Guide for Management Trainers,* AFM 50-19, Department of the Air Force, Washington, D.C., June 1, 1955.)

135

The Case of John W. A case study in human relations involving employee training, with questions for you to answer.

When the Grimes Refrigerator Co. plant switched over from batch spray-painting to a continuous automatic-spray line, the number of painters was reduced from twenty-three to five. All of the displaced painters were placed in other jobs throughout the plant. One of the displaced painters, John W., was assigned to the cabinet department to learn the job of a class B spot-welder.

When John reported to the cabinet department, Bill Mollier, his new foreman, said to him, "I don't know whether you'll stay here for keeps. We're a little slow now, and we really don't need an extra welder. But in the meantime, I'll see that you get a place to hang your hat and a bench to sit at." So for the first few days, all John did was to stand around and watch the other welders. Finally, at the end of the week, Bill told John, "I've got good news for you. Work is picking up in our department and we'll be able to put you to work for real on Monday."

On Monday, Bill assigned John to a welding machine. It was a very simple rig. All the operator needed to know was how to slide a metal refrigerator panel into a jig, clamp on the holding mechanism, and punch an electric switch. The welding was done automatically. When the weld had been made, an air blast automatically ejected the panel onto a moving belt.

"Here," said Bill to John, "watch me do this operation. It's as easy as ABC. A moron could do this job if he'd just learn these three steps. In fact, I sometimes think a moron would be better at it than a normal person." Bill demonstrated the three steps very slowly to John. As he did each step, he explained what was happening. After he'd repeated the operation a half dozen times he got up from the machine and said to John, "Now you try it." John did it right the first time he tried. With Bill standing by, he welded twenty panels without mishap. "There," said Bill, "I told you there was nothing to it. You'll be able to do this job in your sleep." That was the last time John saw Bill to speak to until Friday.

Between Monday morning and Friday, these things happened to John: The air ejection mechanism jammed twice, and he had to get a coworker to show him how to free it. Several panel sheets came to him that looked slightly shorter than the others, but he welded them just the same and sent them ahead to the next operation. On Friday, as he was sliding a sheet into the machine, a sharp edge caught the fleshly part of his thumb and ripped a one-inch gash in it. That was when Bill found time to talk to John again.

1. How do you think John feels about his new job? His new boss?

2. In what way were the incidents that happened to John between Monday morning and Friday afternoon related to his training?

3. What was wrong with the way Bill trained John to operate the welding machine?

4. If you were Bill, what would you have done that he didn't do?

13 THE SUPERVISOR'S ROLE
IN LABOR RELATIONS

What part does the first-line supervisor play in labor matters?

In the eyes of the law, foremen are the responsible agents of their company. Your employer is held responsible for any action you take in dealing with employees or with unions, just as if he had taken the action himself. For this reason, if for no other, it's essential that a supervisor be familiar with the labor contract his company has signed with its union and with the other policies, practices, and procedures that make for good labor relations.

How does a supervisor's authority in labor relations vary according to the company he works for?

A foreman's primary responsibility to his company in labor matters is to protect the interests and the rights of management. How far he can exercise authority in carrying out this responsibility will depend upon the extent to which the front office feels he can act without first checking to see if his decisions are in line with company policy.

In most companies, a foreman may have no authority to adjust wage rates directly; he may be limited to merely reporting a wage rate request and analyzing the job conditions. On the other hand, in most companies a foreman will be expected to take direct and immediate action in the case of willful damage to equipment, unsafe actions, or refusal to follow a work assignment.

But regardless of administrative differences from company to company, the first-line supervisor is usually the first contact between employees and management and between union representatives and management. Since what you do and say in labor matters has such vital consequences to your company's over-all relationship with employees and their representatives, you must be alert to your company's labor practices. Your actions are not confined to yourself and a single employee. They have company-wide impact. Under certain circumstances, your actions could cause your employer to be charged with breaking the contract or even the law.

To be wise in handling your responsibilities, don't depend upon trial-and-error methods. You can be burnt too easily that way. Instead, when there is a point you're in doubt about, make it your business to get the right answers from your boss or from the personnel office. Once you are familiar with how far you can go and what you should do, you won't have to worry about what is right and what is wrong. You'll handle labor relations problems as naturally as you handle mechanical ones. And the surer you are of yourself, the more respect employees, union stewards, and your management will have for you.

What does the term *collective bargaining* include?

When authorized representatives of an employer and the authorized representatives of his employees bargain together to establish wages, hours, and working conditions, this process is called *collective bargaining*. Various labor laws have determined what are fit matters for collective bargaining and what are not. Generally speaking, however, the term *working conditions* is so broad that almost anything that affects an employee at work or the manner in which he carries it out can be included.

Note that the mere fact that a matter, such as establishment of piece rates, is a fit subject for collective bargaining doesn't assure that the union can necessarily control the way it is handled. The union *can* bargain for its position, and management has to bargain in good faith over the issue. But the company does *not* have to accept the union's position. Several considerations will determine its final disposition: the reasonableness of the union demand; the desirability of the demand to employees, management, and stockholders; the ability of the company to pay for its cost; the judgment of management as to its worth; and finally the bargaining strength or weakness of the union or the company.

Does collective bargaining apply only to contract negotiations?

Collective bargaining usually starts with the negotiation of the union agreement and the signing of the labor contract. But it doesn't end there. Supervisors, managers, employees, and union stewards must live with the agreement for the next 365 days or longer. Applying the contract and interpreting its meanings from day to day are what make collective bargaining effective. The contract, like any other contract, is rarely *changed* during its life. But there are dozens, sometimes hundreds, of occurrences between supervisor and employee that need astute judgment as to how the situation should be handled in order to carry out the *meaning* of the contract. It is such interpretation and differences of opinion between management and unions that make labor relations a key foreman headache and responsibility.

Wasn't everything much simpler before the Wagner Act?

There's little denying that a foreman had a much freer hand in dealing with employee matters before the Wagner Act. But there is also considerable evidence that, unions or not, supervision has actually become more intelligent and more effective since the right of employees to organize has been protected by law.

The Wagner Act (correctly called the National Labor Relations Act) describes the conditions under which workers can bargain collectively through their authorized representatives. *The Act did not create any new rights. It was intended to safeguard and enforce existing rights.*

The Wagner Act *does not* set up any specific working conditions (as so many people erroneously believe) which employers must give to their employees. It does not concern itself with the terms of the union agreement. All it does is guarantee that employees may act in a group together—rather than as individuals—if they so desire, in bargaining for their wages, hours, and working conditions.

The supervisor's job has been made tougher, where unions exist, simply because whenever he deals with an individual employee's problem, he must always take into account the whole employee group's position as set forth in the labor contract.

Foremen in the past have been charged with unfair labor practices—of discrimination and intervention? What's this all about?

Foremen are most directly affected by the part of the Wagner Act which prohibits unfair labor practices. Actually, there are five unfair practices, but two most frequently involve foremen:

Interference. This could take place most likely during a union's organizing drive or a National Labor Relations Board (NLRB) representation election. Foremen should be especially careful at that time to avoid (1) any actions that affect an employee's job or pay, (2) arguments that lead to a fight over a union question, (3) threatening a union member through a third party, or (4) dealing without advice from top management with any of the organizing union's officers.

Discrimination. This term applies to any action (such as discharge of an employee, layoff, demotion, or assignment to more difficult or disagreeable work) taken by *any* member of management *on account of the employee's union membership or activity.* To be on safe ground, it's wise not to discuss union matters as such with employees, or to express an opinion for or against a union or unionism. This is good practice off duty as well as on.

Simplest way to avoid charges of discrimination is to disregard completely the fact of an employee's union membership when making decisions regarding his job assignments, discipline, promotions, etc. Before you act, make sure in your own mind that you have separated the man's ability, performance, and attitude toward his job from his stand on unionism or his zeal in supporting it.

Why don't foremen and other supervisors sit in with the management bargaining team at a union contract negotiation?

Bargaining is a delicate matter of strategy and power. It's a little like playing poker. If there are too many kibitzers, a good hand can be spoiled.

If your company does not invite you to sit in on negotiations, don't feel slighted. Not many companies have other than a hand-picked bargaining team of the top plant management group. A survey of 213 companies made in 1957 by the National Industrial Conference Board, New York, showed that only 61 allowed their foremen to sit in on the actual negotiations. In only 15 of these did the foreman actively participate. In 9 they acted as technical advisors, and in 37 they acted as mere observers so they could see what goes on.

What can the supervisor do to help his company negotiate a more workable contract?

Foremen and other supervisors can be a real help to the management bargaining team by submitting specific suggestions beforehand for improving union relationships. In fact, 205 firms in the NICB survey say they encourage such suggestions—especially in the areas of wage payments, seniority problems, and discipline.

How much does the foreman's day-to-day administration of the contract influence contract negotiations?

More than meets the eye. If day by day a foreman neglects or ignores grievances, assigns jobs unfairly, or neglects safety and other working conditions, collective bargaining will be made more difficult. Each time during the course of the year you throw your weight around indiscriminately or take advantage of letter-of-the-law loopholes in the contract, you add to the store of incidents that the union representatives will bring to bear in order to win their demands at contract time.

Take seniority as an example. Suppose you stand on your management right (and the absence of a specific contract clause to the contrary) to assign overtime only to the workers you favor, regardless of their seniority. Once or twice you defend your position by saying that the overtime required the special skills of the two class A operators you held over. But the union observes that several times you've held over class A operators just as convenience: the bulk of the work could have been done by laborers. When contract time rolls around, you can bet that the union negotiators will be in there pitching for a definite clause to spell out exactly how overtime will be distributed.

It's far better to handle your decisions reasonably and equitably during the year so that at contract time the union will accept more general provisions. This leaves the details to be worked out during the year on a mutual basis as the occasion arises. Experience seems to show that the more general type of contract is easier for all members of management to administer.

Union shop, closed shop, what's this all about?

The closed shop was outlawed by the Taft-Hartley law. Under a closed shop, a man had to belong to the bargaining union *before* he could be hired. The union shop is somewhat similar. The difference lies in the fact that a person need not be a union member at the time of hiring. But an employee must (usually after a 30- or 60-day trial period) become a member of the union in order to stay on the payroll.

Under the Taft-Hartley law, the only reason a union may force a company to fire a worker is that he does not pay his union dues. This protects the individual from being discriminated against by his union. In the union shop agreement, it's common for a company also to sign a "checkoff" agreement with the union. This means that the company will collect employees' union initiation fees and dues and turn them over to the union. The employee must first sign an authorization card which gives the company permission to do so.

How does the Taft-Hartley law change the Wagner Act?

The labor law of the land is the National Labor Relations Act (the Wagner Act) as amended by the Taft-Hartley law (Labor-Management Relations Act) in 1947. The T-H law clarified and added to the list of unfair practices which could be charged against management. But more significantly, the T-H law imposed upon unions certain controls over their organizing activities, their internal union organization and their collective bargaining methods.

Under the Act, unions or their agents are forbidden to:

• Attempt to force an employer to discharge or discriminate against former members of the union who have been expelled for reasons other than nonpayment of regular union dues or initiation fees.

• Attempt to force an employer to pay or deliver any money or other things of value for services which are not performed. This outlaws feather-bedding or other make-work practices.

• Restrain or coerce other employees into joining or not joining a union.

• Require excessive or discriminatory fees of employees who wish to become union members.

In addition, individual employees are protected in their desire to bargain or not to bargain collectively:

• They may take up a grievance directly with management—provided that the settlement is in line with the union contract, and a union representative is given an opportunity to be present.

• If they are professional employees, they have a right to vote with a company's other professional employees as to whether they want a collective bargaining unit of their own.

Other significant changes enacted by the T-H law are:

The 60-day notice of contract termination. Either company or union must give the other party 60 days' notice that it wants to end the contract—even though the contract has a definite termination date. During the 60-day period, no employee can strike or slow down; management cannot alter, contrary to the contract requirements, the employment status or working conditions of any employee.

The 80-day injunction. Should a labor dispute, in the opinion of the President of the United States, imperil the health and safety of the nation, procedures are set up so that after proper investigation the President may petition the Federal District Court for an injunction to stop the strike or lockout. During this 80-day cooling-off period, certain other procedures must be followed. Toward the end of the cooling-off period, if the dispute remains unsettled, the NLRB must take a secret ballot of employees to ascertain whether they wish to accept the terms of the employer's last offer. If still unsettled after 80 days, the strike or lockout may resume.

Right to sue for damages. Both companies and unions may sue in federal court for damages caused by breach of contract. Employers may also sue for damages arising out of illegal strikes and boycotts.

Plant guards' units. Plant guards are permitted to form their own bargaining group but may not bargain collectively through a union associated with other employees.

Freedom of speech. Employers and unions are given equal rights to speak their minds freely about each other—except when they actually utter a "threat of reprisal, or force, or promise of benefit." (Note that "promise of benefit" is not considered to restrict a union from describing the potential benefits to be derived from union membership.)

Any other labor laws that a supervisor should know about?

Two laws that it's good to know about are the Walsh-Healey Public Contracts Act and the Fair Labor Standards Act. Generally, your company will watch for compliance, but since the laws influence decisions that affect you, here's a fast rundown:

Walsh-Healey sets the rules for any company which works on a government contract in excess of $10,000. The act forbids hiring boys under sixteen and girls under eighteen. It limits the basic hours of work to eight per day and forty per week. The employer must pay time and one-half for overtime that results. It sets up strict standards for safety, health, and working conditions and also may establish a minimum wage for a particular industry.

Fair Labor Standards (Wages and Hours Law) regulates methods of wage payment and hours of work for any industry engaged in commerce between two or more states. The Law restricts the employment of children over fourteen and under sixteen to nonmanufacturing and nonmining jobs and will not permit the employment of children between sixteen and eighteen in hazardous jobs, including driving or helping a driver of a motor vehicle. The Law sets the minimum wage ($1.00 an hour in 1957) and prescribes that time and one-half must be paid for all hours worked over forty in a week. It also establishes what is "work" and what is not—such as waiting in line to receive pay checks, changing clothes, washing up or bathing, checking in or out. (All this may be considered work in a union agreement if the parties so agree.)

The Wages and Hours Law also sets up guides for determining which supervisors *must* be paid overtime, and which need not. In order to be classed as an "executive," a supervisor must:

• Have as his primary duty the management of a recognized department or subdivision.

• Customarily and regularly direct the work of two or more other employees, exercise discretionary powers, and have the power to hire or fire or make suggestions and recommendations which will be given particular weight as to the hiring, firing, advancement, and promotion of subordinates.

• Not perform "nonexempt" (nonexecutive) work more than 20 per cent of the time.

• Receive a salary of at least $55 per week.

How far does a union shop steward's authority go?

The steward is to the union what you are to the company. It's his union job to protect the rights of union members just as it's yours to protect the rights of management. But in protecting these rights, the union shop steward has no authority to run your shop or to tell you or any employee what to do.

You *may* get the impression that a steward is telling you what to do. A new steward may even feel that it *is* his job. All he has authority to do is to *advise* you or an employee of how he understands the contract to limit your actions and decisions. Unfortunately, in the past many shop stewards knew more about the union contract than some foremen did. As a result the shop steward was often right in his advice and the foreman wrong in what he did. Nevertheless, it goes without saying that you are the department executive, and you are not obligated to share your responsibility with anyone.

It is good practice, however, to keep the steward informed of what you are doing—so that he can make his position known. It also keeps him from thinking you're trying to pull a fast one on him.

How friendly should a supervisor be with the shop steward?

Be as cordial as you can without giving up your right to run your department. You may personally resent Brown, the steward, especially if he's a continual thorn in your side. But remember, he's an elected representative of his group. When he speaks, he speaks not only as an individual, but also as a spokesman for the employees he represents.

You can gain confidence, if not cooperation, from a shop steward if you let him know what's going on. He has status to protect, just as you do. If you try to keep him in the dark or treat him as if he's insignificant, he may react by showing you just how important he is.

So don't keep him at arm's length. Get to know him as you would any other employee. You and he will have many mutual problems. There's nothing wrong with enlisting his help in solving some of them.

Suppose you are planning to start up a second shift on one of the machines in your department. You intend to post a bidding sheet for a new operator. You lose nothing by telling the steward of the new job opportunity in advance. And it gives you a chance to enlist his help when you say, "Brownie, we're going to be needing a good man to run the No. 6 machine on the second shift. We agree with the union that the job should go to the man with the most seniority who is really qualified to do a good job. But let's see that we get some good men bidding."

Some stewards just won't cooperate. How do you handle them?

A really smart steward understands that it's to his advantage as well as yours to see the department run smoothly with high production and the minimum of unnecessary grievances. Other stewards may view their position as purely a political one and seek every opportunity to make an issue. This way, they think, the membership can see how valuable a service they render. This approach is most typical, thank goodness, of newer stewards who feel they must be hardboiled to do their job.

You can help the aggressive steward blow off his steam if you maintain a constructive approach and show him you understand his problems. After all, his job can be a thankless one. Check yourself, too, to be sure that it's not your own aggressive actions that make the steward hard to get along with. Try to approach each problem, not as a battle between the two of you, but as one that you both are trying to solve in accordance with the labor agreement. Don't say only, "Let's see what the contract says." Show that you, too, are interested in justice for your employees: "Brownie, let's see how we can do the most we can for Al without making a decision that is out of line with the contract."

What should your attitude be toward the union?

Don't be antiunion. Adopt the attitude that unions are here to stay. That once your company has made an agreement with one, your best bet is to work as hard as you can to get along with the union. Don't waste your energy trying to undermine the union. Instead, put your efforts into making your department a better place to work.

It would also be a big mistake, however, to turn over to the union your interests in and your responsibilities to your employees. It's more important than ever, when your company has a union, to show employees that you still consider them your department's greatest asset. If you abandon their interests, you're likely to find employees looking to their union representatives rather than to you for leadership.

Should you be hurt when your employees join a union or display strong loyalties to union stewards and officers?

No. An extensive study of employees' loyalties showed rather conclusively that it's natural for workers to have dual loyalty—to their foremen and to their union leaders. Employees look to their boss for sound business judgments and for the satisfactions that come from doing a purposeful job under good working conditions. Employees look to their union for the social prestige of belonging to an influential group and as a protector of their economic interests and job security. An employee who works for a good company and a considerate boss, and who also is represented by an honest, active union enjoys this relationship. Asking him to choose between his boss and his union would be a little like asking a child to choose between his two parents.

Why is there a grievance procedure? Wouldn't it be better to settle gripes informally without all the red tape?

Most union contracts establish a step-by-step grievance procedure. Experience has shown both management and labor that it's best to have a systematic method of handling complaints. Without a formalized procedure, management (in dealing with unionized employees) would find it difficult to coordinate labor and personnel practices from department to department.

The formal procedure provides an easy and open channel of communications for employees to bring complaints to the attention of supervision. And it guarantees that these complaints won't be sidetracked or allowed to ferment without corrective action being taken. Good supervisors and wise managements know that an unsettled grievance, real or imaginary, expressed or hidden, is always a potential source of trouble. The grievance machinery helps uncover the causes and get the grievance out into the open.

Is there a standard grievance procedure set down by law?

No. The actual grievance procedure will vary from company to company. It will depend upon what the company and the union have agreed upon and have written into the labor contract.

A typical grievance procedure, however, has anywhere from three to five steps:

Step 1. Foreman discusses complaint with employee and union steward.

Step 2. Superintendent and industrial relations manager discuss with union grievance committee.

Step 3. Plant manager and industrial relations manager discuss with union grievance committee.

Step 4. General company management discusses with national union representative and union grievance committee.

Step 5. Dispute is referred to impartial umpire or arbitrator for decision.

It should be emphasized that a serious and prolonged effort should be made by both parties to settle the grievance at each of the steps— including the first.

Why does a supervisor sometimes get overruled?

If a supervisor has made every effort beforehand to be sure his decisions and actions are in line with the company's interpretation of the contract, there can be only three reasons why he should be over-ruled. He may have acted on insufficient or incorrect facts. This is probably the most common reason. He may occasionally be made the sacrificial lamb when the company realizes at the third or fourth step of the procedure that *its* interpretation of the contract won't stand up to the union's position. Or both he and the company may be overruled by the arbitrator at the last step.

Why don't grievances go right to the arbitrator in the first place?

Unions and managements seem to agree on this point: They'd both rather settle their household quarrels between themselves than invite a stranger in to sort the dirty linen. Both parties reason, and rightly, that they know more than anyone else about their affairs. In the long run, union and management must learn how to settle their differences themselves without continually depending upon a third party. It's been said by both union and management that "Nobody wins an arbitration." But when it's needed, peaceful arbitration is far better than strikes or lockouts.

What's the purpose of the NLRB?

The National Labor Relations Board (NLRB) is made up of five members appointed by the President of the United States. Its duty is to:

- Administer the National Labor Relations Act and in so doing,
- Determine proper collective bargaining units.
- Direct and supervise representation elections.
- Prevent employers, employees, and unions from violating the Act by committing unfair labor practices defined in the statutes.

The NLRB is not a Federal court with power to settle disputes. But it makes the major decisions as to how the NLRA should be interpreted. Since it is not a court, you may occasionally read of a company or a union petitioning a Federal district court or the United States Supreme Court to set aside a ruling made by the NLRB. The Federal court, or the Supreme Court, in such a case would have the final say—not the NLRB.

The Case of the Suspended Dyemixer. A case study in human relations involving labor relations, with questions for you to answer.

"Eddie, this is the third time this year you've pumped the wrong mixture into a dipping tank," said Frank, the foreman of a chemical plant to a dyemixer. "I can't understand how you can make such a mistake. You mustn't be paying enough attention to what you're doing. So I'll give you something to help you remember. Punch out now, and don't come back to work until next Monday. And if the same thing happens again, you'll be fired."

Eddie punched out, but before doing so, he checked with his shop steward, Tom Tyler. "We'll see what we can do for you," he was told by the union representative.

That afternoon Tom Tyler spoke to the foreman. "Don't you think that a suspension is a little steep for Eddie? You've never done this to anyone else."

"No," said the foreman. "And nobody else has pumped the wrong tank three times in a year. Our contract says we can take necessary disciplinary action to correct poor performance. Eddie has had enough chances. Now he needs to know we mean business. Besides, Eddie's attendance has been lousy lately. He's been late a couple of times this month and was absent at least once when he wasn't excused. And you should have heard the lip he gave me last week, too. Eddie is getting too big for his britches, and he needs something to put him straight. The suspension will have to stick."

The shop steward's only reply was "We'll see about that."

The union filed a written grievance. When the case came before the plant superintendent, here's what the steward said then: "Sure it looks as if Eddie made a mistake. But when I checked up, it wasn't at all clear to me. Eddie says that Frank's directions were confusing, that he misunderstood. In fact, Eddie says that on one occasion recently, he asked Frank to explain his orders over again and all he got from him was 'You understand what I mean.'

"Besides, when I spoke to Frank about this case, Frank was more interested in telling me all the other things that were wrong with Eddie than about the pumping mistake. In fact, he went so far as to say that Eddie was getting too big for his britches and that he was going to straighten him out. It's my opinion that Frank had it in for Eddie and gave him the business the first phony excuse he could find."

The plant superintendent turned to Frank. "Is this true, Frank? Let's hear your side of the story again."

1. If you were Frank, how would you explain your position?

2. What do you think of the shop steward's defense to protect Eddie?

3. What sort of mistakes do you think Frank made in handling this case? Why?

4. What do you think of Frank's relationship with Eddie? With Tom?

14 ACCIDENT PREVENTION

What causes accidents?

People do. And for a variety of reasons. Sometimes a workman is careless. Sometimes his boss hasn't given him instructions. Sometimes an employee's attitude is at fault. Sometimes his supervisor hasn't helped him understand the dangers involved in his work. Sometimes equipment fails. Sometimes machines are not properly guarded. But always it's a person who could have prevented the accident by proper protective or control action.

One famous study seemed to show that 85 per cent of all accidents are caused by unsafe acts of people. The other 15 per cent were caused by unsafe equipment or conditions. These widely quoted statistics are misleading. Actually, most accidents are caused by a combination of both. The important fact is that a person—you, your employees, the safety engineer, the top managers in your company—is at the root of each accident. Unless you have this conviction, you may find your efforts toward greater safety are ineffective.

Where do most accidents happen?

Accidents can happen anywhere. But the most common places for industrial accidents to happen are:

• Around hand lift trucks, wheelbarrows, warehouses, cranes, and shipping departments. More industrial accidents (nearly one-third) are caused by handling and lifting materials than by any other reason.

• Near metal and woodworking machines, saws, lathes, etc., and transmission machinery like gears, pulleys, couplings, belts, flywheels.

• On stairs, ladders, walkways, scaffolds. That's because falls are the third most common source of industrial injury.

• Any place hand tools are worked with—chisels, screw drivers, hammers, and the like account for 7 per cent of industrial disability.

• Everywhere electricity is used, especially near extension cords, portable hand tools, electric droplights, wiring, switchboards, and welding apparatus.

How do you prevent accidents from happening?

The National Safety Council for years has said that accident prevention depended upon the three Es—engineering, education, and enforcement.

• To *engineer* a job for safety is to design the equipment, lay out the work, plan the job, and protect the individual—all with accident prevention as a first ingredient. Safety guards on machines are one example of engineering. Arranging the job so that employees work in another room from one where toxic fumes are generated by the process is another example. Still another is the wearing of protective eye shields, gloves, or safety shoes.

• To *educate* for safety is to show employees where, why, and how accidents can happen and to develop in them safe work habits and the desire to avoid injury. Helping a worker to analyze the danger spots in his job and training him to build a defense against each is an example of education for safety.

To *enforce* safety is to make an actuality of the slogan, "Safety first." Employees work most safely when they want to be safe, but they need guidance in the form of regulations and discipline to protect safe workers from those who would cause accidents by unsafe acts.

Isn't accident prevention the safety man's job?

Safety engineers do an excellent job of carrying out the three Es of safety. But they would be the first to admit that without the supervisor's help, safety programs would flop. The supervisor is the key safety man, especially in education and enforcement.

Doesn't insurance or workmen's compensation take care of accident costs?

Not by a long shot. A company's liability insurance usually pays only the cost of a workman's compensation for an injury received at work. The cost of liability insurance to a company depends upon how good a safety record the plant has. The difference between a good and bad record isn't peanuts. It means real money. "Workmen's compensation" is just a term applied to the procedure of most state governments for determining how much money an employee should get to compensate him for his injury—assuming that it leaves him temporarily or permanently disabled to some degree.

It's been estimated that for an accident that comes to $340 for compensation, a company pays another $1,400 or $1,500 for related expenses. Examples of related expenses are cost of time lost by employees who stop to watch or assist; time lost by supervisors' helping and investigating the accident, making changes in production schedules, assigning and breaking in new workers; cost of medical care; loss of material, damage to equipment, productive time lost on machines—and not to be overlooked—cost of the insurance that pays for the compensation.

How do you figure cost of an accident?

Here's an example of the cost of a common accident, in which a chemical worker was scalded when a kettle of hot dye slipped from a cable while he was pouring it into a vat:

Compensation paid for burns	$ 208	
Medical expense including first aid	102	
Total "compensation" cost		$ 310
Time lost away from job:		
Injured worker's make-up pay while home 3½ days	35	
Follow-up medical visits	153	
Fellow workmen standing by at time of accident	95	
Supervisor's time	60	
Labor for clean-up	75	
Production loss:		
Down time on operation	80	
Slowed-up production rate of other workers	55	
Material spoiled	67	
Damage to equipment	225	
Total related cost		845
Total cost of accident (not including overhead charges)		$1,115

So you see, even without overhead charges for administrative costs included, this small accident cost several times the "compensation" cost.

With whom does accident prevention begin?

Good supervision is the starting place for an effective accident-prevention program. No amount of machine guards or safety rules will stop accidents from happening if the supervisor isn't absolutely sold that it can be done—and that it's his responsibility.

Take the slogan, "Safety first." What does it mean to you? Does it mean "Safety measures come ahead of everything else in my department," or is it just another motto? Keep asking yourself that question every time you urge a workman toward higher production or better quality. Be sure that you don't ever give quantity or quality priority over safety. If you do, you'll find that your accident record suffers.

Doesn't the individual employee have a responsibility for safety?

People cause accidents. A supervisor can't be everywhere at once. He shouldn't want to be. So in the long run it will be your employees who cause—or prevent—accidents in your shop. But they won't prevent accidents unless you've gone all the way down the line to show them how.

First of all you've got to instill in employees the belief that *they* are the most influential source of accident prevention. Do this, with the aid of your safety engineer if you have one, by discussing the accidents that have happened in your plant. Seize every opportunity to let employees see cause and effect for themselves.

Preaching is not much help. Instead, when an accident happens, talk it over with one—or many—of your employees. Get their ideas of how it could have been prevented. Ask them if similar situations could arise in their jobs. Continually bring the conversation around to the human element.

Second, help your employees to develop safe working habits. People have to be trained to work safely just as they must be trained to work accurately. Few people are just naturally cautious—or know instinctively where danger lies. The first day on the job in a foundry, Tom may be worried most about burns from the hot metal and hardly realize that eye injury, dermatitis, or crushed toes are just as likely to happen. His foreman can start him out right, however, by telling Tom all these things. And by showing him how such accidents can happen. And how to do his job so that they don't happen.

Third step in helping employees to be safe lies in the supervisor's ability to enforce his job instructions for safety. Too many employees think of safety as "Don't do this or that"—as just so many rules and regulations. To get acceptance of job methods—as well as rules—you've got to show why they are necessary. And let employees know of the danger to themselves and your dissatisfaction when they don't follow the guides you've established for them. If you catch yourself saying, "Workers in my department just won't wear their safety goggles," it's no one else's fault but your own. It's up to you to see that they do. Reason and encourage first. But penalize if you don't get conformance.

What is an accident-prone employee?

Examination of safety records often show that only a few employees account for the bulk of the accidents—that the great majority of employees rarely have accidents. Those people who get injured frequently are spoken of as being *accident-prone*. This means that for one reason or another the person has an innate tendency to have accidents. Hence he is prone to injury. Psychologists have shown, however, that only a small percentage of so-called accident-prone employees are *truly* accident-prone. Most of these habitual sufferers can actually be made accident-free by proper job placement, training, and encouragement. So if one of your workers appears accident-prone, don't give up on him. Try to help him develop work habits that will protect him and his fellow workers (see Chap. 22).

How effective are safety posters?

This is a debatable subject. But most authorities feel that "scare" posters on highways have done little to reduce accidents. Posters in the plant can be more effective when they are keyed to your shop's condition and your own safety program. For instance, if your emphasis is on safety goggles this month, posters that reinforce or repeat this emphasis will help. The mistake is to expect a series of posters to do your safety job for you. They'll help a little. But the big job is up to you.

Posters, like other forms of communication, need frequent changes in order to attract fresh attention. It's better to have none than to have a dust-covered one that's been on a bulletin board for two or three months.

Should a supervisor give an injured employee first aid?

That depends upon the practice in your plant and upon your own qualifications. There should be no question, however, about your responsibility to see that an injured employee gets first aid—quickly and properly. Permit only trained people (like graduates of the Red Cross first-aid course) to attend the patient. Know who these people are ahead of time and how to summon them without delay.

If your plant has a nurse or a physician, stay with the injured employee until you're sure that he's under medical care.

What can you do about employees who you think are malingering?

Check with the plant medical department, if you have one. Avoid charging an employee with malingering unless your medical department can support you. Otherwise, you may have a hard time supporting your viewpoint. If a workman feigns sickness, ask yourself what there is about the job or about the employee that makes him want to get away from work so badly that he'll put on an act. In the long run, the answer to malingering lies in better understanding and in improving the employee's attitude (see also Chap. 22).

How do you prevent lifting and materials-handling accidents?

Heavy loads are only one reason for lifting accidents. Most lifting accidents happen because an employee doesn't have the knack of lifting with his legs, rather than his back. If you try to pick something up by bending over it and pulling backward and upward with your arms, it tends to strain the muscles and ligaments in the back. Instead, get as close to the object as possible. Crouch down beside it; if it's a case or carton, get the inside of your thighs as close to it as possible. Get a firm grip with your hands and arms. Keep your back straight as you pull the object toward you. Then simply stand up.

Try this knee-lift method yourself until you get the feel of it. Whenever a new employee enters your department, show him how it's done. Let him practice the lift a few times while you watch him.

Of course, it goes without saying that when loads get too heavy— over 100 pounds for a man or 25 to 40 pounds for a woman, you should instruct employees to get help. This may be another pair of hands, or a lift truck, jack, crowbar, block and tackle, crane, or any handling device that suits the purpose.

Accidents often happen when a workman trips when carrying materials. That's one reason clean floors and aisles are so important.

Accidents that happen while using mechanical lifting devices are frequently the result of overloading or improper usage. Make it a point to check load ratings on slings, cables, and cranes. Don't permit an inexperienced employee to operate any mechanical equipment without first checking him out to show him the right way.

How do you prevent accidents on machinery, machine tools, and power-transmission equipment?

Not only is machinery the No. 2 cause of accidents in manufacturing, it also causes the most severe injuries. Since the turn of the century, both employers and machine builders have done much to protect machine operators through the judicious use of safety guards and devices. But don't take this action for granted. Whenever a new machine is installed in your department, inspect it before it goes into action. Try to be certain in your own mind that a workman would be adequately protected.

Many machine tools cannot be fully protected. So it's a good practice to caution employees about wearing loose clothing, long-sleeved shirts, string neckties, etc., around moving machinery. Stay with new and old employees alike until you're sure that each is aware of the danger his machine holds for him. And he knows how to steer clear of his trouble. Of particular importance is knowledge of how to shut machinery down in a hurry. Drill machine operators until they know enough about "off" and "on" control locations so that they can turn their machines off blindfolded.

How do you prevent falls?

In theory, falls can be prevented 100 per cent. In practice, it's not quite that easy. One big obstacle to perfection in this regard is that employees tend to take falls for granted. It's the mark of a sissy, workmen often say, to worry much about them.

To minimize falling injuries in your department keep an eye out for these causes:

Unsafe floors and work surfaces. See that employees keep floors and work places swept clean. Don't permit spillages to remain unguarded or uncleaned a minute. Your keen interest in this matter helps dramatize its importance.

Unsafe ladders, stairways, and scaffolds. Ladders should never be used if there is any doubt about their condition or suitable length. Stairways should have railings and be well lighted. Scaffolding should be checked by a qualified mechanic or engineer.

Improper footwear. There's a lot of stress on safety shoes to protect the feet. But sensible, low-heeled shoes, with soles in good shape and uppers laced to support the foot are an excellent guard against falls, too.

Unsafe practice. An employee may think you're nagging if you insist he hold onto a railing when going up or down stairs. But if you insist on safe practices when walking and climbing, or especially when working overhead, he'll respect you for your interest in his welfare. That's the point to stress—how safe practices protect him—not just the shop's accident record.

How do you prevent hand-tool accidents?

Squashed thumbs and scraped knuckles by the hundreds of thousands bear painful tribute to the misuse of hand tools. Tools in bad shape, like a chisel whose head looks like a mushroom, should be taken out of service, and repaired or thrown away. Proper tools for the job should be available, and employees should be instructed as to the danger in using the wrong tool for a job—like using a knife as a screwdriver or a file as a drift pin to remove a drill from a chuck.

Some employees, especially those who have not come up through the apprentice ranks, won't know how to handle tools properly unless you show them how. In securing employee cooperation in this, appeal to their sense of professional skill. No one likes to feel he looks like an amateur. So see that a file is used with a handle, never hit with a hammer (it might shatter), thumbs are out of the way of hand saws, open jaws of monkey wrenches are facing you when you pull on the handle.

Portable hand tools all have their own peculiarities, too. Check with the manufacturer's instruction manual to be certain you know, and your employees follow, the maker's guide for safe usage.

How do you prevent low-voltage electric shocks?

The term *low voltage* covers anything under 600 volts. Since deaths due to contact with 110 volts (ordinary house-lighting circuits) are common, it's absolutely foolhardy to take any chances with electrical hazards. Injuries from electrical sources happen from touching live parts, short circuits, accidental grounds, overloads on the system, and broken connections.

Advise your employees to report to you any evidence of hot wires, tingling shocks from machines or equipment, abnormal sparking, frayed insulations, loose connections, or any other electrical fault. Don't investigate the cause yourself. Get the plant electrician—and quickly.

Portable electric power tools should always be grounded before being connected to an electric outlet. This is done by connecting a separate wire between the frame of the tool and a good ground—like a pipeline or I beam. Some plants have grounded, three-prong outlets to accept three-prong plugs, but the existence of a three-prong plug doesn't guarantee the circuit is grounded. Check with the plant electrician on this.

Electricity's safety valves are fuses, fused switches, and circuit breakers. These protect equipment and circuits from overloads. Disconnect switches are dangerous. Do not permit production operators to touch them. That's the job for an electrician.

If one of your employees is knocked out by an electric shock, see that he's removed from the electrical source first (be careful, or others may also be shocked) and then given artificial respiration.

Frequency and severity—what's the difference?

Both are measures of how good your plant or department's safety record is. *Frequency* tells how often accidents have occurred. *Severity* tells for how long a time the injured persons are disabled. The key to each measure is the *lost-time accident*. If an employee is injured and he loses no time from work, the accident is not computed in the records. If he does lose time, it is.

Take this example: Foreman Joe has 50 employees averaging 40 hours work a week each. In twelve months one worker is injured. Total time lost is 37 days.

$$\text{Injury frequency rate} = \frac{1 \text{ injury} \times 1,000,000}{50 \text{ workers} \times 40 \text{ hours per week} \times 50 \text{ weeks per year}}$$
$$= 10 \text{ lost-time accidents per million man-hours worked}$$

$$\text{Injury severity rate} = \frac{37 \text{ days lost} \times 1,000,000}{50 \text{ workers} \times 40 \text{ hours per week} \times 50 \text{ weeks per year}}$$
$$= 370 \text{ days lost per million man-hours worked}$$

Frequency and severity rates for twenty-two manufacturing industries are shown in Fig. 14–1. These are average rates. The actual rates will vary from company to company and from department to department.

What's key-point safety?

Key-point safety is a form of job analysis in which the supervisor lists the key safety hazards on the job and the preventive measure an employee should take for each.

Suppose you were a maintenance supervisor in a chemical plant. You're about to assign a work crew to repair an acid sewer. You'd first fill out a key-point safety-planning card. It might look like Table 14–1.

Next step is to discuss the key points with the operator. He's the one that has to follow them. Have him repeat the instructions—and follow up to see that he practices safety on the job.

If you supervise a job that is done about the same way each day, and consequently has the same hazards most of the time, you'll want to make up a permanent key-point safety card for each job. Post it at the machine or the work place. Quiz workers regularly about it.

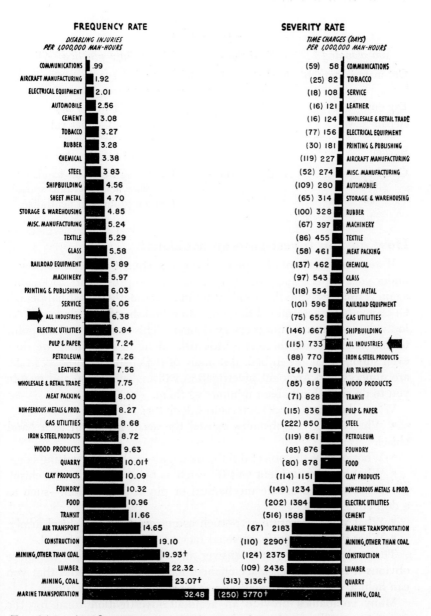

FIG. 14-1 Accident rates in various industries. (*Accident Facts,* 1957 edition, copyright National Safety Council, Chicago, Ill.)

159

TABLE 14-1

Job planning	Hazard	Safe practice
Get material on job	Acid stored in tank	Wear full eye protection and acid-resistant gloves
Dig out sewer	Hand tools	Keep tool handles dry
Repair sewer	Acid splash	Shut off tank outlet valve; proper use of chisels
Backfill	Hand tools	Keep tool handles dry
Clean up	Acid on surface	Use water freely on hands or any place acid splashes; spread lime on ground to neutralize acid

How do you investigate an accident?

If an accident should happen in your department or to an employee under your supervision, one of the best ways to prevent its happening again is to investigate the accident to find out exactly why it happened. Once you have determined this, you can establish safeguards to protect individuals from any unnecessary dangers. This is an important point to understand, since there is a little risk taking in everything we do— even staying at home in bed. But many of the chances employees take are unnecessary. Accident investigation will uncover these and enable you to do something about minimizing them.

When checking on accident causes, look for:

• What object or substance caused the accident?—such as a hand chisel.

• What part of the object did the damage?—such as the cutting edge.

• What kind of accident was it?—such as being struck by the chisel.

• What was the unsafe mechanical or physical condition?—such as a dull edge.

• What was the unsafe act?—such as not grasping the chisel firmly.

• What was the unsafe personal factor?—such as lack of skill.

The easier it is for you to answer any of these questions, the more obvious it is that unnecessary chances have been taken. And that you can help a workman to avoid taking those chances in the future.

Many companies provide an accident investigation form for the supervisor to fill out. A typical one is shown in Fig. 14-2.

How much good is safety clothing if workmen won't wear it?

It's generally been proven that a workman will wear safety goggles and other protective clothing *if* he's been trained to do his work with

Date reported   FOREMAN'S ACCIDENT REVIEW

PLANT NO. 2

Name of injured worker_____Clock No._____
Date of accident_____
Brief description of accident_____
_____
_____

Indicate below by an "X" whether in your opinion the accident was caused by:

Physical causes
_____Improper guarding?
_____Defective substances or equipment?
_____Hazardous arrangement?
_____Improper illumination?
_____Improper ventilation?
_____Improper dress or apparel?
_____No mechanical cause?
_____Not listed? (Describe briefly)_____

Sometimes the injured person is not directly associated with the causes of an accident. Using an "X" to represent the injured worker and an "O" to represent any other person involved, indicate whether, in your opinion, the accident was caused by:

Unsafe acts
_____Operating without authority?   _____Unsafe loading, placement, mix-
_____Failure to secure or warn?   ing, etc?
_____Working at unsafe speed?   _____Took unsafe position?
_____Made safety device inoperative?   _____Worked on moving equipment?
_____Used unsafe equipment or hands   _____Teased, abused, distracted, etc.?
     instead of equipment?   _____Did not use safe clothes or per-
_____No unsafe act?   sonal protective equipment?
_____Not listed? (Describe briefly)_____

Personal causes
_____Physical or mental defect?
_____Lack of knowledge or skill?
_____Wrong attitude?
_____Not listed? (Describe briefly)_____

Actions that I have taken to prevent a similar future accident.
_____
_____

                            Foreman's signature_____

FIG. 14-2 Typical accident investigation form used by supervisors to report their investigations. (Rollin H. Simonds and John V. Grimaldi, _Safety Management_, Richard D. Irwin, Inc., Homewood, Ill., 1956.)

161

it, *if* he understands how it protects him, and *if* everybody—his fellow workers as well as his supervisor—expects him to wear it.

To make safety clothing more acceptable to employees, there are many things you can do:

• Let employees help decide which kind of protection suits the situation best. Discuss the hazardous situation with them first. If working near a degreaser requires wearing a respirator, talk over with them the various kinds of respirators available. Give them a chance to make suggestions as to what they think is best.

• Offer a selection. If an employee says that such and such a safety goggle makes him uncomfortable, it helps if you can offer him a choice of three or four different kinds. "Surely," you can say, "you ought to be able to find one that you like."

• Set an example yourself. If the job calls for hard hats, wear the heaviest, brightest one yourself. Then you can say, "I know that the hard hat looks uncomfortable, Pete. But I hardly even know I'm wearing it any more."

• Get help from the informal leaders in the work group. If you can get an older, respected workman to set the style in safety gear, other workers are likely to follow suit.

• Show you mean business. If workmen can't be cajoled, encouraged, or led to wear their safety clothing, then take disciplinary action. If you're consistent and if the protective equipment is suitable, even most unions will back you up strongly on this point.

What can be done to make safety committees more useful?

If you or your company has organized departmental safety committees, see that the committee has a real job to do. Don't let meetings turn into coffee klatches. And don't use them solely as a sounding board for your inspirational appeals for safety.

Treat the safety committee as a business organization:

Assign specific problems. If your medical department or first-aid room tells you there's been a rash of small cuts on hands and arms, get the committee to investigate this condition to find out what the facts are, where they occur, to whom, etc. Then ask for a specific recommendation on how to correct the situation.

Expect results. Make it clear that being on a safety committee entails more than sitting in on a meeting. Assign area safety responsibilities to the members. Let them assist with inspections (see check list in Table 27–1). Ask for a report of minor accidents in each area. Have the members tell what improvements have been made, what more can be done.

Have members participate on investigations. Talking about safety isn't as effective as getting out on the plant floor to see what's being done about it. Use this opportunity to demonstrate the company's efforts and expenditures for safe working conditions. Emphasize that unsafe practices are just as important to watch out for.

Delegate duties. If the committee plans a safety competition, let them handle the publicity, method of making awards, establishment of rules. They know their fellow employees better than anyone else—and can guess what will work best.

What's the best way to sell safety to your employees?

There are three keys here.

Believe in your product. "Pete, if you'll study your job with me so that you always do it the safe way, I'll guarantee you'll never get a cut or a bruise, let alone lose an eye—as a fellow might who doesn't work safely."

Know your product. "Safety first is more than a slogan here, Mary. There's a safe way and an unsafe way of doing every part of your work. Before you start up your machine, see that your safety goggles are on. Check the tool, is it firmly in the chuck? Now stand clear as you push the button to start the motor."

Show benefits to employees. "Safety practices are designed with one person in mind—and that's you, Al. These practices not only make your job safer, they often make it easier. And we can show you the records to prove that the safety device won't cut down on your earnings. Safety here at work pays off for your family at home, too. They can relax knowing that you are working the safe way, that they needn't fear that someday you'll come home in an ambulance."

The Case of the Smashed Thumb. A case study in human relations involving safety, with questions for you to answer.

Bert broke in at the Carry Wooden Crate Company on a Monday morning. John Brady, his foreman, started the day with a pep talk on safety. "Bert," he said, "this is a relatively safe plant to work in. But there are a couple of places where we've had some serious accidents. One is near the saw bench and the other is at the nailing machine. Don't work at either place unless you're wearing safety goggles and there's an old hand to show you the way to shut down the equipment if something goes wrong.

"Only last week," John went on, "we had a fellow lose his thumb in the saw. And we seem to have a couple of wise guys each year who get smashed fingers in the nailing machine. If you operate both these machines right and with the guards in place, you're as safe as if you were in your own bed. If you don't, you're asking for trouble."

At 3:07 P.M. on Wednesday, Bert got his left hand smashed in the nailing machine.

1. What do you think of John's safety talk? How could he have improved it?

2. What do you think of the Carry Company's safety record? How do you think John could help improve it?

3. Whose fault was it that Bert got his hand smashed? Why?

3

SUPERVISING
PEOPLE

Special Techniques

15 THE KNACK OF GIVING INSTRUCTIONS AND ORDERS

How can you get better results from the instructions and orders you issue?

By being sure your order is the right one for the particular situation at hand. By being specific about what the employee is to do and what kind of results you expect from him.

Your orders are even more effective when you use care in selecting the person most likely to carry them out well. And you add power to your orders by being confident (not cocky) and calm as you deliver them. Finally, your orders will stand the best chance of accomplishing what you intend if you make a practice of checking to be sure they are carried out at the time and in the manner you prescribe.

Should you repeat an order?

Yes, by all means. Repeat your instructions to be certain the employee understands them clearly. All of us are expert at *misunderstanding*. So give a workman an opportunity to ask questions if he's hazy about what you want. In fact, it's a good practice to ask the employee to repeat your instructions back to you. That way you can readily find out where his stumbling blocks might be.

When should you "request" an employee to do something?

As often as possible. It used to be thought that order giving was a one-way street, that all a supervisor had to say was, "I tell you. You do it." Such an attitude today gets you nowhere. Modern employees want and deserve more consideration. And many of them have unions to back up this desire. In addition, we now know lots more about employees' attitudes. For instance, psychologists who study employee behavior tell us that most workers will rate a boss high, and will cooperate more willingly as a result, if the boss gives orders pleasantly. We know, too, that employees like to feel they are offered some say in decisions that affect them and will work harder when they have had a chance to participate.

So there's nothing wrong, much good, with saying, "Alex, will you try to get that machine cleaned up before quitting time?" Or, "Mary, won't you please make an effort to get to work on time Monday?"

Generally speaking, in business, a request carries the same weight as a direct order. But it does impart a feeling that a workman has some freedom of action, that he can question any part that bothers him. And it's especially useful with thin-skinned employees who tend to see every boss as a dictator.

When should you "command" an employee to do something?

Commands are dangerous. But they may be necessary in emergency situations. In case of accident or fire, for instance, your instructions should be direct, clear, and unequivocal to avoid conflicting actions.

Orders should be specific and firm, too, in operating situations requiring active leadership. It's desirable to be especially decisive, for instance, in directing a crew that requires rapid coordination on an unfamiliar job—like supervising a crew that is lowering a 100-ton machine onto its foundations, or starting up a new and complex machine.

But in general, commands cause resentment. It's best to avoid them until you need them. If you use commands only occasionally, your employees will know that you're not being bossy for the sake of showing your authority. They will recognize your change in approach as being necessary and will snap to accordingly.

Is it your fault if an employee misses an order?

Not necessarily. In fact he may be the one who goofed. This points up the wisdom of seeing order giving as a two-way street.

Look at it this way: An order is given only to get something done. You see a situation. You see what the situation calls for. Your job as an order giver is to make sure the person who is to *do* the job sees the situation the same way you do.

For example, say you're foreman of the packaging department in a soap flake plant. You come by the discharge end of a packaging machine that fills and seals boxes of soap flakes. You test-weigh a box and find that it is overweight. From your experience you know that an adjustment of the filling mechanism will correct the situation. The only reason you will give an order is to help the package machine operator see the situation, and the action it calls for, as you do.

How would you give your order? "Wake up, Joe! Shut down your machine and get it fixed." That's not too bad, but it doesn't tell Joe what's wrong or recognize that Joe might know what to do without your telling him. This is better: "Joe, your machine's running overweight. Better shut down until I send the repairman up." Even better, if you have confidence in Joe, is just to hold up a box to get his attention. Then say, "Overweight!" Let Joe take over from there.

So try to look at your orders as solutions to action-demanding *situations*. As situations that both you and your employees must see in the same light if orders are to be carried out willingly and well.

What should you do when an employee willfully refuses to do what you tell him?

First piece of advice, and toughest to follow: Don't fly off the handle. Count to 100 if insubordination makes you want to blow your top. Then ask yourself whether the order was a fair one, whether you've chosen the proper person to follow it. Have you made yourself understood?

If you feel you've done your part, next try to find out what the employee objects to. Get him to be specific: "Well, Pete, what is it that you object to? Why do you think it's unreasonable?" Chances are an employee who is willfully disobedient is looking for an excuse to blow off steam. It may be that if you listen for a couple of minutes, he'll get over his resentment of the order. For that reason, it's smart not to talk about your authority or threaten with discipline. Not then, anyway.

But if an employee is stubborn, if he can't or won't be cooled off or change his mind about doing what you say, you're faced with a disciplinary problem. You still have alternate choices of what to do, so don't be quick about firing, penalizing, or suspending. You may find it wise not to insist—*at that moment*—that he carry out the order. Or you may want to modify the order so that he will accept it. *If you choose to do either of the latter, don't let the matter drop there.*

Find an early opportunity to talk to the employee calmly, constructively, and in private. Don't permit him to think that you were soft or that he got away with something. Let him know you will take disciplinary steps if he doesn't straighten up and fly right. And that you've made a note about the incident in your records (see Chap. 17 on discipline for more information).

Your other choice is to take whatever disciplinary action your plant permits—that same day, while the incident is fresh in everyone's mind. But this is a choice supervisors should avoid if possible. Punishment is a last resort only. That's why it's unwise to force a showdown situation—especially if there are other employees watching or listening, and especially if you'd like to change your mind later on.

Is there anything you can do about a workman who carries out your instructions in a slipshod manner?

There are two effective actions you can take in such a case. First, be sure you have told the worker exactly what you expect his finished work to be. And then follow up to see that it measures up. If it doesn't, insist that it be done over until it's O.K.

A second approach, and one that will win you loyalty and respect, is to offer to show the employee some little knack of your own that will help him do his work in a more professional manner.

Take Rod Peters, who is sealing up corrugated cases of perfume in a toiletries factory. He's having a hard time keeping up with the girls who pack the boxes. So he gets sloppy with the glue brush, smears the cases and puts on either too much or too little glue. Abe True, his foreman, doesn't chew Rod out. Instead Abe says to him, "Having trouble keeping up with the packers? I know, they're pretty fast. Let me show you a trick I learned from Eddie who used to hold this job. See, line up three cases before you swing the glue brush. This way you do three cases at a time.

"Here, you try it. And try to be as neat as you can. Our customers hate to display sloppy-looking cases. And if they're not glued properly, they break open in shipment. So let's see how you make out sealing them this way. I'll be back later in the morning to find out how you're doing."

When should you put an order in writing?

Whenever you change an order that was previously in writing, put the new order in writing, too. Or if you give an order that must be carried over into another shift, it's wise to jot it down in writing—on the bulletin board, in the department log book, or as a note to be passed on to the employees concerned. This is much more reliable than word of mouth.

When instructions are complex and contain variations from normal in amounts and sequence, it's wise to write them down, too. On the other hand, don't depend too much on written orders. Not everyone follows written instructions easily. In fact, if you do write instructions down, look for an opportunity to review them orally with the employee to see if he understands them. That way the written orders serve him as a reference.

Is it wise to let an employee use his own judgment in following your instructions?

Sometimes it's a good idea just to suggest what you want. Then let the employee use his own discretion in carrying it out. This leaves it up to him whether or not anything will be done and how it will be done. For instance, "I wonder if there's anything you can do to get this job finished by quitting time." Or, "It looks as if our scrap record will be off this month. Is there something you can do to get it back on the beam?"

Such an implied order stimulates initiative and cooperation—among more responsible workers. It's a form of delegation, and it helps develop your employees.

The suggestion approach is risky to try with inexperienced or unreliable people. And you shouldn't use it when you have decided in advance exactly what you want done and how. After all, you can't expect your workmen to be mind readers.

Should you let anyone else give instructions to your employees?

Unless you have expressly asked someone else to pass along orders to people who work directly under you (and this should be done only infrequently), it's best to see that you're the only one who gives orders to your employees. Otherwise, your employees will find themselves working for two bosses. And your status and effectiveness will be weakened.

You were hired to direct your employees. That's your responsibility. If someone else tries to take over this part of your job, it's up to you to politely, but firmly, hold onto your rights. If your boss makes a habit of bypassing you in issuing instructions to your employees, you should speak to him at once about it. Be tactful, of course, but unless you convince him that what he's doing works against department morale and efficiency, you're in for trouble.

Employees are paid to work, aren't they? Why, then, should you handle them with kid gloves?

Because in the long run it's easier on the foreman. Actually, giving orders pleasantly and thoughtfully isn't babying employees. It's just common sense to make it as easy as possible for them to say "yes" to what you ask them to do. It's an old adage that "A willing worker does better work."

One reason old-fashioned foremen had trouble with order giving (and consequently cost their companies lots of money by having to fire disobedient workers) was that they overlooked one and sometimes two of the three important ingredients of order giving. It may be obvious that you should tell a workman *what* to do. But it's easy to forget that he may not know *how* to do it—that you must take time out to show him or tell him how to go about it. But the biggest error of all is not to tell him *why*.

Telling an employee why something must be done gives him a reason for wanting to do it. There's a world of difference, for instance, between, "Tim, starting tomorrow I want you to show me personally each piece of off-quality raw material you charge for credit," and "Tim, the purchasing department wants a report on how well our new supplier is meeting specifications with our raw material. For a couple of weeks, I'll have to furnish them with a detailed report. So will you set aside for me each piece of off-quality stock so that I may inspect it? I have to tell the purchasing department exactly what's wrong with it."

Should you give an order when you're angry?

If you can avoid it, don't give orders when you're angry. There's always the possibility that you'll make a threat that you can't, or won't want to, carry out.

You probably know of a case similar to this one:

Ralph, machine-shop foreman, has just been chewed out by his boss for the number of damaged hand tools charged to his department. So as soon as the boss leaves, Ralph blows his stack to his employees. "Next man who turns in a damaged tool, no matter what the reason, he'll pay for it out of his own pocket." So what happens? That afternoon, Stanley, who has been with the company fifteen years and who is as conscientious as can be, accidentally ruins a micrometer. Whom does that put on the spot? Nobody but Ralph!

Is your tone of voice important?

Definitely! Remember the story of the cowboy who said, "When you call me that, smile." Employees are the same way. They'll read your voice like a book to hear whether you're trying to throw your weight around, whether you mean what you say or are just talking through your hat. So when giving an order that's going to be hard to carry out, smile to show that you know what you ask isn't easy. But let the tone of your voice show that you expect it to be done regardless.

Should you ask an employee to do anything you wouldn't do?

You don't have to *do* everything you ask others to do. But, in principle, you should show that you'd be *willing to do* it if you had to.

Giving orders is a hard-rock test of your leadership courage. General Patton used to say that an army of men was like a piece of cooked spaghetti. You can't push it, you can only pull it. You might not have to lead an army, but you should always imply your willingness to stand up where the shots are being received.

If there's a dirty or unpleasant job, be sure you expose yourself to the same conditions your workers do. If they must work in the rain or cold, get out there with them. If they have to get in the muck under a machine, show that you're not above getting your hands dirty either.

This doesn't mean actually doing their work, although many a union doesn't object when the supervisor's efforts are primarily to show his men he's willing to share some of the load with them.

But shouldn't each person be handled differently?

Yes, if you can find time. Some people (women especially) like their boss to be specific about what he wants done. Others desire only an opportunity to raise a question, make a suggestion. Still other people work best when given a free hand. To assign orders accordingly, you'll want to improve your ability to size up people. Then improve your leadership by tailoring each order to fit the individual.

Do you issue group orders differently?

Many people believe that orders given to groups of people are ineffective unless the group is permitted to discuss them and decide how the group can best carry them out. This isn't always practical or desirable, of course. But when issuing orders to groups, keep in mind that the problem of getting across to groups is tens of times harder than that of reaching one person. It's always better if you can find a suitable time and place to discuss the reasons behind the order and to get suggestions from the group as to how it might best be carried out.

One rule to follow in group instructions is to pin down *who* is to do *what.* If you don't, you're likely to find each person waiting for some-one else to carry the ball—the Alphonse-Gaston treatment.

Are there any pitfalls to avoid in giving orders?

Yes. There are many pitfalls to avoid in giving orders and instruc-tions. Here are some of the most dangerous. Avoid:

An offhand manner. If you want employees to take instructions seri-ously, then deliver them that way.

Assuming a worker understands. Give him a chance to ask questions, raise objections. Let him tell you what you have told him.

Too many orders. Don't get order-happy. Make the ones you do issue pay off by keeping them short and specific. Watch your timing, too. Wait until one job is done before asking that another be started.

Conflicting instructions. Check to be sure you're not telling your men one thing, other supervisors telling their employees another.

Choosing only the willing worker. Some people are naturally cooper-ative. Others make it difficult for you to ask them to do anything. Be sure you don't overwork the willing horse and let the hard-to-handle people get out of their share of tough jobs.

Picking on anyone. Employees want the work distributed fairly. Don't take out a gripe or grudge against a particular worker by giving him all the dirty work.

Too much detail. Tell an employee enough about the assignment— but not too much. Sound like double talk? No. Point is that how much you tell depends upon how complicated the job is and how much the employee knows about it. For an old hand, there's nothing more tire-some than having details he already knows explained to him.

Playing the big shot. New foremen are sometimes guilty of flaunting their authority. Older foremen feel more confident, know that you don't have to crack a whip to gain employees' respect and loyalty.

The Case of the Refused Overtime. A case study in human relations involving the problem of issuing orders, with questions for you to answer.

One day in June, a machine-shop foreman asked a number of men in his department to work a few hours overtime. All agreed to stay except Tony. "You'll have to get someone else," said Tony. "I'm painting my house after work these days. Besides, I don't need the overtime money."

"That's got nothing to do with it," replied the foreman. "We have an order to get out tonight. And whether you like it or not, you'll have to stay and help."

"Nothing doing," said Tony, starting to get angry. "My personal time is my own. I work forty hours every week here. If you want me to work overtime, you'll have to let me know in advance so I can plan for it."

"This is an emergency that couldn't have been foreseen," said the foreman. "You'll work tonight or regret it."

"You can't fire me for not working overtime. The union had a grievance on this and cleared it up last year. See you tomorrow." With that Tony put on his jacket and punched out.

1. What do you think of the way the foreman handled this situation?

2. If you were the foreman, how would you have ordered Tony to stay?

3. Should the foreman drop the whole matter or should he make an issue of it? Why?

16 WINNING EMPLOYEE COOPERATION

Why don't some people cooperate?

For a very natural reason: they see no personal advantage in doing so. A terrible attitude? Not at all.

None of us do anything for nothing. We do some things for money, others for lots of other reasons. Joe works well because he likes the feeling of being with a gang of people. Sam works hard because he gets a sense of accomplishment from what he is doing. Mary puts in top effort because her job makes her feel important.

Hardly anyone works for money alone. We all expect different satisfactions in different proportions from our work. So don't be annoyed when a worker's attitude seems to say, "What's in it for me?" That's your signal to get busy and to find some way of providing satisfaction for him on the job.

Why isn't high pay the key to cooperation?

Good pay rates are important, but many companies that have sought the high-wage route to workers' loyalty have been sadly disappointed. Pay means much to employees; yet experience shows it isn't enough.

One big trouble with pay as an incentive is that an employee doesn't enjoy the money while he works. He doesn't get a chance to spend much of his wages at work. Take vacations and pensions. An employee takes advantage of neither while he is actually on the job. Your solution to winning employee cooperation is to uncover an employee's personal needs and then to try to adjust his working conditions so as to satisfy these needs at work.

What satisfactions does an employee seek at work?

Psychologists have observed, and thousands of foremen have verified the fact, that people work for three different kinds of satisfactions:

Physical needs. These are the things that wages take care of—a well-stocked larder and a half-dozen cans of beer on ice, shoes for the kids and a new hat for the wife, a good place to keep the family.

Social needs. These needs are very real—and can be satisfied by a good boss. These needs include a recognition that we can do few things alone, that a group effort produces most things we value. So an employee looks for a chance to be an accepted member of the group he works with. He likes contributing to the group, too. If his foreman is at odds with the work group, a workman is more likely to go along with what the group intends to do than to cooperate with the foreman, even if the foreman is right.

Self-centered needs. These are the needs an individual has to be outstanding. An employee likes to work in places that permit him to show how good a workman he is, that give him a chance for praise and recognition, to show that while he's an accepted member of the team, he's still an important person.

One writer has called the last two needs the "handles on the pay cup." It's a good way to remember them.

What's the best formula for winning cooperation?

The best formula is not to seek one. Despite the simplicity of the three reasons people work, there is no easy road to securing cooperation. Don't be misled into believing there are gimmicks or pat things to say. There are no standard ways to react that, once memorized, will have employees eating out of your hand. If you attempt to outsmart employees, even the stupidest of all will spot your lack of sincerity. And his resistance will go up in proportion.

The best way to achieve cooperation is to change your own way of looking at people until you see in them some of the good and bad qualities you see in yourself. Make a point of being sensitive to people. Pause again and again to imagine how employees think about what you tell them or what you ask them to do. Stop talking, too, and listen to what they say about themeslves, about the other workers, and about you. For not until you begin to *know* people will you be able to put into practice some of the simple ideas expressed here for getting along with people.

Is it wrong to get tough with employees?

Getting tough can be much better than trying to trick your employees into cooperating. At least, if you're tough consistently, they'll know where they stand. But the tough way of getting employees to do what you'd like them to do went out with the Depression—and with the coming of strong unions. If you examine the hard-boiled approach, you'll see that it works on the physical-needs reason for working. The foreman uses fear as his tool when he says, "If you don't do as I say, pick up your paycheck and get out!" This approach was pretty effective when jobs were hard to get. Or was it?

Without dipping too deep into psychology, it's good to know the simple fact that when most people are afraid, they don't always run away and hide. They get aggressive, hard to get along with. Employees motivated by fear become masters of the slowdown and the sand-in-the-gears techniques.

You shouldn't take this to mean that you should be wishy-washy in your actions. Employees cooperate under firm supervision, so long as the supervisor doesn't adopt a "Father-knows-best" attitude and also provides satisfaction for workers' needs.

What kind of supervision gets the best results?

It may seem hard, at first, to believe that supervisors who place less emphasis on production goals actually get higher production from the employees they supervise. This is only one aspect of the picture of the successful supervisor drawn as a result of the study made in 1948 at the University of Michigan. Supervisors in high-production groups were found to have these qualities:

• Their own bosses gave them a freer hand than supervisors in low-production groups.

• High-production supervisors are more employee-centered, spend more time in supervising and less time on mechanical and paper-work details.

• And these same supervisors encourage employees to contribute their ideas on how best to get things done.

Should a supervisor keep a tight hold on the production reins?

Time and time again it's been shown that the supervisor who decides everything himself—what to do, how to do it, when to do it, where it should be done, etc.—gets the least cooperation from the people he supervises.

Are people just plain ornery then? No, that isn't it. The secret lies in the desire of most people to get into the act—to have some say about the decisions that affect them. In some people this desire is stronger than others. But now that you have seen how strong social or group pressures are, you can see how even those employees who are indifferent to participation are swayed by group pressures to cooperate or not.

So if you're having trouble winning cooperation, relax your grip a little. You needn't go all out at first. But give the principle of participation a fair shake.

For instance, if Ziggy has balked every time you've asked him to clean out the machine pit, try this approach, "Ziggy, today's the day the machine pit's got to be cleaned out. I know it's a lousy job, but it has to be done. When would you like to begin—right now or later today so that you can wash up as soon as you're finished?"

Just by offering a choice of time, you've permitted Ziggy to decide something about how the job should be done, even if you still make the big decisions. Next time, you may want to let Ziggy suggest what kind of tools he thinks are best to use, or whether the cleaning should be done with solvents or a steam jenny.

Each person has a limit of how much participation he wants—and how much he can handle. One of the best ways to secure cooperation is to let each person have a say in running his job—up to the point where both you and he are satisfied with the way it's done.

How can you set goals with workers?

Housewives aren't factory workers, but there's an interesting (and true) story about a group of Iowa housewives, which tells you a lot about how to get people to cooperate by permitting them to help you set their own goals. In this case, the researchers were trying to find a way to get Iowa housewives to improve the food value of the meals they served their families. This looked like an easy task. The housewife's own self-interest in taking care of her family would make her cooperate, reasoned the researchers. Best way to get these housewives to use more milk, the researchers said to themselves, was to let a nutrition expert give them the facts. So that's what they tried.

The nutrition expert worked with one group of housewives, did an excellent job of showing how important it was to add more milk to the diet and how easy it was to do. The women were apparently impressed by the talk. But did they use more milk? Only 16 per cent actually increased their milk consumption.

So the research group tried a new method on a similar group of housewives. The same expert met with the women. Only he didn't lecture this time: he held a discussion in town-meeting style. The housewives talked among themselves to decide what they could do to use more milk. The expert answered questions, but let the women run the show. The meetings lasted no longer than before, but the women arrived at the inevitable conclusion that using more milk was something they ought to do. How successful was this free-rein approach? Exactly half of the housewives in the second group were found to be using more milk even one month after the meetings! This was three times the record of the first group. Judge for yourself how much more effective the group participation way was over the first method that depends upon having an expert convince people that his way is best.

The result of this particular experiment has been repeated and verified over and over again in industry. It shows that people cooperate best when the objectives are ones *they want* to achieve, not something they have to reach or else. These objectives should not just be something the boss wants or the company wants.

How do you get employees to want to do things?

Employees like to see for themselves. After all, how many of us take someone else's word for anything? A child won't believe the stove is hot until he burns his hand on it. Even an adult stains his finger to see if wet paint is wet. And a worker who's told, "This is for your own good," wants to find out for himself, too.

Urging people to greater effort occasionally works for great football coaches, like Knute Rockne. But inspiration alone won't get employees to cooperate day in and day out on the job. They'd much rather you outlined the general objectives, then let them decide the strategy of how to reach those objectives.

Take the traditional drive for better housekeeping. What's been your own experience? Have you seen any startling results from a snow storm of posters, pay-envelope stuffers, items in the employee newspaper? The worthwhile results have come only in those departments where the leadership was outstanding. And you can bet that the outstanding supervisor didn't just call his people together and say, "Beginning next week the annual housekeeping contest is on. We're going to try to improve our score by 25 per cent over last year. It will take effort from all of us. And I'm depending upon your cooperation."

Here's what the outstanding supervisor more probably said: "Last year you did an outstanding job of improving the housekeeping in this department. The plant superintendent told me only yesterday how pleased he was with the suggestions for improvements employees in this shop contributed during the last campaign. It will be something we all can feel proud of if this year we do as well as we did last. What do you think we ought to shoot for this year? Were you satisfied with the committee arrangement we used last time, or would you like to suggest a different approach? How often do you think we ought to inspect the department this year—daily or weekly?"

Must you always get participation?

No. If you plan your big targets by asking for and considering the opinions of your employees, they'll understand that there isn't time to handle every decision that way. Participation is a long-range affair. If you show that you want and respect employees' opinion—and that your decisions are affected by these opinions—you'll have achieved the goal of making employees feel they are part of a team. An occasional oversight, an infrequent decision made without their counsel won't destroy the feeling that generates cooperation.

By sowing the seeds of participation generously, you'll also find that you won't have to take over many of the minor decisions that occupy your attention otherwise. Employees who know from experience that their opinions are desired are employees who know in advance how the team (their team and yours) would act if the team had a chance to go into a huddle. And they'll act accordingly (see also Chap. 2).

When can you spot signs of employee objections?

Army leaders for centuries have said that gripes were signs of a healthy condition. The same is true of most industrial situations, too. When employees aren't afraid to speak up or to complain, a foreman can quickly spot objections that stand in the way of cooperation. And take action to remove the objections. So if your employees gripe, be smart. These are the doors you'll have to open if you're to get inside them. So try opening them.

A sign of objection that is much harder to read is silence. When morale in a shop is bad, employees are likely to clam up. Harder still to spot are hidden objections. An employee, for instance, may not say "No" to your face, but he may find excuses not to do what you ask. Signs of hidden resistance show up in answers like this, "I'm not interested," "I'm satisfied where I am," "I'll think it over," "I'll let you know." These are just excuses to put you off from making an issue that will bring his resistance out into the open.

How do you remove resistance?

There are many tacks you can sail to remove resistance. Don't use the same one in every situation. Learn them all so you have a full bag of tools to bring to bear when resistance shows up.

Try a success example. Casey doesn't want to work nights? Tell Casey about Jonesy, who thought he wouldn't like working nights, but who, after trying it for a month, won't work any other shift.

Try making a guarantee. Tom is sure the new method won't work? Tell Tom that if he tries it for a week and he doesn't find it better than the old way, you'll promise he can switch back again.

Try a demonstration. The shop steward thinks the rate on the new job is too tough? Say to him, "Here, let me show you how easy the machine is to operate. It looks a lot harder than it actually is."

Try asking questions. Marie says she can't make bonus? Ask her what she finds hardest about the job, whether she feels it has been properly explained.

Try just plain listening. Sandy won't work overtime today or any other day? Let him rave. Hear all his arguments in a friendly manner. When he's had his complete say, then try persuasion and reasoning.

Must you never say what you think?

It's a mistake to think that you must never say exactly what's on your mind. Some resistance needs a point-blank denial on your part. If George says that he won't sweep around his machine because it's not part of his job, and it is part of his job, then speak up and say so. But don't assume a free hand just because you're right.

Employees, like all of us, hate to be contradicted or told that they're wrong. So use tact when you say, "Just a minute, George. I want to hear your side of this matter so that I'm sure I understand your point of view. But perhaps we'd better clarify exactly what's in your job description before we arrive at any conclusions. I have the job manual on my desk. Let's look at it and see what it says."

Under what circumstances are employees least likely to cooperate?

When, for any reason they are afraid, employees will tend to balk at your instructions. Fear doesn't inspire cooperation. Instead it makes the hackles rise and the hair bristle. So be alert to situations that breed fear. Changes, no matter how slight, are an example of a situation that causes fear and blocks cooperation.

Anything new is something we don't know about, so we tend to be afraid of it. A change in materials, methods, supervision, lighting, even in the toilet paper in the men's room will cause employees to be suspicious—and to get on the defensive.

To counteract this kind of fear, let employees know about changes as far ahead of time as you can. Have a reputation of being available for questions so that an employee will voice his fear to you. "What's up, Jack? How come the change in the lighting in our department? The company planning to replace us with a bunch of women?" asks a workman who knows you'll give him a straight answer.

Fear of layoff, automation, rate cuts, transfers, embarrassment, loss of prestige all block employee cooperation. And the first answer to all of them is the truth, as well as you know. Even an unpleasant fact is an effective antidote to fear. But when you don't know the answer yourself, say so. Don't be afraid to say, "Sorry, I don't know what the story is, but I'll sure as heck try to find out for you."

How do you go about getting cooperation from your associates?

The secret of getting along well with other foremen is much the same as winning cooperation from your employees: find out what they want most from their work, then satisfy these desires. Except that with your associates, it's not so much a problem of providing satisfaction as it is of not blocking their goals and ambitions.

Face up to the fact that, to a degree, you and your associates are competing—for raises, promotions, praise, popularity, and a host of other things. If you compete too hard, or compete unfairly, you won't win much cooperation from your fellow supervisors. And your chances of getting ahead often depend upon your ability to run your department in smooth harmony with those departments that interlock with yours.

To win friends among your fellow supervisors means intelligent sacrifice. Occasionally you'll have to put aside your wish to make your department look good just so that you don't put Ralph, foreman of the next department, behind the eight ball. Willingness to lend a hand when another foreman falls behind and avoiding hair-splitting when allocating interdepartmental charges and responsibilities will help.

Above all, let fellow supervisors run their own shows. Don't try to give orders in their departments or encourage disputes between your workers and theirs.

Just as when an individual employee doesn't play ball with the others, if you don't conform to a reasonable degree, you'll have the supervisory group down on you—and cooperation will be long coming. To turn this group solidarity to your advantage, aim at giving the supervisory organization the advantage of your own positive leadership. Help other supervisors set worthwhile goals, and the chances of your all working together will be improved.

How can you get along best with staff people?

Generally speaking, staff people in your plant are almost entirely dependent upon you and other supervisors for cooperation. And in this case, cooperation will breed cooperation. If you cooperate with staff people, their jobs are made infinitely easier. Their superiors judge them by their success in getting your assistance and upon the degree to which you accept and act upon their advice. So if you cooperate with staff people, you're actually helping them to get more satisfaction from their work. And you can be pretty sure that they'll go a long way toward helping you make a good showing on *your* job.

Wouldn't you like to have a methods engineer report to your boss, "It's a pleasure to work with a foreman like Joe. He never seems to hide things or get his back up when I offer suggestions. He's quick to see how what we're doing will improve operations in the long run. Not that Joe buys everything I say. He doesn't. He's got his ideas too. But together, I think Joe and I are really accomplishing things out there"?

Is it smart to show you appreciate employee cooperation, or should you act as if it's something coming to you?

You *can* overdo your show of appreciation. But neither should employees think you take their efforts for granted. It would be ridiculous, for example, to stand by the time clock congratulating each employee for coming in on time. But it makes sense to look over the attendance record every six months and take a minute to say to each person with a perfect record, "I just reviewed the department's attendance records for the last six months, and I see that you went through those six months without missing a day or being late once. We appreciate that around here. It helps make the department an easier place to work in. Hope you can keep it up."

Yes. It's better to err on the generous side than to get the reputation as a fellow who takes a pound of flesh each day but never so much as says "Thank you."

The Case of Foreman Brown. A case study in human relations involving employee cooperation, with questions for you to answer.

Three chemical operators of the Apex Solvents Co. were washing up at the end of the shift. Here's a transcription of their conversation:

First workman: Where does Brown get off at asking us to give the pumpmen in the blending department a hand? Who does he think he's kidding!

Second workman: Yeah. He ought to know we're on to his line of soft soap by now.

Third workman: What burns me up is that we're expected to do all the cooperating around here. I can't see that the guys in any of the other departments ever pitch in over here.

Second workman: Why should they? They've got their jobs. We've got ours. I say let's stick with our own problems.

Third workman: What's in it for us, anyway? A slap on the back from Brownie. But nothing else in the pay envelope.

First workman: What else do you expect? Brownie gets ahead by taking credit for what we do. It doesn't cost him anything to say "nice going" to us. But I bet he tells a different story to the front office. Makes a hero out of himself.

Third workman: If that's the case, Brownie knows what he can do the next time he asks me to do anything that isn't in my job description!

First workman: That goes double for me.

Second Workman: Me, too!

1. Where has Brownie been wrong in dealing with these workmen?

2. What sort of action will Brownie have to take to get these men to cooperate?

3. Should there be a limit on what an employee is asked to do voluntarily? If so, what kind of a limit?

17 HOW AND WHEN TO DISCIPLINE

What's the real purpose of discipline?

To encourage employees to behave sensibly at work. Just as we have laws in civil life to preserve order and to protect lives and property, so rules and regulations are designed to accomplish the same purpose in the plant. And employees recognize this need. Few would seriously wish to abolish them.

Why do employees resent discipline?

Employees don't object to the idea of rules and regulations. But they frequently object to the way a foreman metes out discipline. In civil life, if a person breaks the law, the policeman only arrests him. He's tried before a jury of his peers who are guided by the rulings of an impartial judge, who in turn determines the punishment.

Now compare the civil procedure for handling lawbreakers with what happens in the plant. As foreman, you're often called upon not only to put the finger on the wrongdoer, but also to hear his case and decide how he should be penalized. To many an employee, this seems unfair because you've acted as policeman, judge, and jury.

So don't take your job as disciplinarian lightly. It's a great responsibility and requires impartiality, good judgment, and courage on your part.

Why do employees break rules?

As in most personnel problems, only a small percentage of workers cause disciplinary problems. People who break rules do so for a number of reasons—most of them because they are not well adjusted. One study of 4,174 discharge cases showed that 62.4 per cent were for personal shortcomings of the employees themselves. Underlying personal characteristics that came up most were carelessness, noncooperation, laziness, dishonesty, lack of initiative, lateness, lack of effort. The foreman's job, as a result, is to help employees to be better adjusted.

The record shows that people break rules less often in shops where the supervisor is a good leader, where he shows a sincere interest in his employees, where employees get more enjoyment from their work. After all, if an employee finds his work uninteresting and his boss unpleasant, is it surprising that the employee will find reasons for being late or for staying away from work altogether?

If the supervisor gives his employees little or no chance to show initiative on the job or to discuss ways the work should be done, he shouldn't be surprised that his employees talk back, goof off, or create a lot of scrap. That's what some people do who can't express themselves any other way.

Sometimes, the real reason an employee breaks rules or is lazy on the job has nothing at all to do with working conditions. Such an employee may be having worries at home—money problems or a nagging wife—or he may be physically sick. You might ask, "What concern is that of the foreman?" It isn't—unless the foreman wants that employee to be more cooperative and productive at work. If you're smart enough to see the connection, then you can do much to improve this workman's performance. Don't snoop in his personal affairs, but do give him a willing and uncritical ear. Let him get to know that you're an understanding person, that his boss is "someone a guy can talk to without getting a short answer or a lot of phony advice."

So when an employee breaks a rule, make discipline your last resort. Instead, search hard for the reason he acts the way he does. Then try to see what you can do to remove the reason.

What kind of handling do employees expect from a supervisor in the way of discipline?

Justice and equal treatment. Being soft, overlooking nonstandard performance, giving chance after chance to wrongdoers *does not* win popularity among most employees. In fact it works the other way to destroy morale. That's because the majority of people who work hard and stay in line are frustrated and disappointed when they see others get away with things. Sure, no one *likes* to be punished. But everyone likes to be assured that the punishment he receives is in line with what he has done wrong ("Let the punishment fit the crime," is the advice given in Gilbert and Sullivan's *Mikado*) and that he's treated neither better nor worse than anyone else for the same fault.

Some people talk about negative punishment, say positive discipline is better. What does this mean?

When you have to penalize someone, that's *negative*. If you can get an employee to do what you wish through constructive criticism or discussion, that's *positive*.

Foremen, more so than employees, understand that disciplining is a nasty task. After all, all a supervisor wants is to run his shop in peace and harmony, to see that things get done right and that no one gets hurt. If he can establish discipline through good leadership, then he won't have to exercise negative discipline through bawling-outs, suspensions, or discharges.

How far can a foreman go in handling discipline?

That depends upon your company's management policy—and upon the labor agreement, if your plant has a union.

Legally, a foreman can hire and fire. But firing is a costly action. To break in a new employee can cost anywhere from $150 to several thousand dollars, in the case of a skilled mechanic. So most companies have tried to approach discipline from a positive direction. And since discipline puts a supervisor in such a responsible position, many companies have carefully spelled out just how far a foreman can go before he has to check with his boss.

Labor unions, in their desire to provide the maximum protection from injustice or unfair treatment, maintain that discipline shouldn't be handled by management alone. Unions contend that they, too, should help decide on an employee's punishment. How much say a particular union will have depends on how successful the union has been in writing this privilege into the contract or in establishing precedents for its participation.

So tread carefully in discipline matters. Find out from your company's policy-level management (your immediate superior, the plant manager, or the personnel manager) just how far the company wants you to go—and how much participation you must permit the union.

Isn't the foreman likely to be no more than a figurehead if he can't take discipline into his own hands?

No. Not if the foreman acts only in accordance with his authority. Trouble comes when you try to throw more weight around than you actually possess. That's when you look foolish!

Hardly anyone anywhere can take action that affects others without at the same time being responsible to still other people. This applies to your boss, who must answer to higher executives and to the company president, who in turn may have to answer to a board of directors.

Being a foreman isn't an easy job. Handling discipline when you know that if you make a mistake you may be reversed or overruled by either your boss or the union makes the job even more difficult. To make it easier, you must become a "legal eagle" on the points of how far you can go before it's wise to check with your boss. Some companies actually formalize this process by having the foreman's superior and the foreman work out a check list so that the foreman knows exactly where he stands on each point. When it's done this way, you'd be surprised how much real authority you have, how many decisions you can make yourself—even though in some cases your authority is necessarily limited. You'll find an example of such a check list on the next page.

Should you act when you're angry?

It's a very unusual person who can think and act sensibly when he's lost his temper. For that reason, it's a good idea for a foreman *not* to take any disciplinary action while he's boiling over. How can this be done? Try one of these:

Count to 100. An oldy, but it works.

Take a walk. Ask the employee to walk over to the window or to your office—anything that takes time. This is especially good, since it gets him away from gawking employees and from familiar surroundings where he's most likely to be recalcitrant.

See him later. Simply tell him you'll speak to him about the matter in a couple of hours. This gives you a chance to cool off, to think the matter through, to check with your boss, if necessary.

How do you decide what to do?

No one can make a decision if he doesn't have all the facts. If a situation arises that looks as if you've got to take disciplinary action, look hard before you leap. Take time to investigate. Let the employee

RESPONSIBILITY AND LIMIT OF AUTHORITY FOR HANDLING EMPLOYEE RELATIONS AND DISCIPLINARY PROBLEMS

(To be agreed upon by a supervisor and his immediate superior)

Authority limits

Class 1. Complete authority. Supervisor can take action without consulting with his superior.

Class 2. Authority is limited to the extent that supervisor must inform superior of any action taken.

Class 3. Limited authority. Supervisor must consult with his superior before taking any action.

New employees	Authority limit classification
Hire additional employees	_____
Accept new employees	_____
Report on probationary employees	_____
Job assignments	
Schedule employees	_____
Make changes in schedules	_____
Transfer employees within department	_____
Transfer employees within plant	_____
Discipline	
Suggest appropriate discipline	_____
Issue written reprimand	_____
Suspend	_____
Discharge for cause	_____
Grievances	
Adjust grievances with employees	_____
Accept written grievances from union	_____
Give written reply to union	_____
Termination and leaves	
Grant leaves of absence	_____
Prepare vacation schedules	_____
Lay employees off for lack of work	_____
Information	
Maintain bulletin boards	_____
Explain company policy to employees	_____
First aid and accidents	
Send employees to first-aid station	_____
Send employees to doctor or hospital	_____
Notify family of injured employee	_____
Prepare report of accident	_____
Safety and good housekeeping	
Take unsafe tools out of service	_____
Correct unsafe conditions	_____
Stop work where conditions are unsafe	_____
Establish housekeeping standards	_____

tell his full story—without interruptions. Check with witnesses for their observations. Look in the company records to see what other foremen have done in the past. Speak to your boss or the personnel manager to get their advice.

For instance, someone tips you off that Will Jones is going to take home a baby stillson wrench in his lunch box tonight. You stop Will at the time clock. Sure enough. There's the wrench tucked underneath a wad of sandwich wrappers. Your first reaction is to fire Will on the spot for stealing. But should you?

Suppose on checking, you found any of these circumstances:

• Will had asked the tool-room foreman for the wrench and received permission to borrow it overnight for a home-repair job.

• Two of Will's coworkers tell you Will had said he was just borrowing the wrench overnight and planned to return it in the morning.

• Will could prove that the wrench was one he actually had bought himself to use on his job.

• When checking with the personnel department, you found that the company had agreed with the union not to fire any ten-year employee for petty thefts. That the most Will's penalty could be for a first offense would be one day off without pay.

Wouldn't any of these facts change your decision?

When should you consult the union on disciplinary problems?

Practices will vary from plant to plant. Some supervisors, however, have found it helps to inform the union immediately of *any* planned disciplinary action. When the supervisor sees that a disciplinary problem has arisen, he holds an informal hearing with the employee with the shop steward standing by. This way, the shop steward is a witness to the situation from the beginning. He can observe that the supervisor's handling of the case is fair. It also makes it harder for the employee to change his story later on—avoids the case where the shop steward says to you, "That's not what he told me."

Unless your company has a practice to the contrary, *you should avoid asking the union or shop steward what you should do or what penalty is appropriate.* You should make it clear that the union representative has been invited only for the purpose of keeping him informed. Keeping order in the shop is *your* job, not the union's, although you may welcome its cooperation.

Do warnings do any good?

Yes, warnings do a lot of good—if you make them more than idle threats. Your warning puts an employee on notice that his performance isn't up to standard. It gives you a chance to explain a rule that he may have taken only lightly before—and to make the penalty clear to him. When you warn an employee, that's the perfect time for you to be constructive, to offer help, to practice positive discipline.

To make a warning a valuable piece of evidence in a union grievance, you should always make a written record of it. You'd be surprised how much weight arbitrators and union officials give to notations that you have written in your pocket notebook, the shop log book, or have inserted in the employee's personnel file.

Some companies make this written notation a formal practice by requiring foremen to fill out a form to be filed by the personnel department. These notations are called *written reprimands,* and copies of the reprimand are sent to the employee and the union.

When should you fire an employee?

As mentioned previously, the foreman's authority is limited by his company's policy and by its agreements with the labor union, if one exists.

Speaking generally, however, some employee offenses are worse than others. Drinking or sleeping on the job, smoking in restricted areas, willfully destroying property, and falsifying time cards are often charges that result in discharge. Less hard to generalize on are offenses like fighting on company property, gross insubordination, etc. But all these wrongdoings have one thing in common—they are single incidents rather than an accumulation of minor offenses. And many of these single acts require immediate action on the foreman's part.

To handle any of these serious offenses, and still leave yourself free from reversal later on, there's an effective kind of action you can take. It's short of discharge, but it gets the culprit out of the plant quickly and legally. This action is called *suspension.* And it follows the advice arbitrators give employees: "Obey first—argue later."

To suspend an employee, you merely say something like this: "Art, you've come to work with a load on. I think you're under the influence of liquor right now and are unfit to do your job. You could be subject for dismissal for being in this shape. I haven't made up my mind yet whether that's what I'll do. But in the meantime, you're suspended. Punch out your time card and don't come back to work until I call you. I'll try to let you know definitely tomorrow."

It's perfectly all right to notify Art's shop steward that you are suspending Art. You can acknowledge that if Art or the steward disagrees with your action, they can file a grievance. But in the meantime, you are suspending Art, pending a final decision of his penalty.

By suspending, you have demonstrated your willingness to enforce your authority when needed. And yet you have protected yourself and the company from looking weak, foolish, or indecisive. If tomorrow, in the opinion of your boss, the personnel manager, or the company's lawyer, you can't make the discharge stick, you and the company are still in an effective position. It's when you cast the die—fire a man and then have to take him back—that you have to eat crow.

When can't you make a discharge stick?

Here are some famous last words: "What's tough about discharging a man? If his work is lousy, or he talks back, or breaks a rule, get rid of him."

Where a union exists, many a foreman with that attitude has ended up behind the eight ball. And his company has been messed up in an arbitration case, had to fork over back pay to a discharged worker, and even faced a charge of an unfair labor practice. Why? Because the crate of eggs that requires the most delicate handling in the collective-bargaining package is the provision for discharge and discipline. Dead beyond recall are the days when a foreman could act and talk tough, when an employee had no recourse but to curse.

As difficult as the discipline problem is, many a discharge or other penalty could be made to stick if the following mistakes weren't made:

No clear-cut breach of rule. In one plant a foreman fired a man for sleeping, only to see his decision reversed by the arbitrator. The union brought out the fact that the foreman had made his observation from 60 feet away. The arbitrator ruled that at this distance the foreman was "likely to see what he wanted to see."

Inadequate warning. Arbitrators frequently feel that a workman is entitled to sufficient warning that his conduct won't be tolerated—even though the rules and penalties are in an employee manual. Typical is the case where an employee has had a record of poor attendance for months without having been disciplined. Suddenly the foreman cracks down without warning and fires him.

Absence of positive evidence. Take this case of loafing—always a difficult charge to make stick: The company went along with the foreman and fired a worker caught loafing. The arbitrator reversed the company because (1) the foreman had not been in the department continually but had popped in and out during one afternoon and (2) the man's job entailed occasional waits for material. Furthermore, the company could produce no time sheets that showed reduced output in black and white. The arbitrator ruled that the foreman might have come into the department at the times the man had been legitimately waiting for materials.

Acting on prejudices. Real or imagined discrimination or favoritism weakens a disciplinary ruling. If a foreman has shown that he has it in for a workman and just waited for an opportunity to hang a penalty on him, an arbitration case may bring this out. If the foreman has let others get away unpunished with the same offense for which he punishes another, he'll have a hard time justifying such unequal treatment.

Inadequate records. The value of written records of warnings and reprimands can't be overemphasized. It's especially valuable for documenting action taken to correct an accumulation of minor offenses. You may not want to discharge a man who's been late the first time—or even the fifth. But when it gets to be a frequent and costly habit, you'll want to take action. Unless you've built up a record of warnings and kept a file of them that can be shown to the union and an arbitrator if necessary, your case will be hard to prove.

Too severe punishment. Many arbitrators recommend "progressive punishment" and look unfavorably on too severe discipline—especially for first offenses. For instance, a foreman in a can company noticed a workman away from his work station 10 minutes before the end of the shift. A look at the employee's time card showed that he had punched out a half minute early. The man was fired because not long before that he had received a written reprimand for doing the same thing. He had been warned that the next time he'd be fired. An arbitrator ruled that a penalty was called for—but not such a tough one. Do it progressively, he said—just a little tougher each time. A lighter penalty would keep an old (seven years' service) and valuable employee on the payroll.

What consideration should be given to an employee's good work record?

There's danger in carrying the rule book too far. Treating each offender equally does not mean that you should not weigh personal factors, too. For instance, what was the worker's *attitude* when he broke the rule? Did he do it deliberately or accidentally? Was he emotionally upset by a circumstance beyond his control (like worrying about a sick child at home)? How long has the man worked for the company? What kind of work record has he had? Remember, it costs money to fire a good employee. Even the civil law courts occasionally suspend sentence or put on probation a guilty person who has been considered a good citizen in the past.

What can you do about absenteeism?

Poor attendance and tardiness are only special cases of the whole problem of securing employee cooperation and disciplining those who don't keep order. Because absences have received so much attention, they point up best the fact that an employee breaks a rule not just for the sake of being bad. Rules are broken for a variety of personal reasons that a foreman can discover only through getting close to his employees. The further you are from knowing your workers, the greater your chance of having disciplinary problems.

Regardless of underlying reasons for unexcused absences, they should be treated like any other case of accumulated minor offenses. Many companies have designed intricate point systems of credits and debits to make penalties for excessive absenteeism almost automatic. Absences and lateness lend themselves to the automatic treatment because they are recorded so well that employees find it hard to find an argument against disciplinary action.

If you were to document, investigate, and follow up other infractions of rules and regulations as well as you take care of absenteeism, you would find that your discipline problems would be at a minimum.

How much should employees know about your discipline policy?

The more the better. Technically, you can make your rules and penalties stick as long as they are posted on bulletin boards, written in union contracts, or expressed in employee manuals. But to be really effective, employees should be reminded (not threatened) of rules from time to time.

It's especially good if you tell them the purpose of the rules. Take a "No smoking" rule. How much more effective it would be if in addition to posting a sign, you told employees something like this:

"You can smoke most places in the plant, but not in Dept. 29. We use a lot of solvents there. If you dropped a lighted match or butt in that department, we'd all go boom! And it would knock the department and maybe the plant out of operation and jobs for a long time. So don't light up in Dept. 29—or even carry a cigarette in there accidentally. We'd hate to do it, but you might be fired on the spot."

Another thought: when you've had to discharge an employee, be sure that the other employees know what the circumstances were and why he was fired. Don't use him as an example. But do convince other employees that you were fair and impartial. Use this opportunity to emphasize that you don't want to discipline—that you want only to see that the department is run smoothly for the benefit of all concerned.

The Case of Joe Kelly and Albert Fonseca. A case study in human relations involving employee discipline, with questions for you to answer.

Carl Rosewell, plant superintendent of the Baby Biscuit Baking Company, received this memo from Albert Fonseca, supervisor of the oven line:

TO: C. Rosewell, superintendent
FROM: A. Fonseca, oven supervisor
SUBJECT: Joe Kelly's grievance
DATE: September 25, 1957

I think Joe Kelly should get three days off without pay. He's been a troublemaker ever since he's been in my department. I told him he had to clean ovens today, but the shop steward told him to keep on doing what he was doing. So when I told him it was none of his business, Joe laughed. Joe has been on the oven operator's job for six weeks and his work is no good. He was late three times last week. But the steward says I've got to give Joe a chance to learn.

When Joe refused to clean ovens, I told him to punch out. I told the shop steward he could file a grievance, so he did. Joe punched in at 6 A.M. and out at 6:55 A.M. He called me last night to find out when he could come back to work. I told him it was up to management and you hadn't talked to the shop steward yet.

1. If you were Al's boss, what would be your opinion of this memo?

2. How could Al have made the memo clearer?

3. What do you think about Al's relationship with Joe? With the steward?

4. Was Al right in sending Joe home? Why?

5. Whom does Al mean by "management"? Is Al part of "management"?

6. What has Joe's attendance got to do with this situation?

7. If you were Al, how would you have handled the case?

18 HANDLING GRIPES AND AVOIDING GRIEVANCES

How much attention should a supervisor pay to employee complaints?

Just as much as is necessary to remove the employee's complaint as an obstacle to his doing a willing, productive job. That's the main reason a supervisor should act as soon as he even *senses* a complaint, gripe, or grievance. A gripe, imagined or real, spoken or held within, blocks an employee's will to cooperate. Until you've examined the grievance and its underlying causes with him, an employee isn't likely to put out very much for you. And if his complaint has merit, the only way for you to get him back on your team 100 per cent is to correct the situation.

Can you settle every grievance to an employee's satisfaction?

No. It's natural for people sometimes to want more than they deserve. When an employee complains about a condition that the facts don't back up, the best you can do is to demonstrate to him that the settlement is a just one—even if it isn't exactly what he'd like.

Jake may want the company to provide him with work clothing on a job which he considers dirty. Suppose you are able to show Jake

197

that the working conditions are normal for the kind of work being done, that other workers in the plant doing the same kind of work provide their own coveralls, and that this practice is common in the industry. Jake *should* be satisfied with this answer. He's getting equal treatment. But there's nothing to prevent Jake from still feeling dissatisfied with the settlement of his complaint. He may still feel the company should provide work clothing.

Look at it this way, though. You didn't give Jake the brushoff. You listened to his argument attentively. You didn't give him a snap answer. You checked with other supervisors in the plant and with the plant manager to see what the company practice was. You found out that the company practice conforms with that of the industry. All this adds up to something of value in you that Jake can see. He can take his troubles to you and get a straight answer. That's good leadership!

Is there danger in trying to talk an employee out of his complaint?

Talk if you will. But don't try to outsmart an employee—even if that's what he may be trying to do to you. Grievances are caused by facts—or what an employee believes to be facts. Clever use of words and sharp debating tactics won't change these facts or dissolve the grievance.

Patience and sincerity are the two biggest keys to settling a grievance. In many cases, just listening patiently to an employee's explanation will result in *his* talking himself out of his grievance.

What is meant by an imagined grievance? If it's a figment of a workman's imagination, why give it serious attention?

Dick, an unskilled machine operator, files a grievance saying that you've been picking on him, accusing him of doing substandard work. As far as you're concerned, he's off his rocker. In fact, you've hardly paid any attention to what he's been doing. Where'd he ever get a notion like that?

Well, where did he? Let's see. Your department has been pretty rushed lately—that's why you haven't seen much of Dick. You've been spending a good deal of your time with two new apprentices that have just been turned over to you for assignment. *You* knew that their presence had nothing to do with Dick or his job. But did Dick?

Here's how Dick looked at the situation: "I've been here four years busting a gut for Joe. So what does he do when they send up a couple of bright young boys? He puts me on the black list. He thinks he's going to freeze me out of my job by not speaking to me for two weeks.

Then when he does, he tells me that the last batch of fasteners I turned out have to be reworked. And first thing this morning he jumps me for breaking a drill. Next thing I know he'll have one of those apprentices showing me how to do a job I've done for four years. Or taking my job on some phony pretext and bumping me back to the foundry. The hell with him! I'll squawk now before it's too late."

Dick has imagined this grievance, hasn't he? He's got the situation all wrong, too. But if Joe doesn't take time out right now to get to the bottom of this complaint, he'll have a real problem on his hands. Joe will make a good beginning by saying, "Dick, if I've been picking on you, it certainly wasn't personal. In fact, if I thought you had any complaint, it was that I hadn't been giving you enough attention. For the last couple of weeks, I've let you pretty much alone because you're an older hand here. I feel I can trust you to go ahead without my standing over your shoulder. But somewhere maybe I've gotten off the beam. Can you tell me what you mean by 'picking on you'? I certainly want to get this idea straightened out."

What's the most important thing you can do when handling grievances?

It can't be said too often: *Above all, be fair.* Get the employee's point of view clear in your mind. If he has an opportunity to make himself understood, his grievance may turn out to be something different from what appears on the surface.

To be really fair, you must be prepared to accept the logical conclusion that flows from the facts you uncover. This may mean making concessions. But if the facts warrant it, a supervisor often has to change his mind or his way of doing things if he's to gain a reputation for fair dealing.

If you find you've made a mistake, admit it. A supervisor isn't expected to be right all the time. But his employees expect him to be honest in every instance—even if it means his eating crow on occasion.

Should a supervisor horse-trade on grievances?

No. Be like a good baseball umpire: *Call each one as you see it.* If an umpire blows a decision, he really lets himself in for trouble if he tries to make up for it on his next call. It should be the same way with grievances. Either an employee has a case or he hasn't. Consider each case on its merits. And don't let the grievances become political issues.

Should a supervisor change his story if he finds the facts won't support his original conclusions?

A supervisor has no other choice if upon investigation he finds he's been off the beam. But he should avoid this embarrassing situation in the first place. Just be sure to *get the facts—all the facts*. Get them straight to begin with—before you give the employee or a shop steward your decision. It costs you nothing to say, "Give me a couple of hours (or a couple of days) to look into this matter thoroughly. Just as soon as I know all the facts, I'll be able to discuss this grievance so that we come up with the fairest solution."

In trying to round up the facts of a case, explore further than just the obvious places. For example, if the grievance involves a dispute over pay, look beyond just the time-card and payroll data. Ask yourself: Has the worker been upset about the jobs he's been assigned to? Has he had his fair share of easier jobs? Have we had occasion to turn him down on a bid for a better job? Does the worker know how to fill in his time card properly? Does he know the procedure for getting credit for machine breakdown time? Have his materials and tools been up to standard?

All these factors could affect a man's pay and should be examined before you commit yourself.

Records are especially useful in assembling the facts and backing you up when presenting your decision to the employee or the union. If your complaint is that a workman's output has been below par, you'll need his records and the records of others to prove it.

Isn't there a danger that if you make a big project out of a grievance, you'll encourage the employee and the union to think it's more legitimate than it really is?

There's that chance. But you've got to risk it. Over the long haul, treating each grievance with care and consideration pays off. That's different, of course, from giving in on a grievance. That might lead employees to believe you're soft and that you'll make concessions just to avoid arguments.

On the whole it is best to follow this rule for handling grievances: *Be businesslike in your discussions.* Talk with an employee someplace where you'll be free from distractions and interruptions. By all means treat the grievance as a private matter; discuss it away from other employees. Once the employee refers his grievance to the union for handling, don't attempt to settle it except in the presence of the union representative.

When you have made your own investigation and are ready to discuss how the grievance should be settled, advise the union steward. Ask him to invite the employee to be present. After all, your reply is to the employee as well as to the union. Even though the employee has gone to his union for representation, you still want to maintain your personal relationship with him. And he can observe for himself that you maintained the initiative, that the steward didn't have to "tell Joe where to get off."

As in any business situation, keep all your discussions on a friendly basis. Avoid discussing personalities. Keep the steward's focus, as well as your own, on the grievance situation. Show him you wish to settle it fairly just as much as he does. Keep control of your temper, even if the employee or steward loses his head. Resist the temptation to blow your top. If you've got to release your feelings, save it until later when you're alone with other management associates. It's all too easy to permit a grievance to fall to the level of a personal squabble between you and the steward. Avoid this at all cost.

When you give your decision on a grievance, how specific should you be? Should you leave yourself a loophole?

A supervisor's paid to make decisions. When the grievance has been fully investigated and you've talked it over with the parties involved, make your decision as promptly as possible. *Be definite in your answer.* State your decision so that there's no mistake about what you mean. If it involves a warning rather than a more serious penalty, for breaking a safety rule, for instance, don't give this kind of reply: "I'll withhold the warning this time, but next time it happens it won't be so easy for you."

Instead, use this clear-cut approach: "There appears to be good reason to believe that Pete misunderstood what I expected of him. So I'll tear up the warning and throw it away. Next time, Pete, you'll get a written warning. And if it happens a second time, it will cost you a week off without pay."

It is also a good idea to make sure that the worker understands the reasons for your decisions. If a union steward is involved, he can relate these decisions to other workers, too. For instance, in the safety warning case in the last paragraph, the foreman might have said: "Ordinarily, ignorance of the rule is no excuse. The rule is in the employee handbook and has been posted conspicuously in the department. Pete's case seems to be different because he asked me about this rule last week, and he misunderstood what I told him about it. I told him that he was to report any injury he got, no matter how minor, to me before he went to the plant nurse. Pete seems to have thought that he didn't have to report the injury so long as he didn't go to the nurse —which he didn't. I've explained it to him now that I want to know about *every* injury—and I'll decide whether we treat it here or send him to the dispensary."

Must you give your decision right away?

No. But don't sit on it forever. Nothing breaks down the grievance procedure like procrastination. If you can't make up your mind on the spot, or need to check even further than you did originally, tell the employee and his steward that you'll give a definite answer "this afternoon" or "tomorrow." Stick to this promise. If you run into an unexpected delay, let them know about it. Like: "Sorry I can't let you know this afternoon as I'd hoped, because the paymaster has been tied up all morning. I won't be able to check the time sheets with him until late this afternoon. But I will let you know first thing in the morning."

Incidentally, where a steward is involved, get your answer back to him directly. It ruins his prestige in the shop if your decision leaks out before you've had a chance to speak to him in person.

Suppose your boss or his superior asks you to hand down a decision on a grievance that you don't agree with. Should you accept responsibility for it?

This is that old "man-in-the-middle" situation. It's bound to come up from time to time. Sometimes you'll find that company practice is easier on the employee than you think it should be. Sometimes just the reverse—it's tougher than what you'd do if you had no one but yourself to answer to. In either case, *don't pass the buck.* If you as a supervisor say that you agree with the employee but that the plant superintendent can't see it your way, you destroy the whole management teamwork. Teamwork that you'll need to back up *your* decisions, too. If company policy is contrary to yours, try to adjust your own thinking so that it coincides.

Should a supervisor help the employee save face if he's had a grievance go against him?

It seems as if it's asking too much for a supervisor to be noble about winning a grievance—especially when the employee or union has been nasty or aggressive in pursuing it. But here again, it's a bad practice in the long run to make the employee eat humble pie. If you help him save face, he may be considerate to you when the tables are turned. If you rub in the decision, you may irk the employee so much that he'll be on the lookout for a gripe that he can't lose.

This shouldn't be interpreted to mean that you must be so downright nice as to appear as if you were sorry you were right. Try saying something like this: "I've checked your complaint from every angle, but it still looks like 'No' to me. You made two comparisons when you stated that I was playing favorites. In each case the facts show that both men you referred to outranked you both in output and quality of production. On my score card they deserve the better assignments. I'm far from glad that I had to say 'No' to you, Fred. But I am glad that you brought your position out into the open. Perhaps now that I know how you feel, I can give you some help to improve your performance so you can do some of the jobs requiring greater skill."

What's the best way to wind up a grievance settlement?

Carry out your part of the bargain and see that the employee lives up to his. Once an agreement has been made, *follow through on corrective action promptly.* You may lose all the good will you've built in settling the grievance if you delay in taking action.

How important is the grievance procedure as such? Wouldn't it be simpler if employee grievances were all handled informally?

Where a union is involved, the grievance procedure becomes a very important matter. The procedure may vary from plant to plant (see pages 146, 147), but in any case your guide should be: *Know the authorized grievance procedure in your plant and stick to it.* It's up to you, too, to see that the steward also observes the provisions of the grievance clause.

Take special notice of what may appear to be tiny technicalities, and be sure *you* observe them. For instance, some contracts call for the foreman to give his answer within twenty-four hours after the complaint has been presented in writing. Be sure you do, so that you can't be accused of stalling, or even lose the grievance entirely on such a technicality.

Of course, it would be desirable if grievances could all be settled in a casual, informal manner. But where a union is concerned, experience shows that it's best to be businesslike and stick to the letter of the contract procedure. On the other hand, don't get so engrossed with the process itself that you overlook the original purpose of the grievance procedure—to settle grievances fairly and promptly.

What effect will the supervisor's attitude have on grievances?

Even if you settle grievances fairly, if your attitude is unfavorable while handling them, you'll defeat the purpose of giving them your attention in the first place. An employee has a right to expect that he can make his complaints known without prejudice. If you make the employee uncomfortable for having raised the question, he'll resent it. If you show in your future actions that you're prejudiced against him for having made an issue, he'll be reluctant to bring his complaints out in the open again. And it's the accumulation of minor grievances, undiscussed and unsettled, that destroys morale and leads to strikes.

What happens to grievances that go unsettled?

Frequently a supervisor may feel that he's taken care of a complaint just by soft-soaping the aggrieved employee. This is a mistake. The grievance will continue to simmer in the employee's mind, even if he says nothing more about it to the supervisor. And his dissatisfaction is contagious.

An unsettled grievance is like one rotten apple in a basket. It spoils the good ones—the good ones don't make a good apple of the rotten one. When an offended or angry employee is dissatisfied, he tends to make other employees lose confidence in the supervisor. He'll talk about his gripe to fellow workers. It may be that others felt the same way he did in the first place. Now that they see he got the brushoff, they'll go along with his line of thinking. An aggrieved employee talks with his family and friends, too. And they're likely to support his version.

When does a grievance go to arbitration?

Most union-management contract agreements call for a grievance to go to arbitration if the grievance cannot be settled at any of the steps of the authorized procedure. Once the complaint has been turned over to an impartial arbitrator, he acts somewhat like a judge. He listens to the facts as presented by both parties. Then he makes a decision. He does not mediate, that is, try to reopen the discussions between the company and the union. Both parties agree to abide by his decision.

What sort of grievances are the most common?

A study of 1,000 grievances made by the American Arbitration Association Labor Tribunal uncovered some revealing data (Table 18–1).

The balance of the grievances involved policy matters of contract interpretation such as wage-reopening clauses, welfare provisions, and union security. Note that this list of grievances shows those which are hardest to settle at the supervisory level, not necessarily the frequency of all grievances. The great majority of all grievances are settled amicably between the foreman and the worker.

TABLE 18–1

Grievance	Per cent
Discipline cases	25
Job evaluation and work assignments	12
Seniority problems, including promotions, transfers, and layoffs	21
Overtime	5
Vacations	5
Application of incentive plans	2
Holidays	2

Where are grievances most likely to occur?

It's hard to pinpoint just what situations are most likely to breed grievances. But there are some indicators for you to follow:

• First of all, don't lose sight of the fact that grievances are symptoms of something wrong with employees, or with working conditions, or with immediate supervision.

• Secondly, employees are most likely to be worried about situations which threaten their security: such things as promotions, transfers, work assignments, layoffs, the supervisor's evaluation of their performance, mechanization or elimination of their jobs, and so forth.

In your dealing with any of these matters, be especially cautious to assure justice. And continually check yourself to be certain you let employees know in advance about changes—changes in methods, materials, machines, wages, hours, working conditions. When *you* know the facts, these changes may seem insignificant. Unless *your employees* know them, changes may appear frightening to them.

It's easy to see that it would be better to prevent grievances in the first place. What can you do to keep from having to wait until one occurs?

The trick lies in smelling out situations that breed grievances. And then correcting these situations. Don't make the mistake of planting seeds of trouble where it doesn't exist, though. A perfectly happy worker may be able to find *something* to complain about if you ask him directly, "What is there about your job that you don't like?" Better leave that type of open-ended prospecting to company-directed attitude surveys (see pages 30 to 32).

These two things will help you to anticipate grievances:

Looking backward. Analyzing past grievances will give you an inkling of where the trouble spots may be in your department. For this reason, it's a good idea to maintain some sort of record of complaints and formal grievances. You can do this by making notations on a page or two of a pocket notebook. From this you'll be able to glean such leading information as, for instance, where the complaints are originating. If your record shows that in the last four months there have been five serious complaints from employees who work on punch presses, that's your signal to find out what's wrong with the punch press job—machines, men, material, time standards, etc. If your record shows that there have been several grievances involving the way you've handled job assignments, then you'd better reexamine your method of assigning work.

Looking forward. Whenever you handle a grievance, don't drop the matter with your settlement. Explore around a little. See if there are other similar situations in the shop. Perhaps this grievance is an indication of how other workers feel now. By searching out causes and taking immediate remedial action today, you may eliminate similar complaints in the future. That way employees will feel, "You don't have to hit Joe over the head for him to get the idea. He's got the knack of sensing what's eating you without your having to make a big squawk about it."

The Case of the Delayed Reply. A case study in human relations involving grievances, with questions for you to answer.

When Lew first brought his complaint to the attention of his shop foreman, Bob Baker, he felt fairly satisfied. "Bob listened to what I had to say about why I should have gotten the overtime rather than the man from the second shift," Lew told his benchmate. "I can't see how Bob can handle it any other way than to give me what's coming to me." This conversation took place the day after Lew had spoken to his foreman.

Three days later when Lew saw that his paycheck didn't reflect any additional money, he spoke to Bob again. "What happened to that overtime pay I spoke to you about? I figured that so long as I didn't hear from you that the company had approved my request. How long do I have to wait for my money?"

"Well, now," said Bob, "I didn't promise you that you'd get the money. All I said was that I'd look into it. But I've been so busy lately that it clean slipped my mind. Tell you what. I'll go up to payroll this afternoon for sure and find out what can be done."

That afternoon Bob checked the matter with the personnel manager and with his boss. They both listened to the facts. Then they showed Bob that a similar case had been settled at a third-step grievance with the union—with no overtime pay for the employee concerned.

Bob didn't look forward to telling Lew that he wouldn't get the overtime, so for a couple of days he avoided going into Lew's part of the shop. The following payday, however, Lew went up to Bob's desk: "I still didn't get the overtime pay. Are you going to do something about it or aren't you?"

Bob then told Lew that he wasn't entitled to the overtime pay. Lew replied, "We'll see about that. I spoke to my shop steward and he's told me to file a written grievance. He said that's the only way to get any action around here. And I can already see that he's right!"

1. Do you think the written grievance could have been avoided? How?

2. If Lew really had no case, will it make any difference in the long run whether he files a grievance or not? Why?

3. How could Bob have improved his handling of this complaint?

4. If you were Lew, what would you think of Bob as a supervisor?

19 SUPERVISING WOMEN WORKERS

Isn't a woman's place in the home?

Some men seem to think so. But if that's your attitude toward women who work in your plant, you're likely to be in for trouble. The fact of the matter is that almost four million women hold jobs in factories as laborers, machine operators, craftsmen, technicians, engineers, and yes—even as foremen and managers. And there are going to be lots more women working. The Bureau of Labor Statistics of the U.S. Department of Labor estimates that women will make up over half the increase in the American labor force between 1957 and 1967.

Why do women work?

Many women simply have no choice. They must work in order to subsist. A lot of women would be much happier if they could stay at home, but the economics of their situation puts them to work. This goes for women who have to pitch in to support the family as well as for single women and widows who have no other source of support.

Sure, some women will go to work in your plant even though they don't really have to have the money. One woman will want the extra income to keep up with the Joneses, or to help pay off the mortgage, or to send her children through college. Another woman will work simply because she can't stand housework. Still another woman, and this is becoming more and more common among women over thirty-five whose children are past school age, will work simply because time at home hangs heavy on her hands.

And of course there are the hundreds of thousands of girls just out of high school whose parents expect them to work until they marry. A large number of these girls find themselves working the rest of their lives.

What's the secret of getting along with women at work?

There's a formula for success in handling women at work, even though it sounds contradictory. *Treat each woman as an individual, but don't have any favorites.*

Women, more than men, value their individuality. So it won't pay to generalize about the gals who work for you. Steer clear of catch-all opinions like, "All women are flighty." It just isn't so. Mary *may* be flighty. But Sue is thoughtful, Peg is dependable, Anita sticks to her job, Thelma never misses a day. So it goes with any trait.

On the other side of the ledger, women tend to be jealous of any advantage you may appear to give to another. Be as fair as you can when making job assignments. See that each girl has the same working conditions and locker facilities. Don't let anyone be able to say that you grant any of the women working for you unwarranted special privileges.

Are women better at some jobs than at others?

Here too, you'll get lots of arguments based upon individual experiences which vary. Nevertheless, it seems pretty certain that women are exceptionally good at jobs requiring:

Quick fingers. Women have shorter thumbs in relation to their other fingers than men do. And their elbows seem to be slightly "knock-kneed." This combination makes women able to do a variety of light assembly work requiring speed and dexterity of hand and arm.

An eye for color. Women are less likely to be color-blind than men. (They differentiate colors from four to sixteen times better.) This makes women naturals for anything requiring color perception such as lacing color-coded wires in electronic assemblies.

Patience. The social scientists have a hard time backing this one up. But plant supervisors insist that women are better than men at sedentary jobs, bench work, and the like. They haven't the tendency to stretch and roam as much as men do. And they seem to have considerable patience for doing highly repetitive work.

If you're alert to each woman's best talents, you can go a long way toward keeping her happy and productive by seeing that she's assigned to the work she does best.

Where do women workers fall short?

Biggest faults management finds with women workers are absences and turnover.

According to a U.S. Public Health Service study, women lose an average of 10.9 days a year from illness, compared with men's average of 7.5 days. Women over fifty have a much better absence record, however, than younger women.

Turnover is also high among women, principally because of marriage and having children. This is borne out by the records which show that turnover among women over thirty-five is considerably lower than for the younger group.

The records for both absenteeism and turnover, then, are against women, but the evidence also shows that there is much the foreman can do in any plant to improve women's performance in either of these categories.

More than the cold statistics, excessive turnover and absenteeism among women should be looked upon as symptoms of poor morale and poor management. Take a look back at the reasons that women work. A woman comes to work for a variety of reasons. If her work doesn't bring her some measure of satisfaction, it's no wonder she'll seize upon sick headaches to stay away from the factory or quit a job where she doesn't get consideration (for a comparison of older women workers with those under fifty years, see Fig. 20–1).

Aren't most women temperamental?

Women really aren't any more temperamental than men: women just show their feelings much more readily. In a way, this is an aid to the supervisor who wants to repair morale in his department. He often doesn't need an attitude survey to find how women feel. They show their attitudes, while men tend to cover them up.

It's true, of course, that a single woman worker, who is not as dependent on her paycheck as a father with five children might be, can be independent and give vent to her feelings more readily. But the Bureau of Business Practice in New London, Conn., makes this observation: "There are emotional men who go in for a lot of petty gossip and bickering, who come apart at the seams under pressure, who sometimes resort to tears—in short, men who neatly match the description of women in business."

Your best bet is to take a woman's show of temperament or emotion for what it is—a revelation of how she feels. Then try to set the kind of atmosphere in your shop that helps her to feel happy and satisfied at work.

Isn't it true that women take jobs away from men?

That's an old charge. Listen to the reply from Raymond B. Parkhurst, vice president of Hughes Aircraft Company, which employs several thousand women: "Women aren't taking jobs away from men. Women have earned their place in industry through skill and adaptability to the job."

The truth of the matter is that prejudice by men and management in industry has generally relegated women to dead-end jobs and lower pay than men. The women in factory work who hold skilled jobs have had to fight for them. And as America's economy expands, industry needs more and more women to fill jobs that the labor supply couldn't fill otherwise.

Can a woman do every job a man can do?

No. She shouldn't be expected to. Not only does she have her physical limitations, but today almost all forty-nine states have laws which limit women's hours of work and night work. Other laws demand specific lunch periods, seats to avoid constant standing, special rest-room facilities, and limits (usually 25 to 30 pounds) on how much a woman may lift. A few states also forbid employment of women for a certain number of weeks before and after childbirth.

Nevertheless, and despite all these restrictions—legal, physical, and moral—the U.S. Census in 1950 reported one or more women in every occupational classification. In fact there were thousands working as welders, draftswomen, painters, and maintenance workers.

Should women receive the same pay rates as men?

Federal laws on minimum wages, hours of work for overtime purposes, and social security don't differentiate between men and women. But only seventeen states, including Alaska, have laws that forbid discrimination in pay rates because of sex. And by and large, the practice of establishing "women's jobs" has crept into the manufacturing scene.

Most progressive companies, however, adopt the policy of equal pay for equal work regardless of the sex of the person who performs it. This doesn't mean that in many situations light work won't still be considered women's work and heavy work men's. But as modern equipment and material-handling devices lessen the load a worker must carry, capable women should be considered when filling almost any job. It's a waste of manpower and often a destroyer of morale among your women workers if you do differently.

Do working women have fewer accidents than working men?

Women *seem* to have fewer accidents at work than men do, although this hasn't been proved conclusively. What is certain is that the accidents men have are more severe. Some people attribute this record to the practice of assigning women to lighter and less hazardous work.

How should women dress for work?

Slacks give a woman at work more freedom of movement. Hairnets or safety caps keep long hair from being pulled out by the roots by moving machinery. Low shoes are easier on the feet during a long working day than spike heels are. Loose bracelets and dangling jewelry get in the way of what she's doing.

If you're charged with telling a woman what to wear to work, emphasize the reasons why. Try to help her see the rules are for her own protection, not just a meaningless whim. Don't let her think that you're intruding on a woman's prerogative to select her own clothing. In general, if your rules are reasonable, if you are discreet and firm in your enforcement, you shouldn't have difficulty with the majority of women workers.

It's wise, when possible, to permit freedom of choice of regulation clothing. For instance, hairnets can be supplied in many types—single or double mesh—nylon or silk—with or without elastic—straight, medium, or bob size—and in eight different colors.

It's also wise to steer clear, if you can, of the sensitive problem of telling Rosie, the Riveter, that her sweater is too tight. In many cases, you won't have to, for other women workers will, as a group, frequently bring to bear social pressure on Rosie that you couldn't begin to exert.

Do women need more attention than men?

Consideration, yes. Attention, no. A woman likes to feel the boss takes a personal interest in her. She appreciates a big hello in the morning. Many like to be called by their first names. But don't confuse this wish for consideration with a desire to fraternize. Studies made by the U.S. Ordnance Department show that only half as many women as men think of the supervisor's *personal* friendship as being important. In fact, most women prefer to maintain a slight social distinction between themselves and their supervisors.

What kind of supervision do women like best?

Women expect tact, courtesy, and consideration. They want the boss to be impartial and to give work orders courteously and respectfully.

An outstanding supervisor, in the eyes of a woman, is one who is considerate of her personal problems and tries to create a pleasant social atmosphere at work. And, given loyalty in return, a woman employee will be a very loyal member of your team (see Table 19–1).

TABLE 19–1   HOW FEMALE PACKERS SEE
THE IDEAL SUPERVISOR *

Characteristic of supervisor	Preference of worker	All workers, per cent	Female packers, per cent
Sex	Prefer men bosses	80	70
Age	Prefer an over-40 supervisor	50	60
Education	Think high school education is enough	60	60
Length of service	Prefer long-service bosses	60	70
Direction of friendships	Want him to find friends among workers	70	60
Supervision desired	Want democratic rather than autocratic supervision	70	60
Knowledge of workers' jobs	Want him to know every job	60	70
Knowledge of his own job	Want him to be expert at his job	50	30
Consideration for workers	Want moderate consideration	50	50
Fairness toward workers	Expect exceptional fairness	50	90
Clarity in instruction	Place high value on this quality	50	30

* From a U.S. Ordnance Corps study in 1955 of 4,141 civilian workers.

Can women be trusted on secret work?

Wartime work and the employment of thousands of women today in defense-contract plants testifies that they are just as good security risks as men.

Why do women complain so much?

They don't—any more than men do. It's just that when a woman has a gripe, she's likely to be more vocal. One big way to forestall emotional complaints among women workers is to be alert to the problems they have at home. When a man comes to work, he can work off his steam on the job itself. But a working mother or wife carries her home responsibilities with her all day. She isn't so likely to find in her work complete release from her worries. That's where you can do a lot just by showing a friendly interest in her problems.

Incidentally, women are famous for complaining about drafts. You know, some want the windows up, others want them closed? Well, there's a reason for this. Dr. C. P. Yaglou of the Harvard School of Public Health has found that physiologically a woman is more comfortable in a warm room (72 to 76°F) than men, who prefer it cooler (62 to 72°F). By the same token, women can stand the heat (78 to 85°F) better in the summertime than men (75 to 82°F).

The Case of Mary V. A case study in human relations involving supervision of women workers, with questions for you to answer.

In a synthetic-materials plant in Michigan, Larry Clark, the packaging supervisor, placed a notice of a job opening for a labeling operator on the bulletin board in accordance with the union contract. When he took the notice down he was surprised to see that the senior bidder was Mary V. The job had never been filled by a woman before because it occasionally involved lifting 50-pound jugs of glue. The state law forbids a woman to lift anything heavier than 35 pounds in the course of her work. Larry called in Mary to his office. "I'm sorry, Mary, you'd be a good person for this job except that it calls for handling the glue jugs. They weigh 50 pounds, and the law won't permit a woman to do that kind of heavy work."

Mary didn't take this explanation gracefully. "Why use the weight angle as an excuse, Larry? Why don't you admit that you don't want me on this job? If you really wanted to give me a fair deal, you'd change the job a little so that one of the men could give me a hand whenever I have to move a jug. Or I could use a lift truck to do it. During the war when labor was short, you were only too glad to change the job a little to make it possible for a woman to do a man's job."

Larry replied, "That was an emergency. It wasn't the efficient way of doing the work. We have to be sure that each operator can do his job without depending upon help from others. Otherwise there would be a lot of confusion. And some of the fellows would complain that they were being asked to do two jobs. Sorry, Mary, but this job will have to go to a man."

"That's what you say to me," said Mary. "But the fact is that you don't want a woman to get ahead around here. Not unless she's one of those cute little new girls who make eyes at you. If it was one of them, you'd have a different story to tell."

1. What do you think of Larry's excuse?

2. What do you think of Mary's suggestion for changing the job content?

3. Can you suggest a course of action for Larry to improve his relationship with Mary?

4. Do you think Mary is unreasonable? Why?

20 SUPERVISING OLDER WORKERS

Who is an older worker?

That depends on your viewpoint. A survey of 163 companies by *Factory Management and Maintenance* magazine in 1958 shows that few people consider a worker to be older until he reaches fifty years of age. But half of the respondents considered a person between fifty and sixty to be older.

Age affects each person differently. But a good rule of thumb is to look for signs of change due to age in *any employee over fifty years old*. Changes may be physical or mental, slight or marked. Changes may affect the older worker's performance for the better or worse. But change there is. And you should be on the lookout for it and adjust your supervisory techniques accordingly.

Why is the older worker more important to industry today than ever before?

Because half of the ten million workers needed by industry in the United States by 1965 will come from the forty-five-and-over age group. That was the conservative estimate of the U.S. Department of Labor in 1957.

Practically no new male workers will come into the national labor pool in the age group from twenty-five to forty-four. This means that most of the other people entering the labor force will be women, or young men under twenty-four. To keep your operations running smoothly, you'll need to make better use of your aging workers and find useful occupations for the over five million men and women who will be available for work.

How do older workers compare with younger workers as to their desire and ability to hold their jobs?

On the all-important matters of job turnover, older workers stand head and shoulders over younger workers. In a recent (1956 to 1957) study made by the U.S. Department of Labor, workers over forty-five were found to be twice as stable as those under twenty-five. Compared with workers under forty-five, workers over forty-five were considerably superior in their ability to stick to a job. And these findings were generally the same for older women as for older men.

Rather tragically, older workers studied had difficulty finding work. Workers over forty-five made up 40 per cent of all job seekers but found only 22 per cent of the available jobs.

That the importance attached to age has significant differences from industry to industry and from town to town also showed up. In Detroit, for instance, older workers' share of the annual hires was only 15 per cent compared with 30 per cent in Seattle. Apparently, the fast-moving heavy work in auto manufacture is judged by employers to be unsuitable for men over forty-five.

All in all, older workers seem to have the nod by a wide margin if you are looking for reliability and stability.

What are an older worker's chief assets?

He has many. According to Dr. William A. Sawyer, formerly medical director of the Eastman Kodak Company and later medical consultant to the International Association of Machinists, AFL, these are the assets an older worker takes to work with him:

Safety. He has far fewer accidents.

Attendance. He has a better absence record. He's sick less often, although his illnesses tend to last longer than those of younger people.

Experience. The variety of his work and his social experiences tend to improve an older worker's judgment and to familiarize him with a variety of work situations.

Loyalty. Broad experience has helped the older worker to recognize good supervision when he gets it—and to reward that supervision with the loyalty it deserves.

Skill. Once acquired, job skills rarely start to fade before a person reaches sixty, often not until much later.

Steadiness. As seen in the previous question, older workers stick to a job better than younger ones.

What are the older worker's chief drawbacks?

According to Dr. Sawyer, an older worker has many liabilities. But his experience and skills often permit him to compensate for them. On the whole, an older worker tends to be:

Slower. No blinking the fact that age slows athletes and workmen down. But while the older person works more slowly, he may make fewer mistakes.

Weaker. His strength fades too, although by now he may have learned to work more intelligently, not harder.

Less resilient. An older worker hasn't the endurance he once had. Fatigue—mental and physical—sets in faster. And what illnesses and accidents he has keep him off the job longer than they would a younger person. But remember, he's less likely to have either happen to him.

Suffering from poor eyesight. The older person's near vision suffers—he may need bifocals to correct it. But if vision also includes the ability to understand what we see, then the older worker isn't much worse off than his sharp-eyed sons.

In what jobs are you most likely to find older workers?

Skilled, rather than unskilled. In the *Factory* survey, 61 per cent of the older workers were holding skilled jobs, 39 per cent unskilled.

How do workers over fifty years compare with younger workers?

Respondents to the *Factory* survey expressed these opinions:

• Male workers over fifty are generally outstandingly better than younger workers in terms of workmanship, attitude, loyalty, response to supervision, dependability, getting along with others, attendance, accident record, effect on labor relations harmony, number of grievances, and over-all performance. Only areas where they rated poorer were output, ease of training (although their performance after training was better), adjustment to change, and frequency and duration of illness (for statistics, see Fig. 20–1).

• Women workers over fifty followed pretty much the same pattern as older men except for getting along with people (not so good) and performance after training (so-so). And while older men required less on-the-job medical attention than younger men, older women needed about the same as younger women.

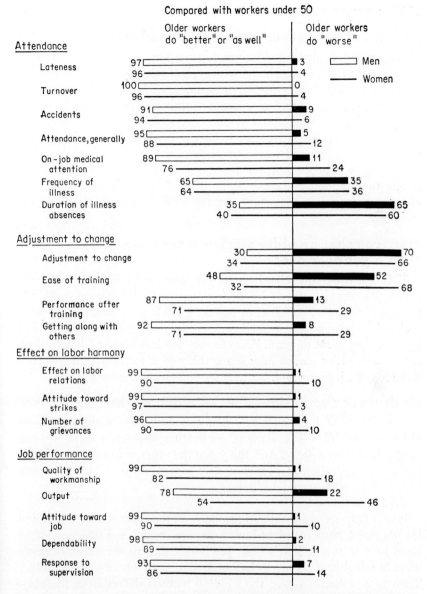

Compared with workers under 50

Older workers do "better" or "as well" | Older workers do "worse"

Attendance

Lateness — 97 / 3 — 96 / 4

Turnover — 100 / 0 — 96 / 4

Accidents — 91 / 9 — 94 / 6

Attendance, generally — 95 / 5 — 88 / 12

On-job medical attention — 89 / 11 — 76 / 24

Frequency of illness — 65 / 35 — 64 / 36

Duration of illness absences — 35 / 65 — 40 / 60

Adjustment to change

Adjustment to change — 30 / 70 — 34 / 66

Ease of training — 48 / 52 — 32 / 68

Performance after training — 87 / 13 — 71 / 29

Getting along with others — 92 / 8 — 71 / 29

Effect on labor harmony

Effect on labor relations — 99 / 1 — 90 / 10

Attitude toward strikes — 99 / 1 — 97 / 3

Number of grievances — 96 / 4 — 90 / 10

Job performance

Quality of workmanship — 99 / 1 — 82 / 18

Output — 78 / 22 — 54 / 46

Attitude toward job — 99 / 1 — 90 / 10

Dependability — 98 / 2 — 89 / 11

Response to supervision — 93 / 7 — 86 / 14

▭ Men
— Women

FIG. 20-1 How older workers compare with workers under 50. From a survey of 163 manufacturing companies employing over 100,000 workers. (Conducted in 1957 by *Factory Management and Maintenance*, McGraw-Hill Publishing Company, Inc., New York.)

219

Does an older worker age all of a sudden?

It may appear that an older employee comes apart at the seams all at once—like the famous one-horse shay. But actually, the aging process is one of gradual decline. As we grow older, we foolishly try to conceal the fact from others and even from ourselves. Then, what has been happening to us over several years is brought to light only when we have a serious illness. If we were to have a physical exam each year, the examining doctor could trace our physical decline as it happens. And would be in a better position to advise us how to adjust our living habits to compensate for our aging. This is why physical exams for older workers are so important—for the worker himself as well as the company.

Is it true that an older worker learns less easily than a younger one?

This is a tricky question because the learning process is so complicated. It's best answered by saying that an older person, with his greater experience, could learn just as quickly as a younger person— *if the older person were as well motivated.* Younger people learn faster because they *want* to learn. Because they see learning as a key to their futures. An older person may see nothing in it for him to learn. He's done his bit, he may feel. So why try to learn something new?

Under what conditions does an older worker learn best?

Knowledge of how well he's doing is especially important to an older person. This is a form of motivation that his experience has taught him to recognize. And the value the older worker places on his pride is so high that, in a learning situation, an error is less acceptable to him than with a younger person.

Take this example:

Pete is fifty-six years old and has been on the same welding machine for ten years. Now his plant buys a gas arc welder and assigns Pete to learn how to run it. Pete's boss, Joe Smith, first shows Pete the many ways in which the gas arc technique is similar to what he's been doing. Then he points out where the welding method differs from the old— and demonstrates what happens if Pete should make a mistake. After Pete has tried out the new machine under Joe's supervision for an hour or so, Joe lets Pete handle it by himself for the rest of the day. First thing in the morning, however, Joe gets together with Pete and inspects the work he's turned out. They agree as to what's acceptable and what's below par. While Joe stands by, Pete reruns the off-quality material until he gets the hang of how to do the job right. Once Pete has the quality problem licked, Joe gives him a pretty specific idea of how fast he's supposed to work. That way Pete can judge for himself if he's turning out enough work.

Day by day Joe lets Pete know how well he's doing as to quality and quantity of work until both Joe and Pete are sure that Pete can handle the job by himself. In other words, Joe hasn't made a nuisance of himself by explaining to Pete the things Pete already knows about his new job. But Joe does emphasize the job's newfangled aspects. And is very definite in letting Pete know how well he's doing.

Under what conditions does an older worker have the most difficulty in learning a new job?

Older adults have the most trouble learning a new skill when that skill conflicts with one they have already learned. Experience grows strong roots. When learning a new skill means cutting off those roots, psychologically the older worker may not be ready to learn something new.

For example, a heat-treater may have acquired great skill over the years in hardening carbon steels. With these steels, rate of heating, control of temperature, and speed of quenching is extremely critical. And the quenching is usually done in water. If you asked this experienced worker to shift his learning gears rapidly by trying to train him to heat-treat high-speed steels, he'd have lots of trouble. High-speed steels aren't nearly as critical to handle as carbon steels, and the speed of quenching differs markedly. And quenching is usually in heated oil.

To make a difficult learning task easier, it's wise to demonstrate to the older worker the similarities between what he's been doing and what you're asking him to do now. For instance, in the case of the older heat-treater, his foreman could show him that the processes for hardening carbon steel and high-speed steel are basically the same, that the differences are mainly a matter of degree. It's always easier for *anybody* to learn if he's moved gradually from the familiar to the unfamiliar.

And here's another point. Rarely is it really necessary for an older worker to learn an entirely new job. It's poor management on your part if you require such a radical change. Why? Because it's just plain smart to keep a man on a job where his previous experience isn't wasted.

At what sort of work will an older person find it hardest to become skillful?

At machine-paced work. Most older workers do much better at jobs they can pace themselves. An older person's loss of speed is often combined with a loss of responsiveness to what a situation demands of him. For instance, a very old person when crossing a street may cautiously look up and down the road to see if there are any oncoming cars. But by the time he evaluates the situation and decides it's safe to cross, he may step into the path of an oncoming vehicle. He simply can't see and analyze a situation fast enough for his decisions to be reliable. The same is true to a lesser degree for almost *any* older worker.

Similarly, many women over fifty have proved to make poor retail salesladies simply because they found it difficult, if not impossible, to pace themselves to the fast-changing sales situation.

For this reason, as a worker's age increases, it's best to assign him to jobs requiring caution and accuracy rather than to those requiring him to react quickly or to keep pace with a machine or a group of faster workers.

How can you motivate the older worker?

By understanding him and helping him to understand himself. As all of us grow older, the gap widens between what we are and what we'd like to be. It's only natural for us to adopt an "I-am-what-I-am" attitude—especially when someone asks us to improve or to change our ways. In fact, the very stability that makes an older worker an asset also makes it harder for him to learn, since this stability is based on his having found contentment with his present lot. So the problem of getting him to want to change, or to do better, resolves itself in *your ability to get him to try.*

To get an older person to try, you must help him to be less critical and less self-conscious of himself. Show him what other older workers are doing—in your plant, if possible. Urge him to talk to others who have changed.

Demonstrate to the older worker, if you can, that even at his worst he'll make fewer errors than a younger person. Let him compare his work records with those of younger persons. If possible, let him make his try at new things in a place where he isn't too conspicuous. It would be a mistake, for example, to announce to the shop, "Old Pete is going to try to learn to operate this newfangled machine." Instead, quietly team up with Pete and make it a problem of both his and your learning something new. Let him see you make mistakes, so he won't feel foolish when he does. Only when he's gained a little confidence, should you let his efforts be spotlighted.

What is it that older employees want from their work?

An older worker isn't much different from anyone else when it comes to looking for satisfaction from his work. His satisfactions differ only in subtle ways such as:

• An opportunity to see his cumulative experience valued and put to use, not thrown aside like an old coat.

• Recognition that his slowing down may affect only one of his capacities, which may be made up for by another of his good points.

• Understanding that job status is still important to him and that changes in pay, title, or position shouldn't be made without giving him due consideration.

• Judgment of his skill and potential on what he is, not on what you may generalize about older people as a group.

How should you advise a worker who is about to retire?

This procedure may or may not be a matter of policy at your company. But one piece of advice seems well worth passing on: *Retirement isn't nearly so bad as most older people anticipate.* According to Dr. Harry Johnson, director of the respected Life Extension Foundation in New York, the idea that most people crack up soon after retirement just isn't so. This opinion is based on a study of 1,546 retired people, and seems to indicate beyond argument that pensioners feel better, not worse, than before retiring and that, if anything, the days pass even more quickly than when they were working.

How can an older worker prepare for a better retirement?

Dr. Johnson has this five-point program to offer:

Be optimistic about your retirement. If you are cheerful, chances are slim that you'll suffer from the retirement blues.

Conserve your health now. Old age won't be much fun unless you're well enough to enjoy it. Best way to assure this is to get a complete physical examination yearly after you reach thirty-five.

Save money for extras. Retirement income including social security may provide only for the bare necessities of life. It's the little extras you can't afford (like a fishing rod, a new camera, or motel rent for a sight-seeing trip) that may make retirement a bore. So start building confidence in your financial future now by buying an occasional share of stock or a small annuity or by setting up a separate bank account.

Insure against a long illness. Most companies don't extend hospitalization or medical-surgical benefits beyond working years. So be prepared to pay for protection after retirement. It's not that sickness is more likely to strike when you're older, but when it does, it's more severe. Disabling illnesses last almost twice as long as when you're younger.

Broaden your social base. As you approach fifty, watch out for a tendency to withdraw from activities outside your home. It's an easy thing to slip into. Instead, check yourself to see if you and your wife still maintain a wide circle of friends. Enter social activities at your church or club. Participate in civic affairs or any action that brings you into contact with people—young as well as old. Not that it's smart to dash around doing things that don't come naturally, Dr. Johnson advises, or to take up a hobby that you're not really interested in just for the sake of having one. Emphasis should be on avoiding the withering of your normal interests because you're growing older.

The Case of Tom Sparks. *A case study in human relations involving an older worker, with questions for you to answer.*

Tom Sparks was fifty-seven. He had been a lathe hand in the shaft department for fifteen years. Truth is that his official title for pay purposes was "lathe operator—turret." But Tom had been around since the days of the overhead-belt drives, and he rarely thought of himself as anything other than a "lathe hand."

One day Tom's boss brought a stranger into the department. "Tom," he said, "this is Mr. Ace, an engineer from the company that made your lathe. He's going to check it over to see if it can be converted to one with a bigger range of speeds, without our having to buy a brand-new one." Mr. Ace looked the lathe over and reported that the conversion could be made. Two months later, the maintenance department mounted a new motor and transmission on Tom's old machine.

Right from the start Tom had trouble with the new setup. It just seemed that he couldn't get the idea that the machine could turn out work as fast as it did. Instead of twenty-five units a day, he was expected to turn out thirty-five a day. Running the lathe was no problem. But loading and unloading that many parts was. He continually lost time between runs. Consequently, his production never reached the expected thirty-five per day.

Finally, after a month with the new drive, Tom went up to his foreman. "You better get someone else to run that lathe the way you've got it fixed up now," Tom said. "I hear there's a job open in shipping that's more to my taste. Will you help me arrange the transfer?"

1. What do you think really bothered Tom about the new setup?

2. If you were Tom's foreman, would you try to persuade him to stay on the lathe job? Why?

3. What could Tom's boss have done to make it easier for Tom to learn how to operate the reconditioned machine?

21 SUPERVISING OFFICE EMPLOYEES

Are office employees a different breed of cats from hourly workers?

From a supervisor's viewpoint, they are. Office workers may have the same number and variety of motives that blue-shirt workers have. But they have them to a varying degree. For instance, job status is of great importance to most white-collar workers, while it is usually only of secondary importance to manual workers. The same is often true of working conditions. On the other hand, wages are of serious importance to both of them.

To supervise office, clerical, and other white-collar workers successfully, you'll have to study their idiosyncracies and deal with them accordingly.

How good is the white-collar worker's morale?

Generally speaking, white-collar workers are pretty cold fish, according to studies conducted by the University of Chicago (see Fig. 21-1). This means that they tend to be neither strongly for nor strongly against their job situation. Net result, however, is that office employees' morale

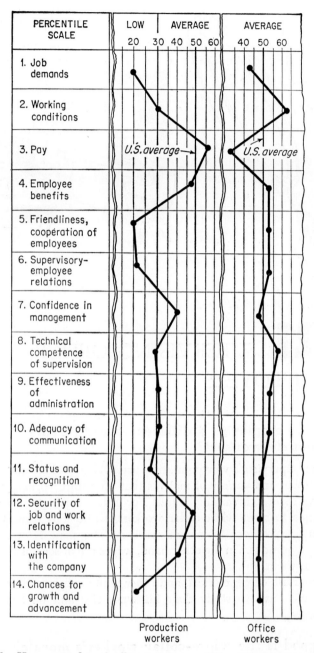

Fig. 21-1 How attitudes of office employees differ from production workers. Heavy zigzag lines show how morale of office employees and production workers is either higher or lower than average for all workers. (David G. Moore and Robert K. Burns, "How Good Is Good Morale?" *Factory Management and Maintenance,* McGraw-Hill Publishing Company, Inc., New York, February, 1956.)

on the whole is better than production workers'. And much of this is attributed to the better working conditions and the correspondingly higher status usually associated with offices.

How important is pay to white-collar workers?

Very important. For years it was a mistaken impression that office workers enjoyed their working conditions and status so much that their wages were of little importance. This isn't true, as the survey figures show. White-collar workers tend to feel underpaid and overworked. Consequently, it's the office supervisor's responsibility to see that the people who report to him are equitably paid. Equitable pay means that people who do the same kind of work in his department get the same kind of pay. Beyond his department, the problem of equitable pay becomes a matter to be settled by company policy.

Isn't it true that office workers are notoriously temperamental?

That's the way the story goes. And there's a certain element of truth to it. First of all, a major portion of office workers are women—and naturally reflect their feminine character (although this has often been greatly exaggerated; see Chap. 19 and Fig. 20–1). Probably more important is the effect of status and the nature of office work.

Most white-collar workers choose that kind of work because it still retains an aura of respectability and dignity not always found in laboring jobs. Is it any wonder that a person to whom social status is important can, with a little help, become a sort of prima donna?

Consider, too, the nature of office work—especially in an accounting situation. In a well-structured system the work must be performed in specific ways—often under close supervision. Strict work requirements and supervisory control create the impression in the employee's mind that his supervisor is technically competent and businesslike. But it doesn't take much to transform this impression into the notion that the organization is cold and like a machine.

Under even favorable circumstances, the supervisor can be regarded as a martinet or, still worse, a kindergarten teacher who treats his employees like children. So you can see you must work hard to guard against creating this impression.

Must white-collar workers be handled with kid gloves?

It helps—as long as there is a firm hand inside them. Remember—white-collar workers choose that kind of work because it implies social distinction. Consequently, they expect their supervisor to act and speak like a gentleman. They won't complain because you're a little stiff and unbending so long as you treat them with genuine respect.

How should you treat the office neurotic?

Every office has one—the poor soul who gets into a tizzy about drafts in the winter, petty jealousies, and imagined insults. Such a problem employee presents a special problem, since other employees will watch closely to see how you deal with him or her. If the office neurotic can get away with murder in other employees' eyes, your healthier specimens will try the same tactics.

You can't ignore the office neurotic. But don't be oversympathetic. Listen to his (or her) gripes politely, but emphasize to him your responsibility to all your employees. Be careful that he doesn't occupy so much of your time that other employees are left to themselves. Try to find ways for him to participate on office committees—where the associations may do him some good and where chances are that he won't be pampered by his coworkers.

Office jobs are routine, often boring. What can you do to relieve the monotony?

Be careful with this one. What may appear to be monotonous work to you may be just what the doctor ordered for your office workers. Unless you see real signs of boredom, don't upset the office applecart by well-meaning, but resented, attempts to liven up the job.

When a worker indicates that he's bored with his job, one sensible move to make is to find ways of varying his daily routine. Can tasks usually done in the morning be shifted to the afternoon? Can he develop for himself a different and more stimulating order of work? Without disturbing the routine of others?

Better still, look for ways to rotate work assignments. If sorting mail is a tiresome job, break it up into smaller pieces so that each of five people share it for only one day each week. Likewise, if the reception desk is a pleasant assignment in your office, don't give this choice plum to only one person. Make it an assignment that several girls can look forward to each week.

In the office, as in the shop, jobs often become boring simply because an employee can't see the point in what he's doing. He feels he's just another cog in a machine. To counteract this form of the blues, sharpen up your listening technique. Ask Joe and Mary for their opinions about office procedures. See if you can't adapt some of their ideas. Let them establish their own way of doing minor tasks. It's said over and over again: To get employees interested in their work you've got to get interested in them.

How do you handle the career-oriented office worker?

The great bulk of office employees are women. Consequently, few of them (in the beginning) view their work as a lifetime career. Handling these employees takes the greater part of your time and your skill. But there is a small, significant group of office employees who desire more from their work than just a place to occupy their time between high school and motherhood. These are career-oriented employees.

The career woman (or man) needs stimulating assignments, a chance to learn—even if there's small chance to get ahead. Be careful not to have this attitude: "What's the point of letting Amy learn how to strike trial balances? She'll never be allowed to become a chief accountant." It's true that in many offices the chances for promotion are limited— especially for women. But nothing dashes cold water into the face of an ambitious person so much as having his boss block his chances for improvement at every turn.

Many people to whom work is a complete outlet will willingly accept broad assignments, won't stand tightly on narrow job descriptions. These willing horses get satisfaction from the importance derived from doing more and doing better. So give them a chance to flex their muscles, so to speak.

What's the chief danger in handling the career man or woman?

You may become so wrapped up in dealing successfully with a career girl that you may do so at the expense of harmony with the bread-and-butter workers in your office. Watch out for developing a crown prince or queen bee in your office. The career girl is a big help, but she's likely to be critical of her fellow workers. She may even take over some of your supervisory load and become bossy. So don't put her in this untenable position. Let other employees know you appreciate her efforts and that you consider her an outstanding employee. But give plenty of your time and consideration to the relatively unimportant people, too. These people make or break the morale backbone in your office.

Do office employees take fringe benefits for granted?

Yes. On the whole, clerical workers don't turn handsprings just because you give them a 15-minute coffee break, for instance. If anything at all, they view fringe benefits negatively. In other words, they're more likely to complain about what you don't give them (and the ABC Co. next door does) than to be much impressed—and grateful—for what you do do for them.

Of what part of their jobs are office employees likely to be most critical?

Your attention to the human side of an office employee's job is likely to be the critical factor of your success or failure in supervising him. Studies show that office employees (particularly women) place high importance on the social and human aspects of the organization. Research at the University of Michigan shows that most supervisors are almost completely unaware of the fact that what office employees like best about their jobs is the kind of people with whom they work. For this reason, you must be especially careful when adding new employees to the work group.

Women, especially, will be critical of others who have better or worse education, dress differently, live in inferior or superior parts of town. The office work group strives for homogeneity. The pressure is strong for conformance. Any newcomer has a hard time breaking down the "typewriter curtain." Off-beat newcomers will find it almost impossible to gain acceptance unless you introduce them gradually—and stand by to give them assurance when needed.

So strive hard to put together people who have similar interests. Don't put too much emphasis on technical skills. A good disposition in a typist will go a long way toward offsetting a slow pair of fingers.

What kind of supervisor do office workers like best?

In a nutshell, office workers prefer supervisors who are (1) considerate of employees' desire to find friends and friendly atmosphere at work, (2) firm and decisive in giving instructions without acting like martinets, and (3) polite and respectful.

Because the office work force is so often dominated by women, you may find Fig. 19–1 a helpful indication of the qualities they like to find in their supervisors.

Why do office workers quit their jobs?

According to the Philadelphia chapter of the National Office Management Association, the reasons vary—according to sex and marital status. The NOMA group checked up on why 1,000 office workers left their jobs in the Philadelphia area. Here are some of their findings:

• A single man is likely to quit within the first year only to resume his education. If he stays with you for a year, he's likely to be permanent—unless somebody offers him more money, a better chance for promotions, or more interesting work.

• A single girl is more than twice as likely to get fired from her job for incompetence than either a single man or a married woman. But if a single girl stays a year, the most likely reason for her to leave after that is for the same reason anyone else does—bigger salary, better opportunity, or more congenial work.

Getting married is nowhere as important a reason for a girl quitting her job as most people believe.

• A married woman usually leaves either because she's going to have a baby or because her husband is transferred. Few married women seem to get fired for incompetence. And very few leave for the reason that single girls and single men do—more money, better opportunity, or more congenial work.

Should you treat your secretary differently from other office employees?

The relationship between a boss and his secretary is a delicate one. Technically, supervising her is just like supervising any other clerical employee. But anyone who's ever had a secretary will tell you that in practice it doesn't work out that way.

First of all, your secretary is doing work for you personally—compared with other kinds of workers who do work as such and are more likely to see their work as being done for the company. And a secretary often has access to confidential matters—both about business and about your own affairs. This makes it difficult to be reserved and impartial in your relationships. On the other hand, you should avoid being too chummy. A dignified distance between boss and secretary will wear better in the long run. Be friendly, but keep your friendliness on the formal side. "Miss Smith" is a good rule from 9:00 to 5:00. If you see her after work, or elsewhere socially, "Gracie" may be all right. In the office it looks better to the rest of the employees—and to outsiders—to be businesslike.

How likely are office employees to be unionized?

While there are notable exceptions, the facts are that there are relatively few office employees who belong to unions. In manufacturing industries, fewer than 8 per cent of all white-collar workers belonged to unions in 1957. And in purely white-collar work, such as in banking, unions have also been notably unsuccessful. In the thirty years preceding 1957, over fifty NLRB representation elections were held for bank employees, but in 1957 the records showed only seven banks with union contracts.

What the future holds is a matter of conjecture. The big unions have avowed that they'll get a bigger share of white-collar workers, especially since the proportion of office and white-collar workers keeps increasing. But chances are that the attraction of unions to white-collar workers will always be less than magnetic. In the main, white-collar workers think differently from production workers about their jobs and status. And office employees will probably continue to view unionism as something beneath their dignity.

Individual cases will differ. Don't be smug in your dealing with office employees because you think they'll never go for a union. Don't think that high pay and flashy fringe benefits will keep unions out of your office. Pay and benefits help—a little. But in the long run, intelligent and considerate supervision is what has kept unions on the other side of the front office.

The Case of the Bulletin Board Notice. A case study in human relations involving supervision of office employees, with questions for you to answer.

When Mr. Bland was hired as supervisor by the claims section of the Granite Surety Corp., he wanted to make a name for himself. He came to the company with broad experience in accounting procedures, and it wasn't long before he had demonstrated his knowledge of the field. In six months he streamlined the tabulating procedures and completely eliminated the need for making hand entries on client file cards. Mr. Bland was often heard to say, "Where there's a machine, there's a better way."

Part of Mr. Bland's improvement program for the claims office was a general sprucing up of the work areas. He persuaded the general manager to repaint the office, install brighter lights, and purchase more modern furniture. The office certainly looked a lot better than it ever had, but some of the old-shoe comforts were lost in the process. Mr. Bland frowned on anything that implied disorder. As a result, he ordered the stenographers to get rid of any pictures formerly pasted on the inside of their typewriter cubicles. Desks had to be cleared every night before going home. But even this wasn't enough.

One day, employees reported to work and found a notice on the bulletin board. It read, "The company has purchased special wax-impregnated dusting cloths. Each employee will be issued a fresh cloth every month. Beginning this week, each employee will wipe down all furniture and woodwork at his work place on Friday before shutting down for the weekend."

That afternoon at 4:15 P.M., Mr. Bland was visited in his office by a committee of three employees. "Mr. Bland," said the spokesman, "we feel we speak for the rest of the office when we say we feel your request that we polish furniture is completely unreasonable. After all, we're employed to perform clerical duties—not menial work."

1. Do you think the employees' complaint was reasonable? Why?

2. What do you think of Mr. Bland's program for improvement of office conditions?

3. In what way could Mr. Bland achieve his objectives and still avoid human relations problems with his employees?

22 HANDLING THE PROBLEM EMPLOYEE

Why worry about problem employees?

Simply because there are so many of them. Authoritative estimates place the number of potential mentally disturbed employees at one out of every four or five American workers.

There are many sociological and humanitarian reasons for being concerned about problem workers. One big reason is that a problem employee is also probably a problem husband, son, or wife. But industry's concern, admittedly, is primarily one of economics. Problem employees are expensive to have on the payroll. They are characterized by excessive tardiness and absences. They are difficult to supervise. And they have a tendency to upset the morale of the work group. Consequently, a supervisor should worry about (1) hiring a problem employee in the first place, (2) handling him on the job so that he reaches maximum productivity with the least disruption of the shop's over-all performance, and (3) determining whether a problem employee has become so seriously maladjusted that he needs professional attention.

Aren't problem employees something new, a kind of reflection on the unsettled nature of our times?

The situation isn't much better or worse than it was forty or fifty years ago. In 1913, the average employment at Henry Ford's plant in Detroit was 14,366. But figures show that 50,488 employees left jobs at Ford that year—an enormous labor turnover! And regardless of Ford personnel policies, this turnover was indicative of the huge number of problem workers who existed even then.

Isn't it wiser to get rid of problem employees than try to rehabilitate them?

It's good business to try to avoid hiring employees who aren't going to get along in your shop. But once a man is on the payroll permanently, it's worth a lot of money to keep him on if you possibly can. In fact, the famous Ford plan of bonus pay and profit sharing was set up in 1914 to try to reduce the excessive cost of labor turnover.

Has anyone been successful in handling problem employees?

Probably the most notable success with problem employees has been that of the Western Electric Company. Back in 1927, the company sponsored a series of research studies aimed at finding the relationship to production of employee working conditions, such as rest pauses and length of work day.

In order to determine how effective the changes were, the researchers started interviewing employees. Then a perplexing change began to take place. Regardless of the mechanical or physical changes made in the working arrangements, productivity seemed to increase. Finally, the researchers realized that as workers were asked for their opinions and were able to register their complaints, these workers became more favorably disposed toward management in general—and actually produced more.

The worthwhileness of letting employees get things off their chest finally proved to be so valuable that Western Electric set up an interviewing (or counseling) program for just that purpose. This talking out their problems changed the nature of the original program to one of employee-adjustment counseling. It began formally in 1936 and supplanted the original program of interviewing for the needs of management.

This discovery of the value of interviewing employees for the purpose of helping them understand their problems is referred to as the *Hawthorne experiment* because it took place at the Hawthorne, Illinois, works of Western Electric. It has provided the basis for much of what we know about getting along with all employees and with problem employees in particular.

How can you recognize an employee with an emotional problem?

There are problem employees, and then there are employees who are *really* problems. The most serious problem employees are those who are emotionally disturbed. And it is very difficult to tell when an employee has crossed over the line into the more serious category. Generally speaking, the symptoms of employees with emotional problems are similar. These people tend to run away from reality. They do this by going on sick leave, by too frequent visits to the dispensary; they believe that their supervisors are against them, blame their continuous failures upon others and other things rather than accepting any blame themselves.

Many problem employees fall into these categories: they are perpetually dissatisfied, given to baseless worries, tire easily, are suspicious, are sure that superiors withhold promotions, that their associates gossip maliciously about them. Some are characterized by drinking sprees, are insubordinate, have ungovernable tempers.

Among themselves, problem employees differ widely, just as more normal people do. But within the framework of their symptoms, they are surprisingly alike in their reactions.

Are emotionally disturbed employees crazy?

Most emotionally disturbed employees definitely are not crazy. In fact, a psychological consultant for Eastman Kodak Company, Ralph Collins, says, "One out of four workers are subject to emotional upsets that visibly disturb their work." Their behavior under certain kinds of stress is not normal. When goaded by fear (such as the threat of a bill collector) or by anger (because of being refused a day off), they may act in a way that you would describe as "crazy." *But they are not* (except for a very few) crazy, insane, or even abnormal.

What about psychotic and neurotic employees?

Both terms sound pretty ominous. But only the employee with a psychosis is seriously ill. Most common type of psychosis is *schizophrenia,* or "split personality." A schizophrenic lives partly in a world of his imagination. Especially when the world seems threatening to him, he withdraws. He may be able to adjust to life, even have a successful career. But when he loses his grip, his problem is way beyond the scope of a layman.

On the other hand, most people are neurotic to a degree. People who have exaggerated fears, who feel the need to prove themselves, or who are irritable, hostile, opinionated, timid, or aggressive (which somewhere along the line describes most of us) have the seeds of neurosis in them. It's when this condition becomes exaggerated that a neurotic employee becomes a problem to his associates and to his supervisor.

A couple of samples of neurotic employees: The lift-truck operator who boasts about his drinking and sexual prowess. The supervisor who gets pleasure from reprimanding an employee in front of others. The mechanic who visits the nurse every other day with some minor ailment. The punch press operator who meticulously arranges his work place in the same manner every day, who can't begin his job unless everything is exactly as he wants it.

What makes problem people problems?

The key lies in the word *adjustment*. Most problems of a neurotic employee are trivial. And he can adjust to them readily. But he may for months, years keep his disturbed feelings hidden—even from himself—then be stricken by a fear that is so great he can't control it. And then he does something that even to himself he can't explain. He has lost, perhaps temporarily, the ability to adjust.

One writer recalls the case of a man who worked on a hand-serviced conveyor.* An industrial engineer studied the job and recommended that the company install a power-loaded conveyor. The man worked on the new conveyor one day, then quit. Why did he do this? Actually his new job was made easier by the power conveyor. But underneath it all, the man couldn't adjust to the power conveyor. It tied him down to one spot and a regular pace. All day he had a sense of working under pressure. He began to fear that if he didn't keep up with the moving line, he'd do something wrong. In other words, the pressure, as he felt it, made the work harder than before.

What sort of management action puts pressure on employees with emotional problems?

All human problems are the result of cause and effect. A supervisor does something and an employee can't adjust—bingo, a human explosion. Typical of some managers who unthinkingly put pressure on workers are:

• The supervisor who thinks it's smart psychology to set production

---

* John Perry, *Human Relations in Small Industry*, McGraw-Hill Book Company, Inc., New York, 1954.

and quality goals just a little higher than an employee can reach. What could be more frustrating?

• The supervisor who thinks it's poor psychology to praise an employee for doing a good job. Is there anything so damaging to a man's morale than to do something well and have it taken for granted?

• The supervisor and management who think that employee relations are better whenever the threat of a layoff hangs over employees' heads.

Are there any problem supervisors?

All too many! Supervisors who preach too much, who are stingy in their interpretation of policy, who assign employees to jobs they particularly dislike, or who continually hold some sort of threat—veiled or otherwise—over their employees' heads.

Then, too, supervisors, especially, are beset with more than ordinary obstacles at work. And not only do they have their own phobias to contend with, they must listen to and try to assuage those of their employees. Is it any wonder that a supervisor occasionally proves himself a problem supervisor by acting irrationally?

What are the signs of a worried worker?

Up until now, we've been discussing the *general* symptoms of problem employees. But you'll be more interested in pinning down the *specific* kinds of behavior that make employees a problem in your shop. That way, you'll be better able to know what to do to aid them. Some specific signs of a worried worker are:

Sudden change of behavior. Pete used to whistle on the job. He hasn't lately. Wonder what's wrong?

Preoccupation. Tom doesn't hear you when you speak to him. He seems off in a fog. When you do get his attention, he says he must have been daydreaming. Is something serious bothering him?

Irritability. Albert is as cross as a bear these days. Even his old buddies are steering clear of him. He didn't used to be that way.

Increased accidents. Bob knocked his knuckles on the job again today. This is unusual. Up until a couple of months ago, he hadn't had even a scratch in five years.

More absences. Rod is getting to be a headache. He wasn't in this morning again. He never was extra dependable, but now we'll have to do something to get him back on the ball.

Increased fatigue. Mary seems to live a clean life and keep good hours. But she complains about being tired all the time. Is it something physical or is she worried about something?

Too much drinking. Ralph was so jittery at his machine this afternoon, I felt sorry for him. And he had a breath that would knock you over. I know he used to like going on the town, but this is different.

What can you do about the problem worker?

Let's make this clear. In this question we are *not* talking about the psychotic person or the one with a serious neurotic disorder. We'll talk about them later on.

You can help the problem employee toward better adjustment only after you have reassured him that you are trying to help him keep his job—not looking for an excuse to get rid of him. No approach does more harm with a person of this nature than the better-get-yourself-straightened-out-or-you'll-lose-your-job attitude on a supervisor's part. You have to believe, and make him believe, that your intentions are good, that you want to help him. Then, you must give him every opportunity to help himself. This approach is called *counseling*.

How do you counsel an employee?

The researchers who conducted the Hawthorne experiments described previously suggested that a supervisor could best counsel an employee if he followed these five rules for his interview:

• Listen patiently to what the employee has to say before making any comment of your own.

• Refrain from criticizing or offering hasty advice on the employee's problem.

• Never argue with an employee while you are counseling him.

• Give your undivided attention to the employee while he's talking.

• Look beyond the mere words of what the employee says—listen to see if he's trying to tell you something deeper than what appears on the surface.

What results should you expect from counseling?

Recognize what you are counseling an employee for. And don't look for immediate results. Never mix up the counseling interview with some other action you may want to take—such as discipline.

Suppose Tom has been late for the fourth time this month. The company rules say he must be suspended for three days. When talking to Tom about his penalty, try to keep the conversation impersonal. Your purpose now is to show him the connection between what he's done and what is happening to him.

Now in the long run you may wish to rehabilitate Tom because he's potentially a good worker. This calls for a counseling interview. And it's better to hold the interview with Tom at a separate time. (Of course, it would have been better to hold the interview before Tom had to be disciplined.)

A counseling interview is aimed at helping an employee to unburden himself—to get worries off his chest. Whether or not the conversation is related to the problem he creates for you at work is not important. The payoff comes as he gets confidence in you—and consequently doesn't vent his resistance and frustrations on the job. Experience seems to show that this will happen if you are patient. Not with every problem employee, of course, but it will with the majority of them.

How do you start a counseling session?

Find a reasonably quiet place where you're sure you won't be interrupted and won't be overheard. Try to put the employee at ease. Don't jump into a cross-examination. Saying absolutely nothing is better than that. If Ralph has become a problem because of spotty work, you can lead into the discussion by saying something like this: "Ralph, have you noticed the increase of orders we're getting on the new model? This is going to mean a lot of work for the shop for a long while ahead. I guess it's meant some changes, too. How is it affecting the operation of your machine? What sort of tooling problems has it created?"

In this case, you are trying to give Ralph an opportunity to talk about something specific and mechanical. If you listen to his ideas, he may begin to loosen up and talk about his emotional problems or his worries.

Another approach is simply to talk to Ralph casually about things he'd be interested in that have no connection with his work. Then let him lead the conversation to the subject that is uppermost on his mind: "Ralph, what do you think of the Braves' chances this year? That's the team you've rooted for, for how many years? Did you used to play ball yourself?"

How many counseling interviews should you have with a problem employee? How long should a counseling interview last?

That's a tough question for a clear-cut answer. For a less serious case, one interview might clear the air for a long time. With employees whose emotional problems are more serious, it may take five or ten 15- to 30-minute conversations just to gain confidence. And with still others, the counseling will have to become a regular part of your supervisory chores with him.

You can readily see that counseling can be time-consuming. That's why it's so important to spot worried workers early. And take corrective action while you can help them with the minimum drag on your time.

As to how long an interview should last—you can't accomplish much in 15 minutes, but if that's all you can spare, it's a lot better than nothing. At the very least, it shows the employee you're interested in his problem. Ideally, an interview should last between three-quarters of an hour and an hour.

How can you best handle these touchy problems objectively?

Make no mistake: handling an employee who has become a problem isn't easy. Sometimes it can become downright unpleasant. And it's only natural to want to duck this responsibility. But the solace you can extract from this is that the sooner you face up to this key supervisory responsibility, the sooner the problems get solved.

To be objective, you must

• Get conditioned to the fact that this is your job and you can't run away from it.

• Look at your task as a fact-finding one—just as in handling grievances.

• Control your own emotions and opinions while dealing with the employee.

• Be absolutely sold on the value of listening rather than preaching.

Finally as a word of caution: *Recognize your own limits in handling these situations.*

How can you recognize when an employee needs emotional first aid?

Dr. Harry Levinson, Director of the Division of Industrial Mental Health, The Menninger Foundation, Topeka, Kans., advises that the basic steps for a supervisor to take in administering emotional first aid are:

• Recognition of the emotional disturbance.

• Relief of acute distress by listening (counseling).

• Referral of cases beyond your limits to professional help.

To recognize the employee who needs help, says Dr. Levinson, look for three major signs:

Extremes. The ordinarily shy person goes even deeper into his shell. The hail-fellow-well-met steps up his social activities to a fever pitch.

Anxiety. If withdrawal or activity brings the employee no relief, he may become panicky, jittery, show extreme tension, flush in the face, or perspire heavily.

Breakdown. If still unable to cope with his anxiety, the problem employee may break down altogether, be unable to control his thoughts, feelings, or actions. His thinking becomes irrational. He doesn't make sense to others. His emotions may become irrational. For instance, the tidy person may become slovenly, the quiet person noisy.

How can you provide relief for the emotionally troubled employee?

Dr. Levinson suggests you may be helpful simply by letting the emotionally disturbed employee know how much his current distress is affecting his job—and how much of this the company will tolerate. After all, a person under strain may add to it materially with fears of what the company might do if and when it discovers his condition. If you can offer some rule of thumb ("Tom, we appreciate the fact that you have something bothering you. And we're willing to go along with your present performance for a couple of weeks or so. But if it doesn't improve after that, we'll have to find a solution.") even if it's not entirely sympathetic, you at least provide something concrete to guide his actions.

If the employee voluntarily brings his problem to you, you can help him most by listening, advises Dr. Levinson. This is more difficult than it appears, he cautions. Listening must mean listening—no interruptions, advice, prescriptions, solutions, pontifications, or preaching.

When should you call for professional help?

Dr. Levinson offers this rule of thumb: *If after two listening (counseling) sessions you seem to be making little headway in establishing confidence, you should report the case (in confidence, of course) to the plant nurse or the company physician.*

If your company has neither nurse nor physician, consult with the personnel manager. There are, in any sizable community, dozens of sources of professional help—psychiatrists, clinical psychologists, and psychiatric social workers to whom the employee can turn in an emergency. And don't overlook the employee's own family doctor.

Dr. Levinson also advises that your approach in referral should be that of opening another door for additional help. Don't ever suggest by action or word that the employee is "crazy," hopeless, or unworthy of attention.

Is an accident-prone employee likely to be emotionally disturbed?

Dr. Gerald Gordon, of the Du Pont company, which has one of the best safety records of any company in the world, has this to say about the subject:

"Our studies have revealed a small group of individuals around whom occupational injuries seem to cluster in disproportionate numbers. Obviously there is something more than hard luck plaguing a man whose career shows a long series of injuries. What's back of his trouble? The answer is that *the accident maker is suffering from a form of mental illness so widespread that it may be found to some degree in most of us.* . . . It is the failure of the employee as a whole person that is the core of his problem. He tends to evade the rules, both of working and of living. . . . In most cases the potential accident victim has a long service record and is well trained for his job. But all too often he's a victim of his own bottled-up emotions, which he turns against himself."

What can a supervisor do about an accident-prone employee?

Du Pont's Dr. Gordon advises that so-called accident-prone employees "can be helped fairly easily if they are discovered early enough and something is done to help them:

"Direct psychiatric work is one way, but this is not always possible if desirable.

"Another approach involves requiring employees to follow safety rules and develop sound work habits. In my opinion, the fact that a worker violates a safety rule is more important than *why* he violates it. Pampering the emotionally disturbed individual only serves to increase his demands and, at the same time, aggravates the severity of his illness.

"If a supervisor openly and honestly exercises his authority to obtain good performance, he is helping both the employee and the company for which they both work.

"On the other hand, a supervisor who evades responsibility for the safety of his men becomes mentally ill himself and spreads this illness to others."

Will counseling help reduce absenteeism?

Most authorities feel that an employee who is chronically absent from work is mentally ill. They reason that the reality of work must be so unbearable to these emotionally disturbed employees that they literally escape from reality by staying away from work.

You can help reduce absenteeism by:

• Firming up your rules about it.
• Being consistent in applying penalties.
• Trying to get at the reasons that an employee is frequently absent.

The last method requires the counseling technique. Widespread absenteeism is cured by getting one person to come to work, then another, and so on. Consequently, it's important that each individual case be followed up promptly. In your discussion of the problem with an employee, be sure to permit him to explain his reactions to the job itself, the people he works with, the working conditions, his tools and equipment, the kind of training he receives, etc. This way, you avoid his feeling that you are placing all the blame on him. And if he is specific in his reactions, you then have specific complaints, rather than vague dissatisfactions, to deal with.

What can you do for the alcoholic employee?

Whatever you attempt, proceed slowly and cautiously. Not every heavy drinker is an alcoholic. And the heavier the drinker, the less likely he is to admit to anyone (even himself) that his ability to handle liquor has got out of his control.

An alcoholic employee is really just another kind of problem employee—only his case is an aggravated one and may need the help of a professional (see next question). Nevertheless, many alcoholic workers have rescued themselves with the aid of Alcoholics Anonymous, an association of exalcoholics who, because they don't preach and because they emphasize the individual's need to face his weaknesses, have perfected the art of listening without being either sympathetic or critical.

Your best bet, however, is to recognize an alcoholic in his early stages. Then use the same techniques to gain his confidence as you would with any other problem employee. Your objective is to provide him with security at work and to help him talk out his problems. If he can be helped to recognize that excessive drinking is a problem he isn't handling, then you can refer him to the company doctor or nurse, who in turn may be able to persuade him to look into Alcoholics Anonymous or to visit a psychiatrist or a special clinic for alcoholics.

To guide you in recognizing alcoholic employees, Professor Harrison M. Trice of Cornell University advises that you look first to the employee's absence record. A sharp rise in over-all rate of absences almost always accompanies the development of drinking problems, he says. In a study of 200 cases of alcoholism in industry, Trice also noted three differences from the normal conception of absences among problem drinkers:

• Absences are spread out through the week. Neither Monday nor Friday absences predominate (probably because the alcoholic is trying to be careful not to draw attention to his condition).

• Partial absenteeism is frequent. A workman often reports in the morning but leaves before the day is over.

• Tardiness is not a marked feature of alcoholism in industry. The widespread notion that a problem drinker comes late to work was not substantiated by Professor Trice's study.

What do the professionals do for problem employees that the supervisors can't?

Two kinds of industrial professionals usually work with mentally disturbed employees who are beyond the supervisor's limits to help adjust:

• The *psychiatrist* is a fully qualified physician who had practiced medicine before qualifying for his specialty. An industrial psychiatrist, because of his training and experience, can diagnose more closely what an individual's trouble is. And prescribe the kind of treatment he ought to have. No supervisor should try to do either.

Actually, few industrial psychologists actually treat their employee patients. They merely try to persuade the employee to seek the kind of psychiatric treatment he needs and also guide the man's supervisor about how to handle him on the job.

• The *counselor,* or industrial psychologist, works with the great majority of emotionally disturbed employees *who do not need full-scale psychiatric treatment.* Because of his specialized training, the counselor's biggest asset is the ability to listen understandingly to an employee's account of his problems. And he has the advantage over the line supervisor, since he doesn't have the authority to discipline, promote, or fire him. Therefore his chances of winning confidence are greater.

The Case of Charlie Zelden. A case study in human relations involving a problem employee, with questions for you to answer.

Fred Wilkes, supervisor of the Century Bronze Co.'s pattern room walked back to his desk with a frown on his face. "Gee," he said to himself, "who ever thought that Charlie would get to be such an old woman? He's getting to be the biggest problem I've got."

Charlie Zelden had come to Century just after World War II. He was a skilled patternmaker of the old school, and Fred had felt lucky in picking up such a good workman. But Charlie hadn't been around long before it became obvious that he had his faults as an employee. He was crotchety and fussy. His tools had to be set up in just the right order. He couldn't work on rush jobs or jobs that required cutting corners. He obviously didn't approve very much of the men he worked with.

Over the years, Fred had felt that Charlie's good points as a craftsman overshadowed his petty gripes and complaints. But in the last year or so, Charlie had become harder than ever to get along with. One day, he'd complain because someone had opened the windows and let in a draft. The next, he'd make a fuss because the engineering department asked for a change that wasn't on his original print. Today, Charlie had said that the light was so poor it gave him a headache. How could Fred expect him to do good work under these conditions?

Day by day, Fred was losing his patience and his sympathy for Charlie. It seemed the more he did to try to help Charlie, the more things Charlie could find that were wrong. What's more, Charlie's talents weren't as hard to do without as they used to be. There were several younger patternmakers who could work rings around him now. And they were a lot easier to get along with.

Fred finally snapped his fingers, then said to himself, "I've made up my mind. Next time Charlie gets out the crying towel, I'm going to turn a deaf ear to him. Or tell him just what I think!"

1. What do you think of Fred's decision?

2. How do you think Charlie will react when Fred tells him what he thinks about him?

3. Why do you suppose Charlie has gotten to be so difficult?

4. If you were Fred, how would you handle Charlie?

4

MANAGING
YOUR JOB

23 PLANNING THE WORK SCHEDULE

The foreman's job is to get out the work. Why should he be burdened with planning and scheduling?

Regardless of how much planning help a supervisor may get from his company's centralized scheduling department, the supervisor just won't be able to turn the work out without detailed planning on his own part.

Turning out the work requires skillful planning right at the department level. Otherwise the supervisor will waste:

* Time—because of avoidable delays.
* Materials—because of haste, spoilage, or unnecessary inventories.
* Machines—because they are not operated to their best capacity.
* Space—because of overcrowding and poor coordination of incoming supplies and outgoing production.
* Manpower—because employees are not fully occupied.

How far ahead should a supervisor plan his work?

Long-range planning should be handled largely by your boss and his superiors. Your target is necessarily much closer at hand. The American Management Association, however, suggests that a supervisor spend 38 per cent of his thinking time on problems that come up the same day,

249

40 per cent for those one week ahead, 15 per cent on those one month ahead, 5 per cent for those three to six months ahead, and 2 per cent for those one year from now.

Check your own habits. If you feel you're too busy to worry about anything but today, chances are you spend most of your time fighting fires that can be avoided by planning a week to a month ahead of time.

Doesn't a supervisor have any say in the company's long-range plans?

He should, even if long-range planning isn't his main responsibility. Many companies make a point of checking with their supervisors about future manpower requirements for proposed schedules, better ways of utilizing equipment capacity, and problems involved in adding shifts. Long-range planning from the top of the organization won't be very successful without a two-way exchange of ideas and information. The more factual and accurate your estimates of future conditions are, the more workable will be the procedures and orders that come back down to you from the company's long-range planners.

In what ways does good planning affect morale?

Employees have confidence in a supervisor who is willing and able to plan their work well for them. One of the worst destroyers of morale is the constant recurrence of emergency situations. Nothing breaks down security like continual crises. Employees don't like change. They fear it and would prefer that the shop was run smoothly all the time. Poor planning adds to that fear. And often hits them where it really hurts—in the pocketbook.

Good planning makes it possible for an employee to go home one night fairly certain of the job he's going to work on tomorrow. It builds his respect for you. He wants the feeling that "they know what they're doing at the plant." If you've shown him that you can schedule work smoothly, an employee will be more willing to pitch in when the occasional emergency arises.

Isn't it true that planning often entails a lot of paper work? Isn't there danger of becoming just another pencil mechanic?

Records and reports are an essential part of planning. But they shouldn't be overdone. Each record should stand the test of "Is this absolutely necessary?" and "Does it give me the specific information, and only that information, I need to plan this job?" The same is true of operating instructions, procedure manuals, and the like. If it takes as much effort to keep them up to date as the effort they save, then do away with them, if you can.

Keep your own planning records simple. Just enough to give you what you need. A large wall calendar is a handy tool. Jot on it the critical items that are coming up in the month ahead. It acts not only as a reminder but also helps you keep your sights on the future.

Another useful device is a pocket notebook with a page for each day of the month. Try to make a habit of writing down in it those items that you must check on from time to time. Put a flag in the notebook a few days before a shipment of supplies is expected, for instance. Then check beforehand to ascertain whether the shipment will be delivered when expected. If it isn't, you've still got time to adjust your plans without waiting to the last minute.

Planning systems are sometimes based on the exception principle. What is it?

Under the *exception principle* of planning, a supervisor sets up a system of records and reports so that recurring problems are handled simply as a matter of routine. These are handled without the supervisor getting into the picture at all. What the supervisor looks for are the exceptions to the routine. He acts only on those items that are unusual or involve change from day-to-day practice.

If a supervisor of a pattern shop, for instance, plans to have fifty forms completed each week during the current month, he'd simply make a daily check of how many forms were finished. Each day he'd enter the number on his calendar (or on a sheet of paper). Whenever the production fell, say, 10 per cent, below fifty forms, he'd note this as an exception that needed his attention. And find out what action was needed to get the production back to normal.

Sound too simple? Actually most record systems are simple in principle. It's when you don't understand them that they get complicated. But even this simple system can warn you of impending trouble. Suppose the pattern-shop foreman put another figure on his calendar each day—the number above or below the production scheduled for the month. If the shop made only forty-nine forms each day, taken one at a time the situation wouldn't look bad. But at the end of ten working days, the shop would be ten forms, or a fifth of a day, behind. This figure is large enough to stand out. And would give the foreman warning in time to step up production to fifty-one forms a day for the rest of the month.

Should you schedule your department to operate at 100 per cent capacity?

No. This is a poor practice, since it leaves no cushion for emergencies. It's best to call on your past experience and plan only for short periods at 100 per cent. No department can run for long in a complicated manufacturing plant without some unforeseen emergency arising. These emergencies may be only unexpected absences or special rush orders. But you must leave room for them.

What should a supervisor do when he is pressured for faster deliveries?

Resist the desire to promise what you can't deliver. Hopes and expectations have no place in planning. Your schedules and promises must be based on fact. Only facts—available equipment and its condition, people and their reliability, material supply and its delivery—can be used as a successful base for planning.

A firm, dependable promise will satisfy most superiors. But don't yield to the temptation to be overcautious. Don't allow for more time than you think the situation actually warrants.

Don't say, for instance, "We can't possibly deliver these parts before the sixteenth," and then finish the job on the eleventh. Others in your plant depend upon the accuracy of your forecasts. If everyone allows too much leeway, that will eat up time and money just as *over-scheduling* might.

Give the best sure date you can figure on. Otherwise you'll lose friends and respect among your associates and your superiors.

When drawing up work schedules, what personnel factors should a supervisor consider?

Planning a work schedule involves many employee variables—all of which must be accounted for in your final plans. Here are some of the most recurrent:

Holidays	Absences
Vacations	Shift rotation
Rest periods	Meal reliefs
Leaves of absence	Quits and discharges
Training time	Time off to vote (where applicable)

How big a job is planning?

A very big one. But you can cut it down to size if you do it in five stages:

Route. Determine the path or sequence the material, work, or task must follow.

Schedule. Set a time for each task of operation to start and finish.

Dispatch. Give the orders (written or oral) to begin work.

Check up. Follow up each job to see that it is proceeding according to plan.

Control. Correct conditions which interfere with your plan. These may be faulty or delayed materials, machine breakdowns, employee trouble of any kind.

If your company has a planning department, what will be the supervisor's main responsibilities?

You'll help most by checking and controlling. And here are some other important things you can do:

• Cooperate with your planning department. It can make your job easier if you'll only let it.

• Follow your schedules carefully. If you know in advance what is expected from your department, you can plan your activities accordingly.

• Find the bottlenecks in your department. Help the planning department to understand how they limit your operations. Many a supervisory complaint about an overload comes down to the fact that he hasn't made the planning department fully aware of the department's limitations.

• Watch the number of setups. Too many reduce your output and raise your costs. When a setup is a long one, check with planning to see if you can produce additional material for stock.

• Notify your superior and the planning department whenever you feel (1) that you can't meet the issued schedule or (2) your department is falling behind schedule.

If your company has no planning department, what can you do to schedule production smoothly and efficiently?

Don't try to fly by the seat of your pants. Work up some sort of schedule and use it as a guide for assigning work and checking up on completions. As each order reaches you, make a rough estimate (based on experience or time study) of how long it will take—the number of man—or machine—hours by operation. Then build up machine loads. At all times, know how many hours of work are ahead of each operator and each machine.

Check regularly with supervisors in the departments before yours and after yours. This way you keep your finger on when to expect goods to work on and when the next department expects goods from you. If your timing gets off, you're likely to have employees standing around waiting for work. Or hear the same complaint from the department that's waiting for goods from you.

Keep an eye constantly on supplies. On a regular basis, check to see that you have enough operating supplies on hand such as raw materials, packaging materials, and any other items which you add to the product in your department.

Each afternoon start checking to see that there will be enough materials and work in process on hand to keep your employees busy the next morning. If you anticipate delays, try to maintain a backlog of low-priority jobs which can be set up and torn down quickly.

What is a Gantt chart? How does a supervisor use it?

The Gantt chart is a very simple device for helping to visualize production progress or machine loading with respect to time. Figure 23–1 is a practical illustration of the Gantt chart used by a departmental foreman for machine loading. Reading from left to right along any horizontal strip indicates the time open (or available) or the time reserved for a certain job.

When a job is scheduled, the foreman estimates the time (in machine-hours) needed. He or his shop clerk then makes a little rectangle (leaving the bottom open) which indicates on the chart the time allotted for the job. Over the rectangle he puts the number of the job. When the job is completed, he draws in the bottom line of the rectangle.

Take the schedule for the 10-inch Hendey, machine No. 497. The chart shows that as of the start of work Tuesday, March 5 (note the V in the date band), there had been scheduled consecutively Jobs 120, 220, 925, 2,312, 248, and 3,814. Jobs 120, 220, and 925 have been completed, as indicated by the heavy lines completing the bottom of the rectangles. Job 2,312 is already half finished (see the heavy bottom line half-closing its rectangle). Jobs 248 and 3,814 haven't been begun. Obviously the Hendey is far ahead of schedule. Consequently the foreman has "overlapped" another job for the Hendey—Job 3,120.

Now look at the 12-inch Pratt & Whitney, Machine No. 76. The foreman has inserted a rush job (2,240) ahead of Job 2,025. As a result, he'll have to block out the time used for the rush job by an X in the future—a full day beginning Wednesday morning.

How can you make a Gantt chart?

To make a Gantt chart for yourself, get a piece of cross-section paper. Divide it up by drawing vertical lines with each block representing an hour, a day, or a shift. The time intervals are up to you and your process. Then draw a series of horizontal lines for each of

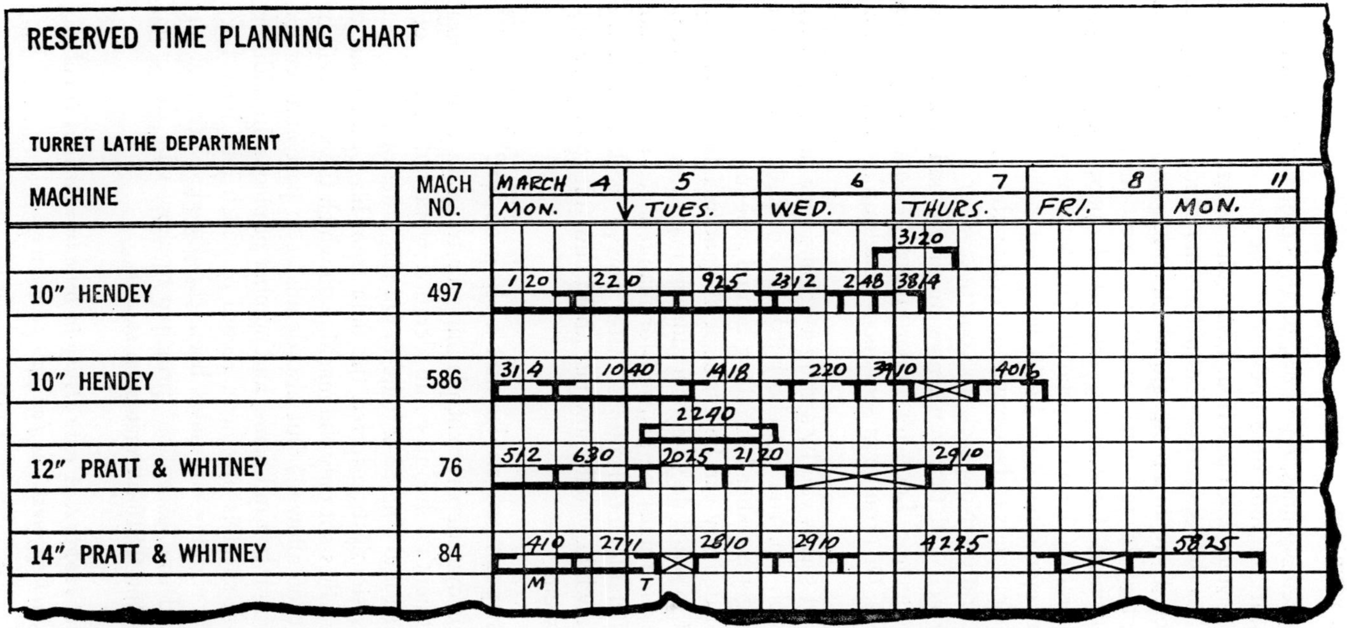

Fig. 23-1. Reserved time planning chart. Used for loading machines and processing equipment. (W. E. Camp, "Planning and Controlling Production," *Factory Management and Maintenance*, McGraw-Hill Publishing Company, Inc., New York, February, 1950.)

the machines, assembly lines, operators, or any other work center you wish to load. Mark in your time intervals at the top as in Fig. 23–1. Then begin with your first operation. Check the orders on hand that can be assigned to that operation. Estimate hours needed to complete the first operation. Draw in a rectangle which corresponds to that time.

Now suppose that this job must have three operations performed on it in your department. Look down your list of operations until you find the next operation. Draw a rectangle for the appropriate amount of time for that operation, only begin your rectangle at some time *after* the first operation is to be completed. Follow the same procedure for the third operation. Now pick up your next order and follow the same process. You'll find that you'll need to juggle and rearrange to find the best sequence. Look for opportunities to combine jobs on similar operations. Or arrange in sequences which utilize the same or similar setups.

The Gantt chart serves you by setting a definite time target for each operation and each job. You can check it hourly or daily to determine whether you are getting ahead or falling behind schedule. And with it, your promises of delivery can be more specific and reliable.

Don't attempt to schedule your operations or machines 100 per cent. Remember that time must be allowed for maintenance and unavoidable or unpredictable interruptions. After you've worked with the Gantt chart for a while, you'll know just about how full you can schedule your department.

How does a supervisor make out a shop order?

If you do your own department planning, or translate your central planning department's schedules into detailed work orders for your department, you'll find Fig. 23–2 helpful. On this order-of-work sheet, the foreman has simply transferred the data from his Gantt chart to a form which specifies not only the machine on which the work will be done (and the time allowed) but also details as to part number and name, employee number and name, and number of pieces. In addition, the order-of-work sheet is used as a record of which jobs have been started, are still running, or have been completed. Note that the foreman has used the "exception" principle to show why the orders numbered 1,418 and 2,810 haven't been started.

The Case of Matt Hopper. A case study in human relations involving work schedules, with questions for you to answer.

When Matt Hopper's boss asked him to see if he couldn't straighten out scheduling bottlenecks in his department, Matt got busy right away. He made a thorough analysis of work loads, manpower requirements, and proc-

ORDER-OF-WORK SHEET

MR. __BRADLEY__   DEPT. __TURRET LATHE__   DATE __MARCH 5__

MACH. OR OPERATOR		ORDER NO.	PART NO.	PART NAME	OPER. NO.	OPER. NAME	NO. OF PIECES		STARTED	RUNNING	FINISHED	REASON NOT STARTED	WILL START
NAME	NO.						TO MAKE	MADE					
10" HENDEY	497	925	B-107356	BRASS BODY-TYPE A	17	ROBERTS	25	25					
"	"	2312	B-03829	" TYPE L	"	"	12	16					
10" HENDEY	586	1040	C-41823	C.I. FLANGE	12	HANSON	30	30					
"	"	1418	C-3182	C.I. HOUSING	"	"	12					GREEN OPERATOR	3/6
12" P.&W.	76	2240	C-42870	C.I. BODY	23	WILSON	20	17					
14" P.&W.	84	2711	S-18703	STEEL SHAFT	7	R. JONES	10	80					
"	"	2810	C-4073	C.I. HOUSING	"	"	12					TOOL TROUBLE ORDER 2711	3/6
12" W.&S.	102	30168	13807	IMPELLER	11	JOHNSON	16	17					
12" W.&S.	103	830	S-8093	STEEL SHAFT	5	T. JONES	30	26					

Fig. 23-2 Order-of-work sheet. Used by supervisor for making work assignments. (W. E. Camp, "Planning and Controlling Production," *Factory Management and Maintenance*, McGraw-Hill Publishing Company, Inc., New York, February, 1950.)

257

ess flow. He designed a form for loading machines and for scheduling work for each operator. And he double checked his plans with his boss and with the production planning department. Everybody agreed that Matt's work schedules ought to now be dependable. Time proved they weren't.

To determine where the difficulty lay, the industrial engineering department sent a methods man in to observe actual practices in Matt's department. Here are some of his observations:

8:00 A.M.: Whistle blows. Of eighteen work places, fifteen are occupied. Only twelve of the fifteen are actually operating.

8:12 A.M.: All work places occupied, fifteen now working.

8:45 A.M.: One work place not occupied, fifteen working, two waiting for material.

9:22 A.M.: Observed one worker watching her neighbor to learn how to work on special job.

11:12 A.M.: Foreman in area. All work places filled, all working.

11:55 A.M.: Fifteen work places occupied, two girls putting on make-up. One girl eating lunch.

12:30 P.M.: Ten work places occupied.

12:35 P.M.: All work places occupied.

1:15 P.M.: One girl reports to nurse with headache.

2:05 P.M.: All work places occupied. Three girls talking with material handler.

3:57 P.M.: Two girls waiting for mechanic to fix soldering irons.

4:17 P.M.: All work places occupied. Seven girls waiting for materials.

1. What do you think may have been wrong with Matt's plans?

2. What are some of the conclusions you'd draw from the engineer's observations?

3. What will Matt have to do to make sure his department meets schedules?

24 TIME–STUDY FUNDAMENTALS

What's the real purpose of time studies?

To figure out ways of saving time or improving its use. And since time is money, saving time helps cut costs in the shop.

Does putting a premium on speed sacrifice quality?

Not if the time studies are set fairly. Skill is a combination of several talents. But to be of commercial value, skill must be applied. Ability to work quickly has proved to be one of the most dependable yardsticks of applied skill.

When setting a time study, it's of first importance that the quality of the unit to be made be very carefully specified. That way the time allowed to do the job is a measure of the craftsmanship needed to do the job according to the quality specifications.

For instance, a time study might show that it takes a standard time of 2.05 minutes to grind a piece to 0.001-inch tolerance and 2.85 minutes to work to 0.0001 inch. The differences in quality desired will show up in the measurement of time needed.

What is meant by *standard time?*

Definitions may differ, but most authorities agree on this: A *standard* is the base time allowed for a defined amount of work to be done to specified quality. *Standard time* is the total allowed time for a job that may include one or more of the defined units of work. Standard time is computed by multiplying the number of good pieces finished by the standard for the particular operation.

For instance, the standard for grinding pieces to 0.001-inch tolerance in the last question is 2.05 minutes. Standard time for a job that requires finishing ten pieces to that tolerance would be

$$10 \times 2.05 \text{ minutes} = 20.5 \text{ minutes}$$

What does *time taken* include?

Time taken is the net actual time worked on incentive. If Pete was assigned the task of grinding the ten pieces to 0.001 inch in the last question and he actually took 17.00 minutes, that would be the time taken. The less time Pete takes to do this job, the more money he saves for the shop. And whether the shop has an incentive plan or not, the more time Pete and others save, the greater the possibility of increased wages for all employees—and lower purchasing prices for customers.

How can the supervisor help save time?

Generally speaking, time studies may only cover the actual work needed to do a certain productive job. Employees may save time on these jobs while the shop as a whole loses time—and consequently money. Time is lost when there are delays. You can avoid delays by seeing that materials are on hand and by supplying employees with the things they need to do their jobs efficiently.

Other delays come about through poor planning and faulty maintenance. Developing the habit of looking ahead and scheduling your shutdowns for repairs goes a long way toward minimizing time lost.

Note that some time standards include allowances for delays. Others do not. It's wise to know if standards in your shop include delays and what they cover. When delays are not included in the standards, it's your responsibility to see that employees get credit for delay time and for necessary extra work.

What is meant by loose standards?

A standard is loose when an average employee working with normal effort is able consistently to undershoot the standard by a very large margin. Most fairly set standards are set with the expectancy that good workers will be able to undershoot them by as much as 25 per cent. Earnings over 133 per cent should be investigated, for they may be loose.

What causes loose standards?

Several factors determine the time allowed in the standard: methods and materials used on the job when studied, the way the job was set up, the way materials were supplied and taken away, the quality specifications, and the method of timekeeping. Changing any of these factors will loosen (or tighten, if the change causes the job to take longer) the standard.

You, as the supervisor, are responsible for observing when any of the original standard conditions are changed. If you slacken your standard of acceptance in order to rush a job through, you help loosen the standard. If you fail to observe and report a change in method or tool used, you help build slack in the standard.

Most foremen are pretty alert to major changes in the way a job is done and quick to report them. But frequently standards get loose, not because of any one big change, but as a result of the accumulation of many minor changes. This is all the more reason you should keep on your toes—and watch for the first signs of a loosening rate—and take action accordingly. This isn't spying, as some foremen seem to think. It's your obligation to the rest of the employees—as well as to the owners who have entrusted the management of their business to you— to protect them from any deviation that inadvertently raises costs and consequently prices.

How do you handle complaints that the standard is wrong?

Time-study men make mistakes. And they do not run the manu- facturing department. That's your job. Along with it goes the re- sponsibility to see that your men get a fair shake.

When one of your employees questions a time-study rate, listen to his objection with an open mind. Perhaps he can tell you about some change in the conditions that does make the rate a wrong one. At any rate, you'll want to get the facts as he sees them.

On the other hand, don't assume the standard is wrong without look- ing carefully at the current job conditions. It may be that methods have been changed, material is off size or condition, the machine is in poor shape, the employee has to hunt for supplies and tools, or he has to wait for jobs.

Ask yourself, too, if you have shown the operator the correct way of doing the job.

Sometimes, of course, investigation shows simply that the complainer just isn't working hard enough to beat the standard.

Isn't there a short cut to the time study?

If you mean, why measure each part of the job separately, why not use the over-all time taken? Then the answer is "No, there is no short cut."

One of the first things Frederick W. Taylor, the father of scientific management, observed was that there was a big difference between what you guessed a workman was doing and what he actually was doing when you watched him carefully step by step. Such breaking down of the job reveals delays and interruptions, which can be eliminated by better management and consequently eliminated from the time allowance. Detailed analysis shows where wrong methods occur and lengthen the time required, or where the effort employed varies widely.

You can have faith in a standard that had been set by detailed breakdown of all the elemental steps of the operation. You're only guessing about standards that have been estimated from an over-all time.

What is meant by *rating*?

Rating is the gauging of the operator's pace as he does the job while observed by the time-study man. The time-study man rates, or compares, the operator's pace with the *normal* pace. The normal pace is, in effect, the *normal* time it would take to do the job.

When an employee is working, he may consciously, or otherwise, work as far below normal as 40 per cent or as much above normal as 200 per cent. The time-study man doesn't wait until the operator works exactly at 100 per cent. It wouldn't be practical. So he rates the operator's pace. And adjusts the actual time measured with his clock by his estimate of the operator's pace.

Take a girl soldering wire-ends to a television chassis. John, the time-study man, times Mary; she makes ten connections. The actual time for each connection is 0.13, 0.12, 0.15, 0.13, 0.12, 0.23, 0.12, 0.12, 0.13, 0.11. John looks the times over and throws out the 0.23 reading as abnormal. Then he totals the remaining readings and divides by 9 to get the average time of 0.12 minute. Now comes the critical phase of time study. John must apply his rating factor.

While he observed Mary making these connections, John mentally compared her pace with what he estimated was a normal pace for that type of operation. His estimate was that she was working at 110 per cent of normal. Therefore the time for the standard becomes not the actual time observed but the rated time, or in this case, 0.12 min/110 per cent = 0.11 minute. You can readily see that no matter how conscientiously or skillfully the rating is made, it is always a matter of opinion. Consequently, it can be a matter of debate. Many of the disputes with labor unions over time studies arise over the rating factor.

If rating is so important, how is it policed?

Integrity of rating is so essential to the acceptance of standards and time studies that time-study people go to great lengths to assure its fairness, reliability, and objectivity. Most time-study men regularly attend rating refresher sessions. In these sessions, they observe motion pictures of operators working at nationally agreed-upon normal pace. One set of films is produced under the supervision of the Society for the Advancement of Management and is generally accepted as standard by most people engaged in setting or arbitrating time studies.

This rating practice helps keep ratings uniform. As a result, good time-study men can judge pace within 1 or 2 per cent. Some firms also help keep their rating estimates consistent by practice-checking operators working against established standards for that company's time-study system.

How do you establish a fair day's work?

Each time-study standard must take into account that it's nearly impossible for a workman to work at a high pace all day long. Fatigue causes most of us to slow up toward the middle of the morning and again toward the middle of the second half of the shift. So a time-study standard must allow time for relaxation. Otherwise it wouldn't be a fair standard. And consequently it would be like asking for more than a fair day's work.

Factors to compensate for relaxation (and to allow for personal time in the washroom, etc.) are usually built into the time standard. This fatigue allowance will vary from about 10 per cent for light bench work to as much as 35 per cent for heavy work, like cleaning molds in a hot and dusty foundry.

For the soldering job mentioned above, the fatigue allowance would be calculated in this manner:

$$0.11 \text{ minute} \times 10 \text{ per cent allowance} = 0.011 \text{ minute}$$

$$\text{Standard time with allowance incorporated} = 0.11 + 0.011$$
$$= 0.121 \text{ minute}$$

Must a job be time-studied to set a standard?

Not if standard data is used. Standard data is simply the recorded summaries of many time studies.

Take the case of a machinist turning down a spindle. Over the years this type of operation has been studied thousands and thousands of times. The standard times for each of separate steps—or elements—in the operation are recorded in charts or tables. These charts can cover practically every possible variation. The table will show the standard time for several varieties of machines and chucks, for carbon and stainless steel, for short spindles and long, for heavy cuts and light, for wide tolerances and narrow.

The time-study man need only analyze the elements in the job, the order in which they are performed, and the number of times they are repeated. Then he looks up in his tables the standard data for each element and adds them up for the standard time for the specific job.

Standard data has proven to be a reliable and often economical way of setting rates.

How much should employees know about time study?

Plenty. If your employees are working on wage incentives, the way in which their earnings are determined shouldn't be kept a mystery.

How do you explain time study to workers?

Building confidence in the honesty of the system is where you should begin. More often than not, once you have shown a workman that you and the time-study man in your department aren't trying to hide something, explanations will be easy. And gripes held to a minimum.

Explanation of time-study methods can be done in group sessions, or you can do it by taking the workmen aside one at a time. In such a case, if you begin with one of the older, more influential, and generally respected employees, he'll be able to help spread the word to others.

Don't talk in generalities, abstractions, or big words. Get right down to cases. Use one of the jobs the employee has worked on as an example. Show him how the job is broken down into elements with a studied time or standard-data time for each.

Don't dodge the issue of rating. Show that rating is designed to protect the workman from a tight as well as a loose rate.

Emphasize that the standard is kept fair by including time for the operator to relax and attend to his personal needs.

Let the employee examine the operation standard and the standard data tables. This will take much of the mystery out of the process—even if he doesn't completely understand the details of the method. Make a point of showing him how important job conditions, methods, and materials are to the standard. This way he'll be more understanding when changes in any one of these conditions changes his standard time.

Impress upon the workman your eagerness to see that he gets credits for extra work or for delays—that your sole interest is to see that everyone makes the best use of his time and that each employee gets all that's coming to him.

All this explanation takes time. But not nearly as much of your time as unreasonable arguments and grievances over standards can cause.

Is there more than one wage-incentive plan?

There are at least twenty-five wage-incentive plans that have been dignified with a name. In the old days some plans were mighty complicated. But the trend today is to keep them simple. This way, not only is the plan easier for the paymaster, but the wage-incentive system is a lot simpler from the employee's viewpoint.

Some of the confusion over wage incentives arises because of the way the money is connected to the time study. Piece rates mean exactly that—so much money per piece. If a workman knows that the piece rate on a mold is 15 cents, he knows he has to make 100 molds that day to make $15. If his base rate is $1.50 per hour, he can see that his earnings are $3, or 25 per cent.

It's more common today to state the standard in time—as so much time per piece (commonly stated in time measurements or in points when the unit-hour * system is used). This way the workman figures his earnings by comparing his actual time taken for the operation with allowed or standard time.

The straight-line incentive system is very popular. It's called "straight-line" because for each 1 per cent production over standard, the employee is paid 1 per cent of his base rate as a bonus. For instance, if the standard time per mold is 6.0 minutes and he finds himself averaging 4.8 minutes per mold, he can easily calculate that his time saving will be 1.2 minutes. Consequently, if he can maintain this pace all day, his incentive bonus will be 1.2/4.8, or 25 per cent.

An older plan that is losing favor, although many companies still use a version of it, is the Halsey Premium Plan. It was also known as

* A unit-hour, or standard hour, is the unit of measure of an operator's effort in doing a normal hour of work. A unit-hour contains 60 standard minutes. In this example, the workman would be producing 75 standard units per hour, or at a rate of 75/60 = 125 per cent.

the Halsey 50-50 Plan because the workman was paid for half the time he saved. If the job was rated for 20 minutes and he took 10, then he got paid for his 10 minutes' work at his base rate plus a bonus of another 5 minutes' pay.

The Gantt plan is also well known. It uses a step bonus for those who make standard. When an operator hits 100 per cent of standard, his hourly base rate is increased so much—say, 10 per cent. When he hits 125 per cent of standard, his hourly rate steps up again—say, to 25 per cent over base.

How good are group incentive rates?

You'll hear a lot of pros and cons about group incentive rates. By pooling all his incentive workers into a group, the foreman can save time making assignments. And this group method cuts down on inspection, timekeeping, and accounting.

But to make the group plan work successfully, you must develop a lot of teamwork among its members. Otherwise, the efficiency of the group tends to be lower than the average efficiency of each employee working individually on incentives. That's because the more highly skilled men tend to slow down if they think they are pulling more than their share in the department. And the fellow who likes to soldier on the job finds a natural cover-up inside the group.

What is *measured daywork?*

Measured daywork really is time study without a wage incentive attached. Jobs are studied and effort measured just as with an incentive system. But no earnings are directly based on the individual's or group's performance against these standards. The foreman uses the standards as an aid to supervision, since they help him plan his work, make assignments, and find out where time is being lost.

Measured daywork is especially useful for indirect labor jobs and for maintenance jobs.

What are *predetermined elemental time standards?*

Predetermined elemental time standards are methods used by industrial engineers and others to measure the time needed for an operator to complete a series of job movements *before* he has actually been trained to do them and *before* anyone observes and times him at the job. These standards have different names according to who developed them. Some of the more prominent are MTM (methods-time measurement), Work Factors, BMT (basic-motion times), ETS (elemental time standards), and DMT (dimensional-motion times).

What is *work sampling?*

Work sampling (also called *ratio-delay*) is another way for measuring work. By making random observations, you can find the ratio of delays, interruptions, or any other work element to the total process time. For instance, if you wanted to find out how much of the time a lift truck was actually out of operation, you'd visit the truck a predetermined number of times a day, say ten. These visits would not be at regular intervals, they would be at random. If in ten days you made 100 observations and during 23 of them the truck was idle, it would be statistically safe to conclude that the truck was idle 23 per cent of the time. You could make the same sort of study on any number of items—so long as you make enough observations and the observations are made at random.

What's the connection between time studies and wage incentives?

Where time studies are used to measure how much a worker produces—and he's paid accordingly—the time studies are said to be part of a wage-incentive plan. Wage-incentive plans enable employees to increase their earnings over their normal hourly rate. Under such a system, the company usually gets its share of an employee's increased productivity two ways: (1) through the assurance the wage incentive gives of the workman fully utilizing his time and effort on the job and (2) by getting maximum usage out of plant facilities and equipment when employees work at optimum effort.

Our national economy gains, too, because effective time-study systems make things cheaper for everyone to buy. Increasing wages by any other method which doesn't depend upon increased output, doesn't help an employee much, either. That's because unless his increases are in *real* wages, they are likely to be followed by price increases (a higher cost of living) that cancels out the raise.

The Case of the Nonincentive Job. A case study in human relations involving time studies, with questions for you to answer.

Jack Burrows had been a press operator at the Pitkin Gear Works for nine years. His foreman for the last three was Bill Sorenson. The two had little or no trouble, and Bill considered Jack a better than average worker, even though he was a bit touchy.

Most of Jack's work was on incentives. He did well and averaged a weekly bonus of about 20 per cent. When Jack had to work on a day-rate job, he was hard to get along with. But he did his assignments well in spite of his grumbling.

There was one nonincentive job, however, that came up regularly three or four times a year. It had never been time-studied although it was a tough one, requiring more than average skill. Bill was in the habit of giving the job to Jack. Jack didn't like this, since it meant he was off incentives for three or four hours each time it came up.

Last week the job came up again. Bill started to give it to Jack, but Jack protested. "Either put that job on incentive or give it to someone else," Jack said. Bill called the time-study department, and a time-study man was sent up immediately.

With the time-study man standing by, Jack began the job at 1 P.M. that afternoon and finished it just before quitting time at 4:25 P.M.

The following day Jack asked Bill what the new rate would be. Bill called the time-study department. He was surprised when the time-study man told him, "The time for that job is 3.25 hours. Jack gave me a hard time yesterday, and I couldn't rate his effort any higher than 85 per cent."

When Bill told Jack what the rate was, Jack blew his stack. "What kind of a racket is this, anyway? I've done that job seven or eight times before and never finished it under three and a half hours. I want that job restudied or I'll never work on it again. Besides, I want back pay for every time I've done it in the past!"

1. If you were Bill, what would you do next?

2. Why do you suppose the job hadn't been time-studied before?

3. What is your opinion of Jack's reaction?

4. Where do you think Bill was wrong in handling the situation up to now?

5. How do you think a similar situation can be prevented in the future?

25 IMPROVING WORK METHODS

What does *methods improvement* mean?

Methods improvement is any change in the way things are being done today that will show up in lower cost or better quality in the finished product tomorrow. The process of methods improvement is simply the organized use of common sense to find better ways of doing work. You need no stop watch, no slide rule, no motion picture camera —only pencil, paper, horse sense, patience, and ingenuity.

More specifically, in methods improvement you put an operation, or a given way of doing a job, under close inspection and analysis. You give it this microscope treatment in order to eliminate every unnecessary step and to find the quickest and best method of performing each of the steps that are necessary.

Is methods improvement known by any other name?

Methods improvement has many names, and it takes many forms. Sometimes it's called *work simplification, time-and-motion study, operations analysis, waste reduction,* or *motion economy.* Some people even believe that mechanization and automation are just advanced forms of methods improvement.

Methods improvement is most generally approached through observing and recording each minute detail of a job, then analyzing the record for ways to do the job better. That's the kind of methods improvement we'll talk about in this chapter. But there are many other approaches (like using motion pictures to observe and record, time-studying, etc.) that can be, and are, used effectively by methods engineers.

Why should the supervisor worry about methods improvements?

Mainly because the squeeze is always on the supervisor to get more and better production at less cost. Work simplification and the like are the most reliable way to increase profits to his company—and to improve wages, salaries, and working conditions as a result.

What can methods improvements do for the supervisor?

The foreman in an efficient shop has an easier job. He needs to spend less time explaining to his superiors the reasons for overtime, delayed deliveries, and high-cost output—and can devote more of his time to supervising his employees and developing their desire to cooperate.

Best of all, the foreman who can advance ways for improving methods gets his light out from under a bushel. It's a wonderful way of gaining favorable attention, which will be weighed when promotions and salary increases are considered.

Where do methods improvements come from?

Any employee can have a good idea. And where a plant has a formal suggestion system, one of its main purposes is to provide a channel for handling employees' ideas. If your plant does not have a suggestion system, you are the most likely one for an employee to bring his suggestions to. Either way, a department whose employees initiate lots of ideas for work improvement makes a supervisor look good. That's one reason why you should encourage them.

The best ideas for work improvement, however, are likely to come from foremen. One authority has estimated that one work-improvement idea from a supervisor is worth ten from an ordinary employee. That's because the foreman has a better overview of the job than a workman. He can see the forest as well as the trees.

In many plants, there is a methods department staffed by methods engineers whose job it is to simplify and improve work procedures. Their job is to help foremen do a better job of lowering costs. They need your cooperation in spotting cost-cutting targets and in making the improved methods work after they are installed. You should form a habit of working hand in hand with the methods department. You can do a lot for them, and they can do much for you.

Can you give some examples?

Sure. Cases in methods improvement can be large or small, simple or involved. Take the job of drilling and tapping a ¼-inch hole. An operator drills first, then sets up and taps. There are two operations performed, but lots of waste effort between operations. Now the job is done with a single tool that has drilling threads on the lower part of the tool and tapping threads on the upper part of the shank. Both operations are done with a single setup.

Another example of methods improvement is in the garment industry. It used to be that a cutter would cut out only one piece of cloth at a time. Now, he stacks as many as a hundred layers of cloth together and cuts out a hundred dresses at a time. He does this with powered shears, whereas in the old days it was done by hand scissors.

Or take this as a case that involves switching to new materials: A plant crates small turbines. It used to take two men an hour to fabricate $9 worth of lumber into a shipping case. Now one man does the job in an hour—using prefabricated, wire-bound crates that cost only $6.

Just by cutting out a job that isn't necessary, precious time and money can be saved. One foreman in a machine shop found by analyzing methods that dozens of machine parts were being finished to higher standards than the actual specification called for. He cut out extra operations by seeing that workmen produced mirror finishes only when specified.

Using a jig or fixture to hold the work in place so that a packer can fold the shipping carton around it with both hands at once saved one plant the equivalent of twelve weeks in labor time in a year.

In the same plant, a man used to haul slat stock from a punch press to a forming machine. Today a simple power-driven conveyor belt costing $3,000 freed this man for more useful assignments in the shop.

Where do you start to look for methods improvements?

Miners say, "Dig where there's the most gold." That's the same as saying, "Look for methods improvements where the most money is spent, where the most people are working, where labor charges are highest, where wasted materials cost most." One big reason for doing so is that your chances to improve methods or eliminate extra operations are most fruitful where a single change will affect repeating operations or operations that are costly to begin with. Another reason is that if your new method indicates a big savings, it's easier to convince others that the change should be made.

Pick a fat target to begin with, not an item that only comes up a few times a month or that isn't in your department more than a few minutes. Look for the jobs that come up frequently, especially the ones you regard as bottlenecks, that take up lots of machine time, that seem to involve lots of chasing around for material, tools, paper work, etc. These are the ones most likely to add up to the big labor charges in your records.

What is meant by breaking down a job?

A *job breakdown* means that you, or any other observer, watches a single job (like filling cans with moth balls) and writes down in sequence each single step (or operation) the workman performs. In the case of can filling, you might record something like this:

1. Pick up empty can with right hand.
2. Look to see if it's upright.
3. Insert under filling spout.
4. Trip filling mechanism with right foot.
5. Fill can (5 seconds).
6. Remove can from pouring spout with left hand.
7. Set it aside.

This is a short breakdown. Some jobs might have as many as fifty or more steps or operations in their breakdown.

Why a breakdown, anyway?

Because it's easiest for you, or for an employee or a methods engineer, to pay attention to one thing at a time. When you make a job breakdown, you list everything that happens—detail by detail—and in the order in which it happens. Then you can study each of the details separately. And unless you've *written down* what you have seen, your breakdown will not be as easy for you to analyze.

What's a flow-process chart?

The flow-process chart is a simple way to pictorialize a job breakdown. It serves as a handy, clear-cut record of how a job was done.

The flow-process chart makes recording your job breakdowns easier, since it uses a kind of shorthand. There are only five symbols to remember:

○ An *operation* is anything that adds value to the product—that changes its physical or chemical characteristics, that assembles or disassembles, that prepares it for another operation, transportation, storage, or inspection. Anything you *do not* classify as a transportation, delay, storage, or inspection is an operation.

⇨ A *transportation* is the work of moving an object from one place to another, to pick up or set aside, etc.

☐ An *inspection* is the work of checking an object for quality, size, weight, or any other of its specifications.

◻ A *delay* occurs when nothing happens to the object, while it is not in storage. An object held in a tote box or bin awaiting the next operation is delayed.

△ A *storage* occurs when an object is kept and protected against unauthorized removal—as in a warehouse.

For further explanations of these flow-process symbols, see Fig. 25–1.

	Wrapping Part	Drill Hole	Typing Letter
OPERATION ○	An operation represents the main steps in the process. Something is created, changed, or added to. Usually transportations, inspections, delays, and storages are more or less auxiliary elements. Operations involve activities such as forming, shaping, assembling, and disassembling.		
TRANSPOR-TATION ⇨	Move Material by truck	Persons Moving Between Locations	Move Material by Carrying (messenger)
	Transportation is the movement of the material or man being studied from one position or location to another. When materials are stored beside or within two or three feet of a bench or machine on which the operation is to be performed, the movement used in obtaining the material preceding the operation and putting it down after operations are considered part of operation.		
INSPECTION ☐	Examine for Quality and Quantity	Review for Accuracy	Checking for Information
	Inspection occurs when an item or items are checked, verified, reviewed, or examined for quality or quantity and not changed.		
DELAY ◻	Material Waiting in "in" Basket	Person Waiting in Line	Waiting for Signature
	A delay occurs when conditions do not permit or require immediate performance of the next planned action.		
STORAGE △	Suspense Copy in File	Material in Warehouse	Filed for Permanent Record
	Storage occurs when something remains in one place, not being worked on in a regular process, awaiting further action at a later date, permanent storage or disposal.		

FIG. 25-1 Flow-process chart symbols with examples of shop and office work. (*Guide for Management Trainers*, AFM 50-19, Department of the Air Force, Washington, D.C., June 1, 1955.)

FLOW PROCESS CHART

SUMMARY						
	PRESENT		PROPOSED		DIFFERENCE	
	NO.	TIME	NO.	TIME	NO.	TIME
◯ OPERATIONS	17					
⇨ TRANSPORTATIONS	4					
☐ INSPECTIONS	1					
D DELAYS	4					
▽ STORAGES	1					
DISTANCE TRAVELED	275 FT.		FT.		FT.	

JOB _Drill, ream, burr, inspect and truck to storage._

☐ MAN OR ☒ MATERIAL _small motor shafts – #2857_

CHART BEGINS _____

CHART ENDS _____

CHARTED BY _Jos. Smith_ DATE _4/8/58_

DETAILS OF (PRESENT / ~~PROPOSED~~) METHOD

	DETAILS	OPERATION	TRANSPORT	INSPECTION	DELAY	STORAGE	DISTANCE IN FEET	QUANTITY	TIME	NOTES
1	Waiting in tote box next machine	◯	⇨	☐	D	▽		1		Part weighs 2½ lbs.
2	Picked up by drill press oper.	◯	⇨	☐	D	▽		1		
3	Loaded into holding fixture	◯	⇨	☐	D	▽		1		
4	Drilled.	●	⇨	☐	D	▽		1		Leland Gifford
5	Removed from fixture.	◯	⇨	☐	D	▽		1		
6	Dropped into portable bin	◯	⇨	☐	D	▽		1		
7	Waits (approx. 2 hours)	◯	⇨	☐	D	▽		1		
8	Trucked to reamer	◯	⇨	☐	D	▽	75	150		By fork lift truck Total wt. – 375 lbs.
9	Picked up by reamer operator	◯	⇨	☐	D	▽		1		
10	Placed in holding fixture	◯	⇨	☐	D	▽		1		
11	Reamed	●	⇨	☐	D	▽		1		Reamer No. 7
12	Ejected by air into tote box.	◯	⇨	☐	D	▽		1		
13	Waits (approx. 1 hour)	◯	⇨	☐	D	▽		1		
14	Dumped into portable bin	◯	⇨	☐	D	▽		150		By operator – hand.
15	Trucked to finishing lathe	◯	⇨	☐	D	▽	50	150		Fork lift truck-375#
16	Picked up by lathe operator	◯	⇨	☐	D	▽		1		
17	Burred on left end	●	⇨	☐	D	▽		1		Polishing lathe No. 3
18	Turned over	◯	⇨	☐	D	▽		1		
19	Burred on right end	●	⇨	☐	D	▽		1		Polishing lathe No. 3
20	Dropped into portable bin	◯	⇨	☐	D	▽		1		
21	Waits (approx. 2 hours)	◯	⇨	☐	D	▽		1		
22	Trucked to inspection station	◯	⇨	☐	D	▽	25	150		Fork lift truck – 375 lbs.
23	Picked up by inspector	◯	⇨	☐	D	▽		1		
24	Inspected.	◯	⇨	☐	D	▽		1		No. 274 gage
25	Dropped into portable bin	◯	⇨	☐	D	▽		1		
26	Trucked to storage in "A" shop	◯	⇨	☐	D	▽	125	150		Fork lift truck -385 lbs.
27	In storage 2 days	◯	⇨	☐	D	▽		150		
28		◯	⇨	☐	D	▽				
29	Note: Operations blacked	◯	⇨	☐	D	▽				
30	in are "Do" operations.	◯	⇨	☐	D	▽				

FIG. 25-2

274

SUMMARY

	PRESENT		PROPOSED		DIFFERENCE	
	NO.	TIME	NO.	TIME	NO.	TIME
○ OPERATIONS	17		10		7	
⇨ TRANSPORTATIONS	4		3		1	
☐ INSPECTIONS	1		1		0	
D DELAYS	4		3		1	
▽ STORAGES	1		1		0	
DISTANCE TRAVELED	275 FT.		250 FT.		25 FT.	

JOB _Drill, ream, burr, inspect and truck to storage_

☐ MAN OR ☒ MATERIAL _Small motor shaft #2857_

CHART BEGINS_____

CHART ENDS_____

CHARTED BY _Jos. Smith_ DATE _4/15/58_

	DETAILS OF (PRESENT PROPOSED) METHOD	OPERATION / TRANSPORT / INSPECTION / DELAY / STORAGE	DISTANCE IN FEET	QUANTITY	TIME	NOTES
1	Waiting in tote box next machine	○⇨☐D▽		1		Part weighs 2½ lbs.
2	Picked up by drill press operator	○⇨☐D▽		1		
3	Drilled	●⇨☐D▽		1		Leland Gifford
4	Dropped into portable bin	○⇨☐D▽		1		
5	Waits (approx. 2 hours)	○⇨☐D▽		1		
6	Trucked to finishing lathe	○⇨☐D▽	100	150		Fork lift truck – 375 lbs.
7	Picked up by lathe operator	○⇨☐D▽		1		
8	Burred on left side	●⇨☐D▽		1		Polishing lathe No. 3
9	Turned over	○⇨☐D▽		1		
10	Burred on right side	●⇨☐D▽		1		Polishing lathe No. 3
11	Dropped into portable bin	○⇨☐D▽		1		
12	Waits (approx. 2 hours)	○⇨☐D▽		1		
13	Trucked to inspection station	○⇨☐D▽	25	150		Fork lift truck – 375 lbs.
14	Picked up by inspector	○⇨☐D▽				
15	Inspected	○⇨☐D▽				No. 274 gage
16	Dropped into portable bin	○⇨☐D▽				
17	Trucked to storage in "A" shop	○⇨☐D▽				Fork lift truck
18	Waits – 1 to 2 days	○⇨☐D▽				Until needed for assembly
19		○⇨☐D▽				
20	CHANGES: Former details 3 and 5 eliminated – can drill without fixture.	○⇨☐D▽				
21	Former details 9, 10, 11, 12, 13, 14, + 15 eliminated by changing drill diameter so that reaming is eliminated	○⇨☐D▽				
22	SAVINGS: 7 operations, 1 transportation, 1 storage, distance traveled 25 ft.	○⇨☐D▽				
23		○⇨☐D▽				
24		○⇨☐D▽				
25		○⇨☐D▽				
26		○⇨☐D▽				
27		○⇨☐D▽				
28		○⇨☐D▽				
29		○⇨☐D▽				
30		○⇨☐D▽				

FIG. 25-2 (continued)

How do you make a flow-process chart?

There are six steps in making a flow-process chart. Try following them on the sample chart, Fig. 25–2.

1. *Choose the job to be studied.* State clearly what the job is and what object (person, part or article, or paper form) you are going to follow on the chart. Stick to that job and the same subject all the way through. Don't change from a person to an object: every detail on the chart must be about the *one* subject. If you want to chart what happens to a person *and* the object he's working on, you'll need a separate chart for each—one that follows the man, the other that follows the part (more about that later).

2. *Pick a starting point and an ending point.* Choose short cycles at first, since they have fewer steps. But once you have decided how much ground you want to cover, write down every step of the job between these two points.

3. *Jot down a short description of each detail.* Don't overlook any detail—no matter how simple or obvious it may appear. Write down each and every operation, transportation, delay, storage, and inspection.

4. *Put in the symbols.* In this example, the foreman has connected the appropriate symbols. Many companies furnish forms that have the five symbols printed in a row at each step. All the foreman does is draw a line connecting the proper symbols from step to step.

5. *Enter the distance and time.* Write the distance in feet for each transportation over one foot. Where the elapsed time seemed especially significant, make a note of it in the time column.

6. *Summarize the process flow.* Do this by counting the number of *operations* in the symbol column and writing the number in the summary block. Do the same for *transportations, storages, delays,* and *inspections.* Enter the total of all distance traveled and total time of the job in the summary block.

How much detail should you include on your process chart?

Better to have too much detail, rather than not enough. Unless the details are recorded, you're likely to overlook them when trying to improve the job method. Once you get the knack of making a process chart, you'll find that it goes very quickly. So don't try short cuts. Include everything.

Will it help to make a sketch of how the job moves?

Yes. If the job involves transportation over sizable distance, a *flow diagram* showing the line of movement helps make the job clearer (see flow-diagram sketch, Fig. 25–3).

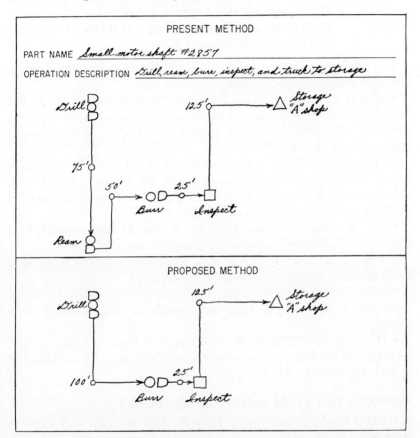

PRESENT METHOD

PART NAME *Small motor shaft #2857*

OPERATION DESCRIPTION *Drill, ream, burr, inspect, and truck to storage*

Drill

125' ———→ *Storage "A" shop*

75'

50' → *Burr* 25' *Inspect*

Ream

PROPOSED METHOD

Drill

125' ———→ *Storage "A" shop*

100' → *Burr* 25' *Inspect*

Fig. 25-3   Flow diagrams for drilling, reaming, and burring a small motor shaft.

How do you find places on the job where methods can be improved?

Ask yourself—and others—questions. Don't assume that the way things are being done today is the best way. Maybe it was a year ago, or even last week. But never come to the conclusion that there isn't a better way. New materials, new tools, new ideas always make a better way possible.

What kind of questions should you ask about the job?

Ask challenging questions, ones that probe into every detail. You're probably familiar with Rudyard Kipling's famous poem:

> *I keep six honest serving men*
> *They taught me all I knew;*
> *Their names are What and Why and When*
> *And How and Where and Who.*

This often quoted poem is your personal key to work simplification. Use it to remind yourself to ask:

• Why is the job done in the first place? Perhaps the job can be cut out altogether. *Why* is each of the details necessary? Give the third degree to each step. Is it really a must, or is it done "because we've always done it that way"?

• What is done? Have you recorded each detail so that you actually *know?* When an operator picks up a part, for instance, he may not only be picking it up, he may be aligning it for insertion into his machine, or feeling the surface for burrs.

• Where is the detail done? Why is it done at that place? *Where* could it be done better, faster, more cheaply, more easily?

• When is it done? Why is it done then? *When* should it be done to do it better, faster, more cheaply, more easily?

• Who does it? Why does this person do it? *Who* might be better equipped, better trained, have more available time to do it more cheaply?

• How is it done? Why do we do it this way? *How* could the method be improved by doing two or more operations at once, by mechanizing it, by using a fixture, etc.?

How can you avoid getting off the beam?

Wishful thinking that "we're doing the best we can" will stand in your way. Avoid making excuses for why things are done in an inefficient way. Dig deep to get the real reasons.

Watch out for words like "maybe," "perhaps," "I think." To make methods improvements, you need facts, not opinions. If a part doesn't fit to another easily, don't accept an answer like, "Maybe it's because it's a little over size." Get a micrometer to see if it is actually over size, how much, and why.

Concentrate on causes, not effects. So the part is three-thousandths over size. You *could* make the other part three-thousandths larger to accommodate it. Or lubricate, or settle for a driving fit. But it's much better to go way back to the job specs, to the machine, to the operator, to your instructions, to find out *why* the part is made over size. Then correct the cause.

In what phase of a job does the greatest room for improvement lie?

In the operations that actually *do* something to the product—shape it, change it, add to it in any way that makes it more worth while. These operations are called the *value-added* operations because they add to the value of the product.

Look at each job as if it were divided into three steps:

Make-ready. This includes the effort and time that goes into setting up the equipment or the machine, or of placing the parts in the machine. A painter makes ready to paint a house by mixing his paint, raising his ladder, spreading his drop cloths, etc.

Do. This is the actual work done that adds value to the product. A painter adds value to the house when he puts a coat of paint on it. A workman adds value to a piece of ⅛-inch iron rod when he cuts it into 2-inch lengths for bolts. He adds value when he heads it. And adds value again when he cuts threads on the other end.

Put-away. This phase covers anything that's done after the "do" is finished. It includes unloading, disposing, storage, transfer, cleanup. When the painter puts away, he takes down his ladder, removes his drop cloth, cleans up any spots on the floor, washes out his brushes, and stores his materials and equipment.

The reason you're advised to concentrate on a "do" operation is that if you eliminate it, you automatically eliminate the make-ready and the put-away associated with it.

What parts of the job are most likely to be wasteful?

Make-ready and put-away details add no value to the product. An operator may spend one minute doing (like drilling), two minutes setting up his tools and clearing them away. Make-ready and put-away details are often easiest to eliminate or speed up through jigs, fixtures, material-handling devices, automatic positioners, etc.

Greatest room for improvement does lie in the "do" part of the job. But this part is frequently the hardest to improve. And since the "do" part adds value and the other two parts do not, you cut out the more obvious waste by concentrating on make-ready and put-away.

How do you develop new methods?

Uncovering delays and finding out what's wrong is a valuable accomplishment, and its worth shouldn't be minimized. But this effort doesn't pay off until you've devised a better way to do the job. There are many approaches from which to choose:

Eliminate. First look for the chance of dropping out the detail or the entire operation. There's no point in wasting time improving methods if the job needn't be done at all.

Combine. Doing two or more things at once saves time. And often it saves additional time by eliminating transportations, storages, and inspections that previously took place between operations.

Change sequence. Frequently you can do things more easily or cheaply by changing the order in which they are done. Ideally a part should be finished, for example, only after the shaping operations have been completed.

Simplify. After you've searched the first three approaches in this list, look for ways of doing the job in a simpler manner. Here's where you try to cut down on waste motions, replace hand operations with mechanical ones, provide fixtures for positioning, chutes for feeding, etc. But remember, don't try to simplify until you've first tried to eliminate, change sequence, or combine.

What is *motion economy?*

Motion economy is the use of the human body to produce results with the least physical and mental effort. It's been given long study by methods engineers and physiologists. Here are some of the principles of motion economy that are generally agreed upon as aids to getting a job done with the least labor:

Motions should be productive. Every motion a person makes should be concentrated on "do" operations, should bring the job closer to a finish. Hands, for instance, should not be wasted by holding the work; they should be released for more productive operations.

Motions should be simple. The fewer parts of the body used, the better. Use a finger and thumb, rather than a whole hand. Grasp an object by reaching with the forearm rather than the whole arm. Motions should be along curved paths, rather than straight lines, since most of the body members swing from a joint in a circular motion.

Motions should be rhythmic. Arrange the work so that it's easy to work with smooth motions. It's easier, too, for hands to move in opposite directions and in similar motion paths.

Make workers comfortable. The work bench, the tool, the chair should all be arranged so that the operator feels comfortable whether his work requires him to sit or stand or walk.

Combine two or more tools. Picking up and laying down tools takes time. It's quicker to reverse a tool with a working edge on either end than to pick up and lay down two separate tools.

Pre-position tools and materials. Having things arranged so that they are already aligned before the operator picks them up speeds up the job. If a part needs to be turned over or around, the job needs positioning.

Limit activity. A person works comfortably within the swing of his arms forward and up and down. If he has to reach or stretch beyond that normal work area, turn around, bend, or stoop, it takes time and is fatiguing.

Use gravity when possible. Materials can be fed by gravity through bins and chutes. This way the part comes out the bottom of the chute right at the worker's hand each time.

What's a Therblig?

The most famous of all motion economy authorities—Lillian and Frank Gilbreth—devised a shorthand of eighteen symbols that can be used to describe any human motion. (Therblig is Gilbreth spelled backwards.) Professional methods engineers use them occasionally, but they are not necessary to you to be effective in your work sim-. plification efforts.

When do you methods-study more than one thing at a time?

Most jobs contain two possible subjects for methods study—the *operator* and the *part* he's working on. Up until now we have been talking about making a flow-process chart for only *one* of the subjects. It is possible to make a flow-process chart that shows what happens to two things simultaneously. In motion-study work, where the methods engineer is trying to find the most economical combination of hand motions, the flow-process chart will frequently contain two columns. In one column is charted what the left hand does, in the other column what the right does at the same time. Such a chart shows when both hands are not working together.

Another valuable two-column flow-process chart is the *man-machine* chart. On this chart the observer records what the operator does and what the machine does. From such a chart, you can determine whenever the machine waits for the man and whenever the man waits for the machine. The first objective in improving methods on machine operation is to see that the machine is used as much as possible. If it's being held up by the operator, you'd try to arrange the operator's job so that he doesn't prevent the machine from running 100 per cent of the time.

If on the other hand, the operator has excessive waiting time, there is always the possibility that he might operate more than one machine at the same time—or devote his waiting time to a productive effort, such as folding boxes, lubricating the machine, etc.

When do methods improvements pay off?

Not until the better method is actually installed. Many a good idea goes for naught just because no one ever acted on it. So when you have an idea for a methods improvement, write it up. And then keep after your boss for a decision. If it's favorable, stick with it until the change has been made. Then do a selling job to show the employees concerned that the method is better and the work is easier and more comfortable. That's the slogan for work simplification—"Work smarter, not harder."

How good are employee suggestion plans for getting ideas from your employees?

It depends upon the company, the way the plan is carried out, and the manner in which the supervisor supports the plan. Some companies have had phenomenal success with plans. Others have laid an egg. The National Association of Suggestion Systems reports that on the average you can expect 238 suggestions per year for every 1,000 eligible employees. And of these suggestions, about 25 per cent will be worth accepting.

To make your company's plan a success, get interested in it. If you adopt a negative attitude, employees will be cool toward the plan, too. Find out what part you play in the plan's administration. And recognize that the degree to which your employees participate will be a measure of how well you stimulate cooperation.

The Case of Bill Sudds and the Methods Engineer. A case study in human relations involving improved work methods, with questions for you to answer.

The Efferson Manufacturing Co. is a first-rate old company that has built a quality line of office accessories for years—inkwells, staplers, dating machines, paper cutters, etc. Recently the company changed hands, and a new management came in to run the plant.

One of the first things the new manager did was to set up an industrial engineering department to study ways and means of improving manufacturing procedures and reducing costs. Mr. Abelson, the industrial engineering manager, was middle-aged, with an excellent record of accomplishment. He had been secured from his previous employer only by the offer of a sizable increase in salary.

Abelson spent the first month on his new job getting his feet on the ground and meeting the various plant foremen. Most of the foremen, who had expected the worst, found Abelson a pleasant surprise. In fact, it was remarked that he seemed to be doing more listening than telling. He certainly gave no evidence of wanting to shake up the plant from bottom to top. There was even some question in the foremen's minds as to when Abelson would begin to earn his keep. Abelson answered that question in February when he began his Methods Improvement Program.

The program began with Abelson calling all the plant foremen together. He carefully explained that the objective of the program was to enable the plant to reduce costs 10 per cent so that products in their highly competitive market could be kept in the line. Abelson said that he expected the foremen themselves to make the greatest contribution to the effort, since they knew more than anyone else about the plant's operations.

After the meeting, Bill Sudds, assembly supervisor and George Keeting, shipping supervisor, talked the program over. It's a matter of record that Bill did most of the talking: "I see that the honeymoon is finally over. I wondered how long Abelson would play cat and mouse with us before he started to tap our brains for all we know. But he'll find it's a long, cold day in July before he gets anything out of me."

1. What do you think of Bill's reaction?

2. How successful do you think Abelson will be with his methods improvement program?

3. If you were Abelson, how would you have gone about selling your program to the foremen?

26 FIGURING AND CONTROLLING COSTS

How important is record keeping to cost control?

Unless you have accurate, available, and up-to-date records, controlling costs is next to impossible. When you say "control," it's the same as saying "keep within limits." If you don't know what the limits are or how well you're holding costs within those limits, how can you take any action?

Isn't there danger in wasting all your time pencil pushing?

Too many records or too much paper work isn't good. A supervisor's main job is to supervise, not to act as a records clerk. But there is a happy medium, and most firms observe it, even though a supervisor sometimes feels he's snowed under by it. One study in Detroit showed assembly-line foremen spending less than 1 per cent of their time on paper work. Another study in a chemical company indicated that record keeping sometimes went as high as 30 per cent. But in the main, it's a rare supervisor who spends more than 5 per cent of his time (or two hours a week) pushing a pencil.

How detailed should cost records be?

To make use of cost records, they should be in enough detail so that the foreman can pick out where his department is out of line and where its performance is satisfactory. You wouldn't get much help, for instance, if all your boss told you was, "Joe. You've got to nip your operating costs. They went 10 per cent over last month." You wouldn't know where to begin. And would probably have to work on hunches.

To determine which costs you ought to know about in detail, find out what costs you are held responsible for. Follow these from month to month. For instance, it's a safe bet that you are held responsible for the following:

Labor costs—direct and indirect. Direct labor varies according to each company's definition, but it generally refers to labor charges for productive employees—those who operate machines, who work on assembly lines, or who fabricate or process materials. Indirect labor usually describes material-handling labor, shipping, and maintenance.

Maintenance and repair charges. This is usually broken down into maintenance labor and maintenance materials—lubricants, replacement parts, etc.

Operating supplies. A foreman isn't usually held accountable for costs of raw materials. But he is responsible for miscellaneous supplies that don't go into the product, like wiping rags, safety clothing, sweeping compounds, etc.

Utilities. Especially in industries (like food plants or chemical or paper plants) where utilities are used in great volumes, a foreman would need to know about his department's use of water, steam, electricity, and fuel.

Waste or scrap. Off-quality material is almost certainly to be pinpointed as a "controllable" cost in your plant.

Many, many more items are often broken out for the foreman's inspection too, like overtime, for instance. An example of one company's cost report to department foreman is shown in Fig. 26–1.

What must you know about accounting?

To understand cost figures, you don't have to know double-entry bookkeeping. But make a point of understanding the accounting terms your company uses. Don't be afraid of appearing dumb. You're a foreman, not an auditor. The accuracy of your accounting department's records often depends on you, so the accountants should be glad to explain their lingo. And if you don't get hep to it, you'll never know

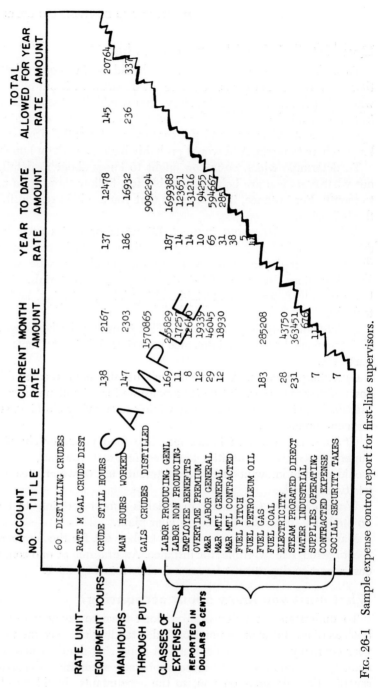

Fig. 26-1 Sample expense control report for first-line supervisors.

whether the expense charges are a true representation of what's going on in your shop.

Won't costs vary according to how much work your department is doing?

Yes. Total costs, studied alone, may have no significance. Suppose labor charges in May were $20,000, then dropped to $15,000 in June. Did you cut costs 25 per cent? You can't tell until you compare the "throughput," or "unit volume," for each month. If the "throughput" were 20,000 units in May and 12,000 in June, then labor costs actually went up.

You'll usually find your costs expressed as "rates"—so many dollars per unit, or per ton, or per gallon, or per dollar value of product. In the case described in the last paragraph, the rate of labor costs in May was $20,000.00 divided by 20,000 units, which is $1.00 per unit. In June it was $15,000.00 divided by 12,000 units or $1.25 per unit. Cost per unit, then, went *up* 25 per cent during the month.

What should you do when your boss says to cut costs?

Some cynical supervisors just run for cover. "Here we go again," is their attitude. "We've been through this too many times to get excited now. This drive for cost cutting will blow over just like all the rest."

Other supervisors get in a sweat, run in six directions at once, lop off a man here, an extra shift there. Anything to cut the total department expense—temporarily at least, even if it affects quality and morale.

A third kind of supervisor takes his time. He doesn't take any action until he's gathered facts and figures. Then he plans a sensible, sure-footed course of attack. He concentrates on the weak spots in the cost armor, gets at the fat where it's easy to cut. His efforts may be unspectacular, may even take a few weeks to show up. But when the record is scrutinized by top plant management, his department is the one most likely to show lasting reductions in cost.

Which supervisor would you like to be? Which supervisor do you think has the most freedom to run his shop? Which supervisor do you thing enjoys his job most? And which supervisor do you think gets the raises and the promotions? Not old "sour grapes!" Not the fumbler! That's for sure.

How can you improve your cost record?

There are five good ways to chop away at costs. Each approach provides you with a different wedge for getting at the roots of each

problem. If one technique won't work, try another—or a combination
of two or three:

Reduce waste. Where can you find waste in materials—raw materials
and operating supplies? How about people, are you wasting their
efforts? Are you getting the most from utilities—or are you wasting
water, steam, electricity?

Save time. Can you speed up or double up your equipment? Will
time studies show you where time itself can be saved? Are you doing
everything you can to get full cooperation from your employees?

Increase output. You can cut cost rates—the cost per unit produced—
by stepping up the throughput in your department. Sometimes there's
a rhythm that goes with high production that's lost with lower production. Sometimes when you cut back, you need the part-time services
of several different people, whereas if you increased output, these same
people would be working 100 per cent of the time. With the higher
output base, cost rates would actually be lower.

Spend wisely. Cutting costs rarely means that you stop spending.
In fact, it's a popular and true expression that "you have to spend
money to make money." And often top management is more alerted to
the need for "spending to save" during a cost-cutting campaign than
at other times. So look for ways to spend money on mechanization or
replacing machines with slow feeds and speeds with newer ones.

Use space more intelligently. Space—for storage, manufacturing,
shipping—costs money. And this cost goes on whether output is high
or low. If you can figure out how to get more use of the same space,
you cut costs. Double- or triple-stacking pallet loads, for instance, cuts
storage charges for space by a half or two-thirds.

When will business get back to normal, so that the pressure for cost cutting will be taken off?

Never. Cost cutting is part of the normal American business economy. It's like death and taxes. There's no escape from the squeeze on
the production supervisor to cut costs. Competition never stands still.
And as soon as a competing company sees that your plant has an edge
in price or in quality, you can bet supervisors in the competing plant
feel the heat for cost reductions or quality improvement the same as
you do. No supervisor anywhere ever "has it made."

How good are one-shot cost-cutting campaigns?

If a cost-cutting drive is a shot in the arm administered to a never-
ending concern for costs, then chances for the drive are pretty good.
If you can recall the six-day bike race with its occasional sprint races,
you'll have a pretty good parallel. The six-day riders raced continu-

ously. But every so often they picked up their pace, and the leader had to sprint faster than the pack for a lap if he wanted to hold his spot out in front.

The "sour-grapes" foreman who looks at each drive as so much nonsense misses the point. New cost-reduction opportunities arise every day. New machines, new materials, new methods, new ideas, new people, new products open more doors to cheaper production than you'll be able to walk through in a lifetime.

Where should you begin your cost-cutting efforts?

Pick the likeliest spots—those which your records show to be out of line with past performance. Be especially critical of operations that show a *trend* upward. Some costs will naturally be up one month, down the next. These may have little real fat in them (although it's worth looking into them to see what causes the variation). Costs that creep steadily out of line might not appear spectacular, but in the long run they hurt most.

One foreman, in checking his cost accounts, noticed that charges for supplies had risen steadily for seven months—up $7.50 one month, up $6.00 another, up $8.00 the next, etc. Month by month the increases were nothing to get excited about. But in seven months this item had shown a net gain of $56.00 *per month!* Even if this expense were now to stay constant at the new level, in a year's time the additional expense would total $672! What was the cause? Seven months ago the purchasing department had changed the supplier of protective aprons all men were required to wear because of the danger from acid splashes. The foreman had heard the men complaining about the inferior quality of the aprons, but he had shrugged it off as just another gripe. Actually, the new aprons were wearing out just a little bit faster than the more expensive kind—but this "little bit more" inched up until it meant $672 per year. How did the foreman correct the situation? He got together with the purchasing agent and the supplier to find an apron that better suited the conditions in the shop—and as a result brought his operating-supplies expenses back into line.

Can you overdo cost cutting?

Yes. It's wise for a supervisor to emphasize economies—even in small things like shutting down motors during lunch time. But if you're penny-wise and dollar-foolish, employees will think the cost effort is a joke. For instance, don't set up a rule that an employee can't get a new pencil unless he turns in a one-inch stub of the old, if at the same time you're spending $100 for new shirts for the bowling team.

Where do you get cost-cutting ideas?

Try these three good sources:

Yourself. Do this by building up a backlog of ideas the year round. Whenever you see something or read about something that might work in your department, jot it down in a notebook or stick it in a folder. Call it your "cost-cutting bank." Then when your attention is drawn to costs for any reason, check over your list to see what might work. (Check Chap. 25 for ways to improve methods and Chap. 35 for ways to get ideas.)

Your employees. Each employee probably knows more about the ins and outs of his job than you do. If you encourage him properly, he's likely to have ideas for cutting corners or cutting waste. Of course, one big way to stop employees from making suggestions is to explain right away why an idea is no good. If you must turn a suggestion down, before you do, examine it from every angle to see if some part of it has value.

Staff departments. If you can pinpoint the areas where cost reduction has the best chance of succeeding, staff specialists like industrial engineers and time-study and methods men frequently can be a big help in devising ways to achieve the reductions. That's their specialty, and they can call on a vast reservoir of examples of how similar reductions have been made in other companies and other departments.

Why are your money-saving ideas sometimes turned down by top management?

Because they don't pay off fast enough. Even though there's nothing much more exasperating to a supervisor than to come up with an idea that might save $250 a year, only to have it rejected by top management, there's often a good reason. If your plan to save $250 a year requires the company to spend $2,000 for new equipment like a conveyor, that means it will take at least eight years for the idea to pay for itself. The cost of financing investments is so great that many companies adopt a policy that a new machine or piece of equipment must pay for itself in five years or less. Some companies insist on a pay-off period of only one year!

What's overhead? Isn't that where the money really goes?

Overhead, or burden, is the charges added to the cost of manufacturing the product. Overhead may include a variety of things right where you can see them yourself—like cost of bookkeeping, mailing, shipping, depreciation of equipment, even maintenance and power if they are not directly apportioned to your unit production. These charges are usually called "factory overhead." "General overhead" includes the cost of advertising, research, selling, etc.

It's common for overhead to be expressed as a percentage of the cost of manufacturing. For instance, say it costs $1.00 to produce a tool in the shop. Factory overhead is 100 per cent, and general overhead is 30 per cent. Here's the way the percentages would be applied:

$$\$1.00 \times 100\% = \$1.00$$
$$\$1.00 + 1.00 = \$2.00 \text{ total factory cost}$$
$$\$2.00 \times 30\% = .60$$
$$\$2.00 + .60 = \$2.60 \text{ total cost}$$

(The method of determining and applying overhead will vary from company to company.)

Now you can understand why a foreman who sees the product turned out in his shop at a cost of $1.00 often feels that the real money is being wasted elsewhere. If you'll look carefully, however, the whole cost picture hinges on how cheaply the product is turned out in the shop. If the shop cost of $1.00 per tool were cut to 90 cents, the total cost would be $2.16 instead of $2.60. That means for a 10 per cent reduction in the direct manufacturing cost, the total cost would be cut 13½ per cent.

Of course, it goes without saying that cost control is just as necessary in all the other company activities as it is in the shop. "It would be foolish to measure shop costs to the fourth decimal point and then spread on the overhead with a shovel," says Phil Carroll, famous cost control authority.

What can you do to cut indirect labor costs?

First of all, let's settle on what indirect labor is. (*Caution:* Definitions will vary in different companies.) According to the accountant, it's all labor not directly applied to the product unit being manufactured. To the supervisor, it's any labor (including his own) that doesn't change the shape, size, or finish of the product. Indirect labor will ordinarily include work done by material handlers, inspectors, maintenance workers, foremen, clerks, superintendents, even works managers.

One way to do something about indirect labor cost is to find out how it normally compares with direct labor charges in your department. Is it one-to-four, one-to-three, one-to-one? If you can get a fix on this ratio or percentage, then you can see whether it's going up or down. And it's likely to go down when you add a new shift or up when you introduce a new piece of direct-labor-saving machinery.

One forging plant found that when it added a new machine, operators then had more time to clean up their work places. As a result, they could do away with the services of a janitor. Time-study analysis and methods improvements are good tools to show up where indirect labor is being wasted. Take a good look at your paper work, too. Maybe it's being overdone, could be reduced enough to drop a clerk.

Why do employees fear cost reduction?

Unless you can sell cost reduction to employees, they are likely to be indifferent at best, rebellious at worst. After all, to employees cost cutting may mean loss of work, overtime, their jobs. They feel that cost cutting threatens their security.

What are some chief criticisms employees have toward cost-cutting campaigns?

Employees working in electrical, textile, and machine-tool industries when interviewed by Fred Rudge, Inc. (management consulting firm) showed a strong conviction that management itself throws away money by poor planning and downright misjudgment as to what's really important—and that applies to supervisors, too.

Here are some direct quotes from workers:

"One man saved the company about $2,000 one day, and the next day he almost got laid off for turning in 20 minutes overtime."

"We put in a new machine, then ripped it apart and sent it away. It probably cost the company $500 to do it. They waste lots of money by not planning the big things."

"They changed construction of this particular item four or five times, got just short of production, and then the whole thing was called off. What that cost I couldn't even guess!"

Sitting as you do on the management side of the fence, you can understand the reason behind many of the moves that look wasteful to employees. But the tip-off for you is that employees frequently don't see the situation the way you do because *no one has taken time to make it clear.*

Your cue to selling cost reduction is to give employees the facts, help them see cost cutting (or profit improvement) as something that helps them, not works to their disadvantage.

What is the union's attitude likely to be?

Here are four common reactions among union leaders:

"Layoffs are prenegotiation steps by the company to scare us."

"These layoffs are aimed to weaken the union."

"Industry is trying to speed up in order to produce the same amount of goods with more profit and fewer jobs."

"Management isn't doing a good job of managing. Why should it tell the workers to do a better job until it mends its own fences?"

Make no mistake about it. If you have a union that actively supports your cost-cutting efforts, you're lucky—and have probably done a good job of showing the true picture of the need to them.

In the face of so many odds, how do you get the need for improvement over to workers?

Remember, biggest fear of both employees and union is immediate loss of jobs. If the big picture means only that jobs will be shuffled, not entirely eliminated, emphasize this point. If there must be layoffs, handle the layoff procedure as well as you can. Show each employee who works for you that you'll do your best to protect *his* job rights (as well as you can in line with the improved methods). Take the lead in talking with an employee about to be laid off to be sure he understands how to handle his insurance and hospitalization, how to apply for unemployment. Can you help him with suggestions about where to get another job? Be sure to tell him about his chances of being recalled to work.

How do you get through employee resistance?

Try these five approaches:

• Talk to employees about cost reduction in terms that are meaningful to them. Get their point of view, or they'll never be able to get yours. In face-to-face conversations, show them how the company's interest in profits is exactly the same as a workman's interest in higher wages and more security. Show that one can't be achieved without the other.

• Get the cost picture down to earth. Don't talk in global terms of standard costs, indirect labor ratios, or even about hard times. If company sales have fallen off, talk in terms of the reduction of specific parts being made in your department: "Where we made 250,000 the first quarter, our schedule calls for only half as much production this quarter." If rising material charges are a factor, pick up a product your employees make and tell them, "Last year, steel for this item cost 55 cents, now it costs 62 cents—a rise of 12 per cent."

• Set specific goals. Don't just say, "We've got to cut costs to the bone." Have a specific program in mind. "Pete, our records show that machine costs have got to be lowered. We'll have to figure a way to use new tools, or change our methods to do this." Or, "Scrap cost us $12,000 last month. This month let's get it down below $10,000."

- Invite participation. Let employees know that you need their help. And that help means more than just cooperation. You'd welcome their ideas about how to go about it.
- Explain why and how. Reasons for a specific change should be spelled out. And employees need your help, too, in deciding how to accomplish the cost-cutting objectives you set.

How should you acknowledge employee suggestions?

If your plant has a formal suggestion system, be sure the employee processes it in writing through the suggestion committee, even if he discusses his idea with you first. Give him what assistance he needs to help work out the bugs. But be sure he goes through the proper procedure to receive full credit and the financial awards his idea deserves.

If your plant has no formal suggestion system, be absolutely sure a workman gets credit for any idea he thinks up or helps to get underway. This is important. Even if it doesn't bring him money, an employee will feel especially cheated if he makes a suggestion and his boss either takes it for granted or lets other people think it is his own idea. So if you want employees to cooperate, show you appreciate their help and want other employees and management people to know about it.

It's always a ticklish situation, though, if an employee suggests a substantial money-saving idea and he gets no financial reward for it. If your plant has no regular way of doing this, you can demonstrate your desire to see him get a share of the savings by going to bat for him with your boss. After that, it's up to the policy of your plant's top management.

Are cost-reduction committees any help?

Many companies have great results using cost-reduction committees to spark a cost-reduction campaign. Committees mean people working together. They provide lots of chances for participation. And committees tap a big reservoir of people for ideas. Doing the job of selling cost can be difficult if you do it alone. If you know others are doing the same thing, it's a boost to your morale.

The Case of Ned Norden. A case study in human relations involving cost control, with questions for you to answer.

Ned Norden had been a plating-room supervisor at the Glossy Trim Company for five years. Ned knew the plating operations from A to Z. When an employee ran into a problem, chances are that Ned would pitch right in. Working alongside the man, Ned would get him out of trouble in no time.

Ned was also known to top management in his company as a man who was willing to cooperate—especially in trying anything new. If the engineers developed a different kind of plating solution, they used to say, "If Ned can't make it work, nobody can."

Since the plating department had been looked upon as process-type operation, the company had never examined the department closely for costs. But when a new comptroller was hired, he put every operation—including plating—under a magnifying glass. His conclusion was that Ned had gotten sloppy about overtime, use of operating supplies, and waste of raw materials. Consequently, Ned was issued a budget for these items at the beginning of the next month.

At the end of the month, Ned's boss called him into his office. "Ned," he said, "In checking over the figures for the plating department this past month, I find you're about 15 per cent over budget. Will you see if you can't bring this back into line as soon as you can?"

The following day, Ned called his work crew together. "Boys," he said, "we've got a real problem on our hands. We have an order from the front office to cut costs in our department 15 per cent. It means there will be practically no overtime for a while. We'll have to watch how often we renew plating solutions. And I want you to keep your usage of sweeping compound, wiping cloths, and aprons to a minimum." Without a dissenting voice, his gang vowed they'd pull together with Ned to make the necessary reductions.

At the end of the next month, Ned was again called into his boss's office. "Ned, I hate to keep making an issue about this cost matter. I know that I rarely have to speak to you twice about any problem in the shop. But the fact remains that your department made no headway whatsoever against costs last month. I'm going to rely on you to make some progress by the end of next month."

Ned again went out to his work group. "Fellows," he said, "you're putting me in a bad light with the front office. We've got to get these costs under control. So I'm depending upon you to give me cooperation."

At the end of that month, Ned's department had cut costs approximately 3 per cent. But by the end of the following month, costs were back to where they were when Ned was first issued a budget. Ned wasn't surprised when he was called on the carpet again. When asked why he had been unsuccessful his reply was, "I can't understand it. I expected the fellows to give me a break. But now I don't know what to do except to get tough."

1. What do you think of Ned's approach to cost cutting?

2. What do you think of Ned's relationship with his employees? Why?

3. If you were Ned, what would you do to get costs back into line?

27 SHOP HOUSEKEEPING

Is the drive for better housekeeping just a frill?

Far from it. Poor housekeeping costs money three ways. It's costly because it interferes with production, because it promotes accidents, and because intermittent cleanup is more expensive than day-to-day good housekeeping. Three testimonials to these conclusions:

• Poor housekeeping breeds poor work habits. Workmanship and product quality suffer. Output frequently falls off. "If one of our shops is having trouble with the quality of its work," says George Hugo, Works Manager for Portland Copper & Tank Works, Inc., South Portland, Maine, "first thing I do is recommend a cleanup and painting job." This isn't foolish. Most authorities agree that employees in a spick-and-span plant do better work.

• The National Safety Council rates housekeeping as the key to accident and fire prevention.

• At a soft-drink plant, girls on the bottling line used idly to paste labels on the conveyor belt while waiting for bottles to come through. The girls were shocked to hear that it cost $12,000 a year to clean the belt because of this habit. When the girls refrained from this practice, the belt was cleaned in half the time at half the cost.

How much does housekeeping cost?

Cleaning up American industry costs over 2½ billion dollars a year, according to some authorities. What it costs in a particular plant will vary from a high in the food industry to a low in the paper-making industry. A rule of thumb would be that for every 200 employees a plant employs, there will be three full-time cleaning people. Of course, this doesn't tell the story of how good the housekeeping is or how much it really costs when you consider the time regular production people may spend housekeeping during the various drives.

What can be done to keep housekeeping costs down?

It may seem like a hard thing to say, but the facts support it: *The excessive cost of housekeeping is directly attributable to workers and their supervisors.* This comes about for three reasons:

• Poor shop layout or unauthorized rearrangement of equipment.
• Improper handling and storage of materials.
• Plain uncleanliness and disorder.

Higher management, of course, must share the blame with its supervisors—especially for poor shop layout and for poor housekeeping that arises from faulty equipment or inadequate sanitation equipment. But even in traditionally dirty industries, like foundry work, responsible, aggressive supervision together with properly motivated employees have ably demonstrated that they can keep the working places neat and clean.

Why are so many employees untidy in their work habits?

Cleanliness and sanitation are earmarks of civilization. Savages from the natives of the Belgian Congo to the American Indians have been notorious for their disregard of the minimum standard of personal and household hygiene. And we too, even today, reflect our uncivilized heritage. We tend, as do most industrial employees, to be oblivious of the dirt we cause through plain carelessness. We need to be sold on the value of good housekeeping before we can ever sell it to plant employees. And we must recognize that good housekeeping isn't something that just comes naturally.

How can you sell a housekeeping program?

Housekeeping isn't something that can be forced on people. But it is something that can be sold. That's because housekeeping has many personal payoffs for those who practice it. When talking about better housekeeping to employees, don't present it in terms of just something the boss wants—"We'll catch the devil if it isn't improved." Instead, show how good housekeeping improves the safety record and makes the shop a safer place for employees to work. Emphasize that house-keeping actually makes production easier and quicker, that clean and neat surroundings take much of the drudgery out of work—and keep clothing cleaner, too. Remember, there is still considerable status attached to the man who can come to work in a white shirt if he chooses.

Nothing is so convincing to an employee as a demonstration of what good housekeeping is—and what it can do for him. Many people are puzzled when told to clean up. Each person has his own standards of what "clean" is, and these standards differ widely. So take a section of your shop and see that it is arranged and cleaned to a minimum of what you judge can be maintained by your regular work force. Don't overlook anything—from wiping out the inside of lamp fixtures to stack-ing tote boxes squarely. Then gather your employees together so they can see what *you* consider good housekeeping. Let them see if you've missed anything, make suggestions, or protest standards they think are unattainable. Then hold them to the accepted standard.

Will daily cleanup replace housekeeping drives?

In many plants good housekeeping has become a way of life because the supervisor has thoroughly indoctrinated his employees. Such an attitude should be your objective, although a once-a-year super-duper clean-up-and-throw-away party is not out of order.

Unless you develop good housekeeping *habits* in your workers, housekeeping will never be anything but a headache. You have to instill in them the same zeal you have. Otherwise, housekeeping will be costly and inferior.

Won't production employees resent having to do their own cleanup?

Some will. They will protest that housekeeping is menial work. Or that they are depriving the sweeper of his rightful job. Or that they aren't paid to clean up. Each of these objections must be met with the facts. Housekeeping need not be menial. Good care of the work place has always been associated with craftsmanship. It is a foundation stone in apprentice training.

In very few cases has improved personal housekeeping deprived a sanitation employee of his job. In most cases it has enabled the sanita-tion worker to become more effective and to show better results from his efforts.

And as to housekeeping being part of the production worker's job, hardly a formal job description has ever been written in which "care of the work place" has not been included.

Poor housekeeping in the plant is the result of poor work habits that have been tolerated by management—primarily the foreman. And the foreman is the primary person in the drive to change these habits.

Suppose the union objects?

Good housekeeping boosts morale. And the success of most unions depends upon group solidarity. So, as in the case of training programs, unions won't generally protest on the basis of principle. But you can expect them to look for reasons to object to anything which may cut down on overtime, the total number of workers, or pay scales. So anticipate these complaints by explaining the objectives and the benefits of your housekeeping ideas. And if the labor union's objections are not allayed by your explanations, consult your boss or the plant personnel department as to what your next move should be.

Is there a relationship between sanitation and housekeeping?

A very direct one exists. It's most obvious, of course, in food plants where the product may be contaminated. But it's also present wherever people work. Dermatitis, one of the most common industrial afflictions, is almost entirely a matter of how clean the shop is kept and how clean the worker keeps himself. In shops where housekeeping is superior, workers tend to take better care of their skin and clothing, too.

What should a foreman look for in the way of cleanliness in locker rooms?

Locker rooms speak eloquently to a workman of his employer's attitude toward him as a person. When they are clean, he knows he has his boss's respect. When they are messy or unsanitary, he feels that his boss thinks of him as so much dirt.

Regardless of whether or not the responsibility for washrooms and locker rooms is assigned to a single supervisor (say, in the maintenance department), be sure you take a personal interest in service-room conditions. Encourage the employees who work for you to keep sinks clean, to throw paper towels in the trash can. Check to see that they don't keep dirty clothing or soiled towels in their lockers very long. If general conditions as to lighting, care of showers, soap supply, etc., are below standard, speak up to your higher management about it. You needn't be a troublemaker in this regard. But recommendations from the supervisor are much more in order than waiting for employees or their union representatives to complain first.

What sort of effect will dress-up maintenance have?

One very effective way to promote better housekeeping is to paint or to spruce up something that employees consider to be almost impossible to keep clean. Painting a boiler room floor, piping, and other equipment is a big step in making a traditionally "Black Hole of Calcutta" a decent place to work. Painting lathes and other machines bright colors is another example. Even the simple trick of painting corners white has prevented the accumulation of trash or soil.

What can be done to correct overcrowded storage space?

Overcrowding of storage areas and of walk aisles is one of the most common sources of poor housekeeping. Top-heavy piling of cartons and cases, boxes that protrude into the aisle, or jammed aisleways look like the dickens, are dangerous to personnel, and slow down production. They are the mark of a poorly run operation.

To reduce overcrowding of material handling and storage, you must first get at the root of the matter. *Is there enough room for what you have to handle?* If there isn't, whatever you do housekeeping-wise may be like shoveling sand against the tide. Final solution to this kind of problem may rest with top management, but you ought to initiate the action. Find out just how much material you do handle. Check to see if inventories can be reduced or better in-process control of material introduced. See whether available storage space and facilities are being fully utilized, or whether temporary storage can be obtained at public warehouses. Present the findings to your boss so that he has factual data upon which to base his decisions about housekeeping affected by storage limitations.

If slipshod storage and material handling are *not* due to insufficient space, then direct your efforts toward better housekeeping to correct it. This may begin with a re-layout of storage areas or with purchase of pallets and pallet-stacking and -handling equipment. Or it may mean a change in your methods of storage by adopting a standardized way of stacking and palletizing. It may also mean a change in the way you handle materials so that there is adequate temporary storage *off* the aisles, and a smooth-flowing system so that materials are moved out of the working areas to warehousing without delay.

And finally, as with all your housekeeping problems, uncluttered material handling and storage will be guaranteed only by how you and your employees utilize the facilities provided. You've got to sell the system to the material-handling employees and to your operators. If there's a right place for cases and a right time to move them, it's up to you to see that they are put there and moved on time. Employees must see why this is important, so that eventually they will handle materials the proper way without having to be told.

What's the best way to handle trash?

Provide plenty of trash receptacles and see that they are emptied regularly. Special flameproof receptacles for flammable materials like oily rags cut down on fire hazards. If you isolate certain wastes for resale as scrap, provide separate containers, well marked, for this purpose. Don't ever permit a workman to throw waste on the floor without correcting him immediately. Housekeeping, like safety (and it is an arm of your safety efforts), cannot be a halfway measure. Employees are sold on it only when your attention to it is persistent and consistent.

Is there any danger in dust?

Dust (and lint or any other fine particles) mixed with air in certain proportions is highly explosive. Dust in air shafts and in elevator and stair shafts also becomes extremely hazardous in case of fire, for it aids the spread of the flames.

To avoid accumulation of dust, see that it is brushed off the upper part of piping and beams. Wipe dust off and away from heated bearings or from radiators or other heated surfaces.

In addition, many manufacturing processes (such as spray painting) and products (like delicate bearings and gyroscope parts) are disturbed by the presence of dust. Sweeping, dry-mopping, and dusting with a cloth tend to move the dust from one place to another, most housewives will tell us. So vacuuming is the only certain way to get rid of it.

How far can a supervisor go in controlling an employee's housekeeping of personal property at work?

A supervisor must exercise some discretion in the matter of an employee's personal property. But the supervisor is correct in setting rules that encourage an employee to keep his locker clean. It's certainly within bounds to announce and hold an occasional inspection.

Many workers have pack-rat tendencies. They will accumulate an unbelievable collection of junk at their work place if permitted. A certain amount of this should be left to the worker's own discretion—if what he has is kept neatly. But you should discourage collection of candy or food wrappers, old newspapers and magazines, etc.

Should a supervisor discipline an employee for poor housekeeping?

Yes. But only as a last resort after you have done everything possible to win him over to the good-housekeeping effort. Of course, you'll want to approach the problem of discipline with caution, being sure that you have properly established the standards of housekeeping desired and made clear to employees the penalty for not observing them (see Chap. 17).

What kind of floor conditions make for poor housekeeping?

Floor surfaces are a frequent source of accidents. Therefore a supervisor should be especially critical of their condition. Encourage employees to report any ruts, holes, or other damage to floors that might cause tripping or truck loads of material to tip over. See that floors are free from dust and other soil. Hold employees responsible for any litter, since what they can *see* about housekeeping will shape their attitudes.

In plants where sanitation is of special importance, or in lunch rooms and locker rooms, look at the floor surfaces more critically. Is there a soil film that isn't removed by ordinary cleaning methods? Are there stain incrustations that will take special treatment to remove? Are baseboards clean? (That's where roaches and other insects lurk.)

Also check to see that material in process is not placed haphazardly on the floor. Be sure that fire extinguishers and hoses are not blocked.

Sometimes a floor can be too clean—when it has been waxed to a polish that makes slipping imminent. Nowadays, you can obtain waxes that improve a floor's appearance while actually being antiskid.

And check to see that machines don't leak oil or other lubricants on the floor. If they do, have sawdust or other absorbents on hand for employee use. And place drip pans under bearings.

What should you look for when making a housekeeping inspection?

Divide your observations into three areas:
• Machines and equipment

Unauthorized arrangements. Have machines, storage areas, or operating areas been changed without approval in such a manner as to make housekeeping more difficult?

Damaged or obsolete equipment. Are there unsightly, damaged, defaced, or improperly guarded machines or other equipment?

Congestion with portable gear. Are air-operated or otherwise portable drills, guns, and tools or movable benches placed so as to hamper personal movement?

Leaks and drips. Are there leaks of air, water, oil, steam, coolant from pipes, tanks, or other containers?

• Materials and storage

Top-heavy piling. Are boxes or pallets stacked so as to tip easily?

Cluttered aisles. Do employees leave boxes, tote pans, skids, or other work-in-process in the aisles so as to be hazardous?

Protruding obstacles. Do racks, bins, benches, or machines stick out into walk-ways or working areas in such a way that clothing might be caught?

Rube Goldbergs. Are there makeshift arrangements of equipment where standard, safer setups are available?

• Cleanliness and order

Dirty floors and walls. Look under tables and benches, into corners and drawers, behind machinery.

Messy equipment. Are machines needlessly unclean? Are chips, scraps, wiping cloths, waste allowed to accumulate?

Unclean rest rooms. Are fountains, washrooms, locker and shower rooms spotless, regardless of their age? Are soap, paper, hot water, and towels available?

Rubbish and litter. Except where they are found in their proper containers, are cigarette butts, paper, bottles, or other rubbish accumulating?

Projections. Do nails, sharp corners, broken glass, or the like project where employees work? Are there hanging wires or broken flooring?

Personal items. Is clothing kept in locker rooms or on assigned racks? Are lunch boxes, pocketbooks, tool boxes kept where they belong?

How can you make a housekeeping inspection effective?

To get more out of your inspections, select different employees to make the inspection with you. Demonstrate your housekeeping standards to them, and let them point out substandard conditions to you. Treat the inspection as an educational exercise as well as a supervisory one. Employees who participate will be better housekeepers—and they may help you enforce housekeeping standards on less responsible employees.

Will a housekeeping contest help?

Contests help spark lagging interest in housekeeping, and they do provide an incentive for employees to do better. Don't depend upon a contest, however, to sustain your housekeeping program the year round. Nothing can substitute for truly changed working habits and continual supervision.

Many companies perpetuate their housekeeping contests so that there is always a competition going on. This tends to lessen the impact of the contest, but it gives the supervisor something to hang his housekeeping sales talk on the year round.

You needn't wait for the company or the plant to start a contest. You can set up a competition within your own department by dividing employees into two teams and letting them draw for names—of baseball teams, horses, etc. Then select a number of inspection points to be rated. Invite an impartial representative from another department to make a weekly or monthly inspection with you and a member of each team. Score according to the number of demerits. Post the standings on the bulletin board. And offer a prize to the winners at the end of six months. This prize can be a very nominal item—like a free lunch at the cafeteria, a placard to hang on the bulletin board, or some other inexpensive gift. Or you may choose only to award a booby prize—such as a broom—to the losers.

Here is an example of a safety and housekeeping check list. Use it as a guide for developing one for your shop.

SAFETY AND HOUSEKEEPING CHECK LIST *

	Condition O.K.	Needs corrective action
Unsafe practices		
Employees operating without authority	____	____
Employees working at unsafe speeds	____	____
Employees making safety devices inoperative	____	____
Employees using unsafe equipment	____	____
Employees lifting improperly	____	____
Employees assuming unsafe positions	____	____
Bulletin boards and safety signs		
Clean	____	____
Readable	____	____
Material changed frequently	____	____
Material removed when obsolete	____	____
Protective equipment and clothing		
Equipment and clothing in good condition	____	____
Equipment and clothing used when needed	____	____
Additional equipment or clothing needed	____	____
Sufficient storage space for equipment	____	____
Floors		
Loose material	____	____
Slippery, wet, or oily	____	____

* Suggested by William S. Walker, American Smelting and Refining Co.

	Condi-tion O.K.	Needs corrective action

Floors

Badly worn or rutted

Garbage, dirt, or debris

Stairways and aisles

Passageways, aisles, stairs clear and unblocked

Stairways well lighted

Aisles marked and markings visible

Lighting

Lamp reflectors clean

Bulbs missing

Any dark areas

Material storage

Neatly and safely piled

Passageways and work areas not blocked

Fire extinguishers and sprinklers clear

Machinery

Machines and equipment clean

Machine areas clean

Sufficient containers for waste materials

Guards on and operating

No drips or oil leaks

Cutoff switches accessible

Buildings

Windows clean and not broken

Painting and upkeep satisfactory

Door jambs clean

Fire doors unblocked

Employee facilities

Drinking fountains clean

Locker rooms and toilets clean

Soap and towel supply satisfactory

Tools

Right tools for the job

Tools used correctly

Tools stored properly

Tools in safe condition

Electrical hand tools grounded, used properly

Ladders in good condition, used properly

Electrical

Motors clean

No exposed wiring

Temporary wiring removed

Switch boxes closed

Proper fusing

	Condition O.K.	Needs corrective action
Pressure		
Gauges working properly	———	———
Cylinders secured from falling	———	———
Pressure vessels inspected regularly	———	———
Steam		
Steam or water leaks	———	———
Insulation condition	———	———
Gases, vapors, dust, and fumes		
Ventilation all right	———	———
Masks and breathing apparatus available where needed	———	———
Dust-collection system satisfactory	———	———
Material-handling equipment		
(Check for cleanliness, safe condition, and operation)		
Cranes, platforms, cabs, walkways	———	———
Chains, cables, ropes, block and tackle	———	———
Industrial trucks	———	———
Railroad equipment—rolling stock, tracks, signals, roadbed	———	———
Conveyors—drives, belt condition, guards	———	———
Elevators, hoists	———	———
Hand trucks and wheelbarrows	———	———
Fire protection		
Hoses and extinguishers well marked	———	———
Hoses and extinguishers not blocked	———	———
Extinguishers inspected regularly	———	———

The Case of Stan Williams' Department. A case study in human relations involving housekeeping, with questions for you to answer.

Employees in Stan Williams' department worked on incentives. Their job was to grind flashings off small gray-iron castings. They had a big work load each day, but the rates were good. So there was little complaining.

Walter Whitney was one of the big money-makers in the department. His bonus averaged 38 per cent. In an especially good week, he might take home almost twice his base pay.

Working conditions in the grinding department were about average for a foundry. There was an adequate dust-collection system, lighting was over 18 foot-candles, and the workmen were furnished goggles, gloves, and leather aprons free by the company. Only trouble was that in the eyes of the plant superintendent the shop was a mess. Grinding wheels were crusted with iron dust, floors were littered with chips and slippery with spilled grinding compounds. Stan Williams lamented this condition, especially since he caught it from the plant superintendent at each housekeeping inspection. "These men have no excuse for being so sloppy," he was told.

"Their rates all include time for cleaning their wheels and sweeping the floor around their work places."

After one such chewing out from his superior, Stan decided to crack down. First man he spoke to was Walter. "The boss has been in here raising Cain again about the way the shop looks," he told Walter. "You'll have to get on the ball from now on. That means you'll have to allow yourself time to clean up each day."

"Nothing doing," replied Walter. "If the old man wants the place looking like the Waldorf, he'll have to hire some sweepers to keep it that way. My job is production, not pushing a broom."

1. What do you think of Walter's reasoning?

2. What do you think of the way Stan handled this problem?

3. If you were Stan, how would you go about improving housekeeping in the shop?

28 MAINTAINING MACHINES AND EQUIPMENT

Why get excited about maintenance?

Poor maintenance is the root of many plant operating problems. Take the case of shipping foreman Ted Weeks. At the peak of his plant's shipping season, he finds himself behind the eight ball. His crew is working overtime every night sealing cases. The truck companies are complaining about tying up their trucks with long waits at the shipping dock. The traffic manager is bellowing about demurrage charges on the boxcars sitting on the siding waiting to be loaded. Worse still, the sales department is in a tizzy about late deliveries and orders canceled because of it.

Ted can't figure how it all went wrong. He had estimated his work load carefully before the season began. He was sure that this year his schedule would work out smoothly. But it didn't. Now he'll catch it from his boss. Whatever went wrong?

Faulty maintenance planning was the culprit. As Ted runs his finger down his time sheets, he notes that on the very first day the shipping department was scheduled full tilt, the power conveyors that boost cartons into the trucks broke down. He'd had to add a couple of men to that operation. And it was a couple of days before the burnt-out motor was replaced. Then on the following day, the hydraulic dock platform had frozen in the "up" position. So the fork trucks couldn't get into the truck bodies, and the trucks had to be loaded by hand that day.

Just when he thought everything would get back on the beam, the automatic case-sealing machine busted a gear and the cases had to be sealed by hand for a day. Since then, it's never run more than three or four hours without developing some kink or other. The maintenance department has had a man up watching it full time.

But that wasn't all to make Ted's month complete. One rainy Tuesday, the roadway into the plant turned into a sea of mud, and a big 50-ton trailer got stuck. No other trucks could get in or out of the plant the rest of the day.

So it went all during the month. One little breakdown followed by another one. And each breakdown upped the labor cost Ted had to charge to the shipping department. He was way over budget now. But worse still was the howl it had stirred in the sales department.

An exaggerated example? Sure. But the point is valid. Down time costs money, wastes time, and causes all sorts of troubles for foremen. And ninety-nine times out of a hundred, down time can be avoided by better maintenance.

Who's at fault when maintenance is inferior?

In most plants the maintenance department is the whipping boy for all breakdown and repair problems. Sometimes this is deserved. Often it is not. That's because the maintenance gang can do only as good a job as the production department will permit. As a result, the responsibility for poor maintenance is far from one-sided. The production foreman has to take his fair share of the blame.

What can the supervisor do to improve maintenance?

He can cooperate with the maintenance department—first, by seeing that employees operate their equipment properly and second, by taking an active interest in the maintenance planning in his department.

Do production employees contribute to poor maintenance?

They surely do. Much equipment wear and tear can be traced to improper operation. Running motors at higher than their rated speed, overloading machines and presses, not enough or too much lubrication, or just poor machine and equipment housekeeping are employee failings. Not that the failure isn't the supervisor's, too. Part of your job training for operating employees is careful, forceful instruction of the *employees'* responsibility for maintenance.

Many employees just don't see the relationship between cause and effect until it's explained to them. A fork-truck driver who makes fast starts with heavy loads may have no idea of what's under the hood of his buggy. When the clutch starts slipping, he blames it on "the maintenance guys."

A belt tender in a bulk chemical plant may look at the job of cleaning sprockets and chains as just a chore to keep the foreman happy. If the employee feels this way, he'll dodge this task whenever he can. As a result, the accumulated powders and dusts will play havoc with chain links and gears—and there will be endless trouble with the belt. And this will be another bum rap hung on the maintenance man.

Not all employees misuse their equipment out of carelessness or laziness. Even the eager beaver can cause repair trouble. There are still thousands of cases each year of conscientious, but misguided workers overlubricating electric motors—and burning out the bearings!

Is down time the only thing that makes maintenance expensive?

Not at all. The cost of repair parts and maintenance labor has skyrocketed in the years since World War II. An index of plant maintenance costs published by *Factory Management and Maintenance* magazine showed that the average cost of maintenance materials alone rose over 50 per cent in the seven years from 1949 to 1957.

Cost of labor and materials isn't the whole story by far. The amount of maintenance required by automatic equipment, and actually performed on it, has risen almost as fast.

Wouldn't it be cheaper to buy new equipment rather than fix up the old?

There's always a point where it's cheaper to replace a machine or a tool than to repair it. Accurate maintenance records may show that a $2,500 pump has had $1,800 worth of work done on it in twelve months. There's no question that it would have been wiser to have bought a new one. It would pay for itself in no time.

Buying new equipment isn't as easy a solution as it may sound, however. It's not uncommon for the cost of a new machine to be many times the original cost of the one it replaces. A machine tool that used to cost $15,000 before the war cost over $100,000 in 1958, and the prices keep going up. Money for these purchases is frequently hard to come by. The United States Government limits the rate at which equipment may be written off against operating expenses. This often prevents a company from buying new equipment without cutting dividends to its stockholders, or actually borrowing money to finance the purchase.

Can the supervisor do anything to speed up maintenance in his department?

Yes. One of the best things you can do is to build a reputation for calling for help only when it's really necessary. Don't cry "wolf," or you're likely to find your hurry-up jobs at the bottom of the master mechanic's priority list. The squeaking wheel may get the grease, but the ever-complaining production foreman doesn't get the fastest or best maintenance.

You can speed up things, too, if you help make ready for the maintenance job. Have your employees clear the trouble area so that the mechanic has room to work. If you can, see that he has good light in which to work. If the machine has to be cleaned before he can inspect it or work on it, have that done ahead of time too. Don't try to take work away from the maintenance crew. But *do* make their work easier and you'll get better service.

What can you do to help plan your maintenance work better?

Biggest mistake is to assume that a call to the maintenance department or a scribbled work order begins and ends your maintenance responsibility. It doesn't, for you can do much toward helping your maintenance department plan its maintenance. Avoid:

Rush jobs. Do a little inspecting of equipment yourself. If a valve is leaking today, don't wait until next Wednesday when it fails completely before requesting a repair job. Nothing upsets good maintenance practice like emergency work. And the usual answer is, "We've taken care of this *temporarily.* Next time if you'll give us a little more notice, we'll try to do a real job on it!"

Niggling call-backs. If the mechanic has been sent up to repair the drive mechanism, try to make sure you show him everything that's wrong while he's on that job. Don't make a habit of calling a couple of days later and saying, "Sorry, Pete, but I meant to have you look at the switch on the drive mechanism yesterday, but I clean forgot about it. And it's giving us trouble now."

Loading many jobs on one order. You know the story of the woman who calls in the painter to paint a room, then says, "As long as you're here, will you touch up this chair? And maybe this table, and this knickknack shelf?" If you try this with the maintenance department, a job they estimate for an hour may stretch into an afternoon.

Sketchy complaints. Try to pin down in your work-order request exactly what's wrong. Don't just say "Machine No. 2 is acting up." Be specific. "The feed on machine No. 2 is erratic. It fails to synchronize with the index mechanism at high speeds." With the latter kind of information, the plant engineer will know whether to send one man or two, the proper kind of tools, and spare parts if necessary.

What's preventive maintenance?

Preventive maintenance (sometimes called PM) involves:

• Periodic inspection of machines and equipment to uncover conditions that lead to production breakdowns or harmful depreciation.

• Upkeep of plant equipment to correct such conditions while they are still in a minor stage.

What can you do to improve preventive maintenance?

Responsibility for PM lies with the maintenance or plant engineering department, but you can do three things to help make their work easier:

Watch maintenance costs yourself. Not just the over-all charges for repairs in your department, if your company furnishes these figures, but also the charges against different pieces of equipment. You can do this yourself without getting fancy. In a pocket notebook, set aside a page for each major piece of your shop equipment. And jot down in it the date of each repair, what it was, and how long it took to repair. Soon, you'll know in detail which machines cause trouble, which ones run up costs—and should be maintained on a preventive basis or replaced.

Check machine performance regularly. No one will expect you to perform a professional maintenance inspection. But you can follow a simple schedule of your own to check operating characteristics of your equipment. When you do this regularly and not by chance, you'll spot many breakdown symptoms—like too much play in shaft or gears, oil leaks, motors running hot, abnormal noises—in time to repair without loss of production.

Allow for preventive maintenance shutdowns in your production planning. Preventive maintenance means planned shutdowns for inspection and overhaul. Once you and your maintenance department have decided how often these inspections should be made and how long they will take, it's up to you to make allowance in your schedule for it. Otherwise, you'll hear the old story, "We wanted to get at your machines last month when we had time, but you said you couldn't afford to lose the production then. Now you're in trouble and we don't have the time to get to you now."

How does good maintenance improve morale?

Good maintenance is like good housekeeping. It shows employees that the company cares. It sets an example for quality for them to follow. It demonstrates that you and the company want to provide the best in tools to work with and in working conditions. And in the end, good maintenance inspires employees to better workmanship.

Are employees interested in maintenance costs?

Probably not, unless you help them see the connection between costs and their own income. Simple demonstrations help. A workman who makes $75 a week may be shocked to find that a 3-inch stainless steel valve costs twice that much. A workman who sees a 5-horsepower explosion-proof motor replaced on his machine may gasp when he hears it costs $250. So here's your chance to make employees maintenance cost-conscious. Remind them of how breakdowns have interfered with their earnings. And when a repair job is done near them, let them see the actual cost. They may respond with "So what! The company has plenty of money to burn." But don't misinterpret what they *say* to mean exactly how they *feel*. They'll be impressed, and all but the hardest to get along with will be more careful in the future.

Isn't poor maintenance sometimes the fault of bad workmanship on the repairman's part?

Lots of times it is. But lots of times his workmanship would be better if he got the right kind of handling when he worked in your department. It's a good bet that Jake, the tinsmith, isn't going to do you any favors if you ride him in front of your own employees. Or if you encourage your employees to criticize him or maintenance in general.

One good way to assure better workmanship is for you to check the repair job yourself, before the crewman packs up his gear and goes off to another job. If you're too easily satisfied, there's not much incentive for him to set high standards for himself. So get together with his boss and agree upon how good the job should be before you feel it's satisfactorily completed.

How can you get more cooperation from the maintenance department?

Try to show them you're on their team. That you don't criticize them to your boss behind their backs. That you understand maintenance is a skilled and demanding job. That they do the best they can, often under difficult circumstances.

Avoid asking for frills, too. It's nice to get that new deflector pan in the plating department, but it doesn't actually need the fringe on top. Requests like these, and other "government" jobs, are often the straw that breaks the camel's back.

When the maintenance department does an especially good job, tell them so. And you can really win them over to your side if you tell their superiors, too. A little written memo makes for a lasting pat on the back.

The Case of the Labeling Machine That Broke Down. A case study in human relations involving maintenance, with questions for you to answer.

Mike Hogan, packing foreman, picked up the phone and dialed the maintenance shop. "Fred, when are you going to get someone up here to fix this labeling machine? We've got the line shut down while the girls set up the hand-labeling table again."

"Sorry, Mike," replied Fred, who was master mechanic for the plant, "but I've got every available man making the changeover on the water condenser. If we don't get that back on the line, you won't have any material to pack by tomorrow."

"That's your problem," interrupted Mike. "It's up to you to get my machine fixed. I've had a work order in on this job for at least a week. Besides, if your men would fix it right, it wouldn't keep breaking down."

"Fix it right! You've got some nerve saying that. The last time we worked on that machine, you said we couldn't do an overhaul. You needed it fixed in fifteen minutes so you could get a rush order out."

"Cut it out, Fred. Sure we rushed you that time, but that was six weeks ago. You've had plenty of time to do something about it since. Either you get someone up here pronto, or I'll go to the Old Man and tell about the continual run around you give me."

Back in his office Fred slammed down the receiver. He turned to his shop clerk. "Run over to the condenser house and tell Jimmy to go up to the packaging department. The labeler's busted again. See what he can do about it."

The clerk said "O.K.," then hesitated a minute. "Fred, you did see that Mike had a work order in on that labeler, didn't you."

"Sure I did," said Fred, "but Mike's such a complainer, I feel it's not much use paying attention to him until he gets excited."

1. What do you think of the relationship between Mike and Fred?

2. What do you think of Fred's way of handling the repair job on the labeler?

3. If you were Mike's boss, how would you go about improving maintenance in his department?

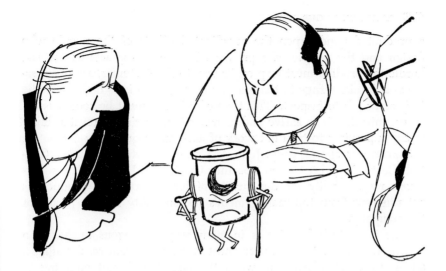

29 SECURING BETTER QUALITY

Who should have final responsibility for product quality —line supervisor or inspector?

Here's a question that gets plenty of batting around in many a plant. And has started many a feud between an otherwise successful supervisor and the inspection department. In the long run, responsibility must be fixed by your company's policy and its interpretation by your boss and his associates. But there's a long-standing rule of thumb that holds the best answer: *Quality must be built into the product. No one can inspect it in.*

Actually few foreman deny that they are responsible for product quality. The jurisdictional disputes arise over who's the best judge of quality—and who has the authority to stop production when quality falls below specifications. And this is something you should try to have your boss make crystal clear for you. Otherwise, chaos will prevail.

Three plant operating executives were asked this same question by *Personnel Administration* magazine. Here is the gist of each man's answer:

Supervisor's primary responsibility. Walter E. Robbins, Jr., Chief Industrial Engineer, Baker & Co., Newark, N.J., says, "The quality of a product depends upon the coordinated efforts of the people who design and the people who produce. The inspector acts as the last hurdle the product must leap on its way to the customer. Many supervisors still take refuge in the old saw that 'our job is to make, it is the inspector's job to inspect.' This type of thinking must be rooted out if an organization is to thrive and grow. It is the primary responsibility of the supervisor to turn out work of acceptable quality."

Supervisor's special duty. John A. Gregg, Director of Quality Control, Coates Board & Carton Co., Inc., Garfield, N.J., says, "The supervisor's responsibility for the quality of his department's products is not different from top management's responsibility for the profits of the company.

"The inspector's function is in many ways analogous to that of a treasurer. He, like the treasurer, must compare present results against an agreed-to standard and, when the operation is not adhering to specifications, report these facts to the proper parties. This means that the inspector should forward this information to the department supervisor, who must make the decision of accepting or rejecting the questionable product.

"The key to quality of product is pride of workmanship, and quality is sharply reduced when the supervisor's duties are transferred to the inspection or quality control personnel."

Sometimes automatically controlled. Morris Tolciss, Factory Superintendent, Presto Lock Co., Garfield, N.J., says, "In those industries where mechanization and automation have been gone into in a big way, the immediate responsibility for the quality of goods lies primarily with the manager of quality control and the designer of the machinery, because the quality safeguards are (or should be) built into the machine or process. For example, weaving machines or printing presses will stop automatically if a thread is broken or if the paper is not properly lined up.

"In other plants . . . it is the responsibility of the departmental supervisor to train his operators so as to obtain the desired quality. Following this, the quality of the finished product becomes the responsibility of the supervisor, with the inspection department functioning primarily as the eyes of top management and the ultimate consumer."

What should you do if there is no inspection department in your plant?

Chances are that there will be an official inspection department *somewhere* in your plant—even if it doesn't carry on its activity in your department. If such is the case, you might first ask the central inspection department for advice in setting up your own quality checks. If you must go it alone, however, try this analysis of your quality problem:

• What is my inspection problem? What do I have to do to maintain quality?

• Shall I assign the inspection to someone as a part-time or a full-time job?

• Shall I do the inspecting myself? If so, how much time can I devote to it?

• Should I try to inspect all the work produced or only a sample of it? Or should I confine myself to the first piece on a new setup only?

Once you have considered these questions and decided on your approach, you can proceed to the next question.

How can you make your own inspections?

Keep in mind these points:

• Set up some specific quality standards, such as dimensions, appearance, etc. Keeping examples of acceptable and nonacceptable work on exhibit helps.

• Put specifications in writing. See that your employees get a copy to guide them.

• Allocate some of your own time for inspection. The total amount isn't so important as doing a certain amount each day.

• Pick the spots where quality can best be made or lost. No point in spending your time checking operations where nothing much can go wrong.

• Make inspection rounds from time to time. Change the order of your trips frequently.

• Select at random 5 or 10 per cent of the pieces produced at a particular station. Inspect each one carefully.

• Correct operating conditions immediately where your inspection shows material to be off grade.

• Consult with employees to determine the reason for off-spec material. Seek their cooperation in correcting conditions and improving quality.

• Check the first piece on a new setup. Don't permit production until you are satisfied with the quality.

• Post quality records, scrap percentages, etc., on the bulletin board to keep employees informed of how the department is doing quality-wise.

How can you get employees more interested in quality?

It's been popular to complain about the "I-don't-care" attitude of some employees. Actually, your viewpoint should be that if an employee doesn't care about quality, it's because you have failed to sell him on its importance.

To get a workman quality-conscious, start right from his first day by stressing quality as well as output. Emphasize that the two must go hand in hand in your shop. Whenever you show an employee how to do a job—especially a new one—be specific as to what kind of work is acceptable and what kind will not meet specifications. Explain the reason behind product quality limitations. And try to give your employees the little knacks of the trade that help to make quality easy to attain.

J. M. Juran * advises this way to show operators how to improve quality: "The need is to convince the operator that a failing on his part will make trouble for some fellow human being—for the assembly operator, the salesman, the customer. Operators who are convinced of the reasons behind rules follow the rules much more willingly than operators who only know that the boss said, 'Do it that way.'"

Can you train employees to produce better quality goods?

Yes. And here's an outstanding example.

At Fieldcrest Mills, Spray, N.C., four "tailing" operators were given 3 weeks intensive training on how to cut down on waste. This was followed up by 12 weeks of close on-the-job assistance and 14 weeks of follow-up. At the end of the first 15 weeks, scrap had been cut 62 per cent, and under normal supervision this reduction persisted for 80 more weeks! And that's not all. You might have thought that all the improvement that could be made in quality had been achieved. It hadn't. Training in quality production was again instituted and a further reduction of 45 per cent in scrap was reached.

What did the company do to attain these results? Basic steps in the program were:

• Present information to operators concerning need for waste reduction.

• Give operators instruction in how to do a better job.

• Keep them informed by graphic aids as to how they are doing.

In addition, the company feels that (1) frank, full, and sincere explanations for changes in methods together with (2) employee participation (at the level of competence) in program activities are the touches that make for long-range success.

---

* J. M. Juran, editor, *Quality Control Handbook*, McGraw-Hill Book Company, Inc., New York, 1951.

What can you do to help the employee understand that the customer is the real quality boss?

Try to provide employees with a customer's-eye view of your product. A workman who handles the same product every day tends to lose his objectivity. He begins to take minor defects for granted. To help him see the product as the cutomer does, get samples of customer complaints (about specific defects) and circulate them in your department. Explain how the customer uses your product—how it will be compared with a competitor's unit and how quality will affect its use. At F. E. Myers & Bro. Company, Ashland, Ohio, foremen and workers are selected to attend training sessions held for distributor salesmen. Employees hear at first hand the reasons for some of the things they do. "Our sales story really opened my eyes. I didn't realize what it takes to sell a pump," said one shop steward after attending the sales course. And the net effect was a greater interest in high quality and lower costs.

At Beech Aircraft Corporation, Wichita, Kans., where damage to aircraft bodies during production is a hazard, this approach is used to stimulate care among operators: "You wouldn't buy a $200 refrigerator with a patch on the door. Would you expect a Beechcraft customer to take an $80,000 plane with a two-inch patch on it?"

When things go wrong with quality in your department, what steps should you take?

Supervisors at an Industrial Management Institute of the University of Wisconsin agreed upon these twelve check points for action:

• Do you explain to each worker exactly what quality is expected on his job?

• When work is rejected, do you make sure that the workers concerned know what is wrong and exactly what is expected of them?

• Have you a plan of close cooperation for the purpose of improving quality with the supervisor of the department from which your work comes and the supervisor of the department to which your work goes?

• Do you get a list of all the defective work in your department each week or month so you can take definite steps to prevent similar defective work during the next period?

• Do you set aside a definite amount of your own time for actual inspection of the work in your department?

• Do you have a system for getting suggestions from your workers on how to improve quality?

• Do you hold regular talks with each of your workers regarding the quality of the work he's doing?

• Are you making full and effective use of departmental bulletin boards for posting facts about quality and defective work and for exhibiting examples of good or bad work?

• Do you keep your workers informed on the cost of defective work in your department?

• Do you have any method for arousing the pride of your workers in their workmanship?

• Have you systematically acquainted each worker with the relation between quality workmanship and job security?

• Do your employees understand the value placed on quality performance when they are considered for raises or promotions?

If you can answer "Yes" to most of these questions, you'll find that quality troubles will stay away from your door.

What is meant by statistical quality control?

Statistical quality control simply means that numbers—statistics—are used *as a part* of the over-all approach for controlling quality. Statistics are tools and in no way relieve supervisor or employee from his concern with quality. Used properly, however, they can be of considerable aid.

What are some of the tools of statistical quality control, and how do they affect the supervisor's job?

Greatly increased demands for precision parts has stepped up the need for better methods to measure and record the accuracy with which manufacturing people meet product specifications. Statistical methods speed up this measuring process. And more and more companies use them in some form or other. Don't let any fear you may have of mathematics prevent you from using statistical methods.

Three statistical quality-control tools are encountered most commonly in the shop:

Frequency-distribution charts. Hold on. It isn't as bad as it sounds. Probably you'll recognize it by its more popular name—a tally card. If you were asked to place an *x* in the appropriate space for every shaft diameter you gauged in a given lot, chances are that you'd come up with a tally that looks something like Fig. 29–1.

In this case the nominal shaft diameter was 0.730 inch with a tolerance of ±0.002. This tally gives you a picture of just *what* and *where* the shaft variations are, instead of merely recording whether a shaft is "good" or "bad." This frequency distribution chart (that's what it is in its simplest form) helps tell you the causes of the variation. The wide distribution in this case indicates tool wobble. A picture which showed

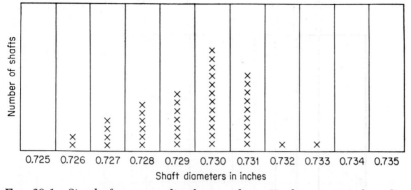

FIG. 29-1   Simple frequency distribution chart. Used in statistical quality control. (Adapted from A. V. Feigenbaum, *Quality Control*, McGraw-Hill Book Company, Inc., New York, 1951.)

parts bunched around a point below or above the nominal 0.730 inch (say, at 0.728) might mean that the setup must be adjusted.

Quality-control chart. This is an hour-by-hour, day-by-day graphical comparison of actual product-quality characteristics. On the chart are limits which reflect the person's or machine's ability to produce, as shown by past experience. Statisticians make use of the knowledge of shop tolerances and analysis of previous frequency distribution tallies to establish these limits. Whenever the inspections plotted on the control chart show that the product is getting outside the predicted control limits, that's a signal for the supervisor or operator to correct what he's doing so that the product comes back into specification.

In Fig. 29–2, the part being made is supposed to measure 0.730 inch. The tolerance specs are ±0.002, or from 0.728 to 0.732 inch. The quality-control statistician has predicted in advance from a frequency-distribution diagram that most production will vary within his control limits—the 0.7285 and 0.7315 lines. When quality stays within these limits, it is said to be "on the highway." It is to be expected that a few products will fall outside the limits into the "shoulder." But when the trend of measurements indicates that product quality is drifting progressively into the "shoulder" area, it's time to check the process. Any product that goes beyond the upper or lower specification limits (goes "into the ditch") is rejected.

Value of the chart lies in telling the supervisor or operator whether he's in bounds or whether he's losing control of the process *before* the process goes completely haywire.

Sampling tables. The trend today has been away from 100 per cent inspection, which is costly and often misleading. (In a 100 per cent check of a load of oranges, does this mean that each orange has been

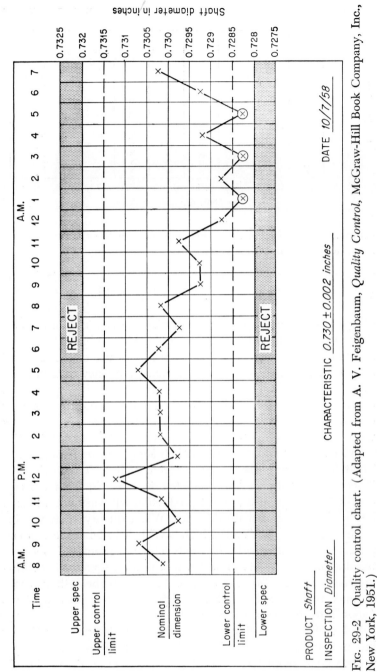

FIG. 29-2   Quality control chart. (Adapted from A. V. Feigenbaum, *Quality Control*, McGraw-Hill Book Company, Inc., New York, 1951.)

inspected for color, ripeness, thickness of skin, appearance? Or does it mean that each orange was inspected for appearance only?) The first solution to less than 100 per cent checking was spot-checking, but this proved unreliable. Today, most sampling is done according to the size of the lot of goods produced and according to tables designed by statisticians for this purpose. These tables guide the quality-control manager in his determination of how large a sample to take and how often to take it.

If your plant uses statistical quality-control techniques, there's probably an authority on the matter on hand. Ask him to explain the details of how your plant's plan works.

The Case of Department A. A case study in human relations involving quality control, with questions for you to answer.

Department A had been at the bottom of the plant list for production for several years. But the department's record for quality had been consistently high.

In the spring of 1958, the plant hired a quality-control engineer with broad experience in the mass-production industries. Immediately he instituted a number of changes in product specifications and in manufacturing standards. In the main, his program proved to be successful due to his ability to sell his ideas to the departmental foremen. That is, every foreman except Jack Hoey from Department A.

Jack argued, "This department has always been tops in quality. We've always been given the tough jobs to do. Sure, we may have been a little slower than others, but that's because we've been more painstaking. If we adopt high-production methods, we'll sacrifice craftsmanship."

Ted Diggs, the quality-control engineer, pointed to the fact that better quality had actually accompanied increased production in some departments. In none had it suffered. Nevertheless, Department A continued to lag behind in output, although it continued to retain its reputation for meticulous workmanship.

After three months with no improvement in production, Jack's boss called him into the office. "Jack," he said, "I'm going to transfer you to Research and Development. In your new job you'll assist a development engineer in setting tolerances on new parts. You won't have supervisory status, but I think the job will be to your taste.

"I'm promoting Tom Oakes to the foreman spot in your old department. He's a quick young fellow who seems able to grasp the fact that production and quality can go hand in hand."

1. Do you think Jack's boss has done the right thing? Why?
2. Why do you suppose Jack has been so obsessed with quality?
3. Do you think Jack will do well in his new assignment? Why?
4. What sort of problems will Tom Oakes face in Department A?

30 PROTECTING YOUR PLANT

What sort of disasters endanger your plant?

Many circumstances endanger the security of your plant. A new competitor or a fall in the market can threaten economic disaster. Theft of property or information could weaken your plant. Fire, wind, or an atomic bomb could destroy it. In this chapter we'll talk about the dangers to your plant caused by the latter—stealing, security violation, fire, storm, or manmade attacks of war.

Just how much of a threat is fire to your plant?

More than many people suspect. Loss of life is shocking to contemplate. And purely from a business viewpoint, a plant destroyed by fire often means hundreds of jobs *permanently* destroyed. That's right. According to *Occupational Hazards* magazine, 71 per cent of all business establishments that are severely damaged by fire fail within three years: 43 per cent never open again, and 28 per cent have to give up within 36 months! So when you hear an employee say, "What do I care if this old plant burns down? It's time the company built a new one," give him an ungarbled account of what fire can do to his job.

What can a supervisor do to prevent fires?

As in most of your work, you help prevent plant fires by getting employees to prevent them. First step for you is to be alert to where fires are likely to start and what good preventive measures are.

Where are plant fires most frequent?

Plant fires, like most fires anywhere, tend to start where few people are or where they're difficult to spot until they've made headway. Few houses are burnt down by sparks from a roaring fire in the living-room fireplace while the room is full of people to watch it. If the fire is caused by a fireplace, chances are that it begins from sparks thrown out the chimney or onto the living-room rug after everybody's gone to bed. It's the same way in the plant. Sparks from a welder's torch can be dangerous (as in the case of the famous General Motors fire at Livonia, Mich.), but much more dangerous are fires that begin where you least expect them.

So look for fire hazards in out-of-the-way places as well as in the obvious spots. Spend some time usefully by probing into corners of warehouses to prevent accumulation of papers and other debris that might make perfect nesting places for a lighted cigarette butt. Look under benches for oily rags stuffed in tight corners, just loaded with the right ingredients for spontaneous combustion. Climb up near the roof to see whether dust is heavy on rafters and pipes—just the stuff to help spread a flash fire that originates somewhere else.

What sort of fire prevention measures should you enforce?

Good housekeeping is one of the best. Where floors, benches, corners, and machines are kept clean and neat, fire has a hard time getting a foothold. Watch out for material piled too close to overhead sprinklers, fire extinguishers and hoses. Material too close to the sprinklers cuts down on their effectiveness. Blocked fire extinguishers may mean the difference between a fire that is put out in a few seconds and one that gets a toe hold in a minute. And never permit a fire extinguisher or fire bucket to be used for any purpose other than to fight fires. Also check regularly to see that they're full.

Check with your safety engineer, personnel manager, or superior to determine the best practices for handling flammable liquids, like solvents of any kind. Some of the precautions will seem sissified, but in the long run, no safety measure with flammable materials can be too extreme.

Don't be lenient with employees who smoke in unauthorized areas. It may seem like a little thing. But it's the carelessly flipped butt *where people don't expect it* that can cause the big trouble.

Set this rule for yourself and your employees: Regard every open light, every flame, every match and cigarette, every bit of oily waste or thimbleful of flammable liquid as potentially dangerous. Discipline taken to enforce safety measures is the least difficult to gain support for from labor unions. So sell each employee on the stake he himself holds in fire prevention in his plant.

How does the National Fire Protection Association differentiate between the different kinds of fires?

The NFPA and the Underwriters' Laboratories, Inc., recognize three kinds of fires:

Class A. Ordinary combustible materials like wood, which are put out by a quenching agent like water.

Class B. Flammable liquids or greases such as gasoline, requiring a blanketing or smothering agent like foam.

Class C. Involving electrical equipment, which requires a non-conductive extinguisher like carbon tetrachloride or CO_2.

What's the significance to the supervisor of the three classifications?

Each kind of fire is fought with a different kind of agent. Most wood and paper fires (A type) are fought with the typical soda-acid extinguisher or a hose—both of which use water as a quenching agent to cool off and wet down the fire.

Oil, grease, and solvent fires (B type) are fought with foam-type, dry chemical, or carbon-dioxide gas extinguishers. These all act to blanket the fire by keeping the air away from it. Water on a fire like this would simply spread the fire around. Lighter oils would float on top of it.

An electrical fire (C type) *could* be put out with almost any kind of extingiusher, but the person holding the hose or extinguisher (if it's soda-acid, foam, or dry chemical) would get a severe, possibly killing, shock. That's why a carbon tetrachloride or CO_2 extinguisher must be used; neither one conducts electricity.

Point is that you need the right kind of extinguisher for each fire. Usually you can depend upon your safety engineer or insurance company to be certain that the most suitable extinguisher is handy to the kind of fire that might start. But you should make a habit of knowing what kind of fire-fighting equipment is in your department, how to use it, and on what kind of fire. Then see that your employees know too.

In case of fire, what should you do?

Experts disagree as to which one of these things you should do first. But they all agree that these three things should be done immediately:

• Report the fire by telephone, or see that the message is carried to the plant or local fire department. Many a building-wrecking fire has gotten away from a person who was sure he could put it out himself.

• See that employees are evacuated. Safety to persons comes before property. See that all employees in the department know of the fire and are gotten out of the building or out of the area—except those officially designated to fight the fire.

• Fight the fire with hand extinguisher or hose. Speed is absolutely essential—thus the need for keeping fire extinguishers unblocked and knowing how to use them.

Before you shut your plant down for an extended holiday or vacation, what precautions should be taken?

Here's what Factory Insurance Associates advise:

In preparation for an extended plant shutdown of this scope, there are some basic and fundamental procedures which are dictated by what is commonly known as just plain horse sense:

• Leave the plant clean by making certain of a thorough house-cleaning just before vacation.

• Check special hazards to make certain that potential fire hazards are eliminated so far as possible.

• Instruct stand-by personnel properly so they will know exactly what to do in case of emergency and where to contact key plant personnel.

• Check all fire protection equipment to assure it is in proper working order and not obstructed.

• Notify fire-control services such as fire department, police department, and central-station supervisory headquarters of the shutdown.

Can anything be done to plan against disaster from flood, hurricanes, and tornadoes?

Your plant can't afford to wait until the sky gets black, the trees start shaking, and the water rises to your door. It will be too late then to take precautions. As with all disasters, the effects of nature can be cut to a minimum by adequate planning beforehand. Important action for you to take is to anticipate the problems that might occur in your department in the event of high winds or water. (Floods and hurricanes will give you plenty of warning—at least twenty-four to forty-eight hours—but tornadoes generally strike without notice.)

Here's a check list of items you should think about beforehand:

• How and where to evacuate or protect employees at the time of the storm.

• What roads and other methods of transportation. your employees may use before and immediately after the storm.

• How you'll control entry and movement during the emergency period.

• Maintaining a list of temporary addresses and telephone numbers of all employees you may want to contact during that time.

• Keeping a record of damage done to your department.

• How you'll protect machines, equipment, and records in your department.

• What kind of emergency supplies you'll need on hand—like tarpaulins, lumber for bracing, roofing paper, etc.

• What utilities (water, gas, electricity) should be turned off in the face of the storm, and who should do it and when.

What about safeguarding government information?

Rules and regulations about the handling of restricted, confidential, or secret government data will be set down by the government security officers, themselves. When in doubt at all, check with your superior or your company's security officer, if there is one. Find out what the restrictions are and see that all safeguards—no matter how foolish or overdone they may look to you—are observed to the letter. Don't make exceptions for anybody. And report to your superiors any violations you observe.

Can a supervisor do anything to prevent sabotage?

Symptoms of sabotage are a little like the evidences of stealing. First of all, make it difficult for just anyone to have access to central power stations, boiler houses, warehouses, or storage of flammable materials. Find out who has authorization to be in potentially dangerous areas. Keep everybody else out. Be on the lookout for employees who roam the plant. If they have no business outside their department, see that they stay there.

Caution: Don't make like an FBI agent. Report any suspicions to your superior, but don't take investigations into your own hands. Most people are honest and loyal. The ones who aren't are very difficult to detect.

Any special measures to take in case of a national emergency such as war?

These measures are up to top management and to the government. There are some standard measures, however, which you can expect most companies to adopt, such as:

• Fingerprinting and photographing all employees.

• Controlling in-plant movements—wearing of identification badges.

• Restricting plant areas—especially power plants, electrical distribution centers, water supply points, and warehouses.

• Preventing unauthorized entry. Fences, screening, floodlights, and guard systems will be checked—especially along railroads, thorough-fares, and water fronts.

• Checking employees at the gate—spot-checking lunchboxes, super-visors signing for packages.

• Reporting procommunist tendencies such as deliberate attempts to destroy material, willful attempts to delay production.

• Safeguarding documents and mail—blueprints, photographs, de-fense orders, reports, etc.—from unauthorized persons and from fire.

What sort of precautions should be taken to protect company information?

Knowledge of what your company's plans are for the future or of your manufacturing processes could, in some instances, be of value to your company's competitors. Lawyers speak of such information as being of "aid and comfort" to competition. You and your company have a perfect right to safeguard this information. So be alert to this danger. Talk to your superior about it. Ask him what kind of informa-tion you can discuss freely with your friends or with plant visitors and what kind of information is best kept confidential.

How much stealing goes on in industry?

A conservative estimate is that employees rob over $500 million a year from industrial plants. The loot ranges from bits of raw material, like a length of copper wire, to expensive hand tools or—where large-scale theft is involved—truckloads of your product.

Doesn't insurance protect a company from these losses?

Frequently. But only if the company can document what has been stolen. Biggest losses occur where a company isn't sure of its inventory balance so that goods and stock leak out in dribs and drabs.

Should the supervisor become a private eye?

Absolutely not. Don't play cops and robbers with employees. Your big responsibility is to make it difficult to steal, to know when things are missing, and to report thefts as soon as you observe them. It's not your job to be a policeman. It's downright dangerous for you to try to be.

What can a supervisor do to stop stealing in the plant?

Plant-wide protection measures are up to top management. But there's lots you can do to discourage employee stealing. The National Industrial Conference Board advises:

• Lock up valuable metals, materials, or equipment at shift end.

Provide cribs for control of nickel anodes, babbitt, copper, and solder. Stow away valuable tools—especially portable hand tools.

• Require all employees, regardless of status, to sign in and out after hours.

• Control the distribution of valuable or easy-to-steal parts on your assembly lines. Distribute only what you need daily.

• Check windows, doors, and other openings regularly for ease of unauthorized entry.

• Watch how frequently employees visit their cars in parking lots. This may indicate the transport of pilfered goods.

• Check the interplant movement of company tools and equipment. Get and request receipts for transferrals of equipment.

• Keep an eye on contractor's maintenance and construction men. They often enter a plant with an empty tool box, leave with a full one.

• Watch scrap trucks while being loaded. Be careful that broken or scrapped tools aren't available to employees who might substitute them for good tool replacements.

• If your company approves, make a practice of signing employee packages that go in and out.

How can you detect hard-to-spot thefts?

Much of the pilferage that goes on around a plant often goes on unnoticed. So it's up to you to set up some checks for detecting when articles are missing. Look for what is called "inventory shrinkage." Suppose you're stocking nuts and bolts. At the end of the month it's usual for about ½ per cent to be unaccounted for. This is normal. But for several months this shrinkage gets bigger, say to 1 or 1½ per cent. This could mean pilferage.

Or investigate unusually high tool replacements. Your own knowledge of tool breakage and material usage should wave a warning flag if the replacements are getting too high.

Keep especially close watch over places where thefts are most likely to occur. For example, sheet aluminum may be hard to steal once it's inside the building. So the place to watch is at unloading docks and related areas at the point of arrival.

What should employees know about stealing in the plant?

By far the easiest and most effective way to combat crime in the plant is to publicize the facts about it. Make sure that employees know that crime—even petty pilfering—doesn't pay. That thefts mean dismissal—or whatever your company's punishment is. Urge employees to report missing articles promptly. The sooner a loss is known, the quicker management can take action. It's also wise to let employees know that the plant will expect cooperation from local police in the event of a theft. And be sure you regard the loss of employees' personal property just as significantly as you do that of plant property.

Should you distinguish between stealing and pilferage?

It's best not to. Take the attitude that a small theft is just as serious as a big one. But don't be so stingy with materials that you force an employee to steal. Giveaways of off-quality products, lending tools for home usage, selling goods at special discounts help deter employees from stealing. And most important of all—set a good example yourself. Employees know when you take home materials and equipment for your own use. When they see these things going on all around them, they say, "Well, if the boss can do it, so can I." Can you blame them?

What kind of an employee steals from the plant?

More than likely the pilferer is an old and trusted employee—one who knows the ropes. By and large he's not a one-time thief, he's a repeater who nibbles here and there. No big-time jobs but a lot of small ones that add up. Remember he's a normal human being—not a kleptomaniac. But he's not fussy. He'll take about anything that's not nailed down—and some that is—and whether he needs it or not. Worst of all, he spreads the stealing virus. Other employees know it's going on. If he gets away with it, they'll try their hand, too.

The Case of the Missing After-shave Lotion. A case study in human relations involving plant protection, with questions for you to answer.

Department 2B in a toiletry factory filled 6-ounce bottles with after-shave lotion. It processed about 100,000 bottles a day. The process was a simple one requiring four machine operators, eight "line" girls who fed bottles and labels and inspected, plus two material handlers and one maintenance man.

For many years it had been the practice in the plant to permit employees to take home as many off-grade bottles of after-shave lotion as they wished to—within reason. This month, however, the department supervisor was alarmed to note that rejects and shortages from his department had risen sharply from ¼ per cent to 1 per cent. At the suggestion of the plant superintendent, the supervisor then set up a "rework" station to recover off-grade bottles and reclaim them for shipment.

At the same time, the department supervisor also posted a notice to the effect that off-grade material could now be bought for 60 per cent off list price. Any employees caught taking bottles of after-shave lotion home without paying for them would be fired.

After the new rule had been in effect six weeks, the supervisor decided to make a spot-check of employees as they left the plant at quitting time. As the shift punched out, he asked each man to open his lunch box and each girl to open her pocketbook for inspection. Fourteen of the employees readily opened their gear for inspection. But one girl flatly refused to have her pocketbook inspected. "You have no right to look at my personal belongings," she said. "I refuse to be submitted to this outrage. It just shows what a cheap company this is."

1. If you were the supervisor, what would you do now?

2. Do you think the girl is right in refusing to have her bag inspected? Why?

3. What do you think of the supervisor's plan to prevent pilfering?

5

HELPING YOURSELF TO SUCCEED

31 RATING YOURSELF
FOR SELF–DEVELOPMENT

What can self-development mean to you?

Just about everything. Not only can it mean the difference between
your holding a mediocre job and your holding a good one, but it can
also mean the difference between your enjoying life and not enjoying
it.

Self-improvement should mean continual growth for you. Not
physical, of course, but mental. It should mean constantly assessing
yourself—as a supervisor and as a person. It calls for setting your personal standards a little higher each year. For as you grow older, experience should tell you more and more about what's truly worth
while and what isn't worth the candle.

True self-development calls for a certain amount of self-*dis*satisfaction. For it's when you become too satisfied with yourself—your performance as a supervisor or as an individual—that your growth stops
and you lose your grip.

So be ambitious for yourself. Work holds high rewards for those who
help themselves along. For mark it well: Over the long haul, your
success will depend upon your own efforts to improve.

How can you know how well you are doing on your job?

To map out a plan for your own self-improvement—the self-propelled road to a higher salary or a better job—the place to begin is with a no-excuses-permitted rating of yourself on your current job. To do so, answer the questions on the Self-rating Job Quiz on the following pages.

To evaluate your score, add up the scores for each of the questions. A total of 70 is par. A score of 100 is tops. Anything below 50 means there's something seriously wrong with your performance.

If your score is between 50 and 70 points, your whole approach to your job needs an overhaul. If your score is in the 70s, better set up a plan now for improvement. If your score is 80 or above, don't take your future for granted. Look again at your low spots—and decide to take definite action to bring them up within the next three months.

How can you improve your education?

Face it, the fellow with the better education has an advantage over the fellow who hasn't. But this doesn't mean that you can't do anything about it. There's plenty you can do to improve your knowledge.

First, examine your own attitude toward further education. Is it strictly negative, sour grapes? If so, better change in a hurry. Convince yourself that you, too, can learn new techniques and accept new ideas. If you *want* to learn, learning is made easier.

Next, pick out the soft spots in your educational armor. Is it reading and writing? Or a weakness with figures? These can be improved quickly through correspondence and home-study courses or in an evening course at a local university. Adult education courses at your local high school also offer help in these areas.

If your weakness is in a technical line—say your company is processing chemicals or constructing complicated electronic equipment, or your job involves simple metallurgy—you can find courses at technical institutes and universities that will help you understand your processes better, even if you don't become an expert.

Caution: You may not be able to take a course in physical chemistry, for instance, if you haven't had a previous course in basic chemistry. So your plan for improvement often may have to be a long-range one. Here's a suggestion, though. You may enroll in an advanced course just as a "listener." This way you get a feel for the subject and its terminology, with only a little prior preparation.

In your programming, don't scatter your efforts indiscriminately.

SELF-RATING JOB QUIZ *

1. Outline employee responsibilities

   Do you as a matter of policy see that each employee knows what you expect from him in terms of output, quality, attendance, and safety?

   (*a*) In specific terms and on a regular basis.   10 points

   (*b*) In specific terms but only when it applies to a
   new employee.   7 points

   (*c*) Vaguely and only when a discipline problem arises.   3 points

   (*d*) Can't remember when you last did this.   0 points

   Score: _____

2. Relationship with your employees

   Do you discuss with your workers your appraisal of their performance and other factors affecting your relationship with them?

   (*a*) Regularly.   20 points

   (*b*) Not on a regular basis.   12 points

   (*c*) Only occasionally.   8 points

   (*d*) Hardly ever.   0 points

   Score: _____

3. Working conditions

   Have you tried hard to see that working arrangements for you and your employees are conducive to good work?

   (*a*) By active, regular steps (inspections, etc.) to
   insure for housekeeping, safety, and discipline.   20 points

   (*b*) By occasional but effective efforts to improve
   housekeeping, safety, and discipline.   14 points

   (*c*) Only when forced to do so by your superior.   8 points

   (*d*) Not in the last twelve months.   0 points

   Score: _____

4. Contacts with other departments

   Do you try (whether or not aided by the company) to become better acquainted with men in other departments and to learn more about their duties?

   (*a*) By taking advantage of every opportunity and
   trying to make more.   10 points

   (*b*) By attending company functions and following
   all contacts.   7 points

   (*c*) By seldom attending company functions and
   failing to follow up contacts.   4 points

   (*d*) By never attending company functions and
   avoiding new contacts.   0 points

   Score: _____

* Adapted from William W. Eaton, "How to Rate Your Company and Yourself," *Factory Management and Maintenance*, December, 1950, p. 105, McGraw-Hill Publishing Company, Inc., New York, by permission of the publisher.

SELF-RATING JOB QUIZ (*continued*)

5. Further education and training
    Have you personally made it a policy to improve your own basic
    education so that it will best benefit you and your company?
    (*a*) By taking night or correspondence courses and
         following a program of self-education.   10 points
    (*b*) By conscientious efforts to train yourself when
         new problems arise on your job.   8 points
    (*c*) By only rare attempts to improve your knowledge
         in the field of your work.   4 points
    (*d*) In no way at all in the last 12 months.   0 points
                                                        Score: _____

6. New assignments and ideas
    Have you searched for ways to contribute new ideas and to accept
    assignments beyond the limits of your current job?
    (*a*) By regularly submitting in writing carefully
         considered ideas, or looking for chances to
         carry out special assignments.   10 points
    (*b*) By accepting additional assignments with enthu-
         siasm and carrying them out with vigor.   6 points
    (*c*) By occasionally suggesting ways informally for
         improving methods in your department.   2 points
    (*d*) By doing just what your job demands and
         nothing else.   0 points
                                                        Score: _____

7. Professional society activities
    Do you belong to, and participate in the affairs of, professional or
    technical societies, like the National Management Association or the
    Industrial Management Clubs?
    (*a*) More than one and attend most meetings.   5 points
    (*b*) At least one and attend most meetings.   4 points
    (*c*) At least one but attend only occasionally.   2 points
    (*d*) No outside activity of this nature.   0 points
                                                        Score: _____

8. Keeping posted on new technology
    Do you make a point of keeping up with the latest developments that
    affect supervision and the technical side of your job by reading busi-
    ness magazines and technical journals?
    (*a*) Regularly on company time and occasionally on
         your time.   5 points
    (*b*) Regularly on company time.   4 points
    (*c*) Rarely.   2 points
    (*d*) Never.   0 points
                                                        Score: _____

SELF-RATING JOB QUIZ (*continued*)

9. Attitude toward company
    When not carrying out specific orders or under active supervision from
    your boss, how do you attempt to use your time?
    (*a*) Exactly as though you were running your own
          business.   10 points
    (*b*) To follow policies and instructions to the letter
          but no more.   7 points
    (*c*) To work effectively only under pressure for
          conformance.   3 points
    (*d*) To look for loopholes to avoid work.   0 points
                                                          Score: _____
                                                          Total: _____

Pinpoint your educational efforts to plug your weak spots. Later on
if you like, you can add frills.

How can you take best advantage of your company's training and development program?

Show that you're interested. In most progressive companies today,
the personnel manager or training director is eager to help supervisors
who want to help themselves. Don't be ashamed to ask for help, or
feel that you'll be revealing a secret weakness. One of the necessary
qualities of an executive is the ability for self-analysis and the determination to improve.

Where can you go for outside help and guidance?

For educational guidance outside your company, try your local
centers for adult education or vocational guidance, a nearby university placement office or extension service. Or write either of the
nationwide management clubs mentioned on page 7. Another source
to try is any nearby chapter of the American Society of Training
Directors.

For information about specific correspondence or technical courses
write to:

• National Home Study Council, 1420 New York Ave., N.W., Washington 5, D.C.

• American Society for Engineering Education, Technical Institute
Division, University of Illinois, Urbana, Ill.

• National Council of Technical Schools, 1507 M St., N.W., Washington 5, D.C.

How can you draw favorable attention to yourself?

Just as you may take for granted an employee who does what he's asked and minds his own business, so too will your company tend to consider you merely average unless you make a special effort to draw attention to yourself.

In the Army there is a saying, "Never volunteer." But plenty of men became heroes by taking this chance. In business, too, you must take chances—stick your neck out—if you're going to go far. So look for opportunities to prepare special reports, to serve on plant committees, to volunteer opinions, and to point out problems.

While you may draw unfavorable comments from your associates if you're too much of an eager beaver, the real danger lies in doing too little and in not making your accomplishments known. Too many supervisors hide their light under a bushel. If you've been making progress in running your department more efficiently, don't brag about it. But do draw attention subtly to this progress by preparing performance reports on a regular basis.

Your outside activities, such as membership in professional societies or civic and service organizations, should be reported to your boss and to your personnel office. Look for every opportunity to get favorable information about you and your accomplishments into writing and into your personnel file.

What will outside reading do for you?

Some people can learn a lot just by reading. Others find it difficult to get much from the printed page. But if you're one of the former, try to set up a planned reading program. Include in it at least one good newspaper (like *The New York Times* or the *Wall Street Journal*), one good news magazine (like *Time* or *Newsweek*), one good management magazine (like *Business Week, Factory Management and Maintenance, The Office Supervisor*), and one good technical magazine or journal that serves your field. Don't just subscribe to them or have your name put on the routing list. Read them—and try to apply what you find in them. In addition, you ought to set up a library of business books for yourself. Suggestions for general management books will be found at the end of this book.

How does your company rate you as a supervisor?

Of course this varies from company to company. But for a very good example of the kind of qualities and performance a first-rate company expects from its managers and supervisors, look at the appraisal chart in Table 31–1, on pages 342 to 345. Try rating yourself. And use your lower ratings as a guide to your self-improvement program.

What is a management-development program?

Management development (it may also be called executive or supervisory development) is the term applied to the systematic inventory, appraisal, and training of management people. Programs vary according to an individual company's policies—sometimes include only top management people and often are not extended to the first-line supervisory level.

If there's a program in your company that applies to you, you'll probably hear about it from your boss. *Caution:* Don't expect your company to take care of your self-development program. It's really up to you.

How can you plan for your self-improvement?

Self-improvement—like the road to hell—is paved with good intentions. To avoid misfires in your ambitions, don't bite off too much at once. Plan ahead for continuing self-development. Check regularly to see what progress you've made. Try to put your plan into writing. The chart in Fig. 31–1 suggests one way to do this.

SELF-DEVELOPMENT SCHEDULE

Supervisor: *Joe Smith*

	WEAK SPOTS	PLAN FOR CORRECTIVE ACTION	WHEN TO DO IT	ACTION COM-PLETE
This Year's Plan	Telling employees where they stand	Prepare calendar with a different workman to be talked to each week	At once	√
	Poor department safety record	Hold monthly meetings with work group	Begin June	√
	Keeping up with job technology	Subscribe to American Machinist	At once	√
Next Year's Plan	No activities out-side of work	Join National Management Association	Next year	
	Speaking in front of groups	Enroll in Dale Carnegie course in public speaking	Next winter	
Fu-ture	Cost estimating	Take correspondence course in accounting	Not scheduled	

FIG. 31-1   Self-development schedule.

How important is your personal growth?

You spend only eight or ten hours a day at work. What you do as a person outside of your job undoubtedly influences the way you conduct

TABLE 31-1 HOW YOUR SUPERIORS LOOK AT YOU *

Typical Form Used by Executives for Rating Supervisors

	Excellent	Good	Average	Fair	Poor
1. *Knowledge of Job*—Familiarity with the various procedures of the work	Exceptional mastery of all phases of his work	Thorough knowledge of practically all phases of his work	Adequate knowledge of particular job	Insufficient knowledge of some phases of job	Inadequate comprehension of requirements of job
2. *Experience*—Skill and practical wisdom gained by personal knowledge	Broad background and training for particular job	A comprehensive background	An adequate background	Has some background but requires direction	Inexperienced or unsatisfactory progress
3. *General Company Information*—Knowledge of major and minor company policies	Thorough understanding and appreciation of all company policies	Knowledge of practically all company policies	Acceptable knowledge of company policies	Limited knowledge of company policies	Does not have enough information to be efficient
4. *Health*—Soundness of body and mind and freedom from physical disease or disability	Robust, energetic	Sufficiently healthy and energetic to handle the job	Sufficiently healthy to handle job but not overly energetic	Frail, affected by pressure	Sickly, affects his work
5. *Enthusiasm*—A positive, ardent, and eager response	Believes wholeheartedly in the company and expresses both orally and in his attitude that belief	Works enthusiastically, not too expressive	Matter-of-fact attitude	Definitely passive or indifferent	Negative in attitude

342

Item					
6. *Personality*—The external mannerisms consciously or unconsciously adopted in meeting situations	Radiant, confident, poised, courteous	Pleasant, forceful	Likeable	Ill-at-ease, not too forceful	Negative, colorless person
7. *Appearance*—Outward impressions made by a person	Superior style, grooming, taste and a sense of the fitness of things	Well dressed and neat	Neat, but not particularly striking	Intermittently careless	Slovenly and untidy
8. *Character*—Integrity of an individual	Has the courage of his convictions and unquestioned habits	Morally sound, tolerant	An average human being possessing average personal weaknesses	A person whose behavior harms no one but himself	A person who is a bad influence on the behavior of the group
9. *Mentality*—Quality of mind, mental power, and creative intellectual ability of a person	Superior ability to think clearly and arrive at sound conclusions	Worthwhile ideas of his own and ability to make useful decisions	Well informed on certain subjects useful in his daily work	Little ability to comprehend, interpret, or grasp new ideas	Unable to reason logically
10. *Sociability*—Sense of mutual relationship, companionship, and friendliness with others	A genuine interest in people and extremely well liked by others	A friendly, pleasant person, happy in a group	Willing to be a part of a group but makes little contribution	Poorly adjusted to the group	Unwilling to be a part of any group activities
11. *Ability to Get Things Done*—Ability to perform, execute, and achieve an assigned task	Completes assignments in the shortest possible time	Completes assignments in unusually short time	Completes assignments in a reasonable time	Slow in completing assignments, or does not complete them	Takes a long time to accomplish little
12. *Cooperation*—An appreciation of collective action for mutual profit or common benefit	Greatest possible cooperativeness	Very cooperative	Cooperative	Difficult to handle	Obstructive

* From William Hodge, "Merit Rating Plan for Executives," *Factory Management and Maintenance*, October, 1953, p. 102, McGraw-Hill Publishing Company, Inc., New York, by permission of the publisher.

TABLE 31-1 HOW YOUR SUPERIORS LOOK AT YOU *(continued)*

	Excellent	Good	Average	Fair	Poor
13. *Acceptance of Responsibility*—Willingness to assume duties	Greatest possible sense of responsibility	Very willing	Accepts but does not seek responsibility	Does assigned tasks reluctantly	Irresponsible
14. *Judgment*—Ability to grasp a situation and draw correct conclusions	Superior ability to think intelligently and use sound judgment	Excellent judgment	Good common sense	Poor judgment	Neglects and misinterprets the facts
15. *Initiative*—Desire and ability to introduce a new course of action	Seeks and sets for himself additional tasks, highly ingenious	Very resourceful	Progressive	Rarely suggests	Needs detailed instruction
16. *Expression*—Ability to articulate and express orally one's thoughts and feelings	Unusually articulate in expressing thoughts and feelings, master of good speech techniques	Speaks well	Nothing about his speech that is distinctive or distasteful	Careless speech habits and mild physical defects	Inarticulate and physical defects
17. *Rate of Work*—The time taken to finish a specific assignment	Greatest possible rapidity	Very rapid	Good speed	Slow	Hopelessly slow
18. *Accuracy*—A high percentage of freedom from mistakes	Highest possible accuracy	Very careful	Careful, no more than reasonable time required for revision	Careless, time required for revision greatly excessive	Practically worthless work
19. *Budget Accomplishment*	Performs within budget even under severe circumstances	Performance almost within budget, little deviation	Performs within budget more than two-thirds of the time and seldom are deviations substantial	Misses budget frequently and deviations are substantial	Almost always misses budget and deviations are often substantial

344

Condition of Department	Extremely orderly	Very orderly	No particular disorder	Disorderliness in department	Department very disorderly
20. Condition of Department	Extremely orderly	Very orderly	No particular disorder	Disorderliness in department	Department very disorderly
21. Handling People—The ability to appreciate, understand, and direct individual differences	Extremely successful in helping and training his men to progress and attain their ambitions	Capable leader	Fails to develop and obtain maximum results from men	Fails to command confidence	Antagonizes his subordinates
22. Developing Assistants—The ability to delegate responsibilities to the right individual	Superior ability in selecting suitable men and training them to assume specific responsibilities	Very capable in recognizing and training subordinates	Good in selection, but little attention is given to training	Allows subordinates to shift for themselves	Hinders the natural development of his men
23. Delegating Work—The assignment of specific responsibilities	Superior ability in recognizing individual's capacities when he assigns tasks	Capable supervisor	Fails to recognize individual's capacities	Fails to see work to be done	Does all the work himself
24. Planning and Organizing—Success in organizing, by delegating authority and planning	Highest possible effectiveness	Effective under difficult situations	Effective under normal circumstances	Lacks planning ability	Inefficient
25. Vision—The power to see and imagine	Superior ability to think creatively, foresee, and imagine	Very capable in anticipating the future	Ability to plan in advance	Overly realistic	Devoid of imagination
26. Selling Company Policies—Company loyalty and an eagerness to tell others	An extremely loyal employee eager to express to outsiders his enthusiasm	A very loyal employee	Passive in his attitude toward company policies	Critical of all company policies	Disloyal and traitorous

yourself at work. Consequently, it's important that as you grow older, you mature as an individual.

To get an indication of whether you are growing up personally, measure yourself against the Maturity Check List in Table 31–2.

Are you satisfied with yourself in areas that *you* consider to be important? Are you making progress where *you* feel you should? Ability to accept yourself is a mark of maturity.

To complete your self-examination, come back to these questions six months from now. That's the value in check lists—to keep checking.

TABLE 31–2 MATURITY CHECK LIST *

Are You Growing Up as You Grow Older?

In the past year	*In your work*	*In your personal and family life*
1. Did you take formal training or instruction to further your progress?	—	—
2. Did you step up your reading?	—	—
3. Did you increase your participation in group activities (company teams, civic associations, church groups)?	—	—
4. Did you improve your ability to handle routine and repetitive activities (correspondence, putting up storm-windows at home)?	—	—
5. Did you at any time review your past activities to determine which are desirable, which ought to be dropped?	—	—
6. Did you find it easier to deal with people?	—	—
7. Did you have fewer emotional flare-ups?	—	—
8. Did you get greater enjoyment out of periods of relaxation and recreation?	—	—
9. Did you devote more time to thinking about the reasons other people behaved the way they did?	—	—
10. Were you more likely to concentrate on one activity until it was completed?	—	—
11. Did you devote more time to, and get greater satisfaction out of, helping others solve their problems?	—	—
12. Did you improve any of your skills or develop new talents?	—	—

* From Mortimer Feinberg, *The Marks of Maturity, A Guide to Personal Growth,* copyright 1956 by Research Institute of America, New York. Used by permission of the publishers.

In the past year	In your work	In your personal and family life
13. Did you come up with some new conclusions about yourself, your personality, your habits?	—	—
14. Did you go in for new and more varied activities, develop new friends?	—	—
15. Did you find yourself making a larger number of independent decisions?	—	—
16. Did you find it easier to live with problems for which you had no immediate solutions?	—	—
17. Did you change some of your opinions and feelings about things?	—	—
18. Did you show a willingness to expose yourself to new experiences?	—	—
19. Did you gain a clearer conviction and a better understanding of the basic truths, religion, or philosophy in which you believe?	—	—

32 HOW TO HOLD GROUP DISCUSSIONS AND LEAD CONFERENCES

Why hold a discussion meeting with employees?

Because employees like meetings as a way of getting information. The spoken word is always more effective than the written word. And employees like the chance to get the story straight from the horse's mouth.

Informal group meetings are an excellent way for you to build participation in your department. It gives you a chance to explain the reasons behind some of the company's actions, and it gives employees a chance to ask questions that are bothering them.

What subjects should be discussed at group meetings?

Group meetings provide an excellent time to spike rumors that are circulating. You could hold a good meeting any time just by saying, "Well, gang, what's the latest rumor?"

Meetings provide good opportunity to bring up production figures, schedules, or new equipment, introduce new employees, comment on jobs well done, make announcements, or have your department meet visitors.

When should you hold meetings with your employees?

It's best to hold meetings during working hours. You can be sure of attendance then. And employees are likely to figure, "If the company is letting us do this on company time, it must be worth while."

The time of day is up to you. Some foremen prefer to hold the meetings just before quitting time so that the shop can be shut down and the employees clean up ahead of time. Others find that a good time is just before lunch.

How often should meetings be held?

That's up to you and your company's policy. Once a week tends to be too often. Once a month is just about right. Meetings should be held regularly, though. If you keep postponing them, the time will fly by without your accomplishing anything.

Are employees paid for attending meetings?

A question to be decided by company policy. But if you require an employee to attend a meeting and it in any way can be construed as helping him to become more proficient *on his present job,* the law considers this to be work, and he must be paid. Most companies make a practice of holding such meetings during working hours, so there is no problem of whether to pay or not.

Where should group discussion be held?

Anywhere that it's quiet and free from distractions. If you have an office of your own or can borrow one for a half hour or so, that's good enough. Some companies provide conference rooms, but even a quiet corner of the shop will do. And don't try to hold a meeting where you'll be bothered by phone calls or other interruptions.

How long should a meeting last?

When asked how long a man's legs should be, Abe Lincoln answered, "They should be long enough to reach the ground." That's the way to look at a meeting. It costs money to take employees off the job. So devote only enough time to accomplish the purpose of the meeting. If you want to announce the production schedule for the next month and answer questions about it, you may be able to finish in 15 minutes. But if you want the group's help in finding a solution to a shop problem, you'd better allow an hour. In any case, set a definite time limit beforehand, announce it ahead of time, and then stick to it.

And be sure to start your meeting on time. It's aggravating for a prompt person to have to wait for you to put the show on the road. Starting late is wasteful, too.

What kind of questions can you expect employees to ask?

Most employees ask questions about their jobs. Pete will want to know if there is going to be a layoff. Tom will ask whether the company is going to provide more working space. Bill will want to know when the new pay rates will come into effect.

Other employees' questions will run the gamut from "Why can't we haul our own finished products in company trucks?" or "Why can't we get more overtime?" to "Why don't we have a plant baseball team?"

Be assured that most employee questions are of the "what-will-this-mean-to-me?" variety.

Should meetings be informal or should they follow *Robert's Rules of Order?*

By all means keep your meetings informal. Let people smoke. Don't be stuffy yourself. A little good-natured kidding sets the stage for some forthright discussions.

On the other hand, a discussion meeting shouldn't be just another bull session. It's up to you to outline the purpose of the meeting to the group clearly, right at the start. And then keep the discussion within the boundaries of the subject matter.

How do you keep a meeting from getting off the subject?

When an employee with an ax to grind gets off the subject, speak up: "John, your point warrants further discussion, but it has little to do with the problem we're talking about today. Will you table it so that we can discuss it another time?"

If a long-winded employee monopolizes the conversation, you'll have to interrupt. Call him by name. Most people stop talking when you do so. Then say something like this: "Ted, we've been glad to get your opinion. Now I want to ask Frank how he feels about the suggestion for improving our scrap record."

How do you draw out the quiet individual?

Wait until the meeting has warmed up, then call on him by name. Try to be sure that you ask him to comment on something on which you feel he has an opinion. Don't ask questions that can be answered by "Yes" or "No." With shy or reticent people, it's best to ask questions that begin with what, why, where, who, when. Say to these people, "Mary, what do you feel is the reason for poor production this month?" or "Sam, what suggestions can you offer for reducing down time on the paper machine?" or "Jack, when have you observed that we run into trouble on deliveries?"

Should you answer any questions directed at you?

In a meeting where your purpose is to hand out information, you're the best person to answer questions. But in meetings where you want employees to participate and think things through for themselves, let them answer questions. If an employee asks you what to do to cut out rework, ask another employee to answer it. Or if you are asked a question, it works very well if you ask the person who asked it, "What do you think?" or "How would you do it?" or "Why do you ask that?"

The purpose of questioning is to encourage employees to think through the problem under discussion. If you do all the answering and all the talking, you'll miss one of the big advantages from group meetings—the sense of participation and two-way communication.

Should a meeting to pass out information follow a particular order?

Each type of meeting best follows a particular sequence. To pass on information, divide your meeting into three parts:

Make your announcement. Tell why the meeting is important to the employees. Tell how it will affect them.

Ask for questions. People who ask questions are your best test of whether what you have said has gotten over. If no one asks questions, try asking some yourself such as, "In what way do you think this change in procedure will affect our output?" or "Ted, how will you go about making the change effective on your job?" or "Mary, what part of this announcement is least clear to you?"

Summarize. Briefly restate your main points plus any clarifying information that was developed during the question period.

What procedure should you follow for a problem-solving meeting?

True participation comes from a meeting where you and your employees decide among yourselves how to handle a shop problem common to all. Such a meeting must follow a fairly inflexible procedure, or the problem will be short-circuited by employees who want to jump to conclusions.

You should try to see that your problem-solving meeting follows, as nearly as it can, these six steps:

Step 1. Decide on the real problem. If you want the group to work on better housekeeping, be as specific as you can. Don't say, "Our problem is to improve housekeeping." It's better to say, "Our last inspection showed that our most serious housekeeping problem is keeping junk from accumulating under work benches. That's what we're going to talk about today."

Step 2. State the facts. Give employees the facts about this particular problem. Try to show them why it's an important problem for them to solve. Say, "I checked last year's record and found that while we did pretty well in every other phase of housekeeping, the bench problem has been a hardy perennial. Besides, the last time the old man came through here, he really blew his stack about it."

Step 3. List advantages of solving the problem. Many conference leaders miss this important step. Here's your golden opportunity to let employees sell themselves on the reasons for solving the problem and to discover what benefits it will bring to them. *You* stop talking at this point and let employees suggest benefits (from better housekeeping in this example), like:

• Make the shop a better place to work.
• Keep the shop clear of roaches.
• Enable us to produce more.
• Keep our stockings from snagging on loose materials.
• Win the housekeeping award for the month.

Step 4. List the obstacles that stand in the way of solving the problem. Get employees to suggest what the troubles are, like:

• Not enough trash receptacles.
• Takes too much time.
• Carelessness.
• Sloppy workmanship.
• Lack of cooperation.

You'll quickly note that at first all the reasons are, in effect, blamed on the company, but gradually the personal reasons come out. When employees begin to realize that part of the responsibility is theirs— that's the beginning of real participation. And cooperation will follow soon. (Note that in this step you *do not* ask for solutions. Hold off the eager beavers until step 5. Only obstacles now!)

Step 5. Suggest possible solutions. Now get the group to look at each of the obstacles they have listed. One by one get suggestions for overcoming each obstacle. You may have as many as five or ten possible solutions for each obstacle.

Suppose, for instance, the group is working on possible solutions to the second item in step 4—"Not enough time." Typical solutions might be:

• Get company to allow more time for housekeeping.
• Plan housekeeping better.
• Prevent benches from getting dirty in first place.
• Clean up as you produce.

Note that again, workers first tend to suggest the *company* holds the solution. Then members of the group start suggesting there are things *they* can do.

Accept every idea that's offered. Don't *you* be the one to turn it down. If you do, the group will think that you have all the answers, will quickly clam up. This is true of steps 3 and 4 also.

Step 6. Decide what to do. This is the action step. Most people want to leapfrog from the statement of the problem to the answer. But the planned conference analyzes the problem systematically—and gets much better results.

In the action step you'll ask the group to study all the possible solutions. "Look at all these possibilities," you might say. "A few are far fetched, others impractical, but some appear to have real merit. What do you think we should do? Which ones should we put into action?"

You'll find the group will throw out some, accept others. They may not come up with the same ones you'd favor. If not, you'll have to abide by their decisions, although you may ask the group to debate a discarded solution which you think has value.

How do you make sure conference members take action on their decisions?

A big reason some employees feel conferences are not much good is that no action is taken on what they agreed upon. So never let a conference break up until the group has pinned down who's going to do what.

Take the housekeeping example. Suppose the group decided to have a committee make regular inspections. That's too vague to guarantee effective action. Pull out those famous questions: *what, where, when, how,* and *who.*

Ask the group, "*Who* should be on the committee? *When* should the inspections be made—weekly or monthly? At the end of the week or in the middle of the week? *What* should they look for? *Where* should they look for it? *How* should they report their findings?"

Suppose that during a conference the supervisor disagrees with an employee suggestion, what should the supervisor do?

If you are acting as conference or discussion leader, it's always more effective if you can get another employee to rebut a suggestion you feel is improper. Or better still, ask the employee who makes a suggestion that you disagree with any of the six key questions such as, "*Why* do you feel that will work, Pete? In *what* way will that get at the real problem? *Where* will that method be most effective?" Then you can turn to other employees and ask them the same questions. If your point of view is really sound, there will be others who feel the same as you. If not, *you* may be wrong.

If during a meeting an employee makes a statement of fact that is not true—and no other member of the group corrects him first—it's proper for you to set the group straight on the facts. Take the housekeeping example again. One employee says that an obstacle is "not enough time." If this group works on piece rates, for instance, and you know that the time study has an allowance in it for keeping the work bench clean, speak up. By all means take advantage of this suggestion to explain how the piece rates include such allowances.

A great value from meetings is that employees feel freer to say and ask things that they might not do alone. You can get an insight into what's bothering them. And speak up to correct misinformation.

Can a supervisor discuss problems with his employees without letting them make decisions? How do you do that?

If you meet with employees to get their opinions or to find out what their attitudes might be, you needn't give up your prerogative to decide how things will be done. Tell the group *at the start* of the meeting that *you* have to make a decision. But that since it will affect them, you'd like to get their opinions on the problem before *you* make up your mind. This is called an "opinions requested" meeting. In it you can follow the problem-solving procedure generally. But be sure to stop before step 6, where decisions for action are made.

You may also just say, "Gang, I'd like to get your opinions on this problem." Take their suggestions as opinions only, with no indication of how you'll finally decide. To draw out the thinking behind what employees suggest, keep asking any of the six key questions.

Should you keep a record of what goes on at a meeting?

Unless you promise the group that the meeting is off the record, it's a good practice to keep notes on the key points brought out during a conference. The easiest way to do this is to use a blackboard or chartboard (an easel with a pad of paper about 2 by 3 feet on it). As you go through each step, write down the points *you* make (steps 1 and 2) and the suggestions the *group* offers (steps 3 through 6) on the board. When the meeting is over, all you need do is copy what's been written on the blackboard, or if you use a chartboard, simply tear off the sheets.

Writing employee suggestions down as they make them is often called the "laundry-list" technique. When an employee sees that you accept each idea and write it down, it stimulates participation. A worker will feel, "At least I've had my say and someone has listened to me." Other employees react, "If Al can say that, there's no reason why I shouldn't get across my point, too."

Must a supervisor be a good public speaker in order to lead a conference well?

No. Conference leading is *not* public speaking. If you know your subject well and have thought about what you're going to say beforehand, that will be enough.

Think about a conference as being nothing other than a large-scale conversation. If you were talking over a problem with two of your workers and a couple more joined the group, you wouldn't find this anything to scare you. About the only thing you'd do differently is to talk a little louder and address yourself to all four. Suppose another three or four workers drifted into the group. About all you'd do is to speak even a little louder and maybe more slowly. You'd probably watch a little more carefully to see if your points were getting across. It's the same way when you lead a conference.

Should you use notes?

Notes will help you have confidence, and they'll keep you on the beam, too. They needn't be elaborate. In fact, they ought to be brief. A good idea is to make up a little 3- by 5-inch file card for each of the subjects you intend to cover. You may have only a couple of phrases or figures on one card, a half dozen on the others. It's all right if the group knows you're using notes. This helps show them you won't waste their time, that you've planned the meeting ahead of time.

Never read what you have to say. Better to stammer and stumble a little than to do that. Employees and others react this way: "If all he's going to do is read this announcement, why didn't he let *us* read it in the first place?" *Only exception to not reading:* when you want to be absolutely certain you are quoting an essential phrase or sentence correctly.

What about humor or funny stories?

Listen to what Dale Carnegie said on this subject:

"Humor is one of the best ways of getting your audience in the palm of your hand. It's also one of the most dangerous techniques of speaking.

"For every natural humorist, there are ten thousand people who linger under the false impression that they are humorists. They can't be funny, but insist on boring everyone by trying. So unless you're absolutely sure that the mantle of Bob Hope or Jackie Gleason has descended on your shoulders, it's smart to avoid most temptations to be funny.

"If you're in doubt about your ability to be humorous—just ask your wife!"

In using visual aids (charts, pictures, graphs, films), to what extent can you rely upon them to tell their own story?

If your employees haven't seen fancy diagrams before, explain how to read them, what points they illustrate, how they prove your point. Make sure everyone can see the exhibit. *You* should know what it looks like, so look at your audience as you describe it. When you've finished with it, put it down so it doesn't distract the rest of the discussion.

Remember visuals are *aids* only. They rarely do the whole job.

What can you do to control the jitters?

Dale Carnegie said: "All speakers, no matter how experienced, feel slight nervousness before they start to talk. Nervousness can be an asset. It is bottled-up energy. Once a speaker gets into his talk, gets excited and animated, this nervousness releases itself in effective energy."

What are some common faults for conference leaders to avoid?

Remember, meetings are for *group* exchange of ideas or plans for action. So conduct your meetings so that every individual gets his chance to get the most out of it.

Don't use the power of your position. Your job is to release the power of the group—through the six key questions.

Don't get angry. The conference leader is effective only when he's patient, understanding, and friendly.

Don't cover too much ground. Be satisfied to do one thing at a time. Hold two or three short meetings rather than one extra-long one.

Don't talk too much. The leader is in charge of the meeting and should guide it along the roads to a solution. But he shouldn't talk more than one-third of the time.

Don't start late. Plan for the right amount of time for your purpose. If you say the meeting will last only 30 minutes, check your watch. After 25 minutes, warn that there's only 5 minutes to sum up. If a solution hasn't been arrived at, schedule another meeting.

How can you get more out of meetings you attend?

When you are a participant, act the way you'd like people to act in your meetings. Offer your comments freely, but don't dominate the conversation. When you disagree, keep personalities out of it. Assist the conference leader by asking the six key questions of other conference members. Remember, you reveal your own attitude when you are a participant. So try to make it a reasonable one. You don't have to be a yes-man in conference. But check your conduct to see whether you're foolishly stubborn or opinionated. (You shouldn't be.) Check your own resistance to new ideas. Listen to hear what *you* can learn from what others say.

Some conferences use case studies and role playing. What's this all about?

In an "announcement" meeting, the conference leader does a good deal of talking and maintains a firm control on the direction the meeting takes.

In a "problem-solving" or "opinions-requested" meeting, he does less talking, but he still guides the meeting firmly along the lines he has chosen.

In a third type of conference, used primarily for training supervisors and managers in handling human relations, the leader exercises only loose control and does little except ask questions, hardly ever offers a comment. This is true of case studies and role playing.

A *case study* is a story (usually true) of an episode that has taken place among employees and supervisors somewhere. The conference leader either tells the story or lets the conferees read it. Then they discuss the case for an hour or so. The leader asks questions like, "Why do you suppose the supervisor acted the way he did? How do you think the employee felt about this matter? If you were the supervisor, what would you have done?" Purpose of this kind of questioning is to encourage participants to examine their own experiences in handling similar matters and to see how other group members think about the technique used. From such meetings, supervisors are able to develop a greater sensitivity toward human relations matters and to improve their relationship with employees and associates accordingly.

Role playing is a variation of the case-study technique. Instead of limiting the meeting to a general discussion, participants actually act out an unrehearsed play about the case. A member will actually assume the role of one of the individuals in the case. He and others then try out their techniques for handling human relations in front of the group. This way a supervisor can get a chance to see how others react to his methods. And he can improve his approach accordingly.

Are there any special precautions to take when showing a film to a group of employees?

Yes. A motion picture film will rarely do the job of conference leading for you. If you use a film, (1) tell the group beforehand what to look for in the film, (2) show the film, and (3) have the group discuss its reactions to the film afterwards.

Try this check list before using a film. If you can't answer yes to all questions, don't use the film:
- Is the film appropriate to the topic under discussion?
- Are you thoroughly familiar with the film? Have you previewed it?
- Is the conference room adequately equipped for showing films?
- Have you prepared an introduction?
- Have you planned a discussion to be conducted after the showing?
- Are the contents of the film in keeping with company policy?

What things should a conference leader check before holding a formal conference?

Figure 32–1 is a check list of things you should do while preparing and planning your conference. This list is designed for formal conferences, but much of it still applies to informal group discussions with employees.

Where can a supervisor find out more about how to lead discussions and conferences?

Try any of these publications:

Auer, J. J., and H. L. Ewbank: *Handbook for Discussion Leaders*, Harper & Brothers, New York, 1954.

Busch, Henry M.: *Conference Methods in Industry*, Harper & Brothers, New York, 1949.

Ellis, William D., and Frank Siedel: *How to Win the Conference*, Prentice-Hall, Englewood Cliffs, N.J., 1955.

Hannaford, Earle S.: *Conference Leadership in Business and Industry*, McGraw-Hill Book Company, Inc., New York, 1945.

Zelko, Harold P.: *Successful Conference and Discussion Techniques*, McGraw-Hill Book Company, Inc., New York, 1957.

CHECK LIST

for conference leader preparation and planning

Have you   *Yes*   *No*

1. Fixed in your mind the objectives to be attained through the conference discussion?

2. Secured, prepared, or thoroughly familiarized yourself with the necessary conference aids:
   - (a) Charts ready?
   - (b) Case studies prepared?
   - (c) Check sheets to be distributed ready in sufficient quantities?
   - (d) Demonstrations predetermined?
   - (e) All special materials obtained?
   - (f) Films to be used previewed and a plan made for their use?

3. Prepared your opening talk?

4. Carefully studied your conference outline?
   - (a) Determined the important points to be emphasized?
   - (b) Considered anticipated responses and group reactions?
   - (c) Determined points at which quick summaries will be made?
   - (d) Considered experiences and stories to be used for emphasis?
   - (e) Determined ways and means of getting conferee participation, stimulating thinking, and creating interest?
   - (f) Considered what the summary of the group's thinking might be?

5. Planned carefully to be sure adequate time has been allotted?

6. Notified everyone concerned of time and place of meeting?
   Checked physical requirements for conducting meeting?
   - (a) Blackboard or chart paper available?
   - (b) Seating arrangement conforms to good conference procedure?
   - (c) Facilities for showing films in readiness?
   - (d) Ash trays provided if smoking is permissible?
   - (e) Chalk, crayon, scotch tape, thumb tacks, erasers, paper, pencils, etc., on hand?
   - (f) Ventilation, heat, light, conferee comfort adequate?

FIG. 32-1 Check list for conference leader preparation and planning. M. Joseph Dooher and Vivienne Marquis, editors, *The Supervisor's Management Guide*, American Management Association, New York, 1949.

33 WRITING FOR BUSINESS

Why is so much importance attached to the ability to write well?

Television, telephone, and radio notwithstanding, writing is still a major form of communication. As industry grows bigger, the need for putting things in writing gets bigger too. And the fellow who can convey his ideas and information to others clearly in writing is the fellow most likely to succeed. Not that a supervisor can dodge the job of writing even if he wanted to. There are memos to be written to the watchman, to the third-shift super, to the boss. There are letters to be written to a sick employee, to business acquaintances, and for a hundred and one reasons. And the supervisor who really gets ahead finds himself preparing reports of his department's activities and progress, or reports that carry his ideas for improvements up the line.

What can better writing do for you?

It has been said, and wisely, that people will judge you not only by *what* you say, but by how *clearly* you say it. It's even more true about what you put in writing. Your memos and letters help create the impression, for good or for bad, that you leave with your associates and your superiors. And even more than creating impressions, your ability to put yourself down in black and white enables you to coordinate your activities with the rest of the management organization.

Don't you need a college education to write well?

No. Any person who applies the rules for grammar that he learned in grade school can do an acceptable job of writing.

Big words and stilted phrases don't really fool anyone. People are interested in what you say, if you are interesting, too. So be yourself in your writing. Don't be afraid to put your words down just the way you'd say them in conversation (well, pretty nearly). Express only one idea at a time. Keep your sentences short, so that you don't tangle the reader in them. Use only familiar words, ones whose meaning you're sure of.

How about spelling?

There's no excuse for spelling words wrong. Dictionaries are easy to use. Check any word you're in doubt of. Most people will excuse shaky grammar if your ideas are clear. But poor spelling or improper usage of words will make you look lazy, or as if you're trying to put on airs that you can't carry.

What are common faults in writing?

Some of the commonest faults observed in letter writing are the easiest ones to avoid. For instance, take these two:

• A letter that rambles. Its purpose is foggy. It starts with one point and turns in another direction. The reader must read through three-quarters of the letter to find out what the writer is getting at. Better be blunt than beat around the bush. Letters that do the latter try the reader's patience.

• Too many big words and jawbreaker phrases. These letters will contain phrases like, "It is requested that the recipient direct his future activities toward reducing his recurrent tardiness else disciplinary action be taken which may result in summary discharge." What this writer means is, "If you don't cut down on your lateness, you'll be fired." Why not say so?

How can you avoid these common mistakes?

If your memo or letter measures up to four qualities, it should accomplish its purpose. Here they are:

• State the purpose of the letter clearly and early. Right in the first sentence, if possible. Certainly in the first paragraph. This way the reader knows from the beginning what you are talking about, the point you want to make. For instance, "Dear Boss: Figures I've been keeping for the last six months show that this department needs a second lift truck. Unless we have one by the first of the year, we will run into heavy overtime. Besides, we won't be able to get shipments out on time."

• Be businesslike. Include only facts, people, and figures that are directly connected with the point you make. Otherwise you waste the reader's time and yours.

• Keep the letter easy to read. Good organization, more than almost anything else, helps a reader to understand you. Be sure that your reasoning is logical in the first place. Then see if each paragraph follows the former one in a logical order. Ask yourself, "Does this make sense?"

Letters are easier to read, too, if the sentences and paragraphs are short. Nothing looks duller than solid blocks of sentences. If you express only one idea in each paragraph, your letters will be shorter and more attractive.

• Do some selling. Your memos and letters needn't be sales letters, but they must be persuasive. If you want someone to go along with your ideas or course of action, you have to show what the benefits will be to him. Say, for instance. "The new lift truck will enable the plant to maintain a perfect on-time shipping record." Or, "With the additional time saved, I'll be able to make the improvements in housekeeping you suggested in your last inspection."

You can be persuasive, too, when you back up your contentions with facts. For example, "A similar estimate was made in department Z last year. Their experience with the new truck showed it paid for itself in nine months."

Should your letter follow any particular order?

A time-tested formula for good letter organization is to divide it into three sections. In the *first paragraph* state your purpose. In the *body* of the letter give your supporting reasons and tell your story. In the *last paragraph* tell the reader the action you want him to take.

What's the best way to begin a letter?

Make the first paragraph of your letter do three things for you:

• Get favorable attention. Set a friendly and courteous tone for the rest of the letter by stating your greeting just as you would when you meet a friend. For example, "Dear Mr. Brooks: Your interest in my last report has encouraged me. I'd like your advice again. . . ."

• Link up with previous letters by date or subject. For example, "When you replied on June 5, 1958, to my memo on cutting scrap loss. . . ."

• Pin down what the letter is about. For example, "As you instructed, I've kept records for in-process scrap loss as well as for loss at final inspection. These records show that addition of another inspection station would reduce total scrap from 7 to 3 per cent."

How much detail should you include?

If you put too much detail in your letter, you'll bore your reader. If you put in too little, he may feel you're weak on your facts. Just the right amount is hard to estimate.

The place for you to start is with your knowledge of the reader. If he's the kind of fellow who's busy, you'd better be brief. If his interest in the subject is considerable, you'd better expand a little to include the type of information you think he wants to know. If he's very familiar with the details already, he may want only the bare facts.

If you stop to think about the reader *before* you write your letter, your chances of being on target are good.

Are there expressions you should avoid?

Some business phrases have been used so often that they have become trite. If you use them, you'll look amateurish, so avoid these trite expressions: *

Old-fashioned	*More up-to-date*
According to our records . . .	We find . . .
As per . . .	According to . . .
Attached please find . . .	We enclose . . . , or We are attaching . . .
At your earliest convenience . . .	Soon . . .
Beg to acknowledge . . .	We acknowledge . . .
Enclosed please find . . .	We enclose . . .
Thank you for your favor of October 7 . . .	Thank you for your letter . . .
In receipt of . . .	We have received your . . .
The writer . . .	I believe . . . , or We think . . .
Thanking you in advance . . .	I shall be grateful for . . .
Regret to inform you . . .	We are sorry . . .
At the present time . . .	Now . . .
Due to the fact that . . .	Since . . . , or Because . . .
In order that . . .	So . . .
In the event that . . .	If . . .
Of the order of magnitude of . . .	About . . .

* Expressions selected from Robert L. Shurter, *Effective Letters in Business*, McGraw-Hill Book Company, Inc., New York, 1954, by permission of the publisher.

Old-fashioned	*More up-to-date*
Pursuant to our agreement . . .	As we agreed . . .
We are not in a position to . . .	We cannot . . .
Consensus of opinion . . .	Consensus . . .
Exactly identical . . .	Identical . . .
My personal opinion . . .	My opinion . . .
In the normal course of our procedure . . .	Normally . . .

How can you be sure you haven't overlooked anything important?

If you write a memo to your boss and he has to telephone you for something you should have included in the first place, that's downright embarrassing. To avoid this, try asking yourself these questions:

Who? Have you pinned down the people involved? Who is affected by your letter—your boss, any of your associates, the person who must carry out or review any action suggested?

What? Remember the detective on the television program who kept saying, "Just the facts, ma'am"? Be sure no one who reads what you write asks that question. In effect your letter should say, "These are the facts of the situation. And here is what I think they mean to you."

Why? Have you explained the reasons behind your suggestion, complaint, or action? For instance, "The monthly report will be two days overdue this month *because* ("because" is your key word) the shop clerk has been busy taking the year-end inventory."

Where? Don't suppose your reader is familiar with the scene of the crime. Tell him where the action takes place. It would be too bad to have a suggestion turned down because your boss assumed you meant it to apply to the plating shop, for example, when you didn't expect it to extend beyond the heat-treat.

When? Did it happen yesterday or last year? Will the change take place next week or next month? Don't make your reader play guessing games. Be specific.

How much? Cost figures quickly bring dreams down to earth. If dollars and cents are involved, include them to make your letter more meaningful.

Should your letter be typed?

You're never wrong if you see that anything you write is typed. It gets your letter off on the right foot. But it isn't necessary. And as you know, it's not always possible to get a letter typed. If a letter is not typewritten, however, it *is* important that you make certain your handwriting is neat and legible.

What about the form of the letter?

There are any number of ways to arrange a business letter. A couple of them are shown on the following page. Take your choice.

For letters or memos written within your own company, you'll want to check the style your company has adopted so that your correspondence is consistent with it.

How many copies?

First rule: Always keep a copy of what you have written. It's good business and makes an excellent reference.

It's also considered courteous—and good business, too—to send a copy of your letter to any person who is mentioned in your letter and who will be affected in a major way by what you write.

What's the difference between a letter and a memorandum?

Except for the form, there is practically no difference. Usually a memorandum is briefer and less formal than a letter. And in many companies it is either typed or written by hand on a printed form that may have these headings:

TO:	FROM:
SUBJECT:	DATE:

Letters are usually more formal than a memorandum, can be either short or long. In business, letters are usually typed, while memos are sometimes handwritten.

When should you write a report?

Whenever you see, do, or propose something that should be recorded permanently.

If your boss asks you to check on the number of absences in your department, a handwritten memo might be sufficient. But suppose your boss asks that you study the absences in your department to see if there's any connection between employees who are habitually late and those who are poor producers. Such a study might take you several days or even months to compile. The results, whether conclusive or not, probably hold widespread interest among higher management people. In such a case, it's to your advantage—and to your company's—for you to prepare a more formal record—a written report.

How should a report be organized?

You can write a report three different ways. Each has its own advantages.

The *logical* method of organization follows step by step the chain of

COMMON LETTER FORMS

Block Form

March 27, 1958

Mr. John R. Bodkin
Manager, Production Control
Silent Gear Company
235 Oak Street
Old Towne, Michigan

Dear Mr. Bodkin:

Thanks for your inquiry of March 15. My superior,
Mr. L. W. Smith, has authorized me to furnish you
with the information you request.

Production rates in the assembly department, which
I supervise, have been 5½% higher since we installed
our job priority system. In addition, we have had
to back order only three jobs since the beginning
of the year. Last year we had a total of 75 back
orders.

I hope this answers all your questions. If not,
don't hesitate to call me.

Sincerely yours,

R. G. Mount
Foreman, Department 121

Semiblock form

June 1, 1958

Mr. Frank Lawson, Superintendent
Superior Axle Company
30 River Road
Northville, New Jersey

Dear Mr. Lawson:

Attached is the report of scrap reduction you
asked me to submit each month.

You may be pleased to note that scrap in Department 312 has been reduced by more than 1/5 over last
month's record.

If you wish to examine the daily scrap records,
you may do so by looking through the "scrap logbook"
maintained permanently in the shop.

Very truly yours,

C. W. Gilchrist
Supervisor, Dept. 312

your reasoning. It's kind of like ticking off the important points on your fingers. You start first with the familiar: "We worked 10,000 hours in our department last month and turned out 50,000 units." Next you go to the less familiar: "Three-quarters of our total production— or over 35,000 units—was produced in the last half of the month." Then to the even less familiar: "Our scrap record, surprisingly, was better during the last half of the month."

Your boss may have been well aware of the first facts in your report, not so much aware of the details you present in the next two sections. On this foundation of facts, you build your logic: "Poor scheduling was a reason production was off in the first half of the month. But apparently, the more our department produces the better the quality of our production." Now for your conclusion: "Next month we'd like to see the planning department load our department at 95 per cent of capacity right from the start. I think it helps us develop a rhythm that gives us better and faster production."

This example is condensed for brevity. In an actual report you might follow each of the key sentences with several paragraphs, plus the necessary documentation.

The *chronological method* of organization begins in the beginning with the first date of what you did or observed and finishes at the end with the last thing you did. This time sequence is limited in value, but it's often useful for reporting the sequence of happenings that led to a grievance, for instance. And of course, this kind of report is easy to organize.

The *psychological method* is the most popular form for reports written in business today. Managers like them because they take less time to get to the point, are consequently easier to read.

The psychological method is almost the reverse of the logical one. The report begins with your conclusions, result, or summary. Following the conclusions are the facts that support your conclusions. These facts demonstrate the reasoning you used to arrive at your conclusion.

The psychological report concludes with an appendix in which you exhibit your calculations, detailed records, observations, etc.

In such a report you might imagine that the reader, say, your boss, looks at the conclusions to get a quick idea of what your results are. If he finds your conclusions hard to believe or understand, he reads the middle part of the report to check your logic. If your reasoning or accuracy is in any doubt, he can check it by going in detail through the exhibits in the appendix.

What elements should go in the written report?

This outline will suit most reports. You needn't follow it to the letter, but it will give you some ideas of what to include, and where.

Cover. Put your best foot forward. If your report is a long one, bind it between manila covers.

Title page. Select a title which tells what the report is all about. And identify yourself as the person who prepared the report, also your department and company and date report is written.

Letter of transmittal. Even though you hand the report to the boss, it's a good idea to insert a formal letter of transmittal. In it briefly state the purpose of the report and why and how it was originated. For instance, "Enclosed for your reaction is a report entitled 'A Comparison of Absences with Production Records for Employees in Department 201.' The report covers the period March 1 to May 31, 1958, and follows the line of inquiry you instructed me to make this spring."

Table of contents. This quickly shows the reader what the report covers. If you number your pages, the contents will also show the length, and perhaps the significance, of your sections.

Conclusions. In addition to summarizing your main findings, include a short synopsis of the purpose of the report and the methods you used to make your observations.

Main body of report. Here you define your problem in detail, tell how you approached it, develop your logic, and support your arguments and conclusions.

Appendixes. Here's where you put the mass of technical data, extractions from time sheets and production records, charts, and diagrams. This is the reading gallery for anyone who is interested in the details of your study. The more of your report you can put back here, the easier your report is to read for a busy executive.

Where can a supervisor find out more about how to improve his business writing?

Flesch, Rudolph: *Art of Readable Writing,* Harper & Brothers, New York, 1951.

Gottlieb, Hans J., B. B. Gamzue, and Milton Kalb: *English for Adults,* Harper & Brothers, New York, 1954.

Gunning, Robert: *The Technique of Clear Writing,* McGraw-Hill Book Company, Inc., New York, 1952.

Linton, Calvin D.: *How to Write Reports,* Harper & Brothers, New York, 1954.

Murphy, Dennis: *Better Business Communication,* McGraw-Hill Book Company, Inc., New York, 1957.

Saunders, A. G., and C. R. Anderson: *Business Reports,* McGraw-Hill Book Company, Inc., New York, 1940.

Shurter, Robert L.: *Effective Letters in Business,* 2d ed., McGraw-Hill Book Company, Inc., New York, 1954.

34 HOW TO MANAGE YOUR TIME BETTER

Are you really too busy?

That's the first question you should ask—and answer—yourself. There's an old story about a farmer who told his wife he would plow the north field the next day. It goes like this:

In the morning he went out to oil the tractor, but he found that he was low on oil. So he went to the storage shed to get some. On the way he noticed the chickens weren't fed. He went to the corn crib to get them some corn, where he saw some sacks on the ground. That reminded him the potatoes needed sprouting, so he started for the potato pit to sprout the potatoes. As it happens, on the way he passed the woodpile and remembered he had to take some kindling to the house. He had picked up a few sticks when an ailing lamb passed by. He dropped the wood and reached for the lamb. He . . .

Guess we don't have to finish the story. It's important only if it means something to you. For instance, does it bear any resemblance to your own methods of operation in the shop? Do you, for example, start out to see the shop clerk, run back to check a tote box of finished parts for quality, stop on the way to talk to a mechanic about a job to be done, then leave him to answer a phone, drop the phone to answer

369

a question from a workman—and never get to see the man you started out to see?

All this may be exaggerated. But it points up a clue to why so many supervisors are too busy to do the job they ought to do. They lack system. So here's the cardinal rule of using your time better: *The more systematic you are, the more effective you will be in the use of your time.*

Where does the time go?

A supervisor's time, according to analyst W. E. Dewey, flies away from him in four different ways:

Routine work. Like checking time cards, filling out pay sheets, distributing pay envelopes, answering mail, etc. These are the little things of your job. But unless you keep an eye on them, they can take a big part of your time—as much as 20 or 30 per cent.

Regular job duties. Like supervising employees, assigning work, training new workers, checking performance, counseling employees. This part of your job is most important. And should get the major part of your attention.

Special assignments. Like when your boss says, "Joe, will you find out how many hours it took to produce that Acme job last month?" or "Will you serve this month on the plant's cost-improvement committee?" These can be the little jobs that show you save time for that extra effort.

Creative work. Like figuring out a new layout for your department or starting a training program to teach your employees new skills. The man who gets ahead often draws favorable attention by what he does about his job on his own initiative.

What can you do to save time?

First find out where your time goes. For a week, keep a running record of what you do. Make it specific—like 8:00, check time clocks; 8:15, call for raw materials; 8:25, supervising in shop; 9:35, fill out time sheets; 10:00, discuss grievances with shop steward; etc.

Next, analyze your time record according to the four categories listed in the previous question. Then add up how much time you spend for each kind of work.

Now ask yourself how much of the *routine work* you can delegate to a clerk or other assistant. You should cut this time for routine work to the bone—say less than 10 per cent of your total time.

Look over your time allotment for *regular job duties.* Are you spending *enough* time on them? Are you doing everything you should? Are you doing some things that can be discontinued for more important efforts? You're the best judge, but you should devote something like 70 per cent of your time to this phase of your job. Supervising, that is. Not stock chasing and running meaningless errands that cheaper help can do for you.

How about your *special assignments?* Are you accepting your share of the miscellaneous duties that crop up? Or are you getting the reputation as a shirker? On the other hand, avoid being so active on side-bar efforts that your regular duties don't get the proper attention. As a rule of thumb, hold your special assignment time to 10 or 15 per cent unless your boss says otherwise.

Finally, does your time analysis show you to be marking time on the job, or are you finding time to do something *creative?* Not only for the eager beaver (who finds that this is the path to promotion) but also for the old-timer, this devotion to trying to find new and better ways of doing things has a pay-off. Your job becomes more interesting— and more rewarding.

To what extent should you try to budget your time at work?

Planning how you'll spend your time is essential to timesaving management. So you'll want to draw up a time budget for yourself. But keep it flexible. A minute-to-minute budget isn't realistic. But it makes good sense to rough out your week ahead on an hourly or half-hourly basis. Try it today. There's a sample in Fig. 34–1. And if it doesn't work out too well the first time, adjust it until it fits you and your work.

How can you manage your time better?

Here are five good tricks to remember:

Make up your mind fast. Not snap judgment, but it's a fact that 85 per cent of the problems that face you aren't worth more than a few minutes of your time. So learn to say "Yes" or "No," "We will" or "We won't." Employees and associates like working with decisive people—even when you aren't right all of the time. And not much saves time like a decisive answer. Time saved for you and your employees.

Be specific about dates. You promise to get out an order "sometime next week." What happens? You're likely to find several deadlines coming due at the same time. If you're specific—Wednesday for Triangle and Thursday for Superior, you've started to systematize your thinking.

Or Pete calls you on the phone. Can he drop by to see you? Any

	MONDAY	TUESDAY	WEDNESDAY	THURSDAY	FRIDAY
8	ROUTINE	ROUTINE	ROUTINE	ROUTINE	ROUTINE
9	Inspection and supervision of operations REGULAR	Individual work with staff REGULAR	Inspection and supervision of operations REGULAR	Individual work with staff REGULAR	SPECIAL WORK
10		Inspection and supervision of operations REGULAR		Control studies and reports REGULAR	Inspection and supervision of operations REGULAR
11			Division staff meeting REGULAR		Our staff meeting REGULAR
12 / 1	L	U	N	C	H
1 / 2	Interviews and contacts REGULAR	Interviews and contacts REGULAR	Interviews and contacts REGULAR	Interviews and contacts REGULAR	CREATIVE WORK
3	Planning and organizing REGULAR	Inspection and supervision of operations REGULAR	SPECIAL WORK	Inspection and supervision of operations REGULAR	
5	ROUTINE	ROUTINE	ROUTINE	ROUTINE	ROUTINE

FIG. 34-1 Plan your time this way—an example of a time budget. (W. E. Dewey, "How to Use Your Time Better," *Factory Management and Maintenance,* July, 1953, p. 230, McGraw-Hill Publishing Company, Inc., New York.)

time, you say. So Pete drops by just when you're up to your ears in a line changeover. Pete doesn't get much attention, your changeover gets the "one-eye-only" treatment, and your time budget suffers.

Control the telephone. It's a monster to foremen in some shops. But it needn't be (if your boss will cooperate). If you can get someone else to answer it for you, do. Then call back when you have the time. Avoid using the telephone for routine messages that can be forwarded through the interoffice mails. And watch yourself so that you don't develop telephonitis and bother others with it unnecessarily.

Write down reminders. Don't trust yourself to remember things to do. Use a sure-fire reminder system. Such as jotting down important jobs to be done on your desk calendar or in a pocket notebook. One foreman we know jots down anything he feels he should remember or act upon on a little sheet of paper. Then tosses it into a desk drawer. Each morning he shuffles the notes to see what he must do out of the ordinary for that day. When it's done, he simply tears up the slip.

Limit chit-chat. Conversation—with employees and fellow foremen— is vitally important to your role as supervisor. But you've got to keep it under control or it will eat up all spare time. So limit casual conversation to a few pleasantries, when you can. Nothing ruins your day so sharply as a couple of 20-minute conversations with your associates about the fish they didn't catch or the status of a do-it-yourself project.

Is a cleared desk top the sure sign of a well-planned job?

The value of a neat desk top lies in the atmosphere of orderliness and efficiency it shows. Beyond this, there is real doubt of its significance. General Lucius D. Clay, former Director of Materiel for the United States Army and subsequently Chairman of the Board of Continental Can Company, has this to say about shiny desk tops:

"All my life I have heard of the executive who has so cleared his desk and arranged his schedule that he has no details to worry about and can devote all his time to what is called long-range planning. I suppose there are such executives somewhere. The only ones I know personally who have reached this condition have long since lost their ability either to administer or to think."

Where does the material come from that piles up on a supervisor's desk?

It comes from three sources—operating data, general reading material, and extraneous matter:

• Operating data includes interoffice memos, work orders, daily operating reports, quality-control records, payroll sheets, purchase orders, and the like. You need these to run the shop and to keep informed about your own operations.

• General reading material includes all sorts of publications, business magazines and technical journals, catalogues, advertising data, books, and pamphlets. These are the things you want to read in the hope of learning something new about your job and to keep you abreast of industrial developments that affect it.

• Extraneous matter includes any of the two previous kind of materials that comes over your desk *that you don't need.* This is the sort of thing that you may have once requested to be sent that has not proved to be worth looking at. You'd be surprised how much of your paper-work problem is of this nature.

What can you do to cut down your paper-work load?

Admittedly, some of the paper work that snows you under originates from sources outside your control. But with these three simple rules you may still be boss of your desk.

Shut off the stuff you don't need. That's the place to begin. Too often, the supervisor himself has asked for something, then neglected to discontinue it after its usefulness was over. For instance, two months ago foreman Joe Smith was chewed out by his boss for letting quality fall off in his department. So Joe started asking each lead man to give him a daily report on the reason for any rejects. Next he got the accounting department to give him a weekly report of his department's scrap-record status. Then he requested each operator to turn in a record each month recording the details of each reject. Within a month, Joe had straightened the situation out. But the paper work continued to flood onto his desk. Not until Joe reexamined his set of controls—and eliminated all but the lead man's report—did he make much headway in clearing his desk.

Set aside the stuff that can wait until later. For reading that appears to be interesting but not urgent, keep a table or bookshelf nearby. This way you can glance through magazines, for example, as they arrive, insert slips or paper clips at articles you want to read further, then put the magazine aside—off your desk—to be read in off moments or at home in the evening. Of course, the big idea with general reading and reference material is to get through it as quickly as you can. Then pass it along to others (like an hourly employee you are grooming for advancement) it will help.

Act fast on important papers. You probably don't have to be told not to sit on a request for information from the plant manager. But it's dangerous, too, to defer action on any essential piece of plant-operating paper work like accounting reports, payroll records, interoffice requests, etc. If you do, you gum up your company's profit-making machine. And draw unfavorable attention to yourself.

How can you organize your workday better?

Key to planning your time lies in your time budget (Fig. 34–1). But since each day presents a set of new problems, you should try to take 5 minutes each morning to plan the day ahead.

Start off by setting a time each day for reading your mail. The earlier you scan it, the sooner you can plan ahead. Every day, make a mental estimate of the time your paper work will take up. Some days routine replies and compliance will take less than half an hour. Other days, one request may take several hours to act on. So it's plain foolish to begin your work without first sizing up the job ahead.

In this regard, make good use of your daily calendar. Use *it* as a daily order of work. List the things you want to do that day, including the specific and nonroutine paper work to be handled.

Another good rule is to dispose of all mail and other paper work before you go home each evening. That way you don't have to face a stack of unfinished work when you come in the next morning.

Is there a better way to take faster action on paper work?

This job of supervising is complex. By now you can see that its many aspects are as intertwined as a ball of yarn after the cat's been at it. Decisiveness, for instance, is a big part of leadership—and it's also essential when it comes to freeing you from your desk so that you can get out on the floor and supervise.

So it's worth repeating: Don't let paper work pile up on you. Try to answer every letter, fill out every report, the same day it comes in. Putting it off only makes the job bigger and harder.

But don't leap into action without thinking a little. See if you can cut down the number of times you must pick up the phone or walk down the hall or into the shop. One master mechanic we know, for instance, keeps six baskets on a table next to his desk. They are labeled—one for each of the people he must see personally each day: his boss, three production foremen, the storekeeper, and the purchasing agent. When this master mechanic goes into action—on the telephone or in a face-to-face visit—he lifts the stuff out of the appropriate basket and takes it with him.

How can you file your papers so you can find them when you need them?

If you take care of your own filing, make it simple. There's been a lot written about files, systems, etc., so we won't discuss them here. But it is a mistake to file something in your office if it is also filed somewhere nearby—in the front office, for instance.

There's one rigid rule for your own filing: Don't label file folders "General" or "Miscellaneous." Instead make file headings definite and specific—"Punch press," "Maintenance records," "Reject reports," "Lubrication instruction," etc. It's easy to letter titles on folders, and folders are cheap. So use many separate folders, not just a few.

If you have a lot of correspondence, it's simple to keep track of what you write by setting up a "correspondence" file. Ask the stenographer to make up an extra copy of letters you write. Then letter a folder for each of the 12 months of the year. Put the extra copy in the appropriate monthly file. After the first year, you can empty the 12-month-old file every month, thus keeping the files from getting too bulky.

In what way does your reading ability affect your time budget?

For the supervisor who is just marking time, the ability to read quickly may not be very important. But for the man who wants to learn as much as he can about his job, reading can become a real barrier to his success. For instance, say your reading rate is 150 words per minute (about average for foremen). If you can double that reading rate to 300 per minute (a very reasonable figure for self-taught speed reading), you'll be able to read twice as much in the same amount of time you now spend for reading. Further, you'll be exposing yourself to twice as many new ideas.

What does it take to be able to read faster?

You must be able to speed up (1) the mechanical, or "seeing," phase of reading and (2) the mental, or "thinking," phase.

• The seeing phase comes first. To do a good job, you may need glasses. This means regular eye examinations by a qualified doctor. And the older you get, the more often you ought to be examined. So if you need glasses, get them—and wear them. They won't do you much good while they're still in your shirt pocket.

Once you've checked your eyesight, the next step is to understand how you read. The eye *does not* move smoothly across the printed page. Actually, it moves in a series of jerks and stops. When your eye moves, it sees only a blur. When it stops (or fixes), it sees. Fortunately, your eye can see (or span) several words at a time. You ought to be able to read "units of production," for instance, in one span.

Most poor readers have a narrow span, need six fixes to read a line of print. With practice, you can read a line in three or four fixes.

• The thinking phase of reading produces the real pay-off. You may perfect your reading mechanically and still have trouble getting the gist of what is written.

To improve the thinking phase, it helps to decide the *purpose* of your reading—*why* you are reading a certain book or article and *what* you expect to learn from it. Your aim is quickly to form a partnership of thought with the writer—to be interested in what he is trying to say and to be alert to his way of saying it. That way you help the writer to get across to you with the least effort on your part.

What slows down your reading speed?

Once you clear up eye defects, these may be the barriers to faster reading:

Narrow span. By a conscious effort you can extend your "eye photograph" so that you need make only three or four fixes per line.

Long fixation. Holding the eye in position too long for each photograph slows you down. You've got to keep forcing your eyes ahead.

Lack of concentration. Don't daydream. Reading means work. Paying greater attention to it will speed you up.

Regressions. Rereading phrases or sentences is one of the worst things you can do. In most cases, what you've missed isn't important. Ability to keep going ahead will depend on your self-confidence.

Inward speech. Saying words to yourself—using your lips or any part of the vocal apparatus—can put brakes on your speed.

Poor vocabulary. A college education isn't necessary. Try building yours by looking up in the dictionary any words you're not sure of.

Weak organization of thoughts. As in decision-making, you read faster when you can sort out the big idea from the trivial.

Lack of practice. This is the toughest of all. Over the years, you and your eyes have developed a lot of bad reading habits. These habits can be hard to break. But lots of practice, as you try harder each time to read faster than the last, will overcome them.

How can you quickly get the main idea of a piece of writing?

You'll find that most fast readers have developed the art of skimming. That is, they deliberately look for the main idea in writing just as a dairyman may skim off the heavy cream from a pail of milk.

The knack of skimming lies in its use as a sort of an advance scout for you. You skim the article to locate the important ideas, then you go back and read them more slowly.

In skimming, you read vertically, running your eyes down the center of a column or page, zigzagging from left to right, picking up key words. Many key words are printed in bold-faced type or are italicized. Other meaningful words are the nouns and the verbs. The descriptive or qualifying words (adjectives and adverbs) are not so important.

Specifically, here's where you're likely to find the main idea:

• In a business letter, the first paragraph frequently tells the gist of the story.

• In a newspaper article, read headlines, then subheads, then the first paragraph. Read further only if you want details.

• In a technical journal or business magazine, read title of the article, blurb, and first paragraph. Then check subheads, bold-face, and italicized type. Also indented material.

• In a reference book or text, start with the preface, introduction, and table of contents. This will tell you a lot about the book without your having to read further. Then read first and last chapters—reading first and last paragraphs of each and skimming the rest of the text. Then treat other chapters which have interest for you in the same manner.

How important is your memory?

A good memory alone won't make you a good supervisor. But you can't be a good one without it. That's because memory is no substitute for good judgment. But it does provide the facts that judgment depends on.

A good memory saves you time. With one, you don't have to grope and fumble for the information you need. Either you have the facts or you remember where to find them. A good memory prevents costly mistakes because what you remember helps you spot things that are out of line with what past records show. And a good memory helps you relax under pressure. There's no need for panicky scrambling to get back the thread of your ideas if your memory is solid. Facts, solidly implanted, are hard to jar loose.

What personal factors affect your memory?

Both your mental and physical condition affect how well you remember facts, faces, names. Fatigue and emotional strain make it hard to learn new things. Even when you're in top-notch condition, your memory may suffer because you accomplish tasks so fast that they have little time to leave an impression on your mind. And as a word of warning: A common sign of physical breakdown, as in old age, is memory trouble. When the body is sick, so is the memory.

Memory is also strongly affected by your work habits. If you're systematic in the way you go about your job, you make it easier to remember job information. That's because sound work habits eliminate confusion and tend to make most of your work repetitive. And repetition (remember how you learned the multiplication tables?) is one of the best memory aids.

How can you remember better?

There are lots of memory systems. Some date back to the Roman times when the Romans learned to remember things by pairing associated things. Basic idea was to carry in mind some easily remembered list of familiar things, then memorize new materials by cross association. You can remember the names of the Dionne quintuplets, for example, by associating their names with the word "Macey": Marie, Antoinette, Cecile, Emilie, and Yvonne.

In general, however, it's wise not to put too much reliance on systems. Better to develop good memory habits (and some essential tricks of the trade) such as these eight:

Get the meaning. We learn much by rote. But it's easier to remember if we see and understand the principle first. Details of your plant's statistical quality control, for instance, are easier to remember if you're already hep to what statistical quality control is all about.

Intend to remember. Read these numbers off to your wife or to anyone near at hand: 17–21–11–19–15–6–10–17. Now ask her to repeat them. Chances are that she can't, because she didn't start out *intending* to remember. So *concentrate* on things you want to recall. *Practice* being a good observer. *Get interested* so that the material isn't as dry as dust.

Look for a pattern. Once you understand the principle of something, try to see if it fits a pattern. If the flow of materials in your shop is counterclockwise and follows a pattern somewhat like a baseball player running the bases, with production control where the pitcher's mound is, how easy this would be for a new employee to remember!

Group and number. Memories work best when they are asked to work on specific things. Grouping items, and numbering them, gives your memory an assist. For example, take those numbers we listed earlier: 172111191561017. At first glance, remembering these looks like a tough job. But take another look: 17211 11915 61017.

Looks easier now, doesn't it? That's because you have broken the fifteen numbers into three somewhat similar groups. You can now easily remember there are three groups. And each group is sized down to what your mind more easily holds.

Use the "uncompleted activities" principle. Once a job has been done, your mind forgets it much more easily than if you hadn't finished it. So if you want to remember something, jot it down on a sheet of paper. Work on it for a short while. Then drop it. Your mind will now hang onto the idea for a long while.

Try the "whole-spaced" learning method. Sounds complicated but it isn't. *Whole learning* means that you get better results when you go through whatever you want to remember from beginning to end. Actually, you can learn a whole poem, for instance, more easily than you can memorize it word by word. *Spaced learning* means spreading out your learning over a period of time rather than trying to cram a lot into one session. *Whole-spaced learning* combines the two techniques.

Be selective. This means only to try to remember what is important.

Fortunately the mind forgets most things very quickly. If it didn't, our brains would be crammed with a hodgepodge of facts. So, if you pick and choose the things you need to have at your finger tips, and make no effort to remember unimportant facts, your mind will be better able to retain the selected ones.

Practice, recite, review. Make a point of using the information you'd remember as often as possible. People who remember names well rarely say, "Glad to meet you." Instead they say, "I'm glad to meet you, Mr. Ylvesaker." Others go even further, ask how to spell and pronounce. Then use the name several times in the conversation. All bears out the value of practicing usage, reciting, and reviewing what you want to retain.

35 HOW TO GET USEFUL IDEAS

**Do you have to be a special sort of genius
to be able to think up good ideas?**

No. While it used to be supposed that creative imagination was a
gift only a few lucky individuals possessed, research seems to prove
that it is something that all of us are born with to some degree or
other. Trouble is that most of us don't make use of it. We tend to
confuse imagination with education. But studies made by the Human
Engineering Laboratories at Stevens Institute of Technology showed
that mechanics, for instance, rate well above average in their innate
ability to think up ideas.

Another misconception that blocks our getting ideas is the thought
that an idea to be worth while must be world-shaking—a big discovery
like the Wright brothers', for example. Much more important in total
volume—and value—of ideas produced are the everyday variety
thought up by supervisors and others on the job in industrial plants.

Here's an example:

A plant was spray-painting bed springs automatically. Drips and
tear drops were a big headache. The engineer tried all the obvious
ideas. He speeded up spraying, then slowed it down. Changed paint

consistency, surface preparation, drying heat, and air flow. No luck. Then the foreman of the operation came up with the bright idea of whacking the springs automatically with a rubber hose. It worked! Paint flew off like dust from a rug when beaten with a rug beater. And the idea saved enough paint, collected in gutters beneath the springs, to paint twice as many springs as before.

What is creative thinking?

It's simply the ability to put your mind to a problem that hasn't been solved by a routine method, then come up with a brand-new solution or batch of solutions. This technique, once learned, can be used anywhere and in any situation.

Here's another sample of unfettered thinking that helps grow good ideas in the minds of ordinary people:

A plant was drilling holes in plastic fittings. As the drill heated up the plastic, the drill kept getting gummed up. The tool designer tried sharpening the drill, a different pitch on the cutting edge, faster speeds. Nothing happened. Then the supervisor suggested that if the plastic were cold enough to begin with, it wouldn't heat up enough during the short drilling cycle to gum up the drill. Now the fittings are kept in a deep-freeze chest next to the drill press. The operator takes out only a few at a time, then drills them while they are still cold and hard. And the plastic shreds easily, doesn't foul the drill.

This example demonstrates a basic principle of creative thinking—the ability to shake off a mental set. Instead of taking the normal approach to a drilling problem—changing the tool—this supervisor was successful because he concentrated on the material. In the case of beating the paint off the bed spring, *free association of ideas* came into play—associating the painting problem with that of getting dust out of a rug.

What isn't creative thinking?

Lots of the things we were taught to do at school actually prevent us from getting good ideas. Logic, for instance. When you examine each thought to see if it's worth while, you tend to veto each idea you have while it's still only a glimmer in your mind. That's why Alex Osborn, founder of the famous advertising agency that bears his name, tells you, "Think the green-light–red-light way."

Suppose you have a problem involving safety. You want to get a new method for preventing accidents on the assembly line. First you apply the *green-light* side of your mind. Try to get as many ideas for preventing accidents as you can think up. Ideas such as a better conveyor,

different assembly tools, doing the job automatically, retraining workers, better lighting, wearing protective gloves, running line at new
speed, deburring parts ahead of time, holding weekly safety meetings,
appointing a safety boss for each line, etc. *While the green light is
on in your mind, don't challenge a single idea you have.* Then, when
you have thought up, say, fifteen ideas, you can switch to the *red-light*
side of your mind. Now you can be hard-headed, logical, realistic.
Now you can challenge each idea as to its practicality. This red-light
thinking is a very valuable part of your mind. You couldn't do your
job without it. But it is not creative thinking. Only the green-light
phase is.

What are the fundamentals of creative thinking?

There are no rules and regulations for getting good ideas. But successful idea-getters find that these seven principles help free your
mind for better ideas:

Narrow down the problem. Too often, we talk vaguely about coming up with the solution to a problem. Take absenteeism. Try to pinpoint it like this: We need the solution to the problem of second-shift
workers who are absent more than three times a year. Being specific
sets up a much better target for the mind.

Learn to concentrate. Put your mental blinders on when you're
trying to be creative. Think of only one problem at a time. If you
worry over a hatful of problems at once, you'll get only flabby ideas.

Be persistent. Good ideas rarely come in the first try. So if you can't
produce any workable solution to your problem today, try hard again
tomorrow, and the next day, too.

Believe in yourself. Self-confidence plays a big part in the search
for ideas. So build up your faith in yourself by practicing getting
ideas—first with things that don't matter much. Then when you face
a tough situation, you'll know you can come through.

Let your unconscious take over. When your mind gets tired out
from thinking, stop for a while. Unconsciously your mind will keep
on working on the problem—for hours, days, months. It can actually
percolate fresh ideas when you are thinking about something entirely
different. That's the explanation for the occasional flash we get out
of the blue.

Keep ideas flowing. When you're thinking up ideas, don't stop as
soon as you have a couple. It's like a run of hot hands in poker. If
you get up to take a break, you may return to the table and find your
luck changed. Same way for ideas: while you're finding it easy to
think them up, don't stop.

Take action. Idea creation may begin with the sudden inspiration.

But nothing much comes of ideas until you put them into action. Crude preparations of penicillin were described in 1929, but nobody followed through on the discovery for a dozen years.

How can you prepare yourself to get better ideas?

Here's sound advice from the world's most successful idea men on basic ways for getting good ideas:

Find the right time of day. The time of day when you're most creative. The time when you feel full of drive. That's when to build up a stockpile of ideas. Later on, when your mind isn't running creatively, you can apply your red-light thinking.

Build up your idea sources. If you're not careful, you'll get into a rut from which no ideas will ever come. Instead, look for ways to freshen up your mind. Like going on trips or lunching with people you don't work with every day. Scan all kinds of magazines, even your wife's, for new ideas.

Don't be afraid to work alone. Lately there has been a fad in believing that only the group approach to ideas pays off. This isn't so. Many a good idea comes from lone-wolfing it.

Schedule practice sessions. With yourself, that is. Unless you drill yourself to produce a bagful of ideas, you haven't decided to be creative. So pick out a simple problem once a day. Like how many uses you can find for a paper plate. Then give yourself 5 minutes to think up as many ideas as possible. If you do this regularly, you'll find yourself becoming more fluent with realistic problems at work.

Don't worry about waste. Accept the fact that many of the ideas you produce will be chaff. It's sometimes wasteful to hunt for inspiration. But it's always wasteful to wait around for the one big flawless idea. Experts in creative thinking advise that only about 8 per cent of the ideas you think up will be practical and of value. That means only two good ones for every fifteen you think up. But two are a lot better than none!

Don't worry about the opinion of others. When you're trying to think up ideas you'll get the horse laugh from lots of people. (Actually, it's only the sour grapes showing.) But a couple of bicycle mechanics named Wright never would have gotten their airplane off the ground if they had accepted the lift formulas believed by the physicists of their day.

Keep your eye peeled for chances. Chance favors the idea seeker. So be alert to any unusual variation in the way things are done at your work. Look for an unexpected turn of events, a surprising result. These may furnish the clues to a sparkling idea.

Sharpen your nose for problems. Listen to gripes. They will tell you plenty about problems which need new solutions. Jot down your own complaints, for instance, about the way things run in your department. Ask the salesmen or the accountants if they see any ways to improve your operation. They'll tell you what they think—and perhaps open your mind to new solutions.

Develop a honeybee mind. Gather your ideas everywhere. Don't be afraid to associate your ideas freely. Let your mind buzz freely from one idea source to another, just as a honeybee buzzes from a rose to a clover to a hollyhock.

Be ready for the hot flash. Relax your mind. After a hard day's work, let it wander. Daydream while you walk home from work. Try a hot shower or restful music. After a good night's sleep, get up an hour early, take a long walk, meditate. Or use the two-day formula. Set your problem aside for a full day. Then hit it hard after a day's rest.

Learn to spot your mistakes. The man who sees his mistake can find out why he made it. Then he can correct it—by learning how to do things differently. This is learning how to get—and accept—new ideas.

Are there any tricks of the trade for getting good ideas?

There are many. And here are the cream of the crop borrowed from some of the world's most successful idea getters:

Organize your approach. Professor John Arnold of MIT suggests you ask yourself when replacing a new machine or process:

• Will it do more? Will it be more reliable, last longer, be easier to repair and maintain, safer and more efficient?

• Will it cost less? Take advantage of cheaper, more automatic production procedures, abundant raw materials, convenient mass-produced subassemblies?

• Will it be easier to sell? To your boss, to staff departments, to the men who install it and the operators who run it?

Split your problem into pieces. Break big problems into smaller ones which follow a logical sequence. It was a milestone, for example, in the design of typesetting machines when the problem was broken down into three steps: (1) composing a line, (2) adjusting line length, (3) redistributing type. Taken as a whole, the problem would have been overwhelming, if not impossible.

Use the blind-man method. Shut your eyes to bring your other senses into play. Try doing things by ear, by smell, by touch. It will open up new channels for your mind to explore.

Use the X method. George B. Dubois, Professor of Mechanical Engineering at Cornell, suggests that if you've split your problem into pieces and still can't get started, try the X method. He means that for each part for which you have no solution, call the solution X, then go on to the next step. If you find enough solutions, the X solution may later become obvious. This is the method General MacArthur used in his island-hopping campaign in the Pacific. When he couldn't conquer an island, he bypassed it, conquered another. The ones he couldn't conquer were left to wither on the vine.

Try the input-output scheme. This is used by the General Electric Company in its Creative Engineering Program. You start the solution of your problem by listing the desired output of your new method— all it should do for you. Then you list all the things that go into the process that are desirable, necessary, and available. Between the two extremes ("input" and "output") are the limitations placed on the idea area. For example, suppose your problem is to cut costs of the manufacture of metal ashtrays. You know you must use electric power, hand labor, and sheet-metal stock. On the output side, the sales department tells you that the ashtray must meet set standards for weight, design, and appearance. And the accounting department gives you a cost ceiling and delivery dates. Now you can cast about among your choices. For instance, your choice of metal may not be limited. Or you may make ashtrays by machine or by hand, with punch presses or stamping presses, in your own plant or in a subcontractor's plant. You can spray or dip the finish on, etc.

Use idea banks and idea museums. That's what Charles Clark, noted brainstormer of the Ethyl Corporation, calls them. He suggests you keep a dream file of clippings, notes, pamphlets, etc., even if you can't work on your idea right at the time. An idea museum? For a plant-operating man it's the shelf of catalogues for equipment and materials he may have right in his office. Another example: a mail-order catalogue. Keep scanning them for ideas.

What are idea needlers?

Idea needlers are actually a check list formalized by Alex Osborn. To find a new way of doing something, go down a list of questions like this:

Adapt? What else is it like? What other idea does it suggest? Does the past offer a parallel? What could be copies (like the ball-point-pen idea used to apply underarm deodorants)?

Modify? Can you change color, meaning, motion, sound, odor, shape?

Magnify? What can you add to it? Can it be made bigger, longer, fatter, heavier?

Minify? What can you remove from it? Can it be made shorter, thinner (copper tubing becomes thinner each year), lighter? Can you break it up or eliminate it altogether?

Substitute? Can you substitute another ingredient or material (like a cardboard instead of a glass container for milk)?

Rearrange? Can you interchange the present components? Or use another sequence? Can you change pace or schedule?

Reverse? Can you use opposites? Or turn it backwards (like putting the eye of sewing machine needle at the point instead of the head)? Can you turn it upside down (like the toothpaste tube that has an extra large cap so that the tube can stand on its head in the medicine cabinet)?

Combine? Can you blend it or use an assortment? Can you combine purposes, appeals, goals, or ideas? (The newest in cameras not only takes pictures but prints them as well.)

Are there any don'ts about getting ideas?

There are several mistakes you can make which will actually prevent you from getting good ideas. Here are the most dangerous:

Beware of self-satisfaction. Harlow H. Curtice, retired president of General Motors Corporation, credits his company's success to the inquiring-mind approach to problems. "This point of view is never satisfied with things as they are," he says. "We assume that anything and everything—product process, method, procedures, or human relations—can be improved."

Steer clear of mind weakeners. Don't be misled by stories of great ideas being brewed in smoke-filled rooms over pots of coffee or bottles of Scotch. These things really dull your mind. You're likely to make decisions out of weariness, rather than from inspiration.

Avoid fatigue, noise, distractions. They sap your strength. Moderation of diet and exercise, together with rest, keeps your body—and mind—sharply honed.

Don't kid yourself with vague ideas. Force yourself to reduce your ideas to specific propositions. Otherwise you're likely to fool yourself with the belief that "one of these days I'll put my thoughts down on paper and I'll be a big success."

Don't hoard ideas. Many a person puts so much effort into protecting his ideas from others who might steal the credit that he never gets another good idea. Sure, there is the risk that someone else will get the credit. But that risk isn't as large as the possibiilty that you will never get another big idea.

What's an idea trap?

One of the most important idea tools you need. It's a pad and a pencil to jot down your ideas. Keep them with you all the time. Ideas are elusive. They'll drift out of your grasp as readily as they drift in. So trap them on paper in black and white.

How can you sell your ideas to your boss?

Here are four good ideas for selling ideas:

Anticipate the sour-grapes attitude. Be prepared to have someone say that your idea is impractical, it's been tried before, or it won't work. In advance, figure out a rebuttal to these dashes of cold water. Be ready to try a new tack, a detour, or a compromise in order to gain a toe hold for your idea.

Create ideas to sell ideas. Treat the sales angle of idea creation as a separate problem. And let your imagination loose on it. Dream up as many schemes as you can *to present* your idea effectively.

Figure out the benefits. Your boss and others will ask, "What's in this idea for me?" So try to win support for your idea by showing how the idea will benefit the company, the job holders, and others.

Make it easy to say "Yes." Waldemar Ayres, formerly Director of Research for the White Sewing Machine Company, advises: "Think through every problem likely to arise in carrying out your proposal. Then provide an acceptable answer to show you've anticipated and planned for every such circumstance. A busy executive has all sorts of worries of his own. If, in order to approve your proposal, he has to stop and solve a problem relating to your baby, the easiest and quickest thing for him to do is to say 'No'."

What's the difference between brainstorming and creative thinking?

Brainstorming is the *group approach* to creative thinking. The term was invented by Alex Osborn, who did much to further the entire concept of idea getting. Usually, brainstorming is a much more limited activity than creative thinking. And is applied to the green-light, or freewheeling, phase only.

How does a group hold a brainstorming session?

A group of from eight to twelve people sit in—people with similar interests but different backgrounds. (You could hold a brainstorming session with a group of your employees. Or you might attend a session composed of foremen and staff people.)

Sessions are usually less than an hour long, often as short as 15 minutes. But concentration is intense.

Goal of brainstorming is to get at least fifty ideas per session. Of these ideas, 6 to 10 per cent may be fruitful.

What are the rules for brainstorming?

Willard Pleuthner, Vice President of Batten, Barton, Durstine, and Osborn, the advertising firm which has wrung the most spectacular successes from his method, gives four rules only:

Don't criticize ideas. There's time for judicial thinking later on, but not while brainstorming. Anybody who pooh-poohs is penalized—pays for a round of coffee or puts a dollar in the kitty.

Welcome freewheeling. The wilder the idea the better. It's easier to tame down ideas than to think them up. A "can-you-top-this?" attitude is encouraged. Participants use others' ideas as jumping-off places for their own.

Strive for quantity. Experience shows the more ideas, the better they're likely to be. Even remote connections and screwy suggestions sow the seed for more fruitful thoughts. And top-of-the-head pace setters break the ice for participants who are more reflective and slower to make contributions.

Combine and improve. Since ideas are like building blocks, panel members are encouraged to suggest how others' ideas can be made better—or how two or more ideas can be turned into one idea that's still better than one alone.

Pleuthner also advises that you be sure ideas gathered at brainstorming sessions be recorded—on tape, on chart board, or by a secretary. He also feels sessions are most productive when held in the morning—if people are expected to work on these ideas later on during the day. But if an employee is to return to routine activity, it's better to hold the sessions in the afternoon. Otherwise the excitement continues during the day and may interfere with performance of regular duties.

How can a supervisor discourage the flow of ideas from his subordinates?

This is so easy a temptation that you should check yourself to see if you're the kind of supervisor whose attitude seems to say to his workers, "You do the working. I'll do the thinking around here." But if you need any further stimulation, take a look at this list of idea killers developed at a meeting of the New York Chapter of the American Society of Training Directors:

- Don't be ridiculous.
- We tried that before.
- It cost too much.
- That's beyond our responsibility.
- It's too radical a change.

- We don't have the time.
- That will make other equipment obsolete.
- We're too small for it.
- Not practical for operating people.
- The union will scream.
- We've never done it before.
- Let's get back to reality.
- That's not our problem.
- Why change it, it's still working O.K.
- You're two years ahead of your time.
- We're not ready for that.
- It isn't in the budget.
- Can't teach an old dog new tricks.
- Top management would never go for it.
- We'll be a laughing stock.
- We did all right without it.
- Let's shelve it for the time being.
- Let's form a committee.
- Has anyone else ever tried it?
- Too hard to sell.
- It won't work in our industry.

36 UNDERSTANDING BUSINESS ECONOMICS

Why must a supervisor be expected to know about economics?

Mainly because this very important subject is so *mis*understood by your employees. Survey after survey of the average American working man shows that, while he's far from a communist, he has a distorted idea about business. He's suspicious about profits—and about his share of them. Scratch hard enough and you'll find that an employee's underlying lack of faith in the capitalistic system is at the root of much of your difficulty with his output and quality. "After all," he figures, "the company makes so much out of my efforts, what difference does it make if I goof off once in a while?"

To correct these vague misconceptions about business economics, it's up to you to know some of the basic truths about the way American capitalism works.

How big are profits?

What's your guess—50, 25, 10 per cent? If you think this way, your estimates aren't far from what the American worker believes are fair, according to national studies made by *Factory Management and Maintenance* magazine in 1946.

Actually, profits, figured as a percentage of total sales, since 1940 have averaged well under 5 per cent for most industries, according to the United States Chamber of Commerce. In 1940, the average profit on sales for all companies engaged in agriculture, mining, construction, manufacturing, wholesale and retail trade, transportation, public utilities, and services was 4.4 per cent. In 1950, it was 4.6 per cent. In 1954, it was down to 2.7 per cent, and in 1955, it was 3.2 per cent.

Or put it another way: Profits as a percentage return of the value of the money invested in the business generally average under 6 per cent, according to the Machinery and Allied Products Institute.

Warning: These are facts. And no matter how you analyze profits of American business, they're liable to add up the same way—in general. *But it is also a fact that in any single year a particularly successful company may earn well over the national average profit.*

Why all the complaining about profits?

Face it. Most of the criticism comes about from labor union charges during bargaining contract negotiations. Profits stated in dollars often run into the millions. Dollar increases in profits compared with previous years may add up to big percentages. In the 1958 bargaining scene in the auto industry, unions were able to point out correctly that some auto companies had made abnormally high profits during the previous few years. But one of the recurrent charges was that profits had "increased by huge percentages" over former years. This was true. But it's misleading. For instance, if a company made only $1 million profit in 1954, this may have represented a 5 per cent profit on sales that year. Say in 1958 the same company made $4 million profit, or 12 per cent of sales for that year. Anyone could accurately say that this company had enjoyed a 400 per cent increase in dollar profits since 1954. But few people would criticize a company for making 12 per cent on its sales effort.

So don't accept exaggerated statements about profits without finding out exactly what they mean.

Do unions oppose profits?

Most unions are as favorably disposed toward corporate profits as stockholders are. And for a simple reason. Employees who work for a successful company stand a better chance of getting high wages than if they worked for a company that makes lower-than-average profits. Few unions today oppose the capitalistic system. They encourage a company to be strong and profitable. What unions *do* want is a larger and larger share of the profits. And employees have been getting this bigger share progressively for over fifty years.

"The worst crime against the working people is a company which fails to operate at a profit," is the way the most famous of all American labor leaders has put it. His name? Samuel Gompers, founder of the American Federation of Labor.

What is it that makes capitalism work so well?

Competition. In other countries, the appeal of socialism has been greater than in America. Socialism means regulation and control of business. Under most forms of socialism, the amount of goods produced is controlled by the government. The manner in which goods are produced and the price people pay for them are also regulated by the government. On the surface, such a system appears to be sensible, fair, and economical. In practice, it has worked well in only a few countries—like Sweden.

Under competition as it is practiced in America, the degree of governmental controls and regulations is limited. Historically, we've gone through periods, like the 1920s, when this regulation wasn't severe enough, and the 1930s, when many people felt the regulations restricted our nation's growth.

Under a competitive economy, anybody is free to go into any business, to produce as much as he likes, and to try to sell these goods where and to whom he wishes for any price he feels the market will bear. The main controls are exercised by the people who do or don't buy his goods at the price he wants—and by the skill in which he runs his business to produce either a profit or a loss.

Here's the way competition may work—say in the manufacture of a plastic water pistol. In 1947, when plastic materials were just becoming popular and available, George B. opened the George Plastic Company. He manufactured 100,000 plastic pistols, sold them at 98 cents each and made a net profit of $20,000. Not bad—over 20 per cent profit on sales. But by the middle of the year, two other fellows, Ralph and Sam, each saw what a profitable business the plastic-water-pistol business is. They each went into business, and each sold 100,000 pistols in 1948 at 79 cents each. Ralph and Sam made $10,000 each, or about 10 per cent profit. But George's business fell off to 50,000 pistols, and he made no profit at all. Next year, he had to find a way to cut his prices or he would fail.

And so the competition continues so long as the water-pistol industry looks attractive from a profit viewpoint. By 1950, there were fourteen different manufacturers. Three of them made a profit of over 10 per cent. Seven made a profit of under 5 per cent. And four made no profit at all. The price of the water pistol was down to 29 cents. Over 30 million were sold each year. And the 29-cent pistol was better than the one George originally sold for 98 cents. This is a hypothetical case. But it is little different from what has happened under our competitive system to electric-light bulbs, fountain pens, gasoline, shoes, radios, clothing, and hundreds of other commodities.

What kind of an effect does supply and demand have on business?

Professors who have studied the intricate workings of the competitive, capitalistic system explain its function on the basis of supply and demand. They say these two forces in our economy are always at work:

Supply. The amount of goods, products, and services that can be brought to the market place, and the cost of bringing them there.

Demand. The appetite the public has to buy, or consume, the products and services available.

These forces act this way:

• The greater the supply of goods available, the lower the cost of producing them. This is what many people mean when they say that mass production is "cheaper."

• The greater the number of people who want a product, the more they will be willing to pay for that product.

• The price of a product is determined by (1) the current supply of the product and (2) the demand by people for it.

Look at the two charts in Fig. 36-1. The upper one represents the supply and demand curves for a new product—say luxury ball-point pens. The solid demand curve shows that as price decreases from $10 to $2, the number of people willing to buy increases from a few hundred thousand to over 2 million. The supply curve shows that at $1 per pen, there are only a very few thousand pens available. But as the price offered per pen increases to $5, the supply could be increased to 3 million. Where the two curves intersect (the equilibrium point), the actual selling price is established. In this particular supply-and-demand market the price would be $2.75, and 1½ million pens would be sold. Now if improvement in manufacturing techniques made it possible to supply pens at a lower cost, a new supply curve would prevail—as shown in the lower chart. The new selling price would be $2, and 2 million pens would be sold.

It is next to impossible to *control* the public demand—except by stimulating it through advertising; although the demand is constantly changing. For instance, at the turn of the century only a few thousand autos were sold in the $5,000 class. Today, several hundred thousand are sold in this price range.

It is possible to *control* the supply curve through improving manu-

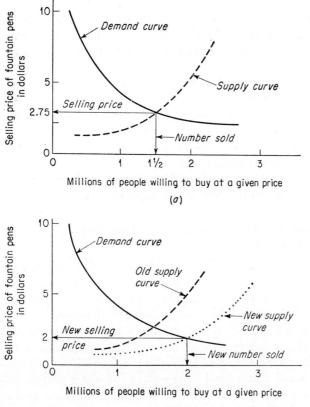

FIG. 36-1   Effects of supply and demand. (*a*) Original situation in hypothetical fountain pen market. (*b*) Changed situation after mechanization lowers supply curve.

facturing and distribution procedures. And by and large, the company that makes things cheaper, or better for the same price, will sell more of its goods—and make a bigger profit.

But rarely, if ever, are prices *set*. The public demand and the manufacturer's production techniques automatically establish the selling price.

In America is competition ever regulated?

To a lesser degree, most businesses are regulated by law—local, state, and Federal. These laws affect minimum wages, amount of unemployment compensation, kinds of safety and health protection, freight rates, selection of shipping containers, and hundreds of other aspects of business most of us take for granted. All this adds up to protection for the public and a fair chance for business to compete.

Certain American industries are regulated more than others. These would include what economists call the "natural monopolies," like the railroads and other common carriers, the water and power companies, telephone and telegraph service, and the like. If these industries were open to free competition, there would be endless duplication of services which would result in a higher cost of these services. Consequently, there is special control over them.

In wartime, too, our free-enterprise system is regulated. Not because under competition more could not be produced more cheaply, but to make certain that the goods and services *needed for war* are produced in sufficient quantities and at the right time.

How much of an investment does it take to provide a job?

Gone are the days when a workman needed only a cheap set of hand tools to make him competitive. Today, a single machine tool may cost anywhere from $10,000 to over $100,000. The more mechanized an industry is, the greater the capital needed to provide each job. Look at Fig. 36-2, which shows for how many workers $1 million will provide a job in various industries. In chemicals, it takes about $20,000 to provide one job. In clothing, only $3,500. *Only* $3,500!

The United States Steel Corporation calculates that in 1956 it took $3,500 *in profits* just to preserve one job for a man working in the open hearth. This was in addition to money already invested to set up the job in the first place. This represents the high cost of depreciation and obsolescence of machines, buildings, and equipment.

How can inflation be controlled?

A highly debatable subject. But no one denies that one of the surest ways to limit inflation is for every employee to produce more. As our population grows, its appetite for a better standard of living grows too. This appetite raises the demand curve for many products. When more and more people want more and more goods and services, it's up to industry to produce them. If our supply curve doesn't change—that is, if it costs just as much to produce as it did before—the increased demand forces prices up. This is inflation!

What all of us—managers and workers alike—must do is to see that our productivity increases along with our demands. As we produce more, costs must go down as demand goes up. This added productivity tends to hold prices in line—and combats inflation. Since 1900, our

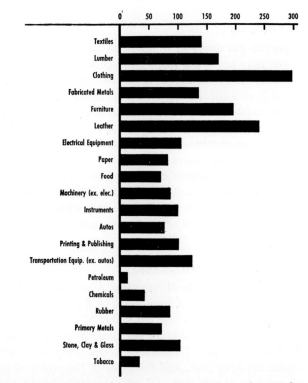

FIG. 36-2 Number of workers per million dollars of capital invested in manufacturing industries. (*Wages, Prices, Profits, and Inflation,* National Association of Manufacturers, New York, 1957.)

productivity has increased an average of only about 3 per cent per year—in spite of increased mechanization and automation.

In what way do taxes affect our economy?

Many people feel that whatever someone else pays in taxes is no concern of theirs. This is merely whistling in the dark. Why? Because the government (Federal, state, and local) is not a *creator* of income: it is at best only a distributor of what *the people* have created. Government gets money to distribute (for the services it provides) through taxation. The more it takes out of our economy in taxes, the less there is for private persons to spend on goods and services. For this reason, many people feel the amount of money the government spends (and consequently the money it collects in taxes) should be watched over closely by all citizens to make certain that the goods and services are the ones most people desire and benefit from. And to be sure these services are provided economically.

Who pays the taxes?

Different people pay taxes at different points of collection. If you drive a car, you may pay a tax when you get a license, whenever you stop for gasoline, and when you drive on certain roads. Another person may not have a car. But he may pay taxes whenever he goes to the movies, buys a pack of cigarettes, or drinks a glass of beer. A business corporation may pay taxes every time it ships a carload of its products, separates an employee from its payroll, or makes a telephone call. So it goes. We all pay taxes in thousands of different ways. And rarely do any of these payments create wealth. True, today the bulk of our taxes goes toward our national defense, to the weapons of war and the men who bear them, and to pay for the debts incurred during previous wars. This is the price of protection—and it runs into billions of dollars each year.

How much do we pay in taxes?

In 1956 Federal, state, and local taxes cost Americans a total of $100 billion—or an average of $2,400 from each of the nation's 42 million families. Individual income taxes netted about 36 per cent of this total. Sales and excise taxes turned over 10 per cent. Property tax ran to 18 per cent. Collection of social insurance from companies and from employees made up 9 per cent. And the taxes on the profits of business corporations came to 21 per cent. All other miscellaneous tax sources provided about 5 per cent of the nation's total tax take.

So you see, in 1956 business profits accounted for 21 per cent of the total tax income *directly*. To say nothing of the share business contributed in sales and excise, property, and social insurance taxes. So it goes every year. And remember—regardless of who pays the tax, in the long run, taxes all come from the individual—in the form of higher prices passed along to him.

Does the average working man get his fair share of the nation's income?

Probably no one believes he gets his fair share. But the facts are essentially this. Since 1929, workers' incomes have risen from something like $64 billion a year to $225 billion today. During the same period, incomes of so-called "propertied" people have increased from $19 billion a year to only about $30 billion yearly. Workers' income has risen 235 per cent, income of propertied people only 58 per cent. These two rates of income tell the story. Working people, today, get the bulk of our personal income total.

What is the single most important factor in multiplying our national wealth?

Tools! Machines and equipment, that is. While America's natural resources are profound, they aren't what set our economy apart from Russia. Neither do our manpower or brains. Our wealth is due to the fact that our political system and our economy recognize the tremendous power of tools.

If you were to match two teams of men in a trench-digging contest, you'd find that the differences caused by the hardness of the earth and the muscle power of the men wouldn't amount to much. And adding more men to one side might speed up the digging only proportionately. But the side with the sharpest and strongest picks and shovels would hold the greatest advantage. Now—consider what would happen if you gave one side a bulldozer. There would be no contest! The strength of the man who operated it would be multiplied hundreds of times by the machine.

It's a fact that motors used in manufacturing accounted for only about 15 million horsepower in 1900. Today, motors carry a load of over 95 million horsepower. It's power like this, hooked up to machines and tools in modern buildings, that gives the American working man his tremendous leverage. And helps him to outproduce any other working man in the world. And to live better as a result.

How can you read a company's balance sheet?

A balance sheet is designed to give a financial picture of a company at a single moment of time. Note that the balance sheet will always have only one date on it—such as December 31, 1958. The balance sheet paints this financial picture by listing the company's *assets*—what it owns or has coming to it, and its *liabilities*—what it owes and has set aside for or has earmarked against depreciation and other contingencies.

An example of a balance sheet is shown on the following page.

• On the *asset* side are first:

Current assets. Assets that can be turned into cash in a hurry if necessary for this corporation include *cash*—held in bank checking accounts to pay bills and employees wages; *marketable securities*—mainly U.S. government bonds, which pay interest and can be converted to cash readily; *accounts receivable*—the amounts customers owe the XYZ corporation, usually collectible within 30 days; *inventories*—all raw materials, supplies, semifinished and finished products which the company has on hand for its operations or to ship to customers;

XYZ MANUFACTURING COMPANY
CONSOLIDATED BALANCE SHEET

December 31

Assets

Current assets		
Cash	$12,954,045	
Marketable securities	4,130,000	
Accounts receivable	8,490,288	
Inventories	10,976,508	
Deferred charges	2,787,254	
Total current assets		$39,338,095
Fixed assets		10,121,816
Other assets		
Investment in subsidiary	$721,759	
Goodwill, patents, etc.	305,559	
Total other assets		1,027,318
Total assets		$50,487,229

Liabilities

Current liabilities	$4,381,296	
Accounts payable	$4,381,296	
Accrued taxes	4,100,322	
Other accrued liabilities	5,546,413	
Total current liabilities		$14,028,031
Reserves		
Reserve for depreciation	$6,939,480	
Reserve for pensions	1,050,000	
Reserve for contingencies	806,441	
Total reserves		8,795,921
Capital stock (stockholders' equity)		
Preferred stock	$9,000,000	
Common stock	9,255,566	
Total capital stock		18,255,566
Surplus income retained in business		9,407,711
Total liabilities		$50,487,229

and *deferred charges*—payments made in advance for services not yet fully rendered, such as insurance, property taxes, rents, etc.

Fixed assets. In this case fixed assets represent the value (at original cost) of plants, buildings, machines, and equipment. It is usual to list these at their original value and allow for depreciation by charging a certain amount (regulated by government) each year to the "reserve for depreciation" on the liability side of the balance sheet.

Other assets. Securities of controlled companies (if any) and good will, patents, trademarks are all assets.

• On the *liability* side of the balance sheet are:

Current liabilities. In this group are *accounts payable*—what the company owes to its creditors for raw materials, services, etc.; *Federal taxes*—usually an estimate of what the company will owe the government at tax time; *other accrued liabilities*—may include state income and other miscellaneous taxes owed, royalties, and salesmen's commissions, for instance.

Reserves. This liability includes a major item for depreciation and obsolescence. Additions to this reserve are the means by which a company spreads out original costs of machines and equipment over a number of years as they become worn out or outmoded. To do this, the company must first estimate the useful life of these machines (in accordance with Federal regulation). And throughout this period the company adds an amount to the cost of its products equal to the original cost of the depreciated items. As is the case with any cost, these costs must be recovered through sale of its products at a price which includes them.

Capital stock. Two kinds of stock, preferred and common, represent the corporation's liability to its owners—the stockholders. The sums assigned represent only a stated value and have no relation to the stock's current market value.

Surplus. This item is largely the accumulated earnings retained in the company. Surplus is not idle cash. It is the money the company has made in profits—and has reinvested in the business to buy new equipment and machines so it can keep up with competition.

On every balance sheet the assets must equal the liabilities. In a company operating in the red, this balance might be achieved by a figure entitled "deficit" rather than one called "surplus."

How do you read a profit-and-loss statement?

A profit-and-loss statement tells you where the company's money came from during the year and how it was spent. The difference between the two is the profit or loss—or net income. Some companies refer to the statement as a "statement of consolidated income."

The profit-and-loss statement covers a stated period of time—usually a year, although many companies now make such a statement every three months.

Typical of the form of most profit-and-loss statements is the sample one on the next page.

- *Operating income* for the XYZ Company comes from:
1. Sales of products or services.
2. Other sources such as royalties.
- *Deducted* from operating income are:
3. Cost of goods sold and other manufacturing charges, usually referred to as "manufacturing expense."
4. General administrative expenses, including sales, advertising, and overhead.
5. Money set aside for depreciation and obsolescence of equipment and buildings.
6. Federal income taxes on operating income.
- The *difference* between the sum of (1) and (2) less the total of (3), (4), (5), and (6) is the *net operating income*.
- In addition, the profit-and-loss statement includes income from other sources, such as:
7. Dividends from stock held by the company.
8. Interest from government bonds.
- Deducted from this other income is:
9. Provision for Federal income taxes on nonoperating income. The difference is *net other income*.
- The sum of net operating income and net other income is the *net income* (profit or loss) for the year.

Do all companies publish financial statements?

No. Only those publicly owned companies who offer their stock in interstate commerce (put their stock on the open market) *must* publish financial statements such as a balance sheet and a profit-and-loss statement. These companies are regulated by the Federal Securities Exchange Commission and must disclose their earnings and their financial condition in a manner established by the Commission. Privately owned companies need not make public their financial position.

XYZ MANUFACTURING COMPANY
PROFIT-AND-LOSS STATEMENT
(Also called "Consolidated Statement of Income")

For year ended December 31

Operating income

(1) Net sales	$88,661,564		
(2) Other operating income	2,000,000		
Total operating income		$88,661,564	

Operating expenses

(3) Cost of goods sold	$65,217,000		
(4) General administrative exp.	14,000,575		
(5) Provision for depreciation of machines and equipment	5,426,550		
(6) Provision for Federal income tax on operating income	2,000,315		
Total operating expense		86,644,440	
Operating income—net			$2,017,124

Other income

(7) Earnings from stock held	$375,320		
(8) Interest from government bonds	418,175		
Total other income		$793,495	

Other expense

(9) Provision for Federal income tax on other income	81,116		
Other income—net			712,379
Net income for the year			$2,729,503
Dividends paid stockholders			$2,010,501
Income retained in the business this year			$ 719,002
Income retained in business at beginning of year			8,688,709
Surplus—Income retained in business at end of year			$9,407,711

Where can a supervisor find out more about business economics?

Try any of these publications:

Allen, C. L., J. M. Buchanan, and M. R. Colberg: *Prices, Income, and Public Policy,* McGraw-Hill Book Company, Inc., New York, 1954.

Hazlitt, Henry: *Economics in One Lesson,* Harper & Brothers, New York, 1946.

Krooss, Herman E.: *American Economic Development,* Prentice-Hall, Inc., Englewood Cliffs, N.J., 1955.

The Mechanics of Inflation, Economic Research Division, Chamber of Commerce of the United States, Washington, D.C., 1957.

Robinson, M. A., H. C. Morton, and J. D. Calderwood: *An Introduction to Economic Reasoning,* Brookings Institution, Washington, D.C., 1956.

37 WHAT A SUPERVISOR'S WIFE SHOULD KNOW ABOUT HIS JOB (FOR WOMEN ONLY)

Isn't the part a supervisor's wife plays in her husband's success exaggerated?

Not at all. No man can separate his home life from his workaday life, no matter how much he may want to. Psychological research shows that a supervisor's disposition at work is likely to be a reflection of how satisfactory his home life is or isn't. And since from time immemorial a wife has set the home climate, she certainly contributes at least 50 per cent to the effectiveness of her husband's career.

In what way can a wife affect the decisions her husband makes at work?

"I take a keen interest in my husband's job," says Mrs. F., "and we discuss his problems regularly at home. But isn't it true that once he gets to the plant, he's on his own? How can anything I do or say help or hinder him then?" Here's how: *A supervisor's job is mainly dealing with people.* Decisions about materials and equipment take less than a quarter of his time. And his boss and his associates are in a position to offer him plenty of help in these areas. But his decisions and his actions regarding people are his big responsibility. If your husband has had an argument with you before he left for work, how well do you think he'll handle his employee relations? If a nagging wife has pinned her husband down at home for weeks, it's a matter of history that he takes out his resentment on the people who work for him. Few things damage a supervisor's or manager's chance for success more than his inability to handle employees—and his associates—wisely and well. If your husband and you haven't worked out an enjoyable relationship with one another, there's small hope that he will be able to work out agreeable relationships with people at work.

Should a wife be blamed if her husband doesn't make a success of his supervisory responsibilities?

It's unfair for a husband to place the blame for *his own* inadequacies on his wife. But every supervisor's wife must ask herself if she's doing everything in her power to aid him in his career.

You don't have to be told that many men unfairly blame their wives for their own failures. You know the "if-my-wife-only-understood-me" type. But all too often there's truth to the charge. Your husband needs your understanding of his job, his good points, and his weaknesses. And he especially needs your help in facing up to his shortcomings.

This mustn't mean criticizing or nagging on your part. But it does mean encouraging him to face up to weaknesses and planning to do something to overcome them.

Here's an example:

Your husband comes home from a hard day. He tells you an employee has put him in a tough spot by spoiling a big job the shop's been working on. He complains to you, "You just can't trust employees today. No one accepts responsibility for doing a job right except me." Is this the time to run your fingers through your husband's hair and tell him how sorry you feel for him? Not quite. Run your fingers through his hair—if that's your particular approach to being nice to the guy you married—but ask him if the problem isn't deeper than "people not caring." Ask him what he's been doing to correct this attitude in the shop. Get him to analyze, for you and for himself, how this particular problem came about. Let him try to suggest preventive action he might have taken to avoid it—or avoid it in the future. *Listening and helping your husband to question himself* are two very effective techniques for having a husband accept his responsibilities for success or failure on the job.

What should you know about a supervisor's job?

If a wife understands that a supervisor's job is primarily the art of dealing effectively with people, she has learned a lot. Any other details are good to know, but not absolutely necessary.

How can you rate your own husband's effectiveness as a supervisor?

Try the quiz in Table 37–1 on your husband. You ask the questions and do the scoring. No fair unless he tells the unvarnished truth. To evaluate your husband's rating, find out where his score puts him:

85–95 points	He's tops!
70–85 points	Good guy to work for
50–70 points	Only so-so
Less than 50 points	He's disliked

If my husband is a boss, why does he need to be careful in how he handles employees?

Fifty years ago, a supervisor could do pretty much as he pleased as far as employees were concerned. Today, an employee represents a large investment in dollars and cents to a company. Your husband's job is to encourage—not tell—this employee to produce a good return on this investment. In today's democracy, no one—even a boss—gets very far by *telling* people what to do. Securing cooperation is a much more subtle and difficult job. One foreman, when interviewed, said the difference today is that "you deal instead of drive."

Should you encourage your husband to be ambitious?

This is one of those "yes-but" questions. Of course your husband needs and should receive your encouragement. He needs a sound foundation of confidence and security from you on which he can build confidence and achievement at work.

But there is the possibility of *too much* ambition—ambition beyond a particular individual's capabilities. If you (or your husband—men are just as guilty) push your husband too far, that's when real trouble begins. He becomes dissatisfied with his accomplishments—and consequently with his job. His work suffers, and so does your home life.

It's most important for you to help your husband size up his abilities objectively. Don't deflate him. But don't let him kid himself, either. For happiness at home and at work, we all need to accept ourselves for what we are. We can't all be president. Neither can we all be department heads or plant superintendents. But we all can learn to get more satisfaction from what we do.

TABLE 37-1 HOW WELL DO YOU RATE AS A SUPERVISOR *

	5 points	3 points	0 points	Enter scores here
1. How well do I know the caliber of work performed by each of my employees?	Very well	Fairly well	Not very well	____
2. How often do I show partiality or favoritism in dealing with my employees?	Seldom	Sometimes	Frequently	____
3. How frequently do my employees feel that they can come to me with their problems?	Whenever necessary	Sometimes	Seldom	____
4. How often do I fail to give my employee clear and definite instructions?	Seldom	Sometimes	Almost always	____
5. How often do I tell an employee *why* he is being asked to do a particular job?	Almost always	Sometimes	Seldom	____
6. How often do I compliment an employee for outstanding work?	Almost always	Sometimes	Seldom	____
7. How often do I "blow up" or lose my temper when an employee makes an error?	Almost never	Sometimes	Frequently	____
8. How well do I understand the work performed by my employees?	Very well	Fairly well	Not very well	____

408

9. How often do I seek the advice of my employees in planning the work?	Frequently	Sometimes	Seldom	—
10. How well do I receive suggestions from my employees?	Open-mindedly	Skeptically	Negatively	—
11. How often do I reprimand an employee in the presence of other employees?	Seldom	Sometimes	Frequently	—
12. How often do I tell my employees in advance about changes which will affect them?	Almost always	Sometimes	Seldom	—
13. How long do I keep an employee waiting for a decision or for information?	A short time	Varies	A long time	—
14. How often do I redo the work of an employee rather than take corrective action?	Seldom	Sometimes	Frequently	—
15. How often do I keep my promises?	Almost always	Sometimes	Seldom	—
16. How anxious am I to advance promising employees?	Very anxious	Apathetic	Opposed	—
17. How often do I try to look at a problem from the employee's point of view?	Frequently	Sometimes	Seldom	—
18. How often do I attempt to shift the blame for my own errors?	Seldom	Sometimes	Almost always	—
19. How often do I go to bat for my employees?	Frequently	Sometimes	Seldom	=
Total:				

* Adapted from "Leadership in Supervision," Veterans Administration, Washington, D.C., 1947.

409

How much sympathy should you give your husband?

Not much disturbs a supervisor who's had a harassing day more than to be greeted at his home by a deluge of complaints. It's a temptation to view your husband as a fellow who's been out in the world meeting interesting people while you've been home sweating over an ironing board and listening to the children fuss. "Before you start telling me about your day," is the way one wife greets her husband, "I've had a rough day, too. Amy spilled ink on the rug, the washing machine I've asked you to fix finally broke down completely, and my nerves are going to pieces." Off to a happy evening, we'll bet.

Sure, wives need and deserve consideration. This is a two-way street. But a wise wife will be careful of her timing. If she's got to unburden herself, it's better to wait until after the dishes are put away and the kids in bed. Over a cool drink she and her husband can exchange experiences—and mutual sympathy. Similarly, avoid raising problems just before bedtime or before your husband leaves for work in the morning. Establish these ground rules for both of you, and life at home and his success at work will be more fruitful.

Many wives of successful supervisors have been criticized for not growing along with their husbands. What can a wife do about this?

Be sensible about this problem. Do your best to grow along with him as he succeeds in business, but don't let fear of falling behind wreck your life. The fact is that except in isolated instances, a supervisor or manager succeeds because he's a good supervisor, not because his wife knows how to wear clothes and can talk politics. Your biggest contribution to your husband and to your home will always be the amount of harmony and constructive self-appraisal you can bring about.

Be assured of this. The chances are a thousand to one that you aren't much different from the wives of the other men your husband works with. Most of them married for love, not money, struggle to meet monthly bills, wash diapers, and have trouble with their in-laws. Don't imagine them as women who have become so efficient that their days are spent in propelling their husbands on to greater things.

It is plain smart, however, for many reasons any doctor or psychiatrist will tell you, not to get into a personal rut. So as your husband moves ahead in business, try to move ahead yourself. Look for activities outside your home. Join a church or civic organization. Take a course in something that appeals to you at your adult education center. Broaden your circle of friends and activities. All this will give you the confidence which you need to meet your husband's associates and their wives and to feel that you are still making life interesting for your husband.

How should you act if your husband's boss invites the two of you to dinner at his home?

Act natural. If you try anything else, you're likely to appear presumptuous or foolish. Put your best foot forward, of course. Wear a dress that you know you look good in, and one that you'll feel comfortable in. But don't go in for heavy make-up or spike heels if you're not accustomed to either. If you don't drink or smoke, don't think you have to just to make a good impression.

In summary, be friendly. Do more listening than talking, but don't be a complete wallflower. Try to enjoy yourself. And remember, your husband won't get fired, or be turned down for his next promotion, if you can't scintillate.

Should you go with your husband to company dances, parties, or a company picnic?

When supervisors' wives are invited, it's a good thing for you to attend company parties and picnics (if your husband asks you to accompany him). Your husband's employees are justifiably curious about his wife. They want to judge for themselves as to whether you're a help or a hindrance, whether you're the reason behind some of his bad faults. When an employee who has met you socially at a company affair can say, "Joe Smith's wife is O.K. She's friendly and not the least bit snooty," your husband has a big plus on his side.

A word about clothes. When you're accompanying your husband to an affair with his employees, try to strike a happy medium. Don't overdress. And don't dress down to his employees' wives.

Another tip: Never try to play hostess unless someone has specifically asked you to. Act as if you and your husband are just another couple being entertained by the company.

So many executives seem to have heart attacks. How can I prevent this from happening to my husband?

In a survey made of 195 plant operating executives by Life Extension Examiners, the health of plant supervisors was shown to be not too different from their counterparts in other phases of business. But four significant differences did show up. Compared with sales and clerical groups, plant supervisors have:
- Better vision.
- Poorer hearing.

- Higher blood pressure.
- More abnormal X-ray findings of heart and lungs.

The last two findings are the ones for you and your husband to worry most about. All executives tend to be too fat. And high blood pressure combined with overweight can bring on heart trouble—especially if there is an abnormal condition there already.

What you can do. Urge your husband (if he's over thirty-five years old) to get a complete physical checkup once a year. Don't permit him to put this off until he feels there's something wrong with himself. And be sure that your husband does what the doctor tells him to.

What can you do with a supervisor who complains of "that tired feeling" all the time?

This sound anything like your supervisor-husband? Norbert De Hart was still a young man—only thirty-four. But he continually pooped out by midafternoon. He wasn't overweight, but examination showed that his poundage had slipped from his shoulders to his waistline. His wife complained that Norbert was always too tired to go out of an evening. Life at home became pretty dull.

If your husband has the same complaint as Norbert, you might try getting him to follow the example of members of the Peoria, Ill., Physical Fitness Foundation. J. A. Bender, physical education specialist and director of the program, advises members to reexamine their habits of exercise, relaxation, and diet.

The value of moderate exercise can't be overemphasized. Not rigorous calisthenics. But corrective therapy, like walking with head erect, chest out, shoulders back, is good. Other exercises include stepping up and down on a 15-inch-high stool—starting at 12 steps per minute and increasing in a month to 72 per minute for 6 minutes, stretching to a bar placed at arms' length overhead in a clothes closet, or doing slow quarter-knee bends.

For diet, ask your family doctor.

How can you help your husband to relax?

One big reason for "that tired feeling" is what some doctors call "tenigue." It's a combination of emotional tension and physical fatigue. Emotional tension is the dangerous culprit.

The National Association for Mental Health offers these eleven sensible guides:

Talk it out. When your husband can confide in you, it releases bottled-up tensions.

Escape for a while. Encourage your husband to get away from it all occasionally. But don't let him make a habit of running away.

Work off anger. It will be lots easier on you and the kids if your husband can take his frustration out on a physical activity, like carpentry or gardening.

Give in occasionally. Try to help him see that if he gives in once in a while, even if he's dead right, this improves his feeling of satisfaction and maturity.

Do something for others. If your husband can devote some of his energy to civic or charitable organizations, it gets his mind off his own worries.

Take one thing at a time. Sometimes, especially for a supervisor, it seems as if the problems have piled up to an insurmountable obstacle. Help your husband to work at one problem at a time, and he'll feel a sense of accomplishment by licking his problems piecemeal.

Shun the superman urge. This is the curse of too-great ambition. You can help by being satisfied with less than the best, the newest, the first. Keeping up with the Joneses is a terrible thing for some men to face.

Go easy with criticism. Since a supervisor must work so much with people, he often feels let down because they don't measure up to his expectations. If he harps too long on this disappointment, he's not being realistic about life. All of us, including him, have our shortcomings. Instead, for every point of criticism, try having your husband cite at least one good feature of the person he feels has let him down.

Give the other fellow a break. Your husband doesn't have to get there first all the time. Every single situation isn't a competition. Most of life's challenges can be better solved by cooperation.

Make yourself available. When things go wrong, we tend to want to withdraw. Actually, for tensions' sake, it's better for us to keep making ourselves available to people. Exposure to others and their points of view is often all that's needed to relax.

Schedule your recreation. Many supervisors drive themselves so hard that they allow little or no time for recreation. Try to plan with your husband some regular activity—like bowling or some other hobby. And see that he devotes a definite number of hours to it regularly.

How can a wife help her husband on his plan for self-improvement?

Be interested. Don't look upon his work or his outside activities as competition for his attention. Try planning his program with him (see page 341). Find ways to help him at home. If he's got to make a speech, act as his audience and as his prompter. If he's trying to improve his relationship with people, let him know when his relations with you improve as a result.

It's unwise (most of the time) to take on the task of educating your husband. He'll resent it just as Abe Lincoln resented Mary Todd Lincoln's efforts. (Do you remember how difficult it was when your husband taught you to drive a car?) Instead of assuming the role of teacher, try to be a coach. Your husband has to carry the ball at work. If you coach him to be confident, to be honest with himself, you'll be far more effective.

38 GETTING ALONG
WITH YOUR BOSS

Should you apple-polish with your boss?

In the eyes of most people, it's despicable to curry favor with your superior by substituting patronizing attention and yes-manship for the main responsibility of getting your job done. Such tactics may meet with short-term success, but in the long run the resentment you stir up among your associates will become a burden that is very difficult, if not impossible, for you to bear.

First be sure of what you mean by "apple polishing." Too often a supervisor whose performance is sub par, or whose skill in human relations is inadequate, accuses his more successful associate of apple polishing. It's hard to get around the fact that the supervisor who does his job well will be appreciated by his boss. And if in addition, his skill in dealing with people includes skill in getting along with his superior, he'll be in especially good graces with his boss. To criticize him is sour grapes. Better that you should reflect on your own approach and try to improve.

Are yes-men successful?

The man who says "Yes" to all his boss's whims may be a comfort to the boss to have around. But he's rarely a true success. This doesn't mean *you* should say "No." The trick to making a hero out of yourself is to find ways to agree with the boss—to find ways to make his ideas and suggestions workable.

Take this example:

You're in a meeting with your boss. He suggests that the way to reduce costs is for each foreman to cut his payroll 10 per cent. You feel that this is an unreasonable proposition. Do you say, "Yes, it's a great idea"? Or do you say, "No, the idea stinks"?

Say neither. To say "Yes" when you disagree is dishonest and only postpones facing up to the problem. To say "No" is tactless—tends to get you a reputation of a noncooperator, a grumbler, or a malcontent.

Try saying something like this, "I agree that we should make every attempt to cut our payrolls. And perhaps a 10 per cent reduction will be possible, although we can't overlook the pressure we're getting from sales to speed up deliveries. Suppose, in addition to taking a long look at our labor cost, we also see what we can do to spread out our production peaks. Perhaps, if we can get the sales department to give a little, we can achieve a lasting reduction in force."

This technique is called the "yes-but" method. It works because you are showing that you accept the principle of the boss's suggestion. And rather than contradict him, you are going along with him to explore ways of making his idea work out. If you use this approach, he'll be more inclined to listen later on to suggestions that run counter to his own thinking at the moment.

How do you stay on the right side of your boss?

Nothing very complicated here. Do your own job well. Stay out of trouble with other departments—such as sales, accounting, engineering—he must deal with. Avoid petty bickering with the other supervisors. For all this you may never get a medal pinned on your shirt, but it will put you well up on his list of supervisors he knows he can depend upon.

What things should you check first with your boss and what matters shouldn't you bother him with?

The usual answer is to bother him only with the big problems and to handle all the routine stuff yourself. But in practice, such a rule of thumb is hard to figure out. Some bosses just can't seem to give up their control of an occasional trifle. If your boss worked himself up from the job you now hold, he may still want to do some part of it which he still enjoys. Such as deciding whether a report form should be on pink paper or blue paper. Sure, it's foolish. But if he shows himself to be a bug on procedural details, better check with him first. It won't be the least bit surprising if he lets you make decisions a hundred times bigger without wanting to know anything about it except the results.

The principle here is that you've got to find out from your own experience just what your boss's delegation habits are. And then follow them.

If you're lucky enough to have a really approachable boss, try the responsibility quiz with him (page 72). It may help both of you resolve the areas where you feel uncertain.

What do you do if your boss asks you to be a stool pigeon?

Chances are slim that he ever will. But if he does, he's the kind of boss you better be careful with. Tell him you'll report to him those activities which come to your attention, and let it go at that.

Don't confuse this issue with your very real responsibility to keep your boss informed of what's going on. Most top-level decisions that go wrong do so because they are based on inadequate information of what people are thinking and saying in the shop. It's up to you to channel your interpretation of feelings and attitudes to your boss so that he can make better decisions. As a matter of fact, much of what employees will tell you is told with the unconscious purpose of having you relay this information upstairs. Of course, you must only talk in generalities—or about *groups* of employees. Never about specific individuals.

Suppose, within a week's time, Mary Jones tells you that she's going to quit because she didn't get a raise, Pete Dow lets you know he's working at another part-time job to make ends meet at home, and Ed Black files a grievance because his wage rate doesn't include his doing the kind of work you're assigning him. What do you tell your boss? You don't tell him that Mary said this, Pete that, and Ed another thing. Instead, you tell him that in the last week you've heard three complaints that indicate that wage rates in the plant are getting out of line. That this is hurting morale. This is information he desperately needs from you. If he wants details, give him only those which don't violate a request by the employee that his conversation be treated confidentially.

What do you do about a boss who's too busy to take time with your problems?

This isn't *all* bad. It *can* mean that he's got so much confidence in you that he trusts you to handle your problems without his help. But the too-busy boss does point up the importance of *timing* when dealing with your superiors.

It can't be stressed too much: Find the right time and place for discussing problems with your boss. If he's irritable on Monday mornings, don't ask for favors then. If he's in a rush late in the afternoon, don't bring a long, involved problem to his attention at that time. Instead, rearrange your own schedule to get to him when experience shows he's the most relaxed and unlikely to be disturbed. One good method is to make an appointment. Call him on the phone. For instance, "Mr. Blake, I've got an inventory problem I'd like to have your guidance on. It will take about a half hour to go over it. Can we get together in your office sometime tomorrow morning—say, between 10 and 11 A.M.?" Your request, put this way, is pretty hard to turn down.

Another tip is to be certain that when you do talk with your boss, you're well prepared to present your problem. If you've left lots of loose ends, he'll feel you're wasting his time. And consequently will find reason to be busy the next time.

Some bosses are just plain impossible. What do you do if you find yourself in a situation like that?

You'll find life a lot easier if you try to make the best of a poor situation. If you grouse about the old man behind his back, ridicule him to others, or try to undermine him, you'll only increase your feeling of incompatibility.

Remember that bosses are human, too. Few of them are mean just for the sake of being mean. A poor boss is really an unfortunate person who is making a mess of his human relations. If you'd study him just as you would a problem employee, you may be able to find a way to improve your relations with him.

Trouble is that too many people generalize about bosses. And forget that each boss is different, because he's an individual. Look hard for his good side and don't take his efforts to be agreeable for granted. And recognize that to most of us, being a leader means exercising authority and giving orders. It doesn't make for popularity. But the weaker and more ineffectual you permit your boss to be in his relations with you, the more you'll suffer in your own contacts with your employees.

How can you tell how you rate with your boss?

There's hardly a supervisor alive who doesn't ask himself this question from time to time. You see the boss stop by Louis' office and chat with him for a half hour, while he passes you by with hardly a nod.

"How come Louis is getting all the attention," you ask yourself, "while I can't get the time of day?" It's a pretty uneasy feeling. No wonder you found yourself unreasonable with Mabel this morning.

You *can* watch some straws in the wind, however, that will tell you what the boss really thinks of your services:

• Do you get raises as frequently as your associates? If you feel that you do, chances are that your boss values your effort. Although he may not put his appreciation into words, he may feel that the pay envelope will speak louder. So don't complain if that's the way he shows his appreciation.

• Does he ask your opinion about matters that affect your department? Even if he doesn't make his decisions in accordance with your suggestions, a boss who shows he's interested in your reactions has shown you that you rate pretty high with him.

• Does he have a hands-off attitude toward your employees? Be thankful for the boss who lets you do all the direct dealing with employees—whether it's favorable or not.

• Does he criticize you when you've made a mistake? If so, he's letting you know where you stand. This way you have a chance to explain why—or to figure out a way so it doesn't happen again. Much worse if your boss doesn't say anything to you, but complains about your efforts to others.

• Does he back you up—even when you're on shaky ground? You can forgive a boss a lot of sins if he's loyal to you with his superiors and associates.

• Does he know much about you and your family? Many bosses find it hard to get personal—even though they are interested in your welfare. So look for the little telltale indications that the boss knows what kind of house you live in, how old your children are, what model car you drive.

If you can answer "Yes" to most of these questions, chances are that your boss rates you as an all-right supervisor. Sure, he probably feels there's plenty of room for improvement. But in the long run, he wouldn't trade you for many other supervisors he's seen.

The trouble with too many supervisors is that they expect the boss to be perfect in his relationships with them. Actually, it's often the other way around. Because you're in the official management family, he may feel that he doesn't have to square every corner with you. Just as when you get home, you drop your company manners—and show your family some of your grouchy side that you've been concealing all day.

Moral? Give your boss half a chance. Don't expect him to fall all over you just because you've done your job. Be satisfied if his good points outweigh his faults. And then see how much this realization will help you get along better with him.

Why are your ideas so often hard to sell to your boss?

Probably because he sees them in a different light. Your viewpoint may be limited to 500 square feet of shop floor, twelve machines, twenty employees, and a mass of today's problems. Your boss probably can multiply your problems by half a dozen—and then complicate them by his conditions for the pressures he feels from topside. So always try to put yourself in the boss's shoes before griping too hard at a rejected idea. More than likely, he'd like to say "Yes" as much as anybody.

What can you do to get your boss to agree with your ideas?

It's been popular to quote, "It's not what you say, but how you say it." There's truth in this adage, but don't ever believe that fancy palaver will ever make a poor idea stick. You've got to have facts and logic on your side—right from the start. And beware of overestimating the pay-off which will come from your ideas. When you do this—or underestimate difficulties—your boss loses faith in your judgment. And may turn down your idea.

E. C. Bill, Administrator of Presentations for Radio Corporation of America, Commercial Electronics Products, writing in *Sales Management,* says, "I am convinced that the fault [of an unsuccessful attempt to sell an idea] usually lies not in the *manner* of presentation, but in *what* is presented."

Mr. Bill suggests that you:

• State exactly what the idea is, in terms that can be grasped by your eleven-year-old daughter. Until you can do this, you don't know what the idea is yourself.

• State the value of the idea to your organization. Answer this question: Why should the owner of your business take X number of dollars and risk them in this scheme rather than in any of the other ways other supervisors are suggesting?

• List on a sheet of paper the advantages of your plan—and the disadvantages of your plan. Be realistic about both.

• Show where your idea will fit into the picture. How much of your plan can you carry out, how much is up to your boss or the cooperation he'll get from others? If most of it depends upon your action, it's easier for him to say "Yes."

• Choose right climate. Be sure that the odds are in your favor.

Regardless of its soundness, it's hard to sell a proposition that means spending money when the emphasis is on holding down expenses.

• Settle for as much as you can get. If you can introduce your program a little at a time, you may be better off. You can work the bugs out of it before a full-scale installation is made.

When should you ask for a raise?

Watch your timing. Keep in mind four things: (1) company policy, (2) company economic situation, (3) your boss's disposition, and (4) your own performance.

If your company has a fixed policy for reviewing and appraising your work and for issuing raises, don't buck the system. Find out when the review period is, what your salary range is (many companies will state that a foreman, for instance, can make from, say, $400 to $500 per month—to go over the top figure, you've got to get the next higher job). Then gauge your actions accordingly.

Of course, it's downright foolish to ask for a raise when your company is in an economic slump. If it's seasonal, wait until times pick up. Even then, don't make your pitch the day after the plant loses a big order.

You needn't be told much about the good and bad times to approach your boss. Be smart about it. Wait a day or a month for the right time —if he tends to be temperamental.

And in every case, be sure that your job, and your work at it, deserves the increase. The days of giving you a raise (other than a general one which everybody may get to adjust to cost of living) just because you've been a nice fellow and stayed with the company for fourteen years are fast drawing to a close.

How do you go about asking your boss for a raise?

Assuming your timing is correct, you'll want to approach the raise problem in much the same manner you would if you were trying to sell your boss a new idea. Here are a few tactics to consider:

Come right out and ask for it. The direct approach will force a "Yes" or "No" answer, so be certain your performance warrants more money before you try it. To be on firm ground, have some facts on hand that can show how your job has grown bigger or your efforts become more effective. "I know the company expects to get a return on all the money it spends—including my salary. So I've made a list of new duties I've picked up since last year. And the shop records show that absences in my department are down 3 per cent over last year, scrap 4 per cent, and direct labor cost per unit has been reduced 0.07 cent."

Explain how much you need the money. Your personal finances tend to be your own affair. You weaken yourself in the boss's eyes by asking for a raise because you can't manage at home. It's much better to be subtle in this area. Let your boss know of your increased responsibility—and how hard you work to keep finances from interfering with your effectiveness.

Wait and see. In many companies, this is the only tack you can follow. But, generally speaking, it's wise for you to put a little pressure on from time to time. For instance, you might say, "I'm not asking for a raise at this particular moment, Mr. Jones, but I'd like to review my past six months' performance with you so that when raises are possible again, I'll be sure that my performance will warrant one."

What should you say when you get a raise?

Be appreciative—but never, never treat it as a handout. Act as if it's something you've earned and consequently deserve. If the raise is smaller than you expected, ask the boss how you can do the kind of job that will deserve more money next time.

SELECTED BIBLIOGRAPHY
FOR FURTHER READING

Allen, Clark Lee, James M. Buchanan, and Marshall R. Colberg: *Prices, Income, and Public Policy,* McGraw-Hill Book Company, Inc., New York, 1954.

Allen, Louis A.: *Management and Organization,* McGraw-Hill Book Company, Inc., New York, 1958.

Apple, James M.: *Plant Layout and Materials Handling,* The Ronald Press Company, New York, 1950.

Auer, J. J., and H. L. Ewbank: *Handbook for Discussion Leaders,* Harper & Brothers, New York, 1954.

Barbash, Jack: *Labor Unions in Action,* Harper & Brothers, New York, 1948.

Barnes, Ralph M.: *Work Sampling,* John Wiley & Sons, Inc., New York, 1957.

Bellows, Roger M.: *Psychology of Personnel in Business and Industry,* Prentice-Hall, Inc., Englewood Cliffs, N.J., 1954.

——— and M. F. Estep: *Employment Psychology: The Interview,* Rinehart & Company, Inc., New York, 1954.

Bethel, Lawrence L., Franklin S. Atwater, George H. E. Smith, and Harvey A. Stackman, Jr.: *Essentials of Industrial Management,* McGraw-Hill Book Company, Inc., New York, 1954.

Bittel, Lester R., Morley G. Melden, and Robert S. Rice: *Practical Automation,* McGraw-Hill Book Company, Inc., New York, 1957.

Black, James Menzies: *How to Grow in Management,* Prentice-Hall, Inc., Englewood Cliffs, N.J., 1957.

——— and J. George Piccoli: *Successful Labor Relations for Small Business,* McGraw-Hill Book Company, Inc., New York, 1953.

Blake, R. P.: *Industrial Safety,* 2d ed., Prentice-Hall, Inc., Englewood Cliffs, N.J., 1953.

Borden, Richard C.: *Public Speaking—As Listeners Like It!,* Harper & Brothers, New York, 1935.

Broaded, Charley H.: *Essentials of Management for Supervisors,* Harper & Brothers, New York, 1947.

Brown, Milon: *Effective Supervision,* The Macmillan Company, New York, 1956.

Busch, Henry M.: *Conference Methods in Industry,* Harper & Brothers, New York, 1949.

Calhoon, Richard P., and C. A. Kirkpatrick: *Influencing Employee Behavior,* McGraw-Hill Book Company, Inc., New York, 1956.

Cantor, Nathaniel: *Employee Counseling,* McGraw-Hill Book Company, Inc., New York, 1945.

Carroll, Phil: *Timestudy for Cost Control,* 3d ed., McGraw-Hill Book Company, Inc., New York, 1954.

————: *Timestudy Fundamentals for Foremen,* 2d ed., McGraw-Hill Book Company, Inc., New York, 1951.

Clark, Charles H.: *Brainstorming,* Doubleday & Company, Inc., New York, 1958.

Crawford, Robert P.: *Techniques of Creative Thinking,* Prentice-Hall, Inc., Englewood Cliffs, N.J., 1954.

Davis, John Richiliew: *Industrial Plant Protection,* Charles C Thomas, Publisher, Springfield, Ill., 1957.

Davis, Keith: *Human Relations in Business,* McGraw-Hill Book Company, Inc., New York, 1957.

Donahue, Wilma, ed.: *Earning Opportunities for Older Workers,* University of Michigan Press, Ann Arbor, Mich., 1955.

Dooher, M. Joseph, and Vivienne Marquis, eds.: *The AMA Handbook of Wage and Salary Administration,* American Management Association, New York, 1950.

———— and ————: *The Development of Executive Talent,* American Management Association, New York, 1952.

———— and ————, eds.: *Effective Communication on the Job,* American Management Association, New York, 1956.

———— and ————: *Rating Employee and Supervisory Performance,* American Management Association, New York, 1950.

———— and ————: *The Supervisor's Management Guide,* American Management Association, New York, 1949.

Dubin, Robert: *Human Relations in Administration,* Prentice-Hall, Inc., Englewood Cliffs, N.J., 1951.

Ellis, William D., and Frank Siedel: *How to Win the Conference,* Prentice-Hall, Inc., Englewood Cliffs, N.J., 1955.

Evans, Chester E.: *Supervisory Responsibility and Authority, Research Report No. 30,* American Management Association, New York, 1957.

Fear, Richard A.: *The Evaluation Interview,* McGraw-Hill Book Company, Inc., New York, 1958.

Feigenbaum, A. V.: *Quality Control,* McGraw-Hill Book Company., Inc., New York, 1951.

Fenlason, Anne F.: *Essentials in Interviewing,* Harper & Brothers, New York, 1952.

Finlay, William W., A. Q. Sartain, and Willis M. Tate: *Human Behavior in Industry,* McGraw-Hill Book Company, Inc., New York, 1954.

Flesch, Rudolph: *Art of Clear Thinking,* Harper & Brothers, New York, 1951.

———: *Art of Readable Writing*, Harper & Brothers, New York, 1951.

Furst, Bruno: *Practical Ways to Better Memory*, Grosset & Dunlop, Inc., New York, 1944.

Gardiner, Glenn: *Better Foremanship*, 2d ed., McGraw-Hill Book Company, Inc., New York, 1948.

——— and R. Gardiner: *Vitalizing the Foreman's Role in Management*, McGraw-Hill Book Company, Inc., New York, 1949.

Gardner, Burleigh B., and David Moore: *Human Relations in Industry*, Richard D. Irwin, Inc., Homewood, Ill., 1952.

Gottlieb, Hans J., B. B. Gamzue, and Milton Kalb: *English for Adults*, Harper & Brothers, New York, 1954.

Gray, J. Seton: *Common Sense in Business*, McGraw-Hill Book Company, Inc., New York, 1956.

Gray, J. Stanley: *Psychology in Industry*, McGraw-Hill Book Company, Inc., New York, 1952.

Gunning, Robert: *The Technique of Clear Writing*, McGraw-Hill Book Company, Inc., New York, 1952.

Halsey, George D.: *Selecting and Inducting Employees*, Harper & Brothers, New York, 1957.

———: *Supervising People*, rev. ed., Harper & Brothers, New York, 1953.

———: *Training Employees*, Harper & Brothers, New York, 1949.

Hannaford, Earle S.: *Conference Leadership in Business and Industry*, McGraw-Hill Book Company, Inc., New York, 1945.

Hazlitt, Henry: *Economics in One Lesson*, Harper & Brothers, New York, 1946.

Hersey, Rexford: *Better Foremanship—Key to Profitable Management*, Chilton Co., Inc., Philadelphia, 1955.

———: *Zest for Work*, Harper & Brothers, New York, 1955.

Heyel, Carl: *The Foreman's Handbook*, 3d ed., McGraw-Hill Book Company, Inc., New York, 1955.

Hutchinson, Eliot D.: *How to Think Creatively*, Abingdon Press, Nashville, Tenn., 1949.

Immer, John R.: *Layout Planning Techniques*, McGraw-Hill Book Company, Inc., New York, 1950.

Ingram, K. C.: *Talk That Gets Results*, McGraw-Hill Book Company, Inc., New York, 1957.

Juran, J. M.: *Management of Inspection and Quality Control*, Harper & Brothers, New York, 1945.

Keller, I. Wayne: *Management Accounting for Profit Control*, McGraw-Hill Book Company, Inc., New York, 1957.

Koepke, Charles A.: *Plant Production Control*, 2d ed., John Wiley & Sons, Inc., New York, 1949.

Krooss, Herman E.: *American Economic Development,* Prentice-Hall, Inc., Englewood Cliffs, N.J., 1955.

Laird, Donald A., and Eleanor C. Laird: *The New Psychology for Leadership,* McGraw-Hill Book Company, Inc., New York, 1956.

——— and ———: *Practical Business Psychology,* McGraw-Hill Book Company, Inc., New York, 1956.

——— and ———: *The Techniques of Delegating,* McGraw-Hill Book Company, Inc., New York, 1957.

Lanham, E.: *Job Evaluation,* McGraw-Hill Book Company, Inc., New York, 1955.

Lee, Irving J.: *How to Talk with People,* Harper & Brothers, New York, 1952.

Leedy, Paul: *Reading Improvement for Adults,* McGraw-Hill Book Company, Inc., New York, 1956.

Lewis, Norman: *How to Read Faster and Better,* Doubleday & Company, Inc., New York, 1944.

Linton, Calvin D.: *How to Write Reports,* Harper & Brothers, New York, 1954.

Lundy, James L.: *Effective Industrial Management,* The Macmillian Company, New York, 1957.

Maier, N. R.: *Principles of Human Relations,* John Wiley & Sons, Inc., New York, 1952.

Mallick, Randolph W., and Armand T. Gaudreau: *Plant Layout,* John Wiley & Sons, Inc., New York, 1951.

Mandell, Milton M.: *Recruiting and Selecting Office Employees, Research Report No. 27,* American Management Association, New York, 1956.

Maynard, Harold B., ed.: *Industrial Engineering Handbook,* McGraw-Hill Book Company, Inc., New York, 1956.

——— and G. J. Stegemerten: *Operation Analysis,* McGraw-Hill Book Company, Inc., New York, 1939.

———, ———, and John L. Schwab: *Methods-Time Measurement,* McGraw-Hill Book Company, Inc., New York, 1948.

McCarty, John T.: *Community Relations in Business,* Bureau of National Affairs, Washington, D.C., 1956.

Michael, Lionel B.: *Wage and Salary Fundamentals and Procedures,* McGraw-Hill Book Company, Inc., New York, 1950.

Moore, F. G.: *Manufacturing Management,* Richard D. Irwin, Inc., Homewood, Ill., 1953.

Morse, N. C.: *Satisfactions in the White-collar Job,* University of Michigan Press, Ann Arbor, Mich., 1953.

Morrow, L. C., ed.: *Maintenance Engineering Handbook,* McGraw-Hill Book Company, Inc., New York, 1957.

Murphy, Dennis: *Better Business Communications,* McGraw-Hill Book Company, Inc., New York, 1957.

Nadler, Gerald: *Motion and Time Study,* McGraw-Hill Book Company, Inc., New York, 1955.

————: *Work Simplification*, McGraw-Hill Book Company, Inc., New York, 1957.

National Manpower Council: *Womanpower*, Columbia University Press, New York, 1957.

Nichols, Ralph G., and Leonard A. Stevens: *Are You Listening?* McGraw-Hill Book Company, Inc., New York, 1957.

Niebel, Benjamin W.: *Motion and Time Study*, Richard D. Irwin, Inc., Homewood, Ill., 1955.

Nunn, Henry L.: *The Whole Man Goes to Work*, Harper & Brothers, New York, 1953.

Osborn, Alex F.: *Applied Imagination*, Charles Scribner's Sons, New York, 1948.

————: *Your Creative Power*, Charles Scribner's Sons, New York, 1948.

Otis, J. L., and R. H. Leukart: *Job Evaluation*, Prentice-Hall, Inc., Englewood Cliffs, N.J., 1950.

Parker, Willard E., and Robert W. Kleemeier: *Human Relations in Supervision*, McGraw-Hill Book Company, Inc., New York, 1951.

Patton, John A., and C. L. Littlefield: *Job Evaluation*, rev. ed., Richard D. Irwin, Inc., Homewood, Ill., 1957.

Payne, S. L.: *The Art of Asking Questions*, Princeton University Press, Princeton, N.J., 1951.

Perry, John: *Human Relations in Small Business*, McGraw-Hill Book Company, Inc., New York, 1954.

Peters, Raymond W.: *Communications within Industry*, Harper & Brothers, New York, 1950.

Pigors, Paul: *Effective Communications in Industry*, National Association of Manufacturers, New York, 1949.

Planty, Earl G., and J. Thomas Freeston: *Developing Management Ability*, The Ronald Press Company, New York, 1954.

Prosser, Charles A., and Phillip S. VanWyck: *How to Train Shop Workers*, American Technical Society, Chicago, 1949.

Randle, C. Wilson: *Collective Bargaining, Principles and Practices*, Houghton Mifflin Company, Boston, 1951.

Redfield, Charles E.: *Communication in Management*, University of Chicago Press, Chicago, 1953.

Riegel, John W.: *Executive Development*, University of Michigan Press, Ann Arbor, Mich., 1952.

Reilly, William J.: *How to Make Your Living in Four Hours a Day*, Harper & Brothers, New York, 1955.

————: *The Law of Intelligent Action*, Harper & Brothers, New York, 1945.

Roberts, J. W., and Clem Zinck: *Methods Improvement and the Foreman*, National Foremen's Institute, New London, Conn., 1951.

Robinson, M. A., H. C. Morton, and J. D. Calderwood: *An Introduction to Economic Reasoning*, Brookings Institution, Washington, D.C., 1956.

Sayles, Leonard R., and George Strauss: *The Local Union,* Harper & Brothers, New York, 1953.

Schell, Erwin H.: *The Technique of Executive Control,* McGraw-Hill Book Company, Inc., New York, 1957.

Schleh, E. C.: *Successful Executive Action,* Prentice-Hall, Inc., Englewood Cliffs, N.J., 1955.

Shurter, Robert L.: *Effective Letters in Business,* 2d ed., McGraw-Hill Book Company, Inc., New York, 1954.

Simonds, R. H., and J. V. Grimaldi: *Safety Management: Accident Cost and Control,* Richard D. Irwin, Inc., Homewood, Ill., 1956.

Smyth, R. C., and M. J. Murphy: *Bargaining with Organized Labor,* Funk & Wagnalls Company, New York, 1948.

Spengler, Edwin H., and Jacob Klein: *Introduction to Business,* 4th ed., McGraw-Hill Book Company, Inc., New York, 1955.

Spriegel, W. R., E. Schulz, and W. B. Spriegel: *Elements of Supervision,* John Wiley & Sons, Inc., New York, 1957.

Upgren, Arthur, and Stahrl Edmunds: *Economics for You and Me,* The Macmillan Company, New York, 1953.

Uris, Auren: *Developing Your Executive Skills,* McGraw-Hill Book Company, Inc., New York, 1955.

————: *The Efficient Executive,* McGraw-Hill Book Company, Inc., New York, 1957.

————: *How to Be a Successful Leader,* McGraw-Hill Book Company, Inc., New York, 1953.

Villers, Raymond: *The Dynamics of Industrial Management,* Funk & Wagnalls Company, New York, 1954.

Voris, William: *Production Control,* Richard D. Irwin, Inc., Homewood, Ill., 1956.

Walker, C. R., R. H. Guest, and A. N. Turner: *The Foreman on the Assembly Line,* Harvard University Press, Cambridge, Mass., 1956.

War Manpower Commission: *The Training Within Industry Report, 1940–1945,* 1945.

Weinland, J. D., and M. V. Gross: *Personnel Interviewing,* The Ronald Press Company, New York, 1952.

Whitehill, Arthur M., Jr.: *Personnel Relations,* McGraw-Hill Book Company, Inc., New York, 1955.

Women's Bureau, U.S. Department of Labor: *1954 Handbook on Women Workers, Bulletin 255,* 1954.

Zelko, Harold P.: *Successful Conference and Discussion Techniques,* McGraw-Hill Book Company, Inc., 1957.

VISUAL AIDS

The motion pictures and filmstrips in the following list can be used to supplement the material in this book. It is recommended that each one be reviewed before use to determine its suitability.

Following each description the name of the distributor is given in abbreviated form, as well as the length of the motion picture in minutes. Unless otherwise indicated, motion pictures are 16mm sound black-and-white films. Filmstrips are usually 35mm and black-and-white with accompanying 33⅓-rpm disc recordings, and their length is given either in frames, as the length of the recording in minutes, or both.

A complete list of names and addresses of distributors follows the list of films.

Motion Pictures

Part 1. About People at Work

Communications. Shows the need for effective communication in industry. (McGraw, 12 min)

Good Place to Work. The story of current and past achievements by industry to improve working conditions and to make factory employment attractive. (NAM, 14½ min)

Making Friends in Plant Communities. Shows how to plan and conduct a plant tour. (NAM, 16 min)

Making Yourself Understood. Analyzes the basic factors of communication. Shows how we can evaluate and criticize all forms of communication and become better communicators and listeners. (EBF, 14 min)

Part 2. Supervising People

Employment Interview. How to get the right man for the job. (McGraw, 11 min)

First Impressions. Why new employees may dislike their jobs and how to make a good first impression on them. (UWF, 21 min)

The Grievance. Illustrates by an actual case how the right of a worker with a grievance is protected under the union contract. (McGraw, 30 min)

Grievance Hearing. A case study of a grievance. Shows how hearings are conducted. (McGraw, 15 min)

The Inner Man Steps Out. The story of a supervisor who tried to follow standard rules for getting along with people, but finds that his efforts back-fire on him. Finally he learns what he has been doing wrong and why. (GE, 35 min)

Interviewing Principles and Techniques. Illustrates principles of good interviewing. (UWF, 17 min)

Instructing the Worker on the Job. Demonstrates the difference between telling, showing, and instructing someone to do a job. (UWF, 14 min)

Introducing the New Worker to His Job. Demonstrates the difference between right and wrong methods of instructing a new worker. (UWF, 16 min)

*Job Evaluation.** How the requirements, duties, and pay of various jobs are determined. (McGraw, 10 min)

Job Evaluation and Merit Rating. Shows that job evaluation is needed to compare requirements for difficult jobs and set rates of pay. (McGraw, 13 min)

Placing the Right Man on the Job. Indicates the necessity for taking individual differences into account. (UWF, 13 min)

Supervisor as a Leader, Part 1. Several workmen tell what they consider to be the qualifications of a good supervisor. (UWF, 14 min)

Supervisor as a Leader, Part 2. Four supervisors discuss the qualities of leadership. (UWF, 13 min)

Supervisory Conferences. Explains the purpose of training programs. (McGraw, 14 min)

You Are There at the Bargaining Table. Presents negotiations between a corporation and a union as they hammer out contract terms. Also shows workers performing typical jobs in the plant. (AMA, 50 min)

- *Safety*

*An Accident Happens to Sam.** Illustrates some of the major types of accidents which occur in industry, why they happen, and how they can be prevented. (NSC, 13 min)

All Out for Safety. Shows foremen and supervisors what to expect at a National Safety Congress and Exposition. Includes industrial scenes cover-ing various aspects of safety training. (NSC, 16 min)

Factory Safety. Points out how good factory safety records are achieved by such measures as rule booklets, safety meetings, stop switches, guards, and attention to minor injuries. (Jam Handy, 10 min)

*Freight Handling Safety.** Freight-car and motor-truck loading hazards, the safe way to open freight-car doors, lowering and anchoring dock plates, handling "sleepers," and using hand trucks. NSC, 11 min)

Handling. A brief lesson on how to avoid accidents when handling heavy sacks and crates. (UWF, 5 min)

How It Happened. Ten episodes taken from reports of actual accidents, plus an epilogue to stress the safety points illustrated. (AT&T, 30 min)

* Correlated filmstrip also available.

Machines. How minor carelessness in handling machinery may lead to accidents. (UWF, 8 min)

Magic Carpet. How to prevent slipping accidents and fire hazards in industry (Waverly, 11 min)

Men Who Come Back. Safety precautions found necessary in most industries, such as machine guarding, good housekeeping, and materials handling. (Ohio, 23 min, color)

Organization. How safety committees can lower the accident rate in industry. (UWF, 11 min)

The Outlaw. Shows results of carelessness in an industrial plant. (ASBE, 30 min, silent)

Plan to Live. Shows the operations in an industrial chemical plant and the safety practices which should be observed (Ind, 17 min)

Safety in the Shop. Dramatizes typical shop accidents and shows how poor supervision or inadequate training may be their real cause. Emphasizes the supervisor's responsibilities in teaching and maintaining safe shop practices. (UWF, 2 min)

Shop Safety. Discusses the causes and prevention of accidents, and safety rules for welding, hoisting, working with machinery and tools, lifting heavy objects, and handling gasoline. (UWF, 28 min)

Working Safely in the Shop. Presents the essentials of shop safety—how to keep a shop safe, how to dress for safety, and safe practices in the operation of the grinder, circular saw, band saw, drill press, jointer, and disc sander. (Coronet, 10 min)

Part 3. Supervising People

The Bright Young Newcomer. Raises the problems created when a bright young newcomer is added to an office group in which the senior woman employee has worked for many years. (McGraw, 7 min)

Call 'em on the Carpet. Shows how to reprimand workers without causing ill will. (NCS, 12 min)

Date of Birth. Presents the actual record of employees in the over-45 age group, indicating that there is less absenteeism, a lower turnover rate, and an equal standard of production among older workers. (Seminar, 16 min, color)

Developing Cooperation. Shows the right and wrong way to supervise employees and how to develop cooperation among workers. (UWF, 15 min)

Discipline: Giving Orders. Stresses the importance of disciplining a person properly and giving orders clearly. (UWF, 15 min)

Discipline: Reprimanding. Shows examples of proper and improper reprimanding of employees by supervisors. (UWF, 10 min)

Experiment. Conveys the idea that people can't be forced to think or act as we want them to, but will respond to a series of gentle pushes. (GM, 12 min)

The Follow-through. Shows the result of a hurried inadequate job of instructing an experienced clerk on operating new equipment. (McGraw, 9 min)

Fragile, Handle Feelings with Care. Story of a typical plant foreman who finds that he has hurt the feelings of his workers by his thoughtlessness. (NSC, 10 min)

The Grapevine. Shows what happens to human relations between management and clerical groups when there is not good communication between them. (McGraw, 8 min)

How Much Cooperation. Discusses what cooperation between supervisor and employees involves. (McGraw, 7 min)

How to Give and Take Instructions. Five basic skills needed for clear and effective communication. (Coronet, 10 min)

Improving the Job. A supervisor asks one of his workmen for suggestions for preventing waste, and methods of improving the job are brought out. (UWF, 9 min)

In the Middle. Raises the problems caused by a change decided on by management that involves acceptance by the clerical force. (McGraw, 7 min)

It's an Order. Shows how to give concise well-worded orders to employees. (NCS, 12 min)

Maintaining Workers' Interest. Shows that the supervisor should be alert to detect and remedy situations in which workers are doing a poor job because their work holds no interest for them. (UWF, 13 min)

Promotion By-pass. Shows the difficulties of a supervisor giving disappointing news to an employee about a promotion that the employee didn't get. (McGraw, 8 min)

Passing the Know-how Along. How to help the experienced worker to break in a man on a new job. (Jam Handy, 15 min, silent)

Retire to Life. The story of a machinist who had looked forward to a retirement of fishing and just plain loafing, but soon felt useless and unwanted. A positive approach to retirement is emphasized. (IFB, 23 min)

Safety in Offices. Dramatization of some of the more common accidents that happen in offices. (Assn, 10 min)

Supervising Women Workers. Discussion between a line supervisor and a foreman of problems encountered in supervising women workers. (UWF, 11 min)

Supervising Workers on the Job. Shows various kinds of poor supervision practices and indicates the value of better methods. (UWF, 10 min)

Part 4. Managing Your Job

The Easier Way. A peg-board device is used to illustrate the principles of motion study. (GM, 12 min)

Flow-process Chart and How to Use It. Shows how to prepare a flow-process chart for the study of work simplification, transportation, storage, and inspection. (UWF, 15 min)

Foreman Discovers Motion Study. Shows the experience of a typical foreman as he comes into contact with motion study for the first time. (Calif, 16 min, b&w or color)

Foreman's Part in Methods Improvement. Shows how a foreman learned about methods improvement and how he applied it to the work of his own department. (MEC, 18 min, color)

Fundamentals of Quality Control. Illustrates the building of distribution curves and their use in controlling quality. (MEC, 16 min, color)

Improved Methods. Case studies in methods improvement with close-ups of each job. (MEC, 16 min, color)

Learning the Principles of MTM. Explains methods-time measurement and how it is used to improve production. (MEC, 18 min, color)

Maintaining Quality Standards. Various scenes emphasize the nature of quality standards, and incidents are shown to demonstrate the role of the supervisor in maintaining quality. (UWF, 10 min)

Methods Analysis.* Shows a job analyst preparing a job specification, discusses several methods of job rating, and describes the work of time-study engineers. (McGraw, 10 min)

MTM for Better Methods and Fair Standards. Shows how an industrial engineer develops a methods-time measurement standard. (MEC, 18 min, color)

More Production through Motion Study. Shows the original and an improved method of performing eleven different jobs and includes effects on production. (Purdue, 25 min, color, silent)

Motion and Time Study. Outlines the concepts of motion and time study and offers specific exercises for class instruction. (USC, 9 min)

Motion Study Applications. Defines and illustrates the most common fundamental hand motions. (Iowa, 17 min)

Motion Study Is Everybody's Job. Demonstrates that motion study can be applied by anyone by pairs of before-and-after pictures. (Purdue, 30 min)

Motor Aptitude Tests and Assembly Work. A subject with unusually good motor ability is compared with a subject of average ability in various tests. After the tests are completed, the two men are shown working at an assembly job in which the factors tested are required. (Penn State, 22 min, silent)

Planning and Laying Out Work. Demonstrates the importance of careful planning by showing the results of poor planning or no planning at all. (UWF, 11 min)

Planning Tomorrow's Methods Today. Analysis of a difficult assembly job and development of a more efficient method. (MEC, 17 min, color)

Production Control, Part 1.* How management regulates production to meeting fluctuating requirements—routing, scheduling, dispatching, and follow-up. Importance of routing, techniques of methods analysis, and gaining employee cooperation. (McGraw, 10 min)

Production Control, Part 2.* The use of the master schedule and the shop

---

* Correlated filmstrip also available.

schedule and the centralized and decentralized forms of dispatching. (McGraw, 10 min)

*Quality Control.** How industry keeps check on the variable factors in manufacturing. The effect of quality standards on manufacturing cost and selling price. (McGraw, 10 min)

Skill and Effort Rating. Demonstrates the principles of performance ratings and shows what indicators to look for. (MEC, 12 min, color)

Skill and Effort Rating. Five films designed to help time-study men improve their proficiency (MEC, silent, color):

> *Office and Light Shop Operations* (9 min)
> *Light Shop Operations* (8 min)
> *Medium Shop Operations* (8 min)
> *Medium and Heavy Shop Operations* (10 min)
> *Heavy Shop Operations* (8 min)

Time Study Methods. An analysis of a representative industrial job. (MEC, 19 min, color)

Work Simplification in Action. Describes an actual work simplification and follow-up program. (Wolverine, 10 min)

- *Plant Protection*

*Cause for Alarm.** The control of fires, how to turn in an alarm, how to meet situations in an emergency, various types of fire extinguishers, and the theory of combustion. (NSC, 14 min)

Guarding against Sabotage. Shows saboteur's techniques, physical and psychological sabotage, and precautions to be taken against sabotage. (UWF, 32 min)

Object Lesson in Fire Prevention. Fire hazards and means of protection in aviation overhaul and repair shops; importance of constant vigilance in day-to-day practices. (UWF, 21 min)

Stop Fires—Save Jobs. Explains and cautions against such industrial hazards as vapors, dust, static electricity, bad wiring, abuse of electrical equipment, and danger in working habits. Stresses three principles of fire safety—fire protection engineering, management cooperation, and employee cooperation. (BCR, 19 min)

Stop the Fire Thief. Causes of industrial fires and how safe practices will eliminate them. (NSC, 13 min)

Target: U.S.A. A demonstration of industry and personnel in action prior to and under an atomic bomb attack. How to protect people and property, build up plant-wide defense, build and allocate shelters, recruit a defense corps, set up first aid stations, and safeguard important records (Cornell, 22 min, b&w or color)

Part 5. Helping Yourself to Succeed

Take a Letter, Please. Burlesques the common faults of people who dictate letters, such as the scatterbrain, the speed demon, the dreamer, and the mumbler. Shows the proper method of dictating. (UWF, 22 min)

* Correlated filmstrip also available.

Eight Parts of a Business Letter. Shows how mail is handled, why business letters are standardized, differences between social and business letters, folding and enclosures, and basic display and arrangement. (Library, 12 min)

Writing Better Business Letters. Emphasizes the three principal characteristics of a good business letter—clarity, brevity, and courtesy. (Coronet, 10 min, b&w or color)

Filmstrips

Fair Wage by Job Evaluation. Illustrates company problems before job evaluation and explains its advantages. (NFI, 90 fr, 15 min, color)

Here's How. Explains how to give instruction to employees, with emphasis on safety. (Zurich, 100 fr, 15 min)

Getting Ready to Instruct. How to prepare to teach a job. (UWF, 94 fr, 33 min)

Human Relations in Supervision. Twenty-four filmstrips and twelve recordings discussing such personnel problems as tardiness, equalizing the load, incompetence, unions, safety violations, and friction between employees (McGraw):

1. *Mary Benson* (insubordination)
2. *A Difference of Opinion* (among supervisors)
3. *Independent Sadie* (insubordination)
4. *Tom, Dick, and Harry* (speed-up claimed by union)
5. *Paul Steele* (insubordination backed by union)
6. *Joe and Bob* (poor cooperation between supervisors)
7. *Alice, Jane, and Agnes* (work assignments)
8. *Al Miller* (practical joker)
9. *Harry Carey* (supervisory responsibility)
10. *George Gray* (disgruntled, insubordinate employee)
11. *Lefty Laws* (incompetent employee)
12. *Sarah Blake* (tardy employee)
13. *John Beaver* (tardy supervisor)
14. *Abbie Swartz* (conflicting orders on rules enforcement)
15. *Tessie Teller* (slowdown ordered by union)
16. *Dewey Jones* (poor leadership)
17. *Frances Moore* (interdepartmental assistance)
18. *Bob Smith* (poor work habits)
19. *Jake Diller* (physically handicapped)
20. *The Three Calendeers* (boondoggling)
21. *Emma Trimble* (training for flexibility)
22. *Jerry Cooper* (AWOL)
23. *Jim Halsey* (violation of safety rules)
24. *Mike and Bill* (friction between employees)

The New Job. Shows the importance of the proper methods of introducing a new employee to his job. (AT&T, 20 min)

Straight from the Horse's Mouth. Outlined supervisory methods for handling personnel problems. (NFI, 108 fr, 15 min, color)

Supervisor Training in Human Relations. Eight filmstrips with 15-min disc recordings (Westen):

> *The Supervisor's Job*
> *Interpreting Company Policies*
> *The Supervisor as a Representative of Management*
> *Induction and Job Instruction*
> *Handling Grievances*
> *Maintaining Discipline*
> *Promotion, Transfer, and Training for Responsibility*
> *Promoting Cooperation*

Supervisory Development Program. A set of eight filmstrips with disc recordings. Shows how to apply sound principles of management and human relations (Vocafilm):

> *Freedom of Opportunity* (13 min)
> *Effective Management* (19 min)
> *Individual Output* (21 min)
> *When You've Got a Problem* (22 min)
> *Getting Ideas Across* (14 min)
> *The Will to Produce* (21 min)
> *Understanding People* (24 min)
> *Individual Adjustment* (21 min)

Supervisory Problems in the Office. Six filmstrips each with an 8-min disc recording (McGraw):

> *Understanding Employee Viewpoint* *Orientation and Induction*
> *Error-correction Talk* *Combating Job Monotony*
> *Motivating the Long-service Employee* *Excessive Supervision*

Supervisory Relations Program. Thirteen filmstrips with disc recordings for the training of supervisory employees (Vocafilm):

> *Inducting the New Man* (22 min)
> *Planning Job Instruction* (22 min)
> *How to Teach a Job Quickly* (22 min)
> *Planning for Safety* (13 min)
> *Getting Production Results* (21 min)
> *Getting Time for the Human Relations Job* (13 min)
> *Today's Requirements for Leadership* (12 min)
> *Solving a Man's Difficulties with His Job* (17 min)
> *Letting Men Know Where They Stand* (19 min)
> *The Reprimand That Builds Morale* (14 min)
> *Handling Grievances at Their Start* (15 min)
> *Supervising Women* (20 min)

Supervisory Problems in the Plant. Six filmstrips with disc recordings (McGraw):

> *Communication* *Discipline*
> *Complaints* *Induction Training*
> *Counseling* *Leadership Techniques*

• *Safety*

Disorderly Conduct. Examples of poor industrial housekeeping show why it is safer to keep a workplace neat, clean, and orderly. (Zurich, 100 fr, 13 min)

Easy Does It. Covers safe methods of handling materials in industry and includes a photoquiz. (Zurich, 100 fr, 15 min)

Giant Hands of Industry. Shows approved hand signals, correct type of hoisting gear, and safety in the operation of cranes. (NSC, 15 min)

A Gray Day for O'Grady. A skeptical supervisor discovers that accidents decrease production and increase costs. (NSC, 82 fr, 15 min)

Human Factors in Safety. A film training course prepared especially for foremen. Six filmstrips with disc recordings (NSC):

Everybody's Different (100 fr, 15 min)
People Are All Alike (119 fr, 15 min)
Teaching Safety on the Job (121 fr, 15 min)
Safety Case Histories (217 fr, 30 min)
Secret of Supervision (106 fr, 15 min)
Teamwork for Safety (116 fr, 15 min)

It's No Joke. Illustrates the dangers of horseplay. (Zurich, 100 fr, 15 min)

Keep It Clean. A summary of practical suggestions on ways to keep industrial plants clean and safe. (NSC, 15 min)

Man-handled. Discusses the safe handling of materials. (Zurich, 100 fr, 15 min)

Mostly Personal. Exposes the personal factors involved in industrial accidents. (Zurich, 100 fr, 15 min)

Safe Handling of Materials. Covers causes of accidents in the handling of materials. (NSC, 15 min)

Safety Management for Foremen. Ten filmstrips with 20-min disc recordings (NSC):

Brain Beats Brawn. Handling materials.
Cause and Cure. Preventing accidents.
Doctor's Orders. Use of first aid.
Follow the Leader. Maintaining safety.
Guard Duty. Safeguarding against mechanical hazards.
Principles and Interest. Maintaining employee interest in safety.
Production with Safety. Training workers for safety.
Right Dress. Proper clothing and personal protection.
Safety Is in Order. Providing safe working conditions.
Stop, Look, and Listen. The work of a plant safety inspection committee.

Sources of Films

ASBE—American Society of Bakery Engineers, Dept. of Visual Education, 208 Third Ave., S.E., Minneapolis

AMA—American Management Assn., 1515 Broadway, New York 36

Assn—Association Films, Inc., 347 Madison Ave., New York 17

AT&T—Films available from local Bell Telephone offices.
BCR—Bureau of Communications Research, 13 E. 37th St., New York 16
Calif—University of California, University Extension, Education Film Sales Dept., Los Angeles 24
CCNY—College of the City of New York, Audio-Visual Extension Service, 17 Lexington Ave., New York 10
Cornell—Cornell Film Co., 1501 Broadway, New York 36
Coronet—Coronet Films, Coronet Bldg. Chicago 1.
EBF—Encyclopaedia Britannica Films, Inc., 1150 Wilmette Ave., Wilmette, Ill.
GE—General Electric Co., Distribution Section, Advertising & Sales Promotion, 1 River Road, Schenectady 1, N.Y.
GM—General Motors Corp., Dept. of Public Relations, Film Section, 3044 W. Grand Blvd., Detroit 2.
IFB—International Film Bureau, Suite 308-316, 57 E. Jackson Blvd., Chicago 4
Ind—Indiana University, Audio-Visual Center, 1800 E. 10th St., Bloomington, Ind.
Iowa—State University of Iowa, Bureau of Visual Instruction, Extension Div., Iowa City, Iowa
Jam Handy—The Jam Handy Organization, 2821 E. Grand Blvd., Detroit 11
Library—Library Films, Inc., 25 W. 45th St., New York 36
McGraw—McGraw-Hill Book Company, Inc., Text-Film Dept., 330 W. 42d St., New York 36
MEC—Methods Engineering Council, 718 Wallace Ave., Pittsburgh 21
NAM—National Association of Manufacturers, Motion Picture Dept., 14 W. 49th St., New York 20
NFI—National Foremen's Institute, Inc., 100 Garfield Ave., New London, Conn.
NSC—National Safety Council, Film Service Bureau, 425 N. Michigan Ave., Chicago 11
Ohio—Ohio Industrial Commission, Div. of Safety & Hygiene, Columbus, Ohio
Penn State—Pennsylvania State University, Audio-Visual Aids Library, University Park, Pa.
Purdue—Purdue University Film Library, Lafayette, Ind.
Seminar—Seminar Films, Inc., 347 Madison Ave., New York 17
USC—University of Southern California, Audio-Visual Services, Dept. of Cinema, 3518 University Ave., Los Angeles 7
UWF—United World Films, Inc., 1445 Park Avenue, New York 29
Vocafilm—Vocafilm Corp., 424 Madison Ave., New York 17
Westen—Westen-Wilcox Sales Agency, 6108 Santa Monica Blvd., Hollywood 38, Calif.
Waverly—Waverly Petroleum Products Co., 460 Drexel Bldg., 1724 Chestnut St., Philadelphia 3
Wolverine—Wolverine Tube Division, Industrial Engineering, 1411 Central Ave., Detroit 9
Zurich—Zurich-American Insurance Companies, 135 S. LaSalle St., Chicago 3

INDEX

Absenteeism, 78–79
cost of, 91
counseling for, 184, 242–243
discipline for, 195
prevention of, by better leadership, 58–59
by better selection, 91–92
by creative thinking, 383
records, of alcoholic workers, 243
of older workers, 217–219
of problem employees, 237
of women workers, 210, 218–219
of younger workers, 218–219
Accident-prone employee, 154, 237, 241–242
Accidents, causes of, 150–151
cost of, 151–152
first aid for, 154
frequency of, 158–159
investigation of, 160–161
and malingering, 155
prevention of, 151–162
electrical, 157–158
falling, 156
hand tools, 157
handling, 155
machinery, 155–156
(See also Safety)
rates, 158–159
review form, 161
severity, 158–159
in manufacturing, 159
for older workers, 217–219
for women workers, 218–219
for younger workers, 218–219
Accountability (see Responsibility of supervisors)
Accounting methods, 285–287
Alcoholic employee, handling of, 243–244
recognition of, 237
Alcoholics Anonymous, 243
Allowance in time study, 263
American Arbitration Association, 204

American Federation of Labor, 393
American Management Association, 249, 359
American Smelting and Refining Co., 304
American Society for Engineering Education, 339
American Society of Training Directors, 389
Anxiety of problem employee, 240
Appley, Lawrence A., 3
Applicants, job, 95–97
Appraisal interviews, 118–121
Apprentice, training, 132–133
Aptitudes, of older and younger workers, 216–217
of women workers, 209–211
tests of, 92–93
Arbitration, 147
Armco Steel Company, 81
Arnold, John, 385
Attendance (see Absenteeism)
Attitude survey, 30–32
Attitudes of employees, changing, 27–29
toward cost cutting, 292–294
defined, 23–24
differences, 25–26
foreman's responsibility for, 24, 29–30
toward foremen, 32
levels, 30–32
toward maintenance, 313–314
office employees, 226–227
older workers, 217, 223
toward pilfering, 330–331
production workers, 33
and temperament, 26–27
understanding, 27
unfavorable, prevention of, 28–29
women workers, 210, 214
(See also Morale)
Authority, 59, 71–73, 83
check chart, 190

439

Authority, for discipline, 188–189
with groups, 19–20
Automation, 53
dispelling fears of, 28–29
Ayres, Waldemar, 388

Baker & Co., 315
Balance sheet, 399
Barth, Carl, 3
Basic-motion times (BMT), 266
Batten, Barton, Durstine, and Osborn, 389
(See also Osborn, Alex)
Beech Aircraft Corporation, 319
Behavior (see Human relations; Motivation)
Bender, J. A., 412
Bill, E. C., 420
Boss, apple-polishing, 415
delegated responsibilities, 416–417
estimate of supervisor, 418–420
getting along with, 415–422
and raises, 421, 422
timing of, 421
selling ideas to, 388, 420–421
talking to, 416–417
and yes-man, 415–416
Bottlenecks in planning, 253
Boy Scouts of America, 50
Brainstorming, 388
rules for, 389
(See also Creative thinking)
Budgets, 286
(See also Cost control)
Bulletin board, 10, 45
Bureau of Business Practice, 210
Business climate, evaluating, 51–53
good, benefits of, 52
supervisor's influence on, 52–53
Business economics (see Free enterprise system)

Camp, W. E., 255, 257
Capitalistic system (see Free enterprise system)
Carnegie, Dale, 355, 356
Case-study technique, 357
Chain of command, 73
Channels of organization, 73
Charts, graphs, and tables, for accident investigation, 161
of accident rates, 159
of accounts, 286
attitudes of employees, 31–32
office and production, 226
of authority and responsibility, 72, 191
balance sheet, 400

Charts, graphs, and tables, budget, 286
comparing older and younger workers, 219
conference leader's check list, 359
cost control, 286
of cost of jobs, 397
for employee performance rating, 113
flow-process, 273–274, 277
diagram, 277
symbols, 273
Gantt order-of-work, 257
Gantt reserved time, 255
housekeeping check list, 304–306
ideal supervisor for women workers, 213
job breakdown for training, 127
job-evaluation factors, 106
job rating, 104, 105
machine-loading, 257
maturity check list, 346–347
normal distribution, 94, 321
organization, 70
personal time budget, 372
profit and loss, 403
quality control, 322
responsibilities of supervisor, 72, 191
safety check list, 304–306
self-development schedule, 341
self-rating performance quiz, 337–339
supervisory performance rating, 342–345, 408–409
of supply and demand, 395
of training methods, 131
training sequence, 129, 135
training timetable, 128
Checkoff of union dues, 141
Clark, Charles, 386
Classification method of job evaluation, 103
Classified work, assignment of women to, 213
Clay, Lucius D., 373
Cleanup campaigns, 298
Clothing, protective, 13–14, 161–162
for women, 212
work, 212
Coates Board & Carton Co., 316
Collective bargaining, 138–140
(See also Labor relations; Unions)
Collins, Ralph, 235
Committee, cost-reduction, 295
safety, 162–163
Communications, 35
action, 39
with boss, 39
dangers in, 38

Communications, employee faith in, 38
and grapevine, 36–37
with groups, 44–45
interference with, 36
with letters (*see* Letters)
and listening, 41–43
meanings, 41
person-to-person, 43–44
personalities in, 41
preferences, 36, 43
with reports (*see* Report writing)
subjects, 38–39
supervisor's role in, 36–44
techniques, 43–45
three-dimensional, 37
written, 44–45
Community relations, 47
business climate, 51–53
company's influence on, 3, 50–51
and newspapers, 48–49
supervisor's influence on, 47, 49–50, 52–53
Competition in business, 393–396
(*See also* Free enterprise system)
Conference leadership, action, securing, 353
case studies, 357
check list for, 359
common faults of, 356
disagreements, handling of, 353–354
films, use of, 358
humor, use of, 355–356
jitters, control of, 356
methods, 350
for information type, 351
for problem-solving type, 351–353
public speaking, 355–356
questions, handling of, 350
rates, use of, 355
records for, 355–356
references, 358
Robert's Rules of Order, 350
role playing, 357–358
visual aids, 356
Conferences, 348
announcement-type, 357
duration of, 349
frequency of, 349
getting more from, 357
information-type, 351
location of, 349
opinions-requested type, 357
problem-solving, 351–353
purpose of, 348
record keeping for, 355–356
subject matter, 348
time to hold, 349

Conferences (*See also* Meetings)
Consolidated income statement, 401–403
Consumer Price Index, 109
Contest, housekeeping, 303–304
Continental Can Company, 373
Contract, union (*see* Union contract)
Control limits in statistical quality control, 321–323
Controls (*see* Cost control; Quality control)
Cooperation, employee, formula for, 177–178
methods for securing, 178–184
pay related to, 176–177
resistance to, 176
removing, 181–182
supervisory, with associates, 183
with staff people, 184
Cornell University, 243, 385
Correspondence courses, 130
Cost control, accounting, methods, 285–287
terms, 285–287
cost-cutting campaigns, 288–289
cost-reduction committees, 294–295
employee attitudes toward, 292–294
of indirect labor, 291–292
overhead, 290–291
policies, 83–84
records, 284–285
report, sample, 286
selling, 289
suggestions from employees, 294
supervisor's relation to, 287–294
union attitude, 292–293
Cost cutting (*see* Cost control)
Cost-of-living raises, 109
Cost reduction (*see* Cost control)
Cost-reduction committee, 295
Cost report, 286
Costs, employment, 86–87
hiring, 87
housekeeping, 296
labor, 285, 291–292
maintenance, 310–311
of thefts, 329
turnover, 89–90
Counseling, absenteeism improvement, 242–243
accident-prone employees, 241–242
alcoholic workers, 244
Hawthorne experiment, 234–235
problem employees, 238–244
Creative Engineering Program, 386
Creative thinking, 382–384
aptitude for, 381–382
and brainstorming, 388–389
discouraging, 389–390

Creative thinking, don'ts for, 387
  idea needlers for, 386–387
  preparation for, 384–385
  selling ideas from, 388
  tricks of trade, 385–386
Creative work, finding time for, 370
Curtice, Harlow H., 387
Customer and quality, 319

Decision making, channels for, 73
  and company policies, 83–84
  failures in, 61
  leeway in, 83
  need for, 63
Delegation of authority, 73, 75–76
Delay symbol in flow-process chart, 273
Demotion of supervisors, 8
Depreciation, 310–311
  effect on cost of jobs, 396
  and preventive maintenance, 312
  reserve for, 400–401
Dimensional-motion times (DMT), 266
Dionne quintuplets, 378
Discharge, 192–194
Discipline, 186
  in absence cases, 195
  attitude of employees toward, 186–187
  authority of foreman, 188–190
  discharge, 192–194
  grievances over, 205
  for housekeeping, 302
  methods for handling, 189–201
  negative, 188
  policy, considerations, 84
  informing employees of, 195
  record, consideration of employee's, 194
  union's role in, 191
  warnings, 191–192
Discussion (see Conference leadership; Conferences)
Dispatching, 253
  (See also Work schedules)
Dooher, M. Joseph, 359
Downtime, 310
Drinking (see Alcoholic employee)
Drucker, Peter, 2
DuBois, George B., 385
Dues, union, checkoff for, 141
du Pont de Nemours, E. I., Company, 48, 49, 241, 242
Dust hazards, 301

Eastman Kodak Company, 235
Eaton, William W., 337

Economics (see Free enterprise system)
Education, PTA, 50
  self-, for supervisors, 336
  (See also Training)
Eisenhower, Dwight D., 62
Elemental time standards (ETS), 266
Emotionally disturbed employee (see Problem employee)
Employee relations (see Human relations; Labor relations)
Employee Relations Bulletin, 7, 8
Employee security, 15, 16, 32
Employee selection, 91–97
Employee suggestions (see Suggestion systems)
Employment references, 97
Escalator clause, 109
Esso Standard Oil Company, 80
Ethyl Corporation, 386
Evaluation (see Job evaluation)
Evans, Chester E., 5, 6
Examinations, physical, 93, 96
Exception principle, 251–252, 256
Exercise for supervisors, 412

Factor-comparison method of job evaluation, 103
Factory Insurance Associates, 327
Factory Management and Maintenance, 104–106, 131, 216, 218, 219, 255, 257, 310, 340, 343, 391
Fair day's work, 263–264
Fair Labor Standards Act, 143–144
Fatigue, allowance for, in time study, 263
  effect on memory, 378
FBI, 328
Federal Securities Exchange Commission, 402
Feigenbaum, A. V., 321, 323
Feinberg, Mortimer, 346
Fieldcrest Milk, 318
Financial statements, balance sheet, 399–401
  profit-and-loss statement, 401–403
Fire extinguisher, 326–327
Fire protection, dangers, 324
  measures, 325-327
  in vacations, 327
Fires, frequency of, 325
  types of, 326
First aid, 154
Flammables, protection against, 326
Floods, protection from, 327–328
Flow-process chart, 272–277, 281–282
Foch, Ferdinand, 58
Follow-up, on absenteeism, 195

Follow-up, of grievances, 206
  in order giving, 169–170
  of training, 132
Followership, 61
Ford, Henry, 234
Foreman's manual, 84
Free enterprise system, capitalism,
    393–395
  competition, 393
  government control of, 395–396
  inflation, 397–398
  investment to provide jobs, 396
  mechanization, importance of, 399
  national income, 398
  profits, 391–392
    misunderstanding of, 392
    size of, 391–392
    union attitude toward, 392
    references, 402, 404
  reports, financial, balance sheet,
      399–401
    profit-and-loss statement, 401–403
  supervisor's knowledge of, 391
  supply and demand, 394–395
  taxes, 397–398
Frequency of accidents, 158–159
Frequency distribution chart, 94,
    320–321
Fringe benefits, attitude of office em-
    ployees toward, 229–230

Gambling, 80–81
Gantt, Henry L., 3
Gantt chart, 254–257
Gantt plan for wage incentives, 266
General Electric Company, 50–51, 386
General Motors Corporation, 325, 387
Gilbreth, Frank B., 281
Gilbreth, Lillian, 281
Gompers, Samuel, 393
Gordon, Gerald, 241, 242
Grapevine, 36–37
Green-light thinking, 382–383
Gregg, John A., 316
Grievances, arbitration of, 204
  attitude of supervisors toward,
      197–198
  common, 204–205
  imagined, 198–199
  methods for handling, 199–204
  prevention of, 205–206
  procedure for, 146–147, 203
  settlements of, 203
  unsettled, 204
  (See also Labor relations)
Grimaldi, John V., 161
Gripes (see Grievances)
Groups, 18–20

Groups, brainstorming with, 388–389
  characteristics of, 19
  communicating with, 44–45
  goal setting with, 19–20, 179–180
  instructions to, 173
  meetings with, 348–359
  psychology of, 65
  training of, 131
  wage-incentive plans for, 266

Halo effect, 119
Halsey, 3
Halsey Premium Plan, 265–266
Harvard School of Public Health, 214
Hawthorne experiment, 234–235
Hiring employees, 91–97
Hodge, William, 343
Housekeeping, and conference leader-
    ship, 351–353
  contests, 303–304
  cost of, 297
  daily cleanups, 298
  discipline for, 302
  dust hazards, 301
  floor conditions, 302
  inspections, 302–306
  locker rooms, 299–300
  personal property, 301–302
  sanitation, 299
  savings from, 296
  selling to employees, 297–298
  in storage areas, 300–301
  support of, by employees, 180
  trash, 301
  union objections, 299
  work habits of employees, 297
Hughes Aircraft Company, 211
Hugo, George, 296
Human Engineering Laboratories, 381
Human relations, 13
  behavior, 14
  good, benefits from, 18
  in groups, 19–20
    (See also Groups)
  motivation, 15–16
  objectives at work, 17
  satisfactions at work, 16
  supervisor's influence on, 20–22
Hurricanes, 327–328

Idea bank, 386
Idea killers, 389–390
Idea museum, 386
Idea needlers, 386–387
Idea trap, 387
Incentives, financial (see Fringe bene
    fits; Wage incentives; Wages)
  nonfinancial (see Motivation)

Index of plant maintenance costs, 316
Indirect labor, cost of, 291–292
Induction training, 125
Industrial Psychology, Inc., 86
Industrial relations department (*see* Personnel department)
Inspection symbol on flow-process chart, 273
Inspections, housekeeping, 302–306
  (*See also* Quality; Quality control)
Instructions, in anger, 172
  attitudes of employees toward, 171–173
  commands, 168
  execution of, 170
  for groups, 173
  methods for issuing, 167–168
  pitfalls in issuing, 174
  refusals, 168
  requests, 168
  suggested, 171
  written, 170–171
International Association of Machinists, AFL-CIO, 217
Interviewing, 94–97
Interviews, appraisal, 118–121
  (*See also* Merit rating)
  errors in, 119–120
  follow-up for, 120–121
  guides for, 121
  halo effect, 119
  sandwich technique, 118

Job analysis (*see* Job evaluation)
Job breakdown, for methods improvement, 272–277
  for training, 125
Job description, 101–102
Job evaluation, 99
  benefits from, 100
  changes in, 110
  drawbacks, 99–100
  and employees, 109–110
  and foreman, 106
  job analysis, 102
  job rating sheet, 104
  job summary sheet, 105
  methods, 103–106
    classification, 103
    factor comparison, 103
    point, 103–107
    ranking, 103
  money values, assignment of, 108–109
  pay related to, 100
  rate ranges, 108
  red-circle rates, 108
  wage patterns, 109
  for white-collar jobs, 107–108

Job Instruction Training (JIT), 125–126, 129
Job Methods Training (JMT), 269
Job security, 52
Job specifications, 94
Johnson, Harry, 223
Juran, J. M., 318

Key-point safety, 159–160
Kipling, Rudyard, 278
Koppers Company, Inc., 65
Kress, A. L., 104–106

Labor, cost of, 86–87, 285
  hiring, 87
  indirect, 291–292
  turnover (*see* Turnover)
Labor Management Relations Act, 7, 141–143
Labor relations, arbitration, 147
  collective bargaining, 138–140
  cooling-off period, 142
  discrimination in, 139–140
  Fair Labor Standards Act, 143–144
  foreman's influence on, 141
  grievance procedure, 146–147
    (*See also* Grievances)
  Labor Management Relations Act, 7, 141–143
  management's rights clause, 141
  minimum wages, 144
  National Labor Relations Act (NLRA), 139, 142, 148
  supervisor's role in, 137–138, 141
  Taft-Hartley law, 7, 141–143
  Wages and Hours Law, 143–144
  Wagner Act, 139, 142, 148
  Walsh-Healey Act, 143
  (*See also* Unions)
Leadership, 57
  and action, 62
  autocratic, 59
  democratic, 59
  free-rein, 59
  group-control, 65
  and human relations, 62
  ingredients of, 58
  poise, 64
  responsibilities, 63
  rewards, 57–58
Learning (*see* Training)
Letters, beginning, 362, 363
  copies, number of, 365
  details in, 363–364
  faults of, 361–362
  form of, 365, 366
  memorandum, 366

Letters, order for, 362
  typing, 364
Levinson, Harry, 240–241
Life Extension Examiners, 411
Life Extension Foundation, 223
Lifting techniques, 155
Lincoln, Abraham, 414
Line organization, 69
Line-and-staff organization, 69–70
  (*See also* Organization)
Listening, 41–42
Locker rooms, 299–300

MacArthur, Douglas, 386
Machine loading, 254–257
Machinery and Allied Products
  Institute, 392
McNair, Malcolm, 63
Maintenance, 308–309
  attitude of employees toward, 313–
    314
  cost of, 310–311
  downtime, 310
  morale, effect on, 313
  planning, 311–312
  preventive, 312–313
  responsibility for, 309–310
  supervisor's role in, 311
Make-ready in job breakdown, 279
Malingering, 155
Man-machine charts, 281–282
Management cycle, 2–3
Management development, defined,
  341
  rating form, 341–345
  schedule, 341
  (*See also* Self-improvement)
Management objectives, 3
Management's rights, 141
Manpower, forecasting, 87–88
  management of, 86
Maslow, A. H., 15
Massachusetts Institute of Technology
  (MIT), 385
Material handling, on flow-process
  chart, 273
  sketching route of, 277
Maturity, check list, 346–347
  in supervisors, 341
Maynard, H. B., Company, Inc., 63
Measured daywork, 266
Mechanization, extent of, 399
Meetings, mass, 45
  staff, 44
  (*See also* Conferences)
Memorandum, interoffice, 44
  writing of, 366
Memory improvement, 378–380

Menninger Foundation, 240
Merck & Co., Inc., 5
Merit rating, 112–117
  consistency in, 114–115
  discrimination in, 116–117
  factors, 112–113
  wages related to, 115
  (*See also* Interviews, appraisal)
Methods Engineering Council Division of H. B. Maynard Company,
  Inc., 63
Methods improvement, blocks to,
  278–279
  defined, 269–270
  examples, 271
  flow-process chart, 272–277, 281–282
  job breakdown, 272–277
  man-machine charts, 281–282
  motion economy, 280–281
  origin of, 270–271
  payoff, 282
  questions to ask, 278
  suggestion systems, 282
  and supervisor, 270
  Therbligs, 281
  value-added operations, 279
  where to find, 271–273
Methods-time-measurement (MTM),
  266
Minimum wage regulations (*see* Fair
  Labor Standards Act)
Monopoly, natural, 396
Monotony in office jobs, 228
Montgomery, Bernard, 61
Morale, of foremen, 33
  levels, 30–33
  maintenance, affect of, 313
  of office employees, 225–226
  planning, effect of, 256
  of production workers, 33, 226
  surveys, 30
  (*See also* Attitudes of employees)
Motion economy, 269, 280–281
  (*See also* Methods improvement)
Motion study (*see* Methods improve-
  ment; Time study)
Motivation, 14–16
  of office employees, 226–227
  of older workers, 222–223
  research, 21
  of women workers, 208
Murphy, M. J., 131
Myers, F. E., & Bro. Company, 319

National Association of Manu-
  facturers, 397
National Association for Mental
  Health, 412

National Association of Suggestion Systems, 282
National Council of Industrial Management Clubs, 7, 338
National Council of Technical Schools, 339
National emergency, 328–329
National Fire Protection Association (NFPA), 326
National Foremen's Institute, 7
National Home Study Council, 339
National Industrial Conference Board (NICB), 140, 329
National Labor Relations Act (see Wagner Act)
National Labor Relations Board (NLRB), 7, 140, 142, 147–148, 231
National Management Association, 7, 9, 338
National Metal Trades Association (NMTA), 107, 112
National Office Management Association (NOMA), 230–231
National Safety Council, 151, 296
Needs, basic, 15–17
 (See also Motivation)
Neurotic employee, 228, 235–236
 (See also Problem employee)
New York Yankees, 19
News of employee interest, 38, 49
Normal distribution, 93, 94, 320–321
Normal pace in time study, 262–263
Normal person, 93

Obsolescences, 310–311
Occupational Hazards magazine, 324
Office employees, characteristics of, 225
 criticism of jobs by, 230
 fringe benefits, 229–230
 methods of handling, career-oriented, 229
 monotony, 228
 neurotic, 228
 morale of, 225–226
 pay, importance of, 227
 preferences of, 230
 reasons for quitting, 230–231
 secretary, treatment of, 231
 temperament of, 227
 and unions, 231–232
The Office Supervisor magazine, 340
Older workers, aging process, 220
 assets, 217–218
 comparison with younger workers, 217–218
 defined, 216

Older workers, drawbacks, 218
 importance of, 216–217
 motivation of, 221–222
 retirement, advice on, 223–224
 training of, 220–222
Operation symbol on flow-process chart, 272
Operations analysis, 269
 (See also Methods improvement)
Orders (see Instructions; Work schedules)
Organization, 67
 channels, 73
 chart, 70
 defined, 68
 foreman's place in, 67
 goals, 68–69
 line and staff, 69–70, 74
Orientation, 125
Osborn, Alex, 382, 386, 388, 389
Overhead, 290–291

Paper work, filing, 375
 handling, 375
 in planning, 250–251
 reading of, 375–377
 reducing, 373–374
 source of, 373
Parkhurst, Raymond B., 211
Participation, 20, 62
 planning for, 181
Patton, George, 61
Pay, attitude of employees toward, 31, 100
 importance of, 20–21
 raises, 115–118
 rates for women workers, 211
 (See also Wages)
Performance rating, of employees, 113
 (See also Merit rating)
 of supervisor, 341–345
 by wife, 408–409
Perry, John, 236
Personality, 60
Personnel department, 92, 96
 and discipline problems, 191, 192
 and grievance procedure, 147
 and problem employees, 241
Physical Fitness Foundation, 412
Picnic, company, 412
Piece rates, 265
 (See also Wage incentives)
Pilfering (see Thefts)
Planning, centralized, 253
 decentralized, 253–254
 exception principle, 251–252
 Gantt chart, 254–257
 machine loading, 254–257

Planning, maintenance, 311–312
  manpower requirements, 87–90
  morale, effect on, 250
  records, simplified, 250–251
  responsibility of supervisor, 249
  (*See also* Work schedules)
Plant protection, dangers, nature of, 324
  from fire, 324–327
  from floods, 327–328
  from sabotage, 328–329
  from thefts, 329–331
  from winds, 327–328
Pleuthner, Willard, 389
Point method of job evaluation, 103–107
Policies, cost-cutting, 83–84
  defined, 78
  discipline, 84
  manuals, 84
  safety, 81
  significance to employees, 81
  written, 79
Politics, 38–39, 50
Portland Copper & Tank Works, Inc., 296
Posters, use of, 45
  (*See also* Visual aids)
Predetermined elemental time standards, 266
  basic-motion times, BMT, 266
  dimensional-motion times, DMT, 266
  elemental time standards, ETS, 266
  methods-time measurement, MTM, 266
Presto Lock Company, 316
Preventive maintenance (PM), 312–313
Problem employee, absenteeism of, 242–243
  accident-prone, 241–242
  adjustment of, 236
  alcoholic, 243–244
  Hawthorne experiment, 234–235
  management pressure on, 236–237
  methods for handling, 238–244
    counseling, 238–244
    relief of, 241
    special problems, 240
  neurotic, 235–236
  number of, 233–234
  psychotic, 235–236
  recognition of, 235, 237–238, 240
  supervisors, 237
Production control (*see* Cost control; Planning; Work schedules)

Profit-and-Loss statement, 401–403
Promotion, 8
  and job evaluation, 110
  and merit rating, 115–117, 119
  to supervisory rank, 8
Protective clothing, 13–14, 161–162
Psychiatry, dangers in lay practice, 29
  and problem employee, 241, 244
Psychology (*see* Human relations)
Psychological research, 15
Psychologist and problem employee, 241, 244
Psychotic employee, 235–236
  (*See also* Problem employee)
Public relations (*see* Community relations)
Public speaking, 355–356
  humor in, 355–356
  jitters, control of, 356
  notes in, 355
  visual aids in, 356

Quality, attitude of employees toward, 317–318
  control charts, 321–323
  and customer, 319
  frequency distribution chart, 320–321
  improvement of, 319–320
  responsibility for, 315–317
  sampling tables, 321–322
  training employees in, 318
Quality control, 321–323
  statistical (SQC), 320–323
  (*See also* Quality)
Questions, how to handle, 350

Radio Corporation of America, 420
Ramond, Albert, 3
Ranking method of job evaluation, 103
Rate range, 108
  (*See also* Job evaluation)
Rating in time study, 262–263
Ratio-delay, 267
Reading, improvement of, 375–377
  for self-improvement, 340
Records, for conferences, 355–356
  for control of absences, 195
  cost, 284–285
  for disciplinary action, 194
  for planning, simplified, 250–251
Recreation, 50
Red-circle rate, 108
  (*See also* Job evaluation)
Red-light thinking, 383
Reference check, 97
Referral of problem employee, 240–241
Regulations, 79–80

Regulations, attitude of employees toward, 186
  grievances about, 201
  infractions, reasons for, 187
  (See also Discipline; Policies)
Religion, 38–39, 50
Repair (see Maintenance)
Report writing, 365–368
  elements in, 367–368
  methods, chronological, 367
    logical, 366
    psychological, 367
  organization of, 365–366
  timing of, 365
Reports, 44
  financial, 399–403
Research Institute of America, 8–9, 131, 346
Responsibility of supervisors, 5–6, 70–71, 73
  check list, 72
Retirement counseling, 217–218
Robbins, Walter E., Jr., 315
Robert's Rules of Order, 350
Rockne, Knute, 180
Role playing, 357–358
Routing, 252
  (See also Work schedule)
Rules (see Regulations)
Rumors, 28–29

Sabotage, 328–329
Safety, and accidents (see Accidents)
  clothing, 13, 161–162
  committees, 162–163
  and community, 50–51
  and housekeeping, 296
  inspections, 304–306
  key-point, 159–160
  policies, 81
  posters, 154
  selling to employees, 153, 163
  smoking rules, 195–196
  supervisor's role in, 152–162
Sales Management magazine, 420
Saltonstall, Robert, 5
Sampling, 321–322
  of work, 267
Sandwich technique in appraisal, 118
Sanitation, 299
  (See also Housekeeping)
Sawyer, William A., 217
Schedule, for job training, 128
  for self-development, 341
  work (see Work schedule)
Schizophrenia, 235
  (See also Problem employee)

Scientific management, 3–4
Scrap, 330
  (See also Waste)
Secretary, treatment of, 231
Security, employee, 182–183, 205
  and morale, 32
Selection, employee (see Interviewing)
Self-improvement, 335
  and education, 336
  and initiative, 341
  and maturity, 341
    check list, 346–347
  performance rating form, 342–345
  quiz, self-rating, 337–339
  reading for, 340
  schedule, 341
  training programs, company, 339
  wife's role in, 413–414
Seniority, 117, 141, 205
Set-ups, cost of, 285
  elimination of, 279
Severity of accidents, 158–159
Shop orders, 257
  (See also Work schedule)
Shurter, Robert L., 363
Simonds, Rollin H., 161
Slowdowns, 28–29
Smoking rules, 325–326
Socialism, 394
Society for the Advancement of Management (SAM), 263
Somervell, Brehon, 65
Specifications in quality control, 321
Spelling, importance of, in business writing, 361
Staff organization, 69, 74, 290
Standard data, 264
  (See also Standards)
Standard time, 260
Standards, in quality control, 317, 318
  in time study, 260
    complaints about, 261–262
    loose, 261–262
    predetermined elemental time, 266
    short cuts to, 262
Start-up (make-ready), 279
Statistical quality control (SQC), 320–323
  (See also Quality)
Stealing (see Thefts)
Stevens Institute of Technology, 381
Stool pigeon, 417
Storage areas, 300–301
Storage symbol on flow-process chart, 273

Strikes, 48, 51–52
Suggestion systems, 282, 294
  supervisor's participation in, 7–8
Superior (*see* Boss)
Supervisor, activities, 5–6
  definition of, 1–2
  and employees, number supervised,
    6–7
  failure, reasons for, 9
  and foremen's unions, 7
  responsibilities, 4–5
  working, 8
Supplies, cost of, 289
  in planning, 251
Symbols for flow-process charts,
  272–277

Taft-Hartley law, 7, 141–143
Tardiness, 184
  of alcoholic workers, 242
  comparisons of older and younger
    employees, 219
  discipline for, 195
Taxes, 397–398
  and depreciation, 310
Taylor, Frederick W., 3, 262
Telephone, use of, 43
Tension, 412–413
Tests, aptitude, 92–93
  psychological, 92–93
Thefts, attitude of employees toward,
  330–331
  cost of, to industry, 329
  discipline for, 191
  insurance of, 329
  responsibility of supervisors for,
    329–331
Therbligs, 3, 281
Time, management of, 369
  analysis, 370
  budgeting, 371, 372, 374
  methods for, 371–373
  organizing, 374
  paper work and, 373–374, 376
  of reading, 377
  saving of, 370–371
  memory and, 378–380
Time-and-motion study, 269
  (*See also* Methods improvement;
    Time study)
Time study, 259
  complaints of, 261–262
  explaining, 264–265
  fair day's work, 263–264
  loose standards, 261–262
  measured daywork, 266
  pace, normal, 262–263

Time study, predetermined elemental
    time standards, 266
  rating, 262–263
  short cuts, 262
  standard data, 264
  standard time, 260
  time taken, 260
  unit-hour, 265
  and wage-incentive plans, 265–267
Time taken, 260
Tolciss, Morris, 316
Tolerance in quality control, 321–
    323
Tornadoes, protection from, 327–328
Training, apprenticeship, 132–133
  benefits, 124
  follow-up for, 132
  group, 131
  indicators, 123–124
  induction, 125
  job breakdowns, 125–127
  Job Instruction Training (JIT),
    125–126, 129
  methods, 131
    for difficult operations, 135
  for quality improvement, 38, 318
  responsibility of supervisor for,
    123
  schedules, 128
  sequence, 128–129, 135
  supervisory, 339
  for supervisory development, 341
  union problems, 133–134
  vestibule, 133
  visual aids, use of, 132
  whole-spaced learning, 379
Training department, 134
Training Within Industry Report,
    127–129
Transportation symbol on flow-process
    chart, 273
Trice, Harrison M., 243
Troublemakers, 29
Turnover, calculations, 90
  in older workers, 219
  rates, 90
  in women workers, 210, 219

Underwriter's Laboratories, Inc., 326
Unfair labor practices, 139–140
Union contract, 140–141
  checkoff provision, 141
  closed shop, 141
  seniority provisions, 141
  union shop, 141
  (*See also* Labor relations)
Unions, 19

Unions, attitude, toward cost cutting, 292–293
  toward discipline, 191
  toward training, 133–134
  authority of shop stewards, 144
  contracts, 140–141
  and grievances, 200–204
  and office employees, 231–232
  and supervisors, 7, 144–145
  (See also Labor relations)
Unit-hour plan, 265
U.S. Air Force, 135, 273
U.S. Bureau of Labor Statistics (BLS), 109, 208
U.S. Census, 211
U.S. Chamber of Commerce, 392
U.S. Department of Labor, 217, 218
U.S. Ordnance Department, 212, 213
U.S. Public Health Service, 210
United States Steel Corporation, 396
U.S. Weather Bureau, 61
University of Chicago, 31, 32, 225
University of Michigan, 178, 230
University of Wisconsin, 319
Uris, Auren, 60

Vacation shutdowns, 327
Vestibule training, 133
Visual aids, 45, 132, 356
  in communications, 45
  films, 358
  safety posters, 154

Wage administration, 108–110
  and supervisor, 115–116, 119
Wage incentives, Gantt task and bonus, 266
  grievances about, 205
  for groups, 266
  Halsey Premium Plan, 265–266
  piece-rate plans, 265
  plans, 265–266
  unit-hour, 265
  (See also Time study)
Wages, determination of, 108
  intangible, 21–22
  in job changes, 110
  and merit, 115–118
  patterns of, 109
  real, 21
  survey of, 108
  (See also Pay)
Wages and Hours Law (see Fair Labor Standards Act)
Wagner Act, 139, 142, 148
Walker, William S., 304
Walsh-Healey Public Contracts Act, 143

Waste, 301
  in creative thinking, 384
  finding, 279
Waste reduction, 269
  (See also Methods improvement)
Wayne University, 5
Western Electric Company, 3, 234
White-collar workers (see Office employees)
White Sewing Machine Company, 387
Whole-spaced learning, 379
Wife of supervisor, and ambitions, 407, 410
  at boss's home, 411
  at company functions, 411
  effect, on health, 411–413
  on tension, 412–413
  knowledge of job, 406, 407
  rating job performance, 407–409
  role in success, 405–406
Wind damage, 327–328
Women workers, accident rates, 212
  aptitudes, 209–211
  assignments, restrictions on, 211
  clothing at work, 212
  complaints, 214
  getting along with, 209
  in offices, 230–231
  pay rates for, 211
  preferences in supervision, 212–213
  reasons for working, 208–209
  on secret work, 213–214
  shortcomings, 210
  temperament, 210–211
Work Factors, 266
Work groups (see Groups)
Work measurement, measured daywork, 266
  predetermined elemental time standards, 266
  work sampling, 267
  (See also Time study)
Work schedules, capacity, per cent of, 252
  deliveries, pressure for, 252
  factors in, 252–253
  Gantt chart, 254–257
  machine loading, 254–257
  shop orders, 257
  (See also Planning)
Work simplification, 269
  (See also Methods improvement)
Working conditions, attitude of employees toward, 297
  effect on morale, 296, 300
  (See also Housekeeping; Safety)
Workmen's compensation, 151
Wright brothers, 381, 384

Writing for business, expressions to avoid, 363–364
  faults in, 361–362
  importance of, 360–361
  letters, 362–366
  memorandum, 366
  orders, 170–171
  references for information, 368

Writing for business, reports, 366–368
  spelling, 361

X method in creative thinking, 385

Yaglou, C. P., 214
YMCA, 7